India Studies in Business and Economics

The Indian economy is considered to be one of the fastest growing economies of the world with India amongst the most important G-20 economies. Ever since the Indian economy made its presence felt on the global platform, the research community is now even more interested in studying and analyzing what India has to offer. This series aims to bring forth the latest studies and research about India from the areas of economics, business, and management science. The titles featured in this series will present rigorous empirical research, often accompanied by policy recommendations, evoke and evaluate various aspects of the economy and the business and management landscape in India, with a special focus on India's relationship with the world in terms of business and trade.

More information about this series at http://www.springer.com/series/11234

Seema Bathla · Elumalai Kannan
Editors

Agro and Food Processing Industry in India

Inter-sectoral Linkages, Employment,
Productivity and Competitiveness

 Springer

Editors
Seema Bathla
Centre for the Study of Regional
Development
Jawaharlal Nehru University
New Delhi, India

Elumalai Kannan
Centre for the Study of Regional
Development
Jawaharlal Nehru University
New Delhi, India

ISSN 2198-0012   ISSN 2198-0020   (electronic)
India Studies in Business and Economics
ISBN 978-981-15-9470-0   ISBN 978-981-15-9468-7   (eBook)
https://doi.org/10.1007/978-981-15-9468-7

Contents

1 Introduction 1
   Seema Bathla and Elumalai Kannan

Part I   Agriculture-Industry-Services Linkages

2 **Post-harvest Food Management, Extent of Processing
   and Inter-sectoral Linkages** 17
   Seema Bathla and Madhur Gautam

3 **Output and Employment Linkages of the Primary, Secondary
   and Tertiary Sectors in the Indian Economy: A Computable
   General Equilibrium (CGE) Analysis** 61
   Nitin Arora and Rahul Arora

4 **The Food Processing Industry in India: Regional Spread,
   Linkages and Space for Farmer Producer Organisations** 81
   K. J. S. Satyasai and Aparajita Singh

5 **Forging Linkages to Promote Agriculture Exports Through
   Contract Farming: A Case Study of Okra Cultivation** 107
   Anjani Kumar and Gaurav Tripathi

Part II   Employment, Investment and Productivity Growth

6 **Temporal and Spatial Patterns in Employment
   and Productivity Growth in the Organised Food Industry** 127
   Seema Bathla and Shiv Jee

7 **Unorganised Food Processing Enterprises in India: Key
   Performance Indicators** 153
   N. Padmavathi and Parmod Kumar

8 **Dynamics of Competition in Food and Agriculture Inputs
   Industries in India: A Mobility Analysis** 183
   M. L. Nithyashree

9   Labour Regulations and Employment Growth
    in the Organised Food Processing Industry in India 193
    Prateek Kukreja

10 Beyond the Polemics: Subcontracting in the Unorganised
    Food Manufacturing Sector in India 209
    Shayequa Zeenat Ali

11 Investment Pattern and Sources of Finance in Micro, Small
    and Medium Agro-Processing Enterprises in India 227
    Santosh Kumar

Part III   External Trade, Competitiveness and Determinants

12 India's Trade in Agro-Processed Products: Revealed
    Comparative Advantage and Its Determinants 255
    Ankur Jain and Elumalai Kannan

13 Trade Competitiveness of the Indian Dairy Industry:
    An Empirical Analysis 273
    Yashobanta Parida, Avinash K. Ghule,
    and Priyankkumar Tulsidas Dudhrejiya

14 Protection Structure and Comparative Advantage in Primary
    and Processed Agriculture Exports 289
    Abhishek Jha and Seema Bathla

15 Protection Structure and Total Factor Productivity Growth
    in India's Organised Food Industry 321
    Seema Bathla

16 Productivity, Competitiveness and Export Performance:
    A Plant-Level Analysis of India's Wearing Apparel Industry 345
    Bishwanath Goldar and Yashobanta Parida

17 Import Content, Value-Added and Employment Generation:
    An Input–Output-Based Analysis of India's Exports 363
    Devender Pratap and Shibananda Nayak

Editors and Contributors

About the Editors

Seema Bathla is Professor, Centre for the Study of Regional Development, Jawaharlal Nehru University (JNU), New Delhi. Before joining JNU, she worked in the Institute of Economic Growth, The Energy Research Institute (TERI) and Delhi University, all premium research institutions of India. She obtained her M.Phil. from Delhi School of Economics and Ph.D. from JNU. She has published six books (five co-authored) and more than 60 research articles in refereed national and international journals. Having keen interest in agricultural issues she has carried out several research studies and undertaken assignments for the World Bank, IFPRI, FAO, UNCTAD, WWF-India and IASRI. She was conferred Jawaharlal Nehru Award for Outstanding Post-Graduate Agricultural Research by the Indian Council of Agriculture Research, New Delhi in 2008. She is also the recipient of Dr. R. T. Doshi award for best paper published in Agricultural Economics Research Review in 2014, 2015 and 2019 and the 2018 Dr. S. R. Sen Biennial Award given by Indian Society of Agricultural Economics for her book on trade liberalization and Indian agriculture.

Dr. Elumalai Kannan is Associate Professor at the Centre for the Study of Regional Development, Jawaharlal Nehru University, New Delhi. He obtained his Ph.D. in Economics from Jawaharlal Nehru University (JNU), New Delhi. He has worked at various reputed organisations such as the National Centre for Agricultural Economics and Policy Research (NCAEPR), New Delhi, International Maize and Wheat Improvement Centre (CIMMYT), New Delhi office, National Council of Applied Economic Research (NCAER), Madras School of Economics, Chennai and Institute for Social and Economic Change (ISEC), Bangalore. He was a visiting scholar at the University of Saskatchewan, Canada. Dr. Kannan has undertaken important research studies on inclusive agricultural growth, stagnation in productivity of important crops in India, agrarian change and farm sector distress, pre and post-harvest losses, contract farming and impact evaluation of agricultural development programmes. He has published several research papers in various reputed journals and contributed to edited volumes on different themes.

Contributors

Shayequa Zeenat Ali National Council of Applied Economic Research, New Delhi, India

Nitin Arora Department of Economics, Panjab University, Chandigarh, Punjab, India

Rahul Arora Department of Economics and Finance, Birla Institute of Technology and Science, Pilani, Rajasthan, India

Seema Bathla Centre for the Study of Regional Development, Jawaharlal Nehru University, New Delhi, India

Priyankkumar Tulsidas Dudhrejiya Ganpat University, Mehsana, Gujarat, India

Madhur Gautam Lead Economist, Agriculture Global Practice, World Bank, Washington DC, USA

Avinash K. Ghule Verghese Kurien Centre of Excellence, Institute of Rural Management Anand, Anand, Gujarat, India

Bishwanath Goldar Institute of Economic Growth, Delhi, India

Ankur Jain Centre for the Study of Regional Development, Jawaharlal Nehru University, New Delhi, India

Abhishek Jha Centre for the Study of Regional Development, Jawaharlal Nehru University, New Delhi, India

Elumalai Kannan Centre for the Study of Regional Development, Jawaharlal Nehru University, New Delhi, India

Prateek Kukreja Indian Council for Research on International Economic Relations, New Delhi, India

Anjani Kumar International Food Policy Research Institute, New Delhi, India

Parmod Kumar Agricultural Development and Rural Transformation Centre, Institute for Social and Economic Change, Bangalore, Karnataka, India

Santosh Kumar Centre for the Study of Regional Development, Jawaharlal Nehru University, New Delhi, India

Shibananda Nayak MSME, Government of India, Cuttack, India

M. L. Nithyashree Division of Agricultural Economics, ICAR-IARI, New Delhi, India

N. Padmavathi Agricultural Development and Rural Transformation Centre, Institute for Social and Economic Change, Bangalore, Karnataka, India

Yashobanta Parida Verghese Kurien Centre of Excellence, Institute of Rural Management Anand, Anand, Gujarat, India

Devender Pratap National Council of Applied Economic Research, New Delhi, India

K. J. S. Satyasai DEAR, NABARD, Mumbai, India

Shiv Jee Centre for the Study of Regional Development, Jawaharlal Nehru University, New Delhi, India

Aparajita Singh FPOs, Research & Consulting, Dvara E-Registry, Hyderabad, India

Gaurav Tripathi International Food Policy Research Institute, New Delhi, India

Chapter 1
Introduction

Seema Bathla and Elumalai Kannan

Since 1991, India has been integrated with global markets, per capita income has risen, urbanization has grown and, therefore, the economy has experienced many shifts. One shift has been in consumer behaviour and food preferences. Awareness of the health effects of alternative foods is growing, too, and demand is rising continually for safer and more nutritious foods and, also, for processed and packaged foods. As consumer demand for non-traditional food products affects the production mix (on-farm activity) and the post-harvest management of farm produce (off-farm activity), the policy and regulatory framework must facilitate the supply-side transition of India's food system and help it adapt to and align with these evolving demand patterns. To meet the growing demand for processed and packaged foods, investment in processing of agricultural produce must be encouraged, the food value chains organized, and the regulatory environment for food safety strengthened.

The current thrust of agricultural policy in India is to double farmers' real income by 2022–23. To achieve this target, the government must transform the food system by raising the value of production realized on the farm. Simultaneously, the system has to shift to growing high-value products (fruits, vegetables, livestock and dairy products and fish). The system must also raise the value realized for these products through the downstream processing and service segments of the post-harvest agriculture food value chains.

Equally important for a transforming economy, although less appreciated, is the contribution of a modern food system to growth and employment. Value addition, processing and food services can be powerful sources of growth in the non-farm economy—including manufacturing and services—and a major source of employment for the rural labour force (World Bank 2008). In the USA, agricultural production or value-added constitutes about 1% of the gross domestic product (GDP), whereas the food industry accounts for almost 6%; agricultural employment makes

S. Bathla (✉) · E. Kannan
Centre for the Study of Regional Development, Jawaharlal Nehru University, New Delhi, India
e-mail: seema.bathla@gmail.com

© The Author(s), under exclusive license to Springer Nature Singapore Pte Ltd. 2021
S. Bathla and E. Kannan (eds.), *Agro and Food Processing Industry in India*, India Studies in Business and Economics, https://doi.org/10.1007/978-981-15-9468-7_1

up about 1.4% of total employment, but the post-farm food economy almost 8% (USDA 2020). In developed countries, the structure of the food system changes continually as the role of manufacturers, processors and food services in both value-added and employment grows larger relative to that of farmers (Gollin and Probst 2015).

How is India's food system evolving? Are its current policies and institutions appropriate? The research evidence shows that the role of agribusiness is expanding, and that retail shops and supermarkets are stocking an increasing variety of processed and prepared foods. But we do not fully know the size or structure of the agribusiness sector or the magnitude of the forward linkages of agriculture with other sectors in terms of output and employment generated directly or indirectly. Because estimates are unsubstantiated, or based on weak evidence, debate breaks out often over popularly quoted figures, including for simple indicators such as backward output linkages—the share of the agricultural produce that is processed, or the extent of processing of the agricultural produce—or post-harvest losses. Few studies rigorously assess the magnitude of changes in the entire food value chain (Sarkar 1995; Bhattacharya and Rajeev 2013). Is the investment in agriculture, industry and services adequate? How can we improve the intersectoral interlinkages? Can contract farming between farmers and industry or arrangements with farmer producer companies (FPC) or farmer producer organizations (FPO) that aggregate produce strengthen backward linkages?

The central government considers the food processing sector important to the economy, and it has made the sector a policy priority. To accelerate the return on investment and meet the growing consumer demand for diverse foods, the central government offers several incentives: a five-year tax holiday for new agriculture-processing units and a 35% tax deduction for five years; reduced import duty on processing machinery; no corporate taxes on profits from export sales; and automatic approval for 100% foreign direct investment (FDI) on most items. Capital investment in large projects and processing firms, investment in mega food parks and 100% greenfield investments are exempt from excise duty (Government of India 2017). During the COVID-19 pandemic, the Ministry of Food Processing Industries introduced a scheme for the creation and expansion of food processing and preservation capacities under the Pradhan Mantri Kisan Sampada Yojna. Financial assistance in the form of grants-in-aid of 35–50% of the project cost subject to a maximum of INR 50 million is proposed to be given to cooperatives, FPOs, micro, small and medium enterprises (MSMEs), etc. to encourage investments in various segments in rural areas. These incentives aim to raise agricultural productivity by improving farm prices and making them more stable, and reduce wastage by enabling the processing of produce unsuitable for wet markets into more value-added consumables. Other aims are to increase returns to farmers and food enterprises; diversify into crops needed for processing; and, potentially, transform traditional "food crops" into "cash enterprises".

The exports from this segment are again an important outlet for agricultural output: exports of processed foods and beverages constitute almost 48% of rapidly expanding agricultural exports, almost doubling in (real) value over the past three years, and its share in total exports is close to 12% (Goyal et al. 2017). Exports may grow further with growing urbanization, increasing per capita income and integration with world markets. To reap these benefits, the Government of India approved the first Agriculture Export Policy in December 2018. The policy aims to increase agriculture exports to INR 4.5 trillion (USD 60 billion) by 2025 by making the trade regime stable, diversifying exports by products and destinations, and promoting perishables and high-value-added products. A sum of INR 14 billion (USD 187 million) has been allocated to set up specialized, produce-specific clusters in states (Government of India 2018). India's food processing sector contributes about 14% to the manufacturing GDP; it employs nearly 13 million people directly and 35 million people indirectly. From 2010 to 2014, the food and beverages segment of the organized manufacturing sector accounted for 14% of employment and 8.3% of output, although the inter-state differentials were large.

Several challenges confront India's food processing sector, however. The foremost is that the unorganized (informal), low-productivity enterprises make up more than 80% of enterprises and employment but contributes only 20% of the gross output. This has serious implications for growth. Both "push" and "pull" factors explain the high labour absorption by the unorganized sector. Workers in small enterprises have low productivity, and they work in poor conditions with hardly any social security or other benefits; also, they face threats from imports and foreign competition (Rao and Dasgupta 2009; Goldar and Aggrawal 2010; Sharma and Bathla 2012).

Another challenge is the steady decline in labour intensity in the organized foods and beverages industry—from 0.68 on average during the 1980s to 0.10 in 2014–15. It is slightly above 0.06, the average estimated for overall manufacturing, implying that the food industry has the potential to absorb labour, albeit at a slower pace (Bathla 2018). Recently, the capital intensity in many industries has been high, and it seems to have lowered employment growth in the organized segment of the economy (Das et al. 2009). This deceleration must be analysed in the context of the increasingly capital-intensive nature of production; increase in the real wage to rental price of capital ratio; stringent labour laws and regulations; subcontracting, which has forged linkages between the organized and unorganized segments; and changing government policies, including on exports and imports (Sen and Das 2014).

The unorganized enterprises are dominated by micro and small family-run units in rural areas that operate at a low scale and without adequate finance, technology, skilled labour or social security benefits. Employment and productivity growth in these enterprises have been adversely affected by foreign competition, import surge and non-tariff measures such as food quality and safety (Banga and Bathla 2012). Could India's small enterprises grow if provided adequate finance and subcontracting linkages with large firms? Is subcontracting in India's unorganised food manufacturing sector exploitative or productive? Would protection on processed food products through high import tariffs or non-tariff barriers help the smaller units?

The organized foods and beverages segment has had a constant 8% share in total manufacturing output and capital, raising it as another challenge. Besides, total factor productivity growth (TFPG) was low during the 1980s and early 1990s (Mitra 1999; Mitra et al. 2002; Hashim et al. 2009). It improved in the late 1990s and early 2000s to

1.42%, but decelerated again to 0.95% in 2014–15 (Goldar 2017). The inter-industry and inter-state differentials in investment, employment, productivity and technical efficiency are large (Das et al. 2009; Bathla 2014). The competitiveness of industry is hindered by large inefficiencies in the resource use, high cost of production and packaging, safety and quality issues, irregular access to finance, and inadequate investment in the marketing, transport, and cold chain infrastructure for perishables (Sidhu 2005; EPW 2004, 2005).

India's exports of agricultural commodities have been growing, but its export basket comprises mainly low-value, semi-processed commodities (rice, wheat, spices and marine products). The tariff structure of agriculture exports is high, though the nominal rate of protection (weighted) fell from 45.7% in the 1980s to 11.2% in the 1990s for agriculture and from 97.4 to 29.9% for the food industry (Nouroz 2001). In estimating trade protection from 2004–05 to 2013–14, Saini and Gulati (2017) show that the domestic prices were below export parity prices for primary products (cereals, oilseeds and fruits) and above import parity prices for processed products (sugar and skimmed milk powder). These processed products lack comparative advantage. Agricultural exports, though globally competitive, have slowed due to non-tariff measures—food quality and sanitary, phytosanitary and health-related issues—in the key markets of the US, European Union (EU), and the Association of South East Asian Nations (ASEAN) (Mehta 2005; Prasad 2017).

How can India address the growing incidence of rejection on account of food safety and quality? Kannan and Birthal (2010) support dismantling the high protection levels in dairy products to raise employment and improve performance in the dairy industry. Kumar et al. (2020) opine that the foremost requirement is to enhance compliance at the farm level. They find that adoption of food safety measures by dairy farmers in the eastern state increased milk yield by about 1% and profitability by 2.3%. There is also a need to devise some institutional mechanism in the Agriculture Export Policy (GOI 2018) to address non-tariff measures imposed on India's exports.

To address these challenges of agriculture and food industry exports, first, we must examine the composition of India's agriculture exports and imports and its comparative advantage in processed (value-added) products relative to primary (raw) products. Second, we must understand why processed products lack export competitiveness: is it because the industry is protected, or it is inefficient, or other countries bar India's agriculture exports? The productivity of the agro-industry has grown; is that because of domestic demand or reduced protection has raised the exports of value-added products? Further, manufacturing is integrated into global value chains to boost export competitiveness. And interest has been growing lately in analysing its ability to reinvigorate growth and employment in the economy and the processes that need to be followed (Banga 2016; Ray and Miglani 2020). However, the challenge is the integration of primary and processed food-beverages exports into global value chains, which is very low at 5.1% and 1.9%, respectively (Bathla and Jha 2020).

These issues were discussed at a national seminar on *Intersectoral Linkages, Productivity, and Competitiveness in India's Agro and Food Processing Industry* during 21–22 September 2019 at Jawaharlal Nehru University, New Delhi. The seminar was organized by Jawaharlal Nehru University and supported by the Indian

Council of Social Science Research, New Delhi. Eminent scholars in the areas of agriculture, industry and labour market issues presented papers at the seminar. Based on the comments received, these papers were revised and compiled into this book. Its 17 chapters explore three inter-related themes: agriculture–industry–services linkages; employment, investment and productivity growth; and external trade, competitiveness and productivity in the organized and unorganized sectors of the manufacturing industry.

1.1 Agriculture–Industry–Services Linkages

The four chapters under this theme examine the linkages between agriculture, industry and services in the economy. They focus on the magnitude of the processing of agriculture produce in the manufacturing sector, backward and forward output and employment linkages and ways to strengthen these through FPCs and FPOs and contractual arrangements with the food industry.

Seema Bathla and *Madhur Gautam* set the stage by discussing the structure and size of India's agriculture and food-beverage industry, intersectoral production linkages and by estimating the extent of agriculture produce that is processed. The analysis is based on the data on organized manufacturing from the Annual Survey of Industries (ASI) and the data on unorganized enterprises from the National Sample Survey (NSS) for the period from 2000–01 to 2011–12.

Very little agricultural produce is processed, though the quantum is expected to increase in view of rapidly increasing incomes and the changing consumption patterns in favour of processed food. To align with the evolving demand patterns, India's food system requires a policy and regulatory framework that facilitates a smooth transition on the supply side. The increasing awareness of the health effects of alternative foods, and the demand for safer and more nutritious foods, requires greater attention to the regulatory environment for food safety and the organization of food value chains. The rising demand for processed and packaged foods requires an enabling environment to attract investment in the processing of agricultural produce and strengthening the linkages between agriculture, industry and services.

Using a computable general equilibrium model, *Nitin Arora* and *Rahul Arora* analyse the intersectoral employment and output linkages in the economy. Economic reforms, liberal trade and industrial policies have brought about a perceptible structural shift in the Indian economy and transformed it from an agriculture-based economy to one dominated by the services and manufacturing sectors. India's services-led growth can pump demand, but the primary and secondary sectors must both grow substantially for the supply side to progress. Since all the sectors cannot be allocated equal amounts of resources, as proposed in the balanced growth thesis, balanced growth may be brought about by unbalancing the economy through high-linkage sectors. Authors follow a nuanced approach to identify the sectors that have the potential to absorb the maximum labour and improve production levels in the economy through backward and forward production linkages.

K. J. Satyasai and *Aparajita Singh* examine the size and spread of the food processing industry in India and explore the role of FPOs or FPCs in strengthening the agriculture–industry linkages and in benefiting producers and consumers. Food processing units account for 12% of all units. Mostly family-based own account enterprises, they are encumbered by poor margins, problems of scale, limited markets for their products and poor bargaining power in factor and product markets. Aggregation and the leveraging of institutional innovations such as FPOs can reduce the transaction costs of own account enterprises and their acquisition cost of inputs and improve their sale of finished products. Facilitating access to finance would help FPOs grow. A case of the north-eastern states is evaluated to highlight the emerging role of FPOs.

Anjani Kumar and *Gaurav Tripathi* analyse the benefits of contract farming in okra and the farm-level adoption of food safety practices. The chapter uses farmers' survey data collected from Pune and Satara districts in Maharashtra, and it shows that participation in contract farming is significantly influenced by variables such as caste, education of household head, number of visits by government extension officials, number of visits by private extension officials and the number of extension visits by farmers. Given the participation, contract farmers earn relatively higher profits, stemming mainly from higher yields and lower production costs, and contract farming is found to significantly and positively impact the adoption of farm-level food safety measures. The benefits of contract farming are context-specific, however, not a one-size-fits-all solution for agricultural production. Therefore, appropriate policy strategies and mechanisms need to be designed to promote this institutional measure in agricultural commodities, especially in high-value crops.

1.2 Employment, Investment and Productivity Growth

The six chapters on this theme deal with trends in employment; investment; total factor productivity (TFP); efficiency; subcontracting; labour market flexibilities/rigidities; and competition in the organized, unorganized and MSME sectors. These papers analyse the progress made due to the capital-intensive mode of production and their effects on employment and TFPG.

The authors analyse in detail the credit constraints being faced by MSMEs, increasing competition, subcontracting of small units, growing labour market rigidities and falling labour intensity. The analyses—at both the all-India and disaggregated state level—aim to comprehend location-specific factors that determine employment and productivity in the agro and food segments within manufacturing. The authors recommend interventions such as bringing about complementarity between the organized and unorganized sectors, making finance available, upgrading the skill and technology used by MSMEs and reforming the stringent state-specific labour laws.

Seema Bathla and *Shivjee* provide an overview of the temporal and spatial patterns in employment and partial productivity growth in the organized foods and beverages industry in India from 1980–81 to 2014–15. The authors also determine the industry's position in relation to organized manufacturing overall. The analysis—conducted for the period from 1980–81 to 2014–15—indicates that the industry has grown steadily since 1980–81 and that the improvement has been perceptible since the 2000s, the second phase of reform.

The authors identify large temporal and spatial differences with respect to the number of factories, persons engaged, investment and gross value-added (GVA), and they point out higher levels of labour productivity and capital intensity in the processed food industry in Bihar, Gujarat, Himachal Pradesh, Karnataka, Madhya Pradesh, Maharashtra, Punjab, Rajasthan and Uttar Pradesh. Despite improvement in the rate of productivity growth, the food industry lags the non-food segment in terms of labour productivity and capital intensity.

Capital productivity has almost converged, but significant gaps remain in wage rates and labour productivity in favour of the non-food industry. The increasing substitution of capital for labour within food has deepened capital and reduced labour intensity—from 0.68 during the 1980s on average to 0.10 during 2010–2015. This fall is worrisome, as it may imply that an increase in the output of the food industry has not generated adequate growth in employment and hence led employment elasticity to fall. Another issue is capacity utilization, captured through capital per GVA, which rose to 4.89 on average (2010–14) from 2.07 (1980–89).

Padmavathi N. and *Parmod Kumar* examine the structure and composition of the unorganized food processing enterprises in India and explore inter-state disparities using data from two recent rounds of the NSS (67th, 2010–11 and 73rd, 2015–16). They show that the unorganized food enterprises are labour-intensive and that the sector is undergoing a structural transformation—it is moving away from establishments to self-owned enterprises, which has helped labour productivity grow rapidly. In turn, labour productivity is positively and significantly associated with the capital–labour ratio, energy intensity and emoluments per worker. However, states having a relatively larger share in enterprises and workers have performed poorly with respect to labour productivity and the capital–labour ratio. The authors reiterate that though food enterprises have the potential to alleviate rural poverty, the insignificant share in the workforce in relatively lower-income states—Assam, Bihar, Odisha and Madhya Pradesh—may erode non-farm employment opportunities. Registered units that hire workers and have access to credit are more productive, and policy intervention and programme incentives are needed to reduce the inter-state disparities in the growth of food enterprises.

Competition promotes the adoption of new production techniques and facilitates improvements in production quality, efficiency and productivity. Employing a mobility analysis, and using firm-level data from the Prowess database of the Centre for Monitoring the Indian Economy from 2004–05 to 2015–16, *Nithyashree M. L.* examines competition in the food, agriculture machinery, fertilizer and pesticides segments. The stability in firms' rank in industry, obtained by a new turnover index, indicates that except for the machinery sector, competition increased in other sectors. The transition matrix for firms' mobility shows little mobility for the food and pesticides industries. The mobility of firms plays a role in achieving dynamic and effective competition, as is shown by the persistent skewed market concentration in the fertilizer industry and by the scale efficiency in the machinery industry.

Prateek Kukreja analyses the slow pace of growth in industrial employment in view of labour market rigidities. Kukreja delineates the labour regulations and amendments in the organized manufacturing sector undertaken by the central and state governments and uses a state-wise index to evaluate the progress on reforms in labour regulations. The author finds that the organized food and beverage industry employed nearly 1.85 million people in 2016–17 but, as in the non-food industries, mostly on contract. This could be to escape the strict provisions of the Industrial Disputes Act, 1947. The number of contract workers rose from 1.21 million in the early 2000s to 3.40 million in 2015–16. The popular notion is that strict dismissal norms inhibit employment creation, but it is contradicted by the empirical finding based on the generalized method of moments. By increasing the use of contract workers, employers may circumvent the cost of firing regular workers, as stipulated by law, and the cost of compliance, overall, with labour laws. The labour demand is also significantly affected by the increasing wage rate and growing capital intensity. Developing skills commensurate with industry needs can accelerate the pace of job creation.

The National Manufacturing Policy, 2011 treats food processing as the "sunrise" sector of the economy. *Shayequa Zeenat Ali* contends that this sector has immense potential to absorb the surplus labour from agriculture. A few, large, organized, highly productive units co-exist with a large number of small, unorganized, less productive enterprises in the sector, however, and forging linkages between these two sections are necessary to raise productivity. Subcontracting is a type of linkage that can stimulate growth in unorganized enterprises. Sometimes, unorganized food units subcontract for a large firm, and Ali examines the determinants of such a decision and the gains or losses therein. Based on data from three rounds of the NSS (61st round, 2000–01; 66th round, 2005–06; and 73rd round, 2015–16), the findings indicate that subcontracting in foods and beverages has been increasing. The urban directory manufacturing enterprises (DMEs) have higher growth and labour productivity than own account manufacturing enterprises (OAMEs) and non-directory manufacturing enterprises (NDMEs), and they are most likely to engage in subcontracting. The compensation to labour in urban DMEs turns out to be high; the only exception is dairy units, where compensation is higher in rural DMEs. The results favour subcontracting as it has enabled higher productivity and growth in the unorganized food enterprises.

Santosh Kumar investigates the pattern of investment in agriculture-processing MSMEs by focusing on the sources of finance. Kumar uses unit-level data from the Small Scale Industries (SSI) survey (1972–73 and 1987–88) and the SSI/MSME Census (2001–02 and 2006–07). The analysis is carried out by type of enterprise in rural and urban areas according to the three-digit National Industrial Classification (NIC). The SSI survey considers registered units only, but the Census surveys both registered and unregistered units; therefore, the data are not comparable, though broad trends can be discerned.

In 1972–73, the number of registered small-scale agriculture-processing enterprises was 26,252 and the total workforce 306,000; these numbers rose, respectively, to 195,000 and 983,000 in 1987–88. The subsequent surveys show that the number of agriculture-processing MSMEs rose from 2.276 million in 2001–02 to 6.413 million in 2006–07 and the number of workers from 7.106 million to 17.669 million; however, investment per enterprise declined by about 1% per annum during the first period (1972–73 to 1987–88) and increased by 3.77% per annum in the subsequent period (2001–2007). Real investment per enterprise in registered agricultural processing enterprises, INR 0.66 million in 1972–73, decreased to INR 0.55 million in 1987–88.

The subsequent census surveys of registered and unregistered units show an increase in real investment per enterprise from INR 98,000 in 2001–02 to INR 122,000 by 2006–07 at 2011–12 prices; these also show that intra-enterprise differentials were large. The rate of growth was high in dressing and dyeing of fur and fur articles; tanning and dressing of leather; luggage handbags; saddlery and harness; beverages; spinning, weaving and finishing of textiles; tobacco; other food; meat; fish; fruits and vegetables; oils and fats; and footwear units—but lower in other groups. The two-stage least squares (2SLS) analysis shows that investment is determined by the importance of institutional loans, profit earned, availability of raw material and energy. The authors call for easing credit constraints and modernizing small enterprises to accelerate investment—and, hence, employment and agricultural growth—and root out poverty.

1.3 External Trade, Competitiveness and Determinants

The six chapters under this theme delineate the composition and direction of India's exports and of its imports of primary and processed agriculture products, and the changes in their protection structure and comparative advantage, export intensity of imports and determinants of exports. A few papers delve into the composition and size of India's agriculture exports and into the role of the exports of processed agriculture products in firms' performance. To make its food industry efficient and globally competitive, India has taken policy initiatives to lower protection levels by altering tariff and non-tariff measures on agriculture and processed foods. Keeping these initiatives in view, a disaggregated industry- and firm-level analysis is attempted.

Ankur Jain and *Elumalai Kannan* categorize 224 agriculture products—into animal products, including fish; cereals, oilseeds and vegetable oils, horticultural products; processed agricultural products; and agricultural raw materials—and find that their export composition changed between 1998 and 2018. There has been a recent increase in the export share of non-traditional products such as lettuce, grapes, cloves, jams and jellies; these products appear to have huge export potential.

India has a revealed comparative advantage in animal products: human hair, whether unworked or not; silk waste, including cocoons; and crustaceans, whether in shell or not. In the case of horticultural products, its revealed comparative advantage was higher for seeds of anise, badian, fennel and coriander, followed by mate and coconuts, Brazil nuts and cashew nuts. Among cereals, oilseeds and vegetable oils, India has revealed comparative advantage to exports of rice, groundnuts not roasted or otherwise, and other fixed vegetable fats and oils. In the case of processed agricultural products, India has a revealed comparative advantage in oilcake and other solid residues; vegetables, fruits, nuts, and other; and unmanufactured tobacco.

Further, major agricultural exports are more or less in line with their revealed comparative advantage. However, only 34% of products have revealed comparative advantage, and FDI and the exchange rate are found to positively affect revealed comparative advantage. The broad implication is that more focus needs to be given to those products which have comparative advantage to export. In particular, processed agricultural products should receive special attention as they have potential to generate income, employment and value addition. Commodity-specific programmes aiming at export development may be useful towards achieving these ends.

Yashobanta Parida, Avinash K. Ghule and *Priyank Kumar Dudharejiya* narrow down the analysis to dairy exports to examine their major markets, trade direction and competitiveness. Taking the period from 2001 to 2016, they find that South Asia, the Middle East and Southeast Asia are the major destinations for India's dairy products. India became a net exporter of dairy products after 2000, but it remains a minor player despite being the largest milk producer in the world. Much of its dairy-related international trade occurs with one country, the UAE, and it depends on France for imports with regard to some products. Given the changing contours of foreign markets, India's reliance on a few countries for international trade invites certain risks. These may be minimized by keeping a close eye on changing business conditions worldwide and focusing particularly on the relevant countries.

The nominal protection coefficient reveals that the Indian dairy industry is not competitive enough in exporting to the world. The reason could be that the export prices of India's dairy products exceed the world export price. Nevertheless, India is relatively competitive in terms of exporting cheese and curd. The results based on autoregressive distributed lag (ARDL) estimates show that the world per capita income is one of the key determinants responsible for increasing dairy exports, while the exchange rate also plays a significant role in enhancing dairy exports. The results also show that the higher unit price of dairy products adversely affects dairy exports, while diminishing the tariff rate of products can increase exports to some extent. The study concludes that there is considerable scope for enhancing the international trade performance of the dairy industry by focusing on the production of cost-effective and quality dairy products. Also, international cooperation and policy dialogue should be strengthened to restrict export (including input) subsidies provided by developed countries. Negotiating exceptions to the non-tariff and technical barriers to the dairy trade would also help, as would promoting the production of clean milk and improving traceability with the help of technological interventions.

Taking the analysis further, *Abhishek Jha* and *Seema Bathla* probe the quantum of agriculture exports and imports at the four-digit level by bifurcating products into primary (low processing) and value-added (high processing) categories. From 2001 to 2017, the share of primary (raw) agriculture exports in total agricultural exports has increased, due mainly to the export of meat and basmati rice, but the share of highly processed agriculture exports has remained static. In the case of imports, not much change is seen except in the case of processed palm oil and edible oils. This is validated by results obtained from the Galtonian regression, which show little structural transformation in India's external trade in agriculture (raw and processed) commodities.

Processed food products have a lower comparative advantage than primary exports, but they enjoy greater protection. It may imply that India's policy of lower support to primary agriculture commodities does not allow farmers to gain from higher prices in the world markets. And high protection accorded to processed commodities (produced by industry) negates the gains to consumers from low world market prices. The food industry must enhance its price competitiveness through requisite technology, policy and skills and also participate in the domestic and global agriculture value chains.

To what extent has protectionism affected productivity growth and efficiency in the organized food industry? *Seema Bathla* attempts an answer by using the estimates on the level of protection (measured using the average applied tariff rate and nominal rate of protection in Jha and Bathla, this book). Bathla finds that though protectionism in agriculture has fallen, it is more than one for several commodities under the exportable and importable hypotheses. This has helped India become a net exporter of agricultural products, but the pace of increase in exports and imports of processed products tends to be slow. The estimated TFPG in the organized foods and beverages industry improved between 1980–81 and 2014–15. An increase in productivity growth can be attributed to a reduction in the protective regime, but it is more influenced by factors operating within India's economy. A slow pace of growth in processed food exports can be explained by the increasing incidence of non-tariff measures—the topmost include food quality and sanitary, phytosanitary and health-related issues.

To make a sufficient dent on poverty in the Indian economy, high growth in manufacturing needs to be accompanied by the creation of ample employment opportunities. *B. N. Goldar* and *Yashobanta Parida* argue that export-oriented, labour-intensive manufacturing industries need to be focused on to boost manufacturing sector growth and concomitant large-scale job creation. The authors consider the wearing apparel and exports industry and show that fast growth in global exports, which reflect fast growth in global demand, positively affects the export performance of India's wearing apparel industry. Also, industry- and plant-level analyses find that domestic industry growth positively affects export performance. It may, thus, be inferred that policies that promote the wearing apparel industry's growth—through, say, infrastructure development—will automatically boost its exports. This may perhaps be true also for other domestic labour-intensive industries.

Devender Pratap and *Shibananda Nayak* focus on another, yet inter-related, aspect of the exports of manufactured goods. The authors maintain that the global fragmentation of production has led to an increasing trade in intermediate goods in the manufacturing sector. Trade in intermediate goods has necessitated the extent of import intensity and domestic value addition in output and exports of specific countries, globally participating in the joint production sharing. Clearly, developing countries need to assess the extent of domestic value addition in their exports.

The authors analyse the changes in the import intensity of exports from India at four points in time—1989–90, 2003–04, 2006–07 and 2007–08—based on the flows in the input–output table and on items distinguished by both domestically supplied inputs and that sourced through imports. The import content or intensity of exports for the manufacturing and services sectors rose during these periods. The contribution of manufacturing and services exports to total direct and indirect value-added (TVA) declined steadily from 86.9% in 1989–90 to 78.5% in 2007–08. In contrast, total employment (direct and indirect jobs) increased from 35.57 million in 1988–89 to 78.91 million in 2006–07 and then decreased slightly to 63.66 million in 2007–08. Surprisingly, the foods and beverage sector within the manufacturing industry has a negligible contribution to import content of exports.

All the research-based papers are comprehensive in providing insights into the growing importance of the agriculture and food processing sectors in India to meet the diversified consumer demand, potential to absorb labour, accelerate output and exports and enable higher growth in the agriculture and services sectors through backward and forward linkages. The chapters illustrate distinct facets of the agriculture and processed foods sectors across the organized, unorganized and MSME segments during the past two decades, and bring forth the topical ones: intersectoral linkages, with little benefits to agriculture; falling labour intensity; increasing capital intensity and credit constraints; persisting rigidities in the labour market and growing subcontracting; the unchanging share of value-added exports in total agriculture exports and competitiveness; and continuing food safety and quality issues. Besides, the state- and firm-level analyses suggest new dimensions—each having implications for increasing employment, productivity and efficiency in the processed food sector—for drawing policy inferences. All the chapters call for an integrated approach that relies on a market-oriented economy backed by effective policy interventions. The book will immensely benefit academicians, students and policy-makers interested in agriculture, food manufacturing and international trade.

References

Banga, K. (2016). Impact of global value chains on employment in India. *Journal of Economic Integration, 31*(3), 631–673.

Banga, R., & Bathla, S. (2012). Impact of trade on labour markets in the unorganised sector in India: An empirical approach. In K. Pushpangadan & V. N. Balsubrahmanyam (Eds.), *Impact of growth on development: India's record since liberalization.* New Delhi: Oxford University Press.

Bathla, S. (2014). Agro-industry: The food processing sector. World Bank Study (2014) *Republic of India: Accelerating agricultural productivity growth.* Washington D.C.: The World Bank.

Bathla, S. (2018). Productivity in food processing industry under varying trade regimes: Analysis across the Indian states. In A. Mitra (Ed.), *Economic growth in India: Its various dimensions* (Essays in Honour of Prof. B. B. Bhattacharya). Hyderabad: Orient BlackSwan.

Bathla, S., & Jha, A. (2020). Indian agriculture and agro processing in the global value chains. In A. K. Mishra, A. Kumar, & P. K. Joshi (Eds.), *Transforming agriculture in South Asia: The role of value chains and contract farming*, Chapter 15. Routledge Publication.

Bhattacharya, T., & Rajeev, M. (2013). *Identifying the high linked sectors for India: An application of import-adjusted domestic input-output matrix*, Working Paper No. 329. Bangalore: Institute of Social and Economic Change.

Das, D. K., Wadhwa, D., & Kalita, G. (2009). *The employment potential of labor intensive industries in India's organized manufacturing*, Working Paper No. 236. Indian Council for Research on International Economic Relations (ICRIER).

Economic and Political Weekly (EPW). (2005). Food processing: More recommendations. Editorial. *Economic and Political Weekly, 40*(20), 164.

Economic and Political Weekly (EPW). (2004). Food processing policy: Still in the making, editorial. *Economic and Political Weekly, 39*(48), 5069

Goldar, B. (2017). Growth, productivity and job creation in Indian manufacturing. In U. Kapila (Ed.), *India's economy pre-liberalisation to GST: Essays in honour of Raj Kapila* (pp. 619–652). New Delhi: Academic Foundation.

Goldar, B., & Aggrawal, S. C. (2010, September). *Informalisation of industrial labour in India: Are labour market rigidities and growing import competition to blame?* Working paper. New Delhi: Institute of Economic Growth.

Gollin, D., & Probst, L. T. (2015). Food and agriculture: Shifting landscapes for policy. *Oxford Review of Economic Policy, 31*(1), 8–25.

Government of India. (2017). *Consolidated FDI policy circulars of 2017*. Ministry of Commerce and Industry, Government of India.

Government of India (GOI). (2018). *Agriculture Export Policy*. Department of Commerce, Ministry of Commerce and Industry, Government of India.

Government of India—Ministry of Food Processing Industries (GoI-MoFPI). https://mofpi.nic.in.

Goyal, T., Mukherjee, A. M., & Kapoor, A. (2017). *India's exports of food products: Food safety related issues and way forward*. ICRIER, Working Paper No. 345.

Hashim, D. A., Kumar, A., & Virmani, A. (2009). *Impact of major liberalization on productivity: The J curve hypothesis*, Working Paper No. 5/2009. Department of Economic Affairs, Ministry of Finance.

Kannan, E., & Birthal, P. S. (2010). Effect of trade liberalization on the efficiency of Indian dairy industry. *Journal of International and Area Studies, 17*(1), 1–15.

Kumar, A., Mishra, A. K., Saroj, S., Sonkar, V. K., Thapa, G., & Joshi, P. K. (2020). *Food safety measures and food security of smallholder dairy farmers: Empirical evidence from Bihar, India*. Wiley: Agribusiness. https://doi.org/10.1002/agr.21643.

Mehta, R. (2005, June). *Non-Tariff barriers affecting India's exports. Research and information system for the non-aligned and other developing countries*. RIS Discussion Paper No. 97. Research and Information System for Non-aligned and Other Developing Countries.

Mitra, A. (1999). Total factor productivity growth and technical efficiency in Indian industries. *Economic and Political Weekly, 34*(31), M98–M105.

Mitra, A., Varoudakis, A., & Veganzones, M. A. (2002). Productivity and technical efficiency in Indian States' manufacturing: The role of infrastructure. *Economic Development and Cultural Change, 50*(2), 395–426.

Nouroz, H. (2001). *Protection in Indian manufacturing: An empirical study*. Macmillan India Ltd.

Prasad, H. A. C. (2017, January). *Reviving and accelerating India's exports: Policy issues and suggestions*, Working Paper No. 1/2017-DEA, Government of India Ministry of Finance Department of Economic Affairs Economic Division.

Rao Chandrasekhara, N., & Dasgupta, S. (2009). Nature of employment in the food processing sector. *Economic and Political Weekly, 44*(17), 109–115.

Ray, S., & Miglani, S. (2020). *India's GVC integration: An analysis of upgrading efforts and facilitation of lead firms*. Working Paper 386, ICRIER.

Saini, S., & Gulati, A. (2017). Price distortions in Indian agriculture, International Bank for Reconstruction and Development and World Bank.

Sarkar, S. (1995). Size structure of agro-industry: A linkage analysis. *Indian Journal of Agricultural Economics,50*(4) (October–December), 634–648.

Sen, K., & Das, D. K. (2014). *Where have all the workers gone? The Puzzle of Declining Labour Intensity in Organized Indian Manufacturing, Development Economics and Public Policy Working Paper Series WP No. 35*. Institute of Development Policy and Management, School of Environment, Education and Development. UK: University of Manchester.

Sharma, R. K., & Bathla, S. (2012). *Economic and social viability of agro-processing industry in India. Research study*. New Delhi: African-Asian Rural Development Organization (AARDO).

Sidhu, M. S. (2005). Fruits and vegetable processing industry in India: An appraisal of the post-reform period. *Economic and Political Weekly*, 3056–3061.

USDA. (2020). *Agriculture and food statistics: Charting the essentials, Economic Research Service (ERS) of the United States Department of Agriculture (USDA)*. www.ers.usda.gov/data-produc dts/ag-and-food-statistics-charting-the-essentials. Accessed April 18, 2020.

World Bank. (2008). *Agriculture for development*. Washington, D.C.: The World Bank Report.

Part I
Agriculture-Industry-Services Linkages

Chapter 2
Post-harvest Food Management, Extent of Processing and Inter-sectoral Linkages

Seema Bathla and Madhur Gautam

2.1 Introduction

The state of transformation of India's food system is reflected in the changes taking place in the size and scale of the agro-processing and agro-services sectors, and their inter-linkages with agricultural sector. Knowledge gaps are, however, extensive given the diversity in economic activities, a large and varied consumer base, domestic and trade policies that influence the growth of the sector, and regional differentials. This chapter delves into three important questions, which are the prerequisites to understand the evolving food system in India—both on-farm, in terms of production mix, and off-farm, in the post-harvest management of farm produce. First, what is the size of agribusiness in the non-farm economy in terms of output (measured as gross value added) and employment? Second, what is the share of agricultural output that is processed, and what is the nature and extent of agricultural inputs (domestic and imported) used by the manufacturing and service sectors? And finally, what are the magnitudes of inter-industry (agriculture-industry) and intra-industry linkages?

It brings together available data from multiple sources covering a wide range of economic activities that comprise the post-harvest agri-food management system. The availability or accessibility of such data often constrains the needed analysis.

This chapter draws on a background paper for a World Bank report on "Unlocking Agribusiness for Inclusive Growth, Jobs, and More: Policy and Investment Priorities" 2016. The findings, interpretations, and conclusions expressed in this paper are those of the authors and do not necessarily reflect the views of the Executive Directors of The World Bank or the governments they represent. The World Bank does not guarantee the accuracy of the data included in this work.

S. Bathla (✉)
Centre for the Study of Regional Development, Jawaharlal Nehru University, New Delhi, India
e-mail: seema.bathla@gmail.com

M. Gautam
Lead Economist, Agriculture Global Practice, World Bank, Washington DC, USA
e-mail: mgautam@worldbank.org

17

This chapter is no exception to such data limitations. We begin in Sect. 2.1 with a description of the approach, methodology and data sources used, as well as the limitations that currently available data impose in arriving at a more comprehensive picture. Section 2.2 sets the context for the remainder of the chapter by looking at the evolving consumption patterns, volume (quantity and value) and form (raw or processed) of agricultural exports and imports, and how has this composition and the overall structure of the agro-processing and agro-services sectors changed over time. Section 2.3 looks into the share of agricultural production that is processed and provides estimates on the inter-sectoral production linkages. Section 2.4 summarizes the main findings and their policy implications.

2.2 The Methodological Approach, Data Sources and Limitations

The main focus of this chapter is on the changes taking place in the post-harvest food management system for crops, livestock and fisheries-based food products. Agriculture, however, contributes more than just food supply to the economy; it also supplies essential non-food raw materials for substantial segments of the industrial and service sectors. For comparability, and where feasible, estimates are provided for the broader agricultural domain, coined in the Indian national accounts statistics as "agriculture and allied activities," and includes forestry in addition to crops, livestock, and fisheries. Accordingly, the broader agro-based estimates include post-harvest activities for non-food crops (such as textiles from natural fibres, and tobacco); non-food livestock products (such as leather and leather products); and wood-based products (such as furniture manufacturing) in addition to food crops related activities.

Post-harvest management and agribusiness is defined to encompass all activities including aggregation of farm commodities, packaging, sorting, agro-processing, distribution of food and food products (wholesale and retail trade) and food service (hotels-restaurants) activities. The analysis considers both the formal and informal sectors in an attempt to provide as comprehensive a picture as possible, but is naturally constrained by the availability of relevant data. Despite tapping all reliable sources, some gaps remain as certain data simply do not exist. Nevertheless, the estimates presented in this chapter provide a more comprehensive picture than any other study we are aware of.

Two points in time, 2000–01 and 2010–11 are chosen for the analysis, mainly driven by the desire to maintain comparability between the formal (organised) and informal (unorganised) sectors. While data on the formal processing industry are available on an annual basis, the data on the informal processing sector are available only at discrete intervals (every 5 or so years). Another motivation for looking at two points in time is to illustrate the changes taking place in the food system, with the selected years covering a particularly dynamic period for the Indian economy during which it emerged as one of the fastest growing economies of the world.[1]

The analysis of the size and structure of the agro-processing and the agro retail business uses data on the number of workers, units (factories or enterprises), value of fixed assets, gross value added (GVA), output and inputs used in each of the selected industry/sector. These variables are directly observable in the data, which makes computation of the relevant indicators straightforward.

The extent of processing of major agricultural commodities (EPA) is based on the volume of individual commodities used as inputs in the post-harvest processing and food service industries. The agricultural produce used as input in each post-harvest industry is considered (using detailed 5-digit national industrial classification, or NIC codes) to arrive at reasonably reliable estimates for the major commodities produced in India. EPA is then estimated as the ratio of the aggregate value of each commodity used as input in post-harvest activities to the total primary production of that commodity (in quantity and value terms), after deducting seed usage and wastage from the gross level of production.

While EPA is seemingly straightforward to define, arriving at a meaningful empirical estimate can be tricky. A wide range of activities can be considered as "processing"—from the minimalist cleaning of grains to very high levels of processing (such as prepared or ready-to-eat foods). A common source of confusion in discussions on EPA, typically in the context of value addition through agro-processing, is the lack of clarity on what is meant by processing. To avoid such confusion, it is important to distinguish between different levels of processing to understand how the food system is evolving. As such, the approach adopted is to classify agriculture-based products under three broad categories of foods depending on the level of processing they undergo. The three categories are as follows.

The first level is unprocessed food, that is all products whose final sale is in their raw, or natural, form. These foods may involve cleaning, grading and packing, but are essentially purchased by the final consumer in their primary form. These post-harvest activities likely add some value (insofar cleaner and higher graded produce commands a price premium in the market), but they are not the level of processing implied in a discourse on post-harvest food management activities, such agro-industrial manufacturing or food services. The foods included in this group are nevertheless typically high value (from farm production value point of view), including horticulture (fresh fruits and vegetables), eggs, and certain spices.

The second level is primary processing. A large volume of agricultural produce requires some form of basic processing, such as grinding, milling, hulling, shelling, and even drying. This processing typically transforms products that are not edible in their raw form (such as grains) to a more edible form (such as flour or consumable pulses, etc.) but the value added is relatively small. This category is important to

---

[1]The choice of the second year, 2010/11, instead of 2009/10 (which would mark the 10 year period) is deliberate because India suffered one of the worst droughts in recent history in 2009. To avoid picking a negative outlier year, which may unduly distort the trends, 2010/11 is chosen for comparison.

distinguish from foods consumed or purchased in raw form, but it also needs to be distinguished the third, or secondary, level of processing. This secondary level of processing results in a significant modification of in the form of the agricultural commodity, and typically also adds significantly higher value.

Ignoring primary processing as a distinct category would, on the one hand, raise the unbelievable spectre of "very low level of processing" of agricultural output. For example, rice and wheat account for a large share India's agricultural production, but neither is consumed in its raw form—paddy (the raw form of rice, with husk) is not consumed directly, nor is wheat typically consumed as whole grain (the same is the case with almost all cereals). Paddy is milled into rice and wheat into flour, entailing some degree of (primary) processing. On the other hand, generically classifying all such produce as processed would also be misleading by conveying the impression that a very large share of the produce is being processed (typically assumed to mean a higher level of processing than milling/husking), and subjected to significantly greater value addition than may be the case.

To arrive at a more relevant, and more precise, estimate of the extent of agricultural produce that is processed, we distinguish between primary and secondary levels of processing. This avoids defining processing to mean everything from rice-husking to making cheese to fully prepared or ready-to-eat meals. Maintaining this distinction between the levels of processing helps to arrive at a cleaner estimate of EPA.

Further, it is important to note that while the extent of primary processing per se is of less direct interest, completely ignoring the agriculture inputs to primary processing may result in an underestimate of EPA. This may be if a potentially significant share of the produce *indirectly* enters secondary processing as an intermediate input (that is, as output from primary processing). For example, a bread maker may purchase wheat directly to mill the grain in-house. In this case, the share of wheat grain going directly to the bread maker would be an accurate measure of EPA. However, other bread makers may choose to purchase wheat flour from the milling industry rather than purchase wheat grain directly for own milling. In this case, the share of wheat that ends up indirectly as flour input to secondary processing will be missed if all of the grain going to the primary processing industry is ignored.

To avoid such mis-measurement, EPA is defined as the sum of two components: (a) agricultural produce used directly as input in the secondary processing industry. And (b) the proportionate share of agricultural production used in the primary processing industry (readily identified in the National Industrial Classification codes as 106 and 107) that is eventually used as intermediate input by the secondary processing industry. The proportionate share is derived as the share of primary processing industry output used as input in the secondary processing industry multiplied by the ratio of raw agricultural produce (typically grain) used as input to produce the primary processing output (all in value terms).

Finally, to assess how the structure of the food system is changing, secondary processing is further sub-categorized using a finer distinction of the level to which food is processed. This is possible only on the demand side, using data from the nationally representative household consumption surveys. Using data on individual commodities consumed, secondary processed foods are further sub-categorized into three levels—low, medium and high. That is, changes in consumption levels of a total of five categories of foods (unprocessed, primary processed, low secondary, medium secondary and high secondary processed), are estimated to get a sense of the trends in the composition of the food system.

Low level secondary processing includes products with value addition that is more than primary processing, but still relatively modest, such as pasteurizing, heating, fermenting, slaughtering and crushing (e.g. butter, curd, meat, fish, and sugar). The medium secondary level of processing adds higher value as direct raw inputs are mixed with other primary or secondary processed products to make final products (e.g. biscuits, bread, ghee, ice cream, and jams). The high-level secondary processing includes products with the highest value-added activities and includes ready-to-eat foods, prepared, frozen and packed meals, and processed foods which typically involve significant supportive investments in plant and machinery (such as cold chains) or services (such as restaurants).

The backward and forward production linkages between agriculture and manufacturing (through agro-industries) and services (through retail trade) are estimated based on the usage of agriculture inputs in the respective processing and retail activities. The inputs used in each industry (extracted at 5 digit NIC code level) are segregated into five categories, namely (a) raw agricultural commodities; (b) agricultural commodities with low value addition; (c) agricultural commodities with moderate value addition; (d) agricultural commodities with high value addition; (e) agricultural inputs (fertilizer & pesticides), machinery and equipment; and (f) non-agricultural inputs. The categorization is done to estimate both inter-sectoral (agriculture and industry) and intra-industry (within agro-processing) linkages. The latter is important as some of the final products of the food industry may be used as inputs for further processing industries. For the organized sector, inputs are also separated as indigenous and imported raw materials to see the source of intermediate processed inputs, providing an indication of the potential for substitution.

The data used in this study are from the following sources:

1. Unit level data on organized manufacturing from the Annual Survey of Industries (ASI), Central Statistical Organization (CSO), Ministry of Statistics and Programme Planning, Government of India (GOI) at two points of time, 2000–01 and 2011–12 (GOI-ASI 2000–01 and 2011–12).

2. Unit level data on unorganized manufacturing from quinquennial National Sample Survey (NSS) from the 56th round (2000–01) and the 67th round (2010–11) of the Unincorporated Non-Agricultural Enterprises (excluding construction), conducted by the National Sample Survey Organization (NSSO) (GOI-NSSO 2000–01 and 2010–11).

3. Unit level data on the tertiary sector based on quinquennial NSS for the 57th round (2001–02) on Unorganized Services, excluding Trade & Finance, and the 67th round (2010–11) for Service Sector enterprises. It is important to note that the former round excludes wholesale trade, implying that he two the two data sets are not fully matched.

4. National income across broad economic sectors, the total value of output from agriculture and allied activities, and the value of processed food items from that National Accounts Statistics (GOI-NAS), published by the CSO from 2000–01 to 2011–12.

5. Export and Import of major agricultural commodities from 1996 to 2011 from COMTRADE, and area and production of major agricultural commodities from FAO and Agricultural Statistics at a Glance, Ministry of Agriculture, GOI.

6. Consumption expenditure across broad items are taken from the GOI-National Household Consumer Expenditures surveys carried out during 1993–94 (50th round), 2004–05 (61st round), and 2011–12 (68th round) by the national sample survey organization (GOI-NSSO 1993–94, 2004–05 and 2011–12).

The current values of fixed assets, input and output are converted to 2004–05 prices using gross fixed capital formation deflator for manufacturing given in the GOI-NAS). For other variables, the wholesale price index of all commodities is used to convert all values to 2004–05 prices. The agro- and food-related sectors in manufacturing and services are identified using the National Industrial Classification (NIC) codes at 3, 4, and 5-digit levels for both manufacturing and retail activities. Due to changes in the definition of some of the codes, a comparable time series data on key performance indicators in agro, food and beverage industry is constructed on the basis of a concordance matrix to reconcile the changing codes and definitions between NIC-2004 and NIC-2008. The industries falling under NIC (2008) 3-digit codes, namely, 016, 101–108, and 110, are categorized as food and beverage processing. The broader set of agro-processing industries is defined as those included in the food processing sector plus the industries under the codes 120 (tobacco), 131, 141, 142, 2021, 2098, 2825 (Cotton textiles, wool textiles, agricultural inputs and machinery and food processing equipment and their repairs).

In the services sector, activities include wholesale and retail trade, NIC codes 561, 562, 563 (hotels, motels, restaurants, beverages); 750 (veterinary activities); 4620, 4630, 4653 (wholesale trade in livestock, processed food and agricultural tools and equipment); 4711, 4722, 4723, 4781 (retail trade in food and beverages); and 46,101, 46,692, 46,695, 52,101 and 52,102 (wholesale trade in fertilizers, agrochemicals, textiles and warehousing-refrigerated and non-refrigerated). Appendix 2.1 gives the complete list of agro-processing industries, and wholesale and retail food services included in the analysis for the study.

The data on inputs used in the manufacturing and tertiary sectors are as per commodity classification codes for Annual Survey of Industry (ASI) (ASICC), also used for NSS, which have been further replaced by the National Product Classification for Manufacturing Sector (NPC-MS) codes. For each of the selected industry/enterprise, the quantity and value of inputs used is extracted at 5-digit level for 2000–01 and 2011–12 and is reconciled using a concordance matrix between the two rounds.

Finally, as in the case with NIC 2004 and NIC 2008, a concordance matrix is used to reconcile the NIC 2008 codes with the 2008 Standard International Trade Classification (SITC) codes (for export and import data) to make the data comparable and consistent over the study period. Based on the value of each input used, input coefficients (IC) are estimated by taking the ratio of value of input and output separately for agriculture and agro-processed products to represent the extent of backward and forward (inter-sectoral and intra-industry) production linkages. As noted earlier, the comprehensiveness of this analysis is constrained to a certain extent by the availability of some types of data, as well as some limitations in the data that are available. Appendix 2.2. lists the main data gaps encountered.

2.3 The Evolving Food System: Consumption, Trade, and Scale of Agro-industry

This section looks at the changes taking place on the demand side of the food system. To assess if structural imbalances may be emerging on the supply side, specifically in the processing sector, changes in the nature and composition of agricultural exports and imports are also analysed. An imbalance in trade patterns, for example, between unprocessed and processed foods, might reflect underlying frictions which may be constraining the domestic processing industry to respond to the emerging demand pressures.

2.3.1 Consumption Patterns

The share of food in the average total household consumption expenditures is still substantial at 41% (in terms of monthly per capita expenditures or MPCE). While the *share* has come down from 60% in 1993/94 and 47% in 2004/05, in *absolute terms* the real MPCE on food has grown at the rate of 4% per year between 2004/05 and 2011/12.

Rising incomes are clearly fuelling demand for food items, but how is the consumption basket changing? To assess this, consumption is categorized into five groups based on the extent to which the individual food items are processed. Appendix 2.3 gives a detailed list of food items included in each category. This categorization demonstrates the shift in consumption patterns away from low-value grains or other primary commodities to high value foods, and increasingly towards food with higher value addition. Changing consumption foods by the extent of their value addition has important implications, from food grain demand projections, to the strategic approach to developing the sector.

Estimates of changes in food consumption patterns are given in Table 2.1, which shows the shares of each category of food in the monthly per capita expenditures (MPCE) between 1993–94 and 2011–12 (using the 50th−68th round NSS consumption expenditure surveys). The bottom row (shaded) shows the level of total food consumption (MCPE) in each of the survey years. The table also shows the annual

Table 2.1 Changes in food consumption patterns in India

	Share of total MPCE			Annual rate of growth (2004–05 prices)		
	1993–94	2004–05	2011–12	1993–04	2004–11	1993–11
Unprocessed	13.7	15.6	14.8	0.48	3.28	1.6
Primary proc.	43.9	38.8	32.9	−1.77	1.58	−0.5
Low secondary proc.	34.2	35.8	37.8	−0.26	4.84	1.7
Medium secondary proc.	4.44	6.04	5.59	2.14	2.89	2.4
High secondary proc.	3.72	3.71	8.87	−0.72	17.83	6.1
Total MPCE (Rs.) (2004/05)	369.3	342.8	451.9	−0.68	4.03	1.1

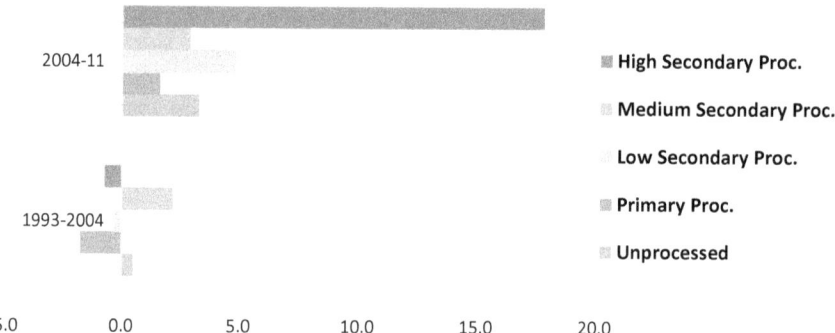

Fig. 2.1 Annual growth rates for real monthly per capita consumption expenditures, 1993/94–2011/12. *Source* GOI-NSSO consumption expenditure surveys, various years

growth rate for each food category (last four columns). Figure 2.1 visualizes the annualized growth rates between the three survey rounds.

Increase in the income of households and urbanization are expected to be associated with consumption patterns shifting towards more diversified and processed foods. The share of expenditures spent on unprocessed and primarily high value produce (e.g. horticultural products), has remained relatively stable over the past 20 years at about 15%, implying that the consumption of these foods has grown in line with the rapidly rising overall expenditures. The shares of foods with primary processing has declined significantly, with real absolute expenditures also declining over the long run—this group is comprised of low-value cereals or staples.

A notable shift in recent years (post 2004/05) is the rapid growth in the share of foods with secondary levels of processing. The combined (low-, medium-, and high-) secondary processed foods accounted for the *majority* share of the consumer basket in 2011/12 (at 52%). The bulk of this demand is still concentrated in lower end of the secondary processing scale, with expenditure levels growing at a brisk almost 5% per year between 2004/05 and 2011/12. Foods subjected to medium level of secondary processing had the lowest share in 2011/12, but their demand still grew faster than primary processed foods. The share of the high processed foods is also still relatively low, but the demand for these foods is growing the fastest—their share more than doubled between 2004/05 and 2011/12, with expenditures levels growing at a spectacular rate of almost 18% a year.

These trends confirm that rapid changes are taking place in the food system. The demand for primary commodities such as horticultural products is growing twice as fast as the demand for cereals and cereal products. The demand for processed foods is rising even faster, and rapidly shifting towards highly processed and prepared foods. Long-term trends (growth rates from 1993 to 2011) show a similar pattern: a distinct shift away from primary processing (food grains/cereals) towards (a) fresh fruits and vegetables—calling for both diversification of agricultural production and investment in post-harvest infrastructure, better management of high value fresh produce value chains, and ensuring food safety and standards, and (b) processed foods—with both low and high levels of secondary processing, parts of the food system that offer significant potential for non-farm jobs and income growth. These trends call for a closer scrutiny of the food processing sector to identify potential constraints to investment in the sector. These patterns are consistent with the growth of more nutrient-dense unprocessed horticulture products, income-elastic livestock and other foods with low level of processing, as well as a rapidly growing preference for fully prepared meals and cooked foods—all which additionally require ramping up the efforts to ensure food safety.

2.3.2 Trade Patterns: Composition of Food Exports and Imports

The changing food habits of Indian consumers are expected to also influence the pattern and composition of food trade (exports and imports). The trends may reflect rising imports of processed or high value foods, with exports increasingly concentrated in primary or low-value products (which may suggest a structural balance). Alternatively, they may simply reflect diversifying consumer tastes for products that are not produced domestically.

Trends in India's net exports are shown in Fig. 2.2, which shows the net export value (i.e. exports less imports) of agricultural and non-agricultural commodities, averaged over two periods—2000–05 and 2006–11. India has improved its trade surplus in agricultural exports, even as the deficit in non-agricultural commodities worsened over the same period. Overall, the share of agriculture (food, beverages and tobacco only) in total exports fell from 12.06 to 9.10%, while imports occupied a much lower and also a falling share (from about 4.7–3.2%). These data point to India's revealed comparative advantage in agricultural exports (see Balassa 1965 for a discussion on revealed comparative advantage).

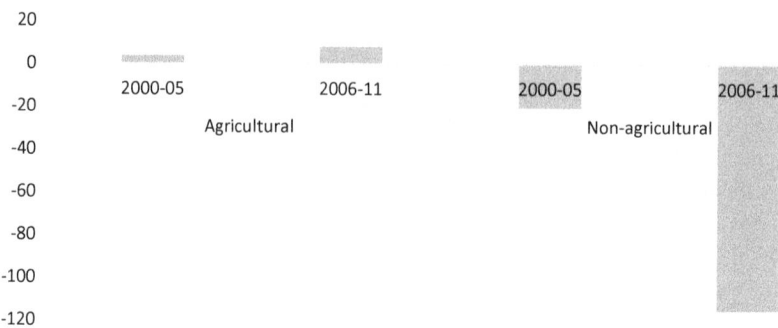

Fig. 2.2 Net exports of agricultural and non-agricultural commodities (US Dollar, Millions)

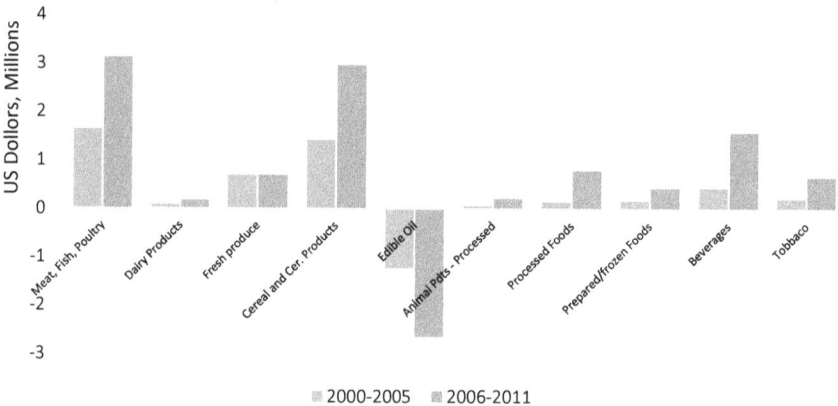

Fig. 2.3 Net exports by food commodity group

The commodity wise composition of net exports, Fig. 2.3, shows that net exports have increased for each commodity group, irrespective of the degree of processing. Importantly, exports are more diversified than imports. Consistent with Fig. 2.1, we find the largest shares of commodity exports are for fresh meat (including live animals, 19% on average between 2006 and 2011), cereals and cereal products (19%), and oilseeds (13%). Imports are heavily concentrated in edible oils, accounting for just over half (50.4%) of all food imports.

Two important observations emerge from the data on exports and imports between 2000 and 2011. Although the volume of *net* exports of fresh produce (raw fruits, vegetables, nuts, etc.) appears relatively small in Fig. 2.3, substantial volumes of fresh produce are both exported and imported, with the former slightly higher in value than the latter. Fresh produce is the second highest share of both imports (34%) and exports (22%) among traded agricultural commodities—India is clearly exporting more of some commodities (surplus of traditional fresh produce) while importing others (perhaps reflecting widening preferences of consumers for newer and different foods). It may also reflect a "bridging" problem whereby fresh produce that cannot be stored across seasons is exported in the surplus season only to be re-imported in the lean season. The second observation is that, contrary to common perception, India's net exports of processed foods (processed, prepared and beverages) have risen overtime, although their shares are modest relative to other food groups. In fact, with the exception of edible oils, all animal and plant based processed foods show positive and growing net exports. An important conclusion that emerges from these trends is that it does not appear to be the case that imports of processed foods are rising in response to consumer demand. Falling net exports (meaning rising processed food imports) would raise concerns about the emerging constraints or otherwise distorted development of the food processing industry, but the current analysis does not suggest this to be the case.

2.3.3 Structure and Trends of Agro-processing and Services

Both manufacturing and tertiary sectors have a dualistic structure: a relatively smaller (in number of units) but more capital-intensive organized segment coexists with a pervasive and relatively labour-intensive unorganized segment (also called the unregistered or informal firms or enterprise sector) (World Bank 2014). Appendix 2.4 gives details on the structure and size of the agro-processing industry, the food processing industry, and the agro-wholesale and retail trade sectors (for which data are available) for 2000–01 and 2011–12. Both agro-processing and food processing manufacturing sectors are dominated by the unorganized sector in terms of number of enterprises and workers. But in terms of gross value added (GVA) and investment, the unorganized sector stands way below the organized segment.

A closer look at the composition of manufacturing sector shows that a substantial share of manufacturing is dependent on agriculture (for processing of food products, manufacture of non-food agro-based products, or manufacture of inputs and machinery used in agriculture). The GVA of the combined organized and unorganized agriculture-linked industries is estimated to be a sizeable 29.4% share of total manufacturing sector. Of this, food processing accounts for 11%, non-food agro-processing for 12%, and the input industry for an additional 6% of total manufacturing GVA (Fig. 2.4).[2] Considering the organized and unorganized segments individually, agro-based manufacturing accounts for a substantial 24% share of the organized sector GVA, but in unorganized manufacturing, it dominates with a share of 60% of GVA. In terms of structure, the organized sector is balanced across the three types of industries—food processing, non-food agro-based, and inputs industry. But the unorganized sector is heavily concentrated in the non-food agro-processing sector, with the biggest components being fibre-based manufacturing (47% share), followed by wood products (20%).

---

[2]The reported figures are percentages of the combined GVA of organized and unorganized manufacturing sectors, of which 70% is organized and 30% is unorganized.

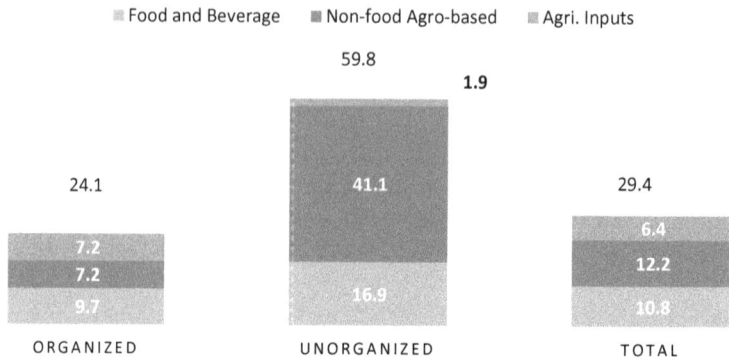

Fig. 2.4 Share of manufacturing gross value added from the food, non-food agro-based, and agriculture input industries, 2011–12

In the services sector, as noted the analysis is restricted to unorganized food services for 2010/11. The 2004/05 informal sector survey did not include information on wholesale or retail trade, so the data on the unorganized sector in that year are limited to food service establishments (restaurants, bars and catering services), veterinary services, and storage/warehousing services (henceforth referred to as FVS). For 2010/11, data on wholesale and retail trade in food, beverage, livestock and tobacco products are available, so a fuller accounting of the food service sector is possible (that is, FVS + WR). To get a sense of the share of FVS in the food services sector, the data shows that the FVS accounted for about 26% of the total value of FVS + WR. In other words, the unorganized food-related services sector is dominated by trading activities.

Changes over time can only be assessed for the FVS segment, showing a modest expansion in the number of establishments (3%) and in employment (2%), but a decline in fixed assets (almost 3%). Total output value (GVA) grew at an annual rate of about 4% between 2004/05 and 2011/12. From the 2010/11 NSS, food services (that is, FVS + WR) as a share of all trade, hotels, restaurants and storage activities in the unorganized sector is estimated to be about 26%. Within these activities, retail trade dominates (accounting for 60% of GVA contributed by this segment), followed by food services (restaurants, food catering, etc. at about 26% of GVA) and then wholesale trade (about 13%).

To overcome the lack of survey data on the organized services sector, an indirect method is used to arrive at an (admittedly crude) estimate of the size of total agro-based services. For this, the value of GDP contributed by the trade, hotels/restaurants and storage services from the National Accounts Statistics (which includes both formal and informal sectors) is compared with the total GVA estimated from the 67th round of the NSS (only the informal sector). This shows that the unorganized sector accounts for about 40% of the total (organized and unorganized) value added by trade, hotels/restaurants and storage services for 2010–11. Assuming that the share of agro-related services in total service activities is the same in the organized and the unorganized sectors, about 26% of the total trade, hotels and restaurants, and storage activities (which contribute a non-trivial 17% to the national GDP) are accounted for by agro-services.

The total contribution of food-related services (as defined above to include FVS + WR) to the total economy is thus estimated at 4.4%, which is almost the same as the share of the agro-related manufacturing sector of 4.6%.[3] These findings highlight the broader role agriculture plays in the overall structure of the Indian economy. Thus, while the direct share of agriculture in GDP is about 14% of real GDP, the indirect contribution of the sector (in terms of value added through industry and service sector linkages) which is not readily visible in the traditional sectoral aggregates from national accounts (i.e. agriculture, industry and services), is another substantial 9.0%. It is important to reiterate that because of the data limitations noted above, these are underestimates of the entirely of indirect effects. Even so, it appears that *at least* one-fourth of the manufacturing and services sectors, equivalent to about 9.0% of the national GDP, are agro-based. Clearly, what happens in agriculture matters to a substantial share of the economy and population, especially for jobs, beyond those immediately dependent on it.

2.4 Extent of Processing of Agriculture and Inter-sectoral Production Linkages

Fast growth in agri-business suggests that the food system is transforming in response to consumer demand. Yet, a persistent concern of policy makers is that it is not happening fast enough. The perception is that only a small fraction of agricultural output is processed, leaving significant unexploited opportunities to add value (which would translate at least partially to higher rural incomes) and create non-farm employment.

To understand how much of agricultural output is being processed, EPA is estimated for major agricultural commodities most commonly used as raw material (or inputs) in the industry/enterprise sector. A specific interest of this study is the level of secondary processing. The value of agricultural products used as inputs in processing is divided by the respective value of primary production for each commodity to estimate EPA. The aggregate EPA is based on the weighted average using share of production value as weights, after making allowances for losses and other uses.

The analysis of the backward and forward production linkages between agriculture, industry and service sectors is also done at two points of time, 2000 and 2011. Backward linkages are a result of the demand from agriculture for intermediate goods (e.g. agricultural machinery and inputs), and forward linkages result from

---

[3]In sum, in addition to the direct contribution of agriculture to the 2010–11 GDP of about 14.5%, the sectors indirect contribution through forward and backward linkages to the manufacturing and service sectors is estimated to be an additional 8.5%. Thus, influencing about 23% of the GDP, agriculture continues to play an important role in contributing to overall economic growth.

the use of agricultural output as input into the downstream agro-processing industry and the tertiary/service sectors. Backward and forward linkages are important indicators of the "leveraging" effect of agriculture in the broader non-farm economy, often referred to as production and inter-industry linkages. Focusing on the agro-processing and food service businesses, their linkages with agriculture and intra-industry linkages are estimated as the total value of (agriculture) input required to produce one unit of (industry or service sector) output. This is done by categorizing the value of total agri-commodities used as inputs in the industry into (a) primary (unmilled) commodities (b) commodities with value addition/processing (milling), and (c) non-agro manufactured and other inputs.

The proportion of the value of input to the value of output, or input coefficients, are estimated for each industry. The agriculture-based inputs used in an industry/enterprise are classified as agricultural inputs (unprocessed) and agro-industry inputs (processed to at least some degree). This helps in accounting for the proportion of agricultural output that is used to produce intermediate products which are then used for further processing. This distinction helps understand the intra-industry, or forward linkages that may not at first sight be obvious. For example, some enterprises may use already processed agricultural commodities for further processing, such as converting processed milk into dairy products such as cheese, or wheat flour into edible products such cookies and bread. In such cases, as one agro-industry unit uses raw material from another agro-industry unit, it may superficially show weak or no linkages with primary agriculture; yet in reality, it is critically (albeit indirectly) dependent on agriculture for its key input (e.g. raw milk or wheat grains), without which the industry would not exist. Further, a breakdown by the source of the inputs, namely indigenously sourced or imported, allows estimating separate input coefficients (IC) for indigenous and imported inputs to shed light on the extent to which an industry is dependent on external markets for raw materials/inputs. This separation is possible for the formal sector in 2011–12 as the ASI surveys provide this information.

It is important to note a significant shortcoming in the data on the unorganized sector which constrains the analysis of temporal trends. While it is possible to segregate raw materials used in each industry by the level of processing (unprocessed or agriculture input and processed or agro-industry input) for the organized sector for both years (2000–01 and 2010–11), for the unorganized sector this distinction is possible only for 2000–01 (NSS 56th round), but not for the 2010–11 (NSS 67th round). This is because, as noted earlier, the survey for 67th round was changed to capture data only on five major inputs used in each industry, without identifying the type, nature or source of product represented by each of the five input values. As such, for the unorganized sector it is possible to get only a snap-shot at the start of the decade, but how the unorganized sector has evolved in terms of EPA remains unknown. Similar data for the food service sector, do not exist, so the analysis is restricted to the manufacturing/processing sector.

2.4.1 Extent of Processing of Agriculture Commodities

To estimate EPA, the output of primary agricultural commodities is first adjusted to account for seed, feed and wastage (SFW).[4] This adjustment to the gross value of output for individual commodities is based on the SFW estimates from the Central Institute of Post-Harvest Engineering and Technology (CIPHET), Ministry of Agriculture, reported in the Annual Reports of the Ministry of Food Processing Industry, and in Ghosh (2014). Using the adjusted production levels, EPA is estimated for the major crops that are reported as inputs for both the organized and unorganized manufacturing sectors in 2000–01, and for the organized sector in 2011–12. The estimates in both value and quantity terms provide similar estimates, so for presentational convenience, the discussion below is only for EPA estimates in value terms.

The analysis reveals, as expected, that cereals undergo the highest level of processing (whether primary or secondary) among all commodities considered. As shown in Appendix 2.5, the EPA for paddy in the organized sector is estimated to be 34.7%, for wheat it is 18.4%, and for maize 43%. In the unorganized manufacturing sector, in 2000–01, about 13.0, 3.3 and 0.1% of paddy/rice, wheat, and maize was processed, respectively. These estimates appear low, considering the earlier discussion that most cereals cannot be consumed in their raw product form. This may be because the surveys do not capture the full extent of primary processing, such as home-based processing by farm/rural families. In addition, a significant proportion of wheat and paddy/rice are procured by the government to maintain food stocks and it is not clear how these are further processed.

The magnitude of (primary) milled food grains (cereals and pulses) that are used for further (secondary) processing in the organized industry is estimated at 3.8% for rice; 3.1% for wheat and maize (Appendix 2.5). The level of processing is higher in 2011–12 compared to 2000–01, but still remains quite low. In unorganized manufacturing (2000–01), the estimates are 1.09% for rice; 2.96% for wheat and 1.05 for maize. The share of pulses is higher: 9.41 and 10.1% of the production of gram and other pulses in 2011–12. Pulses also had a higher percentage of processing in the unorganized sector in 2000–01 (5.38 and 5.47%, respectively).

Commodities other than food grains are processed to varying degrees. Among fruits, about 3% of grapes and mangoes, but less than 1% of apples and bananas produced are used in the industry for processing. Selected spices (chillies and pepper) and vegetables (peas, cucumber and beans) show substantial levels of EPA at 35, 81, 64, and 31.8%, but most of the other vegetables have low processing. A high percentage of oilseeds are also processed in organized manufacturing—soybeans at 100%; sunflower at 49%; safflower at 33%; followed by sesame at 15%, and linseed and groundnut at 7% each. As expected, cocoa beans, coffee, cashews, walnuts and jute hold a substantial share of output that is processed (varying between 38 and 62%).

---

[4]Wastage is common for agricultural produce, typically due to weather conditions, pests, transport or other such physical and losses. In addition, a part of the produce is retained for seed and feed by a majority of the farmers.

Table 2.2 Extent of processing of agricultural products (%)

	Un-organized 2000–01	Organized 2000–01	Organized 2011–12
Any level of processing (primary or higher)			
A. All agri-commodities processed/VOP agriculture	–	–	14.14
A.1 Fruits-vegetables/VOP fruits-vegetables	–	–	2.65
A.2 Other crops/VOP other crops	–	–	15.64
A.3 Food grains processed/VOP food grains	6.10	9.65	26.74
Secondary processing (beyond primary)			
B.1 Food grains processed/VOP food grains	–	–	4.30
B.2 Agriculture products processed/VOP agriculture & allied	2.40	2.90	7.60

Note Based on weighted average of the aggregate value of output (from NAS, CSO) for commodities reported in ASI or NSSO data. Aggregate output for all commodities adjusted for wastage using CIPHET wastage ratios

Aggregating across commodities up to the sectoral level, Table 2.2 provides aggregate EPA for all commodities and for food grains, derived as a weighted average for all commodities in the respective groups (using share of production value as weights). Considering any level of processing (primary or higher), the weighted average EPA for all products processed in the organized sector in 2011/12 is estimated at 14.14%. Of these, nearly 70% is accounted for by food grains, whose formal sector EPA is estimated at 26.96% for 2011/12. The EPA for fruits and vegetables is low at 2.65%, and other crops (including oilseeds, spices, beverage crops, etc.) is estimated at 15.74%.

Comparable estimates for 2000–01, for both the organized and unorganized sectors, can be estimated only for food grains because of changing NIC classifications, which do not allow calculating comparable estimates for other commodities. For food grains, the percentage subjected to any level of processing in 2000–01 in the organized sector estimated to be 9.65%, with another 6.1% processed in the unorganized sector.

As indicated earlier, a particular interest is to assess the level of agriculture production that is processed beyond the primary level—that is processing and value addition beyond the minimal level such as milling of cereals and pulses. Following the approach outlined earlier, the two step calculation is applied as follows. First, all commodities that are used as inputs directly in secondary processing (that is, all non-milling) activities are measured in terms of their direct input values to the processing industries. Second, the raw material (agricultural output) equivalent embodied in the milled food grains (i.e. outputs of primary processing) that used as inputs for further processing (that is, beyond the milling industry in secondary processing) is measured as the ratio of the value of raw agricultural inputs to the value of total primary milling industry output. Adding these two estimates (inputs used directly in secondary processing and the pro-rated input used in primary processed inputs for secondary processing) provides a more accurate estimate of total agricultural production that is used as input to the secondary level of processing.

The EPA estimates for food grains (estimable only for the organized sector for 2011–12) and for the aggregate of all agricultural products processed are given in rows B.1 and B.2. Food grains are separated out given their large share in overall agricultural production in India. The estimates for EPA in 2000–01 for the unorganized and organized sectors are found to be quite similar (at 2.4 and 2.9% respectively). However, there was a substantial jump, more than doubling of EPA in the formal sector between 2000–01 and 2011–12, from 2.9 to 7.6%. Lack of data for the unorganized sector prevents arriving at a firm conclusion on the trend in EPA for that sector, assuming that it grew at a similar rate, and given that the EPA for unorganized in 2000–01 was close to the EPA for the organized sector, one guesstimate for the unorganized EPA for 2011–12 is 6%. That would bring the total share of agricultural output processed to between 13 and 14%, which is substantial but still with significant scope for increasing. For example, EPA for China and the United States is estimated at 23% and 65%, respectively (Ghosh 2014).

These estimates provide important insights in the government's pursuit of value addition and pathways for doubling of farmers' incomes. Clearly the structure of Indian agriculture, with its heavy focus on cereals, places a large tax on the value addition through agro-processing as the scope (reflecting final demand) for food grain-based processed products remains relatively low. This is consistent with the estimated primary and secondary EPA estimates, which shows that despite a substantial share of food grains going into low (primary) level processing (milling), a much smaller fraction undergoes further value addition in terms of secondary processing. Other commodities show a significantly higher level of secondary processing. This is evident from a comparison of the sector wide estimates of secondary to primary processing for food grains (4.3:26.7) compared to all commodities (7.6:14.1); that is the ratio of secondary to primary processing is much higher for non-food grain crops. Among the non-food grain crops, it is important to note, however, that the extent of horticultural crops being processed remains quite low. The latter likely reflects a combination of structural problems, with limited value chain infrastructure (e.g. limited temperature controlled transport and storage), and a preference for fresh foods by a majority of the consumers, as was also noted in the changes in consumption trends.

Comparing the estimates arrived at in this study with existing estimates, it is important to note the methodological differences. The estimates derived here may not exactly be comparable with the estimated 6.42% and 0.34% EPA for the organized and unorganized segments for 2010–11 in Ghosh (2014). The higher estimates of EPA in this study may be due to difference in the methodology, assumptions made, number of commodities taken, level of aggregation of inputs at 3 and 5-digit industrial codes, and segregation of milled and unmilled cereals as industrial inputs. Nevertheless, the findings do validate the need to augment processing activities in both organized and unorganized segments given their enormous potential for raising agricultural incomes and creating new jobs. Importantly, the estimates derived here also confirm that India's food industry is far behind China and USA where the EPA is about 23% and 65% respectively (Ghosh 2014).

2.4.2 Estimate of Production Linkages

The estimated input coefficients (IC) are presented in Table 2.3a, b for the organized sector in 2000–01 and 2011–12, and Table 2.4a, b for the unorganized sector 2000–01 and 2010–11. Some business activities are grouped together for ease of presentation. For organized agro-processing, the backward production linkages went up substantially from 1.6% in 2000–01 to 13% in 2011–12. In food processing, for 2011/12, the share of inputs sourced directly from primary agriculture was the highest for the non-descript post-harvest activities at 60%, followed by grain milling and other products (28%), processed meats and fish (22%) and processed fruits, vegetables, oils and fats (17%). The direct backward production linkage of beverages, leather and wood industries is low, at less than 5%.

Restricting attention to direct backward linkages misses the substantial degree of intra-industry linkages, reflecting further complicated forward and backward linkages. For both agro-processing and food processing aggregates, the indirect agro-industry linkages are significantly higher than the direct primary agriculture linkages. For the broader agro-processing sector, intra-industry IC at 33% is almost twice the direct IC at 13%. Food processing also has a substantially higher IC for agro-industry inputs than for direct primary agriculture. This is important because relying only on direct linkages may be mis-leading. For example, it is odd to find no direct input from agriculture into dairy products, but when intra-industry links are accounted for, indirect agriculture-based input (as processed dairy output) is very high at 73%. Similarly, other food and beverage industries in general have much higher agro-industry ICs, including grain milling, animal products (meats and fish), and textiles. A higher IC for intra-industry is also consistent with the previously observed rising trends in consumption towards food products with high value addition and ready-to-eat products.

Another important finding is the pattern of IC for non-agro-based industry across different industries. So, while food processing in general has low ICs for non-agro-industry ICs, these are significantly higher for the non-food agro-processing sectors, since machinery and other industrial inputs are used more intensively in these activities (e.g. in the agriculture input, textile and wood products industries). An alternative perspective on the estimated ICs is the potential leveraging impact of agricultural inputs and how these ripple through the economy for much higher accumulated total impacts. Given that in all the industries considered, not only food but also other agro-processing industries, agricultural raw materials are essential for the existence of the industry. As such, low ICs (both direct and indirect) may reflect a small contribution as input provided by agriculture, but critical nature of these inputs means that these low ICs in reality reflect their large leveraging effects in industrial value added and, relatedly, employment.

The extent to which these backward and forward impacts are materialized is dependent on the existing structural, policy or institutional impediments. These impediments would likely encourage the processing industry to rely more heavily on

Table 2.3 Production linkages in organized agro-industries during 2000–01 and 2011–12 (at current prices, Rs. billion)

Description (NIC 1998)	Value of all inputs	Value of output	Value of agric. input	Value of agri-industry input	Value of non-ag industry input	Other inputs	Total IC	IC agric	IC agro-industry	IC non-agro-industry	Other inputs
	1	2	3	3.1	3.2	3.3	1/2	3/2	3.1/2	3.2/2	3.3/2
(a) *Organized manufacturing 2000–01*											
Post-harvest activities (140)	73.9	77.6	38.1	0.0	17.1	18.7	0.95	0.49	0.00	0.22	0.24
Processing and preserving of meat, fish, fruits, veg. oil (151)	288.0	309.5	39.4	15.1	115.4	118.1	0.93	0.13	0.05	0.37	0.38
Manuf. of dairy products (152)	130.8	145.3	3.2	77.6	22.0	28.0	0.90	0.02	0.53	0.15	0.19
Manuf. of grain mill products, starch products, animal feed (153)	363.2	401.4	4.6	143.0	130.1	85.5	0.91	0.01	0.36	0.32	0.21
Manuf. of other food products (154)	431.8	527.5	3.8	225.7	91.3	111.0	0.82	0.01	0.43	0.17	0.21
Manuf. of beverages	72.1	90.1	0.6	14.7	14.4	42.5	0.80	0.01	0.16	0.16	0.47
Manuf. of tobacco products (160)	76.2	118.7	0.5	22.8	19.8	33.2	0.64	0.00	0.19	0.17	0.28

(continued)

Table 2.3 (continued)

Description (NIC 1998)	Value of all inputs	Value of output	Value of agric. input	Value of agri-industry input	Value of non-ag industry input	Other inputs	Total IC	IC agric	IC agro-industry	IC non-agro-industry	Other inputs
	1	2	3	3.1	3.2	3.3	1/2	3/2	3.1/2	3.2/2	3.3/2
Spinning, weaving and finishing of textiles (171)	623.5	768.1	38.1	0.1	339.7	245.5	0.81	0.05	0.00	0.44	0.32
Manuf. of other textiles (172)	53.8	67.4	1.4	0.0	26.9	25.5	0.80	0.02	0.00	0.40	0.38
Manuf. of wearing apparel, except fur apparel (173)	60.7	73.7	0.1	0.0	32.4	28.2	0.82	0.00	0.00	0.44	0.38
Manuf. of articles of fur (181)	129.7	166.0	0.0	1.7	63.8	64.3	0.78	0.00	0.01	0.38	0.39
Manuf. of knitted and crocheted apparel (182)	0.2	0.2	0.0	0.0	0.1	0.1	0.80	0.00	0.14	0.30	0.36
Tanning; manuf. of leather products; dressing and dyeing fur (191)	35.2	39.2	3.8	2.0	13.8	15.7	0.90	0.10	0.05	0.35	0.40

(continued)

Table 2.3 (continued)

Description (NIC 1998)	Value of all inputs	Value of output	Value of agric. input	Value of agri-industry input	Value of non-ag industry input	Other inputs	Total IC	IC agric	IC agro-industry	IC non-agro-industry	Other inputs
	1	2	3	3.1	3.2	3.3	1/2	3/2	3.1/2	3.2/2	3.3/2
Manuf. of footwear (192)	50.2	60.1	2.3	2.2	19.5	26.2	0.84	0.04	0.04	0.32	0.44
Saw milling and planning of wood (201)	1.7	2.2	0.4	0.0	0.8	0.6	0.77	0.19	0.00	0.34	0.24
Manuf. products of wood, cork, straw and plaiting materials (202)	16.7	20.0	1.2	0.0	7.8	7.7	0.84	0.06	0.00	0.39	0.38
Manuf. of paper and paper products (210)	141.2	187.1	8.4	2.8	52.7	77.4	0.76	0.05	0.02	0.28	0.41
All agro-industry	**7485.5**	**9269.0**	**152.6**	**539.8**	**2948.2**	**3845.1**	**0.81**	**0.02**	**0.06**	**0.32**	**0.42**
Food and beverages	**1359.8**	**1551.3**	**89.8**	**476.0**	**390.3**	**403.6**	**0.88**	**0.06**	**0.31**	**0.25**	**0.26**

(continued)

Table 2.3 (continued)

Description	Value of input	Value of output	Indigenous RM									Imported RM		
			Value of agric input	Value of agro-industry input	Value of non-agri industry input	Other inputs	Total IC	IC agric	IC agro industry	IC non-agro industry	Other inputs	IC agric	IC agro industry	IC non-agro industry
	1	2	3	3.1	3.2	3.3	1/2	3/2	3.1/2	3.2/2	3.3/2	3/2	3.1/2	3.2/2
(b) *Organised Manufacturing 2011–12*														
Processed food, meat and dairy (016–108)	6697.35	7414.9	1757.9	2804.6	91.0	3212.4	0.90	0.24	0.38	0.01	0.43	0.01	0.04	0.00
– Post harvest activities (016, 0893)	569.44	604.6	359.8	68.4	0.5	140.7	0.94	0.60	0.11	0.00	0.23	0.00	0.00	0.00
– Meat, fish, animal feed (101, 102, 108)	460.12	518.4	116.1	244.8	9.9	89.4	0.89	0.22	0.47	0.02	0.17	0.00	0.01	0.00
– Fruits and vegetables; oils and fats (103, 104)	1935.98	2076.3	359.4	660.6	45.9	1189.8	0.93	0.17	0.32	0.02	0.57	0.00	0.13	0.00
– Dairy products (105)	796.54	870.2	1.5	637.2	5.8	148.7	0.92	0.00	0.73	0.01	0.17	0.00	0.00	0.00

(continued)

Table 2.3 (continued)

Description	Value of input	Value of output	Value of agric input	Indigenous RM			Total IC	IC agric	IC agro industry	IC non-agro industry	Other inputs	Imported RM		
				Value of agro-industry input	Value of non-agri industry input	Other inputs						IC agric	IC agro industry	IC non-agro industry
	1	2	3	3.1	3.2	3.3	1/2	3/2	3.1/2	3.2/2	3.3/2	3/2	3.1/2	3.2/2
– Grain mill and other food products (106, 107)	2935.27	3345.5	921.1	1193.7	28.9	1643.8	0.88	0.28	0.36	0.01	0.49	0.01	0.01	0.00
Beverage and Tobacco (110, 120)	573.1	808.9	31.0	212.9	69.3	259.9	0.71	0.04	0.26	0.09	0.32	0.00	0.00	0.01
Textiles (131, 139, 141–143)	2288.1	2983.7	32.2	1452.9	479.3	323.7	0.77	0.01	0.49	0.16	0.11	0.01	0.02	0.03
Leather and footwear (151, 152)	294.36	359.1	33.6	69.9	29.9	160.9	0.82	0.09	0.20	0.08	0.45	0.01	0.00	0.06
Wood and paper products (161, 162, 170)	701.93	838.9	30.9	187.5	149.4	334.2	0.84	0.04	0.22	0.18	0.40	0.01	0.05	0.06

(continued)

Table 2.3 (continued)

Description	Value of input	Value of output	Indigenous RM									Imported RM		
			Value of agric input	Value of agro-industry input	Value of non-agri indu stry input	Other inputs	Total IC	IC agric	IC agro indu stry	IC non-agro industry	Other inputs	IC agric	IC agro industry	IC non-agro industry
	1	2	3	3.1	3.2	3.3	1/2	3/2	3.1/2	3.2/2	3.3/2	3/2	3.1/2	3.2/2
Agriculture input (2012, 2021, 2821, 2825, 2826, 25,932, 28,132)	1813.05	2289.6	6.5	52.0	742.7	1011.9	0.79	0.00	0.02	0.32	0.44	0.03	0.00	0.09
Wood and cane furniture (31,001)	13.25	18.3	0.0	6.1	2.6	4.6	0.73	0.00	0.33	0.14	0.25	0.00	0.00	0.00
Repairing of agro industry equipments (33,122, 33,124, 33,126, 33,127)	2.97	4.4	0.0	0.0	1.3	1.7	0.67	0.00	0.00	0.30	0.38	0.00	0.00	0.00
All manufacturing	57,760.2	47,974.6	0.0	0.0	0.0	0.0	1.20	0.00	0.00	0.00	0.00	0.00	0.00	0.00
Agro processing	12,384.1	14,718.0	1892.0	4785.9	1565.5	4140.8	0.84	0.13	0.33	0.11	0.28	0.01	0.03	0.02

(continued)

Table 2.3 (continued)

Description	Value of input	Value of output	Value of agric input	Value of agro-industry input	Value of non-agri indu stry input	Other inputs	Total IC	IC agric	IC agro indu stry	IC non-agro industry	Other inputs	IC agric	IC agro industry	IC non-agro industry
				Indigenous RM									Imported RM	
	1	2	3	3.1	3.2	3.3	1/2	3/2	3.1/2	3.2/2	3.3/2	3/2	3.1/2	3.2/2
Food and bev processing	7097.2	7948.0	1765.2	2928.1	150.7	2253.3	0.89	0.22	0.37	0.02	0.28	0.01	0.04	0.00
Agri input manufacturing	1813.1	2289.6	6.5	52.0	742.7	1011.9	0.79	0.00	0.02	0.32	0.44	0.03	0.00	0.09

Source ASI, GOI

Table 2.4 Production linkages in unorganized agro-industries during 2000–01 and 2010–11 (Rs. billion at current prices)

	Value of input	Value of output	Value of agri.input	Value of agri ind. input	Non-agri. input	Other inputs	Input/output (IC)	IC agric.	IC agri-industry	IC non-agric.	IC other
	1	2	3	3.1	3.2	3.3	1/2	3/2	3.1/2	3.2/2	3.3/2
Unorganized manufacturing 2000–01											
Post-harvest activities (16)	0.347	0.531	0.218	0.000	0.055	0.074	0.654	0.411	0.000	0.104	0.140
Processing/preserving meat, fish, fruits, veg, oil (151)	61.271	74.055	51.449	1.535	0.429	7.858	0.827	0.695	0.021	0.006	0.106
Manufacture of dairy products (152)	24.528	31.337	0.093	19.450	0.128	4.857	0.783	0.003	0.621	0.004	0.155
Manufacture of grain mill products, starches and starch products, prepared animal feed (153)	151.700	196.570	2.595	111.702	2.021	35.382	0.772	0.013	0.568	0.010	0.180
Manufacture of other food products (154)	92.468	129.472	5.926	66.592	0.723	19.227	0.714	0.046	0.514	0.006	0.149
Manufacture of beverages (155)	6.864	13.043	0.082	1.922	0.794	4.066	0.526	0.006	0.147	0.061	0.312

(continued)

Table 2.4 (continued)

	Value of input	Value of output	Value of agri.input	Value of agri ind. input	Non-agri. input	Other inputs	Input/output (IC)	IC agric.	IC agri-industry	IC non-agric.	IC other
	1	2	3	3.1	3.2	3.3	1/2	3/2	3.1/2	3.2/2	3.3/2
Manufacture of tobacco products (160)	13.367	37.411	0.012	8.187	0.738	4.430	0.357	0.000	0.219	0.020	0.118
Spinning, weaving and finishing of textiles (171 rev)	65.730	107.600	0.722	4.853	60.960	−0.805	0.611	0.007	0.045	0.567	−0.007
Manufacture of other textiles (172)	31.454	64.439	3.756	0.150	18.988	8.560	0.488	0.058	0.002	0.295	0.133
Manufacture of wearing apparel, except fur apparel (181)	41.210	116.411	0.010	0.000	5.184	36.017	0.354	0.000	0.000	0.045	0.309
Manufacture of articles of fur (182)	3.801	5.129	0.027	1.637	20.982	−18.845	0.741	0.005	0.319	4.091	−3.674
Manufacture of knitted and crocheted apparel (173)	6.842	10.387	0.001	1.590	1.824	3.427	0.659	0.000	0.153	0.176	0.330

(continued)

Table 2.4 (continued)

	Value of input	Value of output	Value of agri.input	Value of agri ind. input	Non-agri. input	Other inputs	Input/output (IC)	IC agric.	IC agri-industry	IC non-agric.	IC other
	1	2	3	3.1	3.2	3.3	1/2	3/2	3.1/2	3.2/2	3.3/2
Tanning and dressing of leather; manufacture of luggage, handbags, saddler and harness; dressing and dyeing of fur (191)	7.138	10.094	2.096	1.591	1.454	1.997	0.707	0.208	0.158	0.144	0.198
Manufacture of footwear (192)	7.934	14.485	0.140	2.400	3.721	1.672	0.548	0.010	0.166	0.257	0.115
Saw milling and planning of wood (201)	22.894	31.201	18.891	0.001	0.193	3.809	0.734	0.605	0.000	0.006	0.122
Manufacture of products of wood, cork, straw and plaiting materials (202)	29.805	76.969	16.019	0.184	6.612	6.991	0.387	0.208	0.002	0.086	0.091
Manufacture of paper and paper products (201)	13.791	19.083	0.135	0.119	11.464	2.072	0.723	0.007	0.006	0.601	0.109
Agro-processing	617.377	1001.664	102.172	221.913	221.913	136.272	0.616	0.102	0.222	0.222	0.136
Food and bev processing	337.178	445.008	60.363	201.201	4.151	71.463	0.758	0.136	0.452	0.009	0.161

(continued)

Table 2.4 (continued)

NIC 2008	Description	Value of input	Value of output	Value of main five inputs	Input coefficient (IC)		IC agri-industry
		1	2	3	½	3/2	3/2
Unorganized manufacturing 2010–11							
016–108	Processed food, meat & dairy	728.37	939.59	55.85	0.78	0.06	
016 and 0893	*–Post-harvest activities*	5.72 178.08	6.36	0.51	0.90	0.08	
101, 102, 108	*–Meat, fish, animal oil and feed*	178.08	219.01	14.03	0.81	0.06	
103 and 104	*–Processed fruits-vegetables, vegetable and animal oil*	67.28	75.77	5.47	0.89	0.07	
105	*–Dairy products*	32.98	41.00	2.51	0.80	0.06	
106 and 107	*–Grain mill and other food products*	444.29	597.43	33.30	0.74	0.06	
110 and 120	Beverage and tobacco	45.29	99.57	2.75	0.45	0.03	
131, 139, 141–143	Textiles	267.38	708.75	21.43	0.38	0.03	

(continued)

Table 2.4 (continued)

NIC 2008	Description	Value of input	Value of output	Value of main five inputs		Input coefficient (IC)		IC agri-industry
		1	2	3		½		3/2
151 and 152	Leather and footwear	20.13	36.03	1.42		0.56		0.04
161, 162 and 170	Wood and wood products, paper and paper products	168.91	288.33	12.23		0.59		0.04
2012, 2021, 2821, 2825, 2826, 25,932, 28,132	Agriculture inputs-fertilizer, pesticides, machinery	46.61	64.59	3.42		0.72		0.05
31,001	Wood and cane furniture	100.42	164.27	7.54		0.61		0.05
33,122, 33,124, 33,126, 33,127	Repairing of agro-industry equipment	7.73	20.08	0.23		0.38		0.01
	Agro-processing	1384.87	2321.24	104.89		0.60		0.05
	Food and beverage	741.27	965.34	56.47		0.77		0.06
	Agriculture input Mfg	46.61	64.59	3.42		0.72		0.05

Source 56th and 67th round, GOI-NSSO

imports for raw materials. This is an empirical question, and the findings (for organized sector in 2011–12, the only sector and year for which this is possible) suggest
that while the food industry does indeed imports, both raw materials and processed
inputs, the IC for these import linkages is found to be 5% for processed inputs
and 0.5% for primary agricultural inputs. The highest IC is 13% for the imported
fruits-vegetables and oils-fats, which could be due to their specific nature and taste.
Overall, the agro- and food industries are relatively less import reliant, suggesting
that it is not the case that the processing industry is substituting imported inputs for
domestic inputs to any significant extent. Greater reliance on domestic inputs means
that investment in agro-processing would largely benefit domestic producers through
backward linkages.

2.5 Summing Up and Implications

Given the important role that agri-food value chains and agribusiness can play in
promoting the economic transformation, the objective of this chapter is to gain a
better understanding of the size and nature of the evolving post-harvest management
and agribusiness sector in India. The sector is defined to include farm commodities,
and all packaging, sorting, agro-processing, distribution of food and food products
(wholesale and retail trade) and food service (hotels-restaurants) activities.

The analysis of the evolving demand patterns show rapid changes are underway in
the food system. In 2011/12 over half (52%) of all consumer expenditure is estimated
to be on processed foods. Importantly, the trends in demand patterns highlight a
clear shift from cereal based products (the bulk of primary processed products) in
two directions: One is a shift towards unprocessed horticultural products, reflecting
more diversified diets with growing importance of fresh foods. The second is an even
more rapid shift towards processed foods, with the demand for highly processed and
prepared foods growing at the fastest pace (a phenomenal 18% a year between 2004
and 2011).

These long-term trends in demand have significant implications for policy: the
shift from primary processing (food grains/cereals) places a premium on accelerating
the pace of reform of the agricultural marketing system and promoting freer intra- and
inter-state commerce of agricultural produce. In addition, the rapid growth for fresh
fruits and vegetables calls for both diversification of agricultural production with
investment in post-harvest infrastructure, better management of high value fresh
produce value chains, and ensuring food safety and standards. The rising demand for
more processed foods, which is expected to accelerate further with sustained income
growth and a rising middle class, offers significant potential for generating jobs and
income growth in the post-farm segments of the food system. It underscores the need
for a closer scrutiny of the food processing sector to identify potential constraints
to investment in the sector. These patterns are consistent with the growth of more
nutrient-dense unprocessed horticulture products, income-elastic livestock and other
foods with low level of processing, as well as a rapidly growing preference for fully

prepared meals and cooked foods—all of which also require ramping up the efforts to ensure food safety.

One indicator of potential frictions facing the domestic agro-processing industry may be that the rapidly growing demand for processed foods, as reflected in the observed trends in consumer expenditures, is being met by imports. The analysis of the trade data, however, shows that this is not the case. India's net exports of processed foods (processed, prepared and beverages) have risen over time—with the exception of edible oils, all animal and plant based processed foods show positive and growing net exports. Nor does the evidence suggest an overwhelming or growing share of fresh food in net exports.

Agro-processing and food service sectors constitute a sizable share of the overall manufacturing and service sectors (in terms of gross value added or GVA). Agro-related manufacturing is a substantial 29.4% of the GVA for manufacturing—accounting for about a quarter of the formal sector and an overwhelming two-thirds of the informal sector manufacturing output. Of this, about 11% is from food processing activities, 12% is from non-food agro-processing activities and an additional 6% is from agro-input industries. Similarly, the study estimates that about 26% of the hospitality, trade (wholesale and retail) and storage service economy is directly food-related. To put these estimates in perspective, in 2011/12, while the share of agricultural and allied activities in national income was 14%, the agro-processing industry contributed an additional 4.4% and food-related services an additional 4.6% to the aggregate GDP, implying that about 23% of India's economy in 2011/12 was directly or indirectly related to agriculture. Viewed from the leveraging perspective, this means that every Rs. 10 produced in agriculture stimulates an additional Rs. 6.4 in the downstream food system comprising agro-processing and foods services.

Comprehensive estimates of the extent of agricultural produce that is processed can be derived only for the organized sector for 2011/12. Taking all the crops grown in India, about 14.4% of agricultural output is estimated to be processed in organized food industry, considering any type of processing (including primary and secondary). In this, as expected, food grains processing is estimated to be the highest at 26.4%. The EPA for food grains in 2000/01 is estimated to have been at 9.7%, indicating a substantial increase over the decade. Data to derive a similar estimate for the unorganized sector are not available for 2011/12, but considering that the share of unorganized sector (at 6.1%) was about 40% of the total (organized and unorganized) EPA for food grains in 2000/01, it is likely that the 2011/12 the total EPA was likely significantly higher than the estimated 26.4 for the organized sector alone.

A particular interest in this study is to estimate how much of agricultural output is subjected to beyond the primary level of processing. This is because including primary processing may provide a misleading sense of how the agro-processing industry is progressing, considering, one, that all food grains have to undergo some form of primary processing to make them fit for human consumption, and two, that primary processing is a very basic and low valued added processing activity. Restricting attention to secondary processing, the EPA in the organized secondary processing industry (defined to include direct inputs of all agricultural commodities to secondary processing industry plus the imputed agricultural input from the output of primary processing that is further used as intermediate input in the secondary processing industries) is estimated at a lower level of 7.6% for 2011/12. While still low, this is a significant increase, more than doubling, from the secondary processing EPA estimate of 2.9% in 2000/01. The unorganized sector EPA cannot be estimated for 2011/12, but the estimate for 2000/01 is 2.4%, which is similar but slightly lower than the EPA for the organized sector. If it is assumed that the growth in the EPA for the unorganized sector is similar to the growth in the organized sector, then a unorganized sector EPA for 2011/12 would be about 6.8%. Using a slightly conservative estimate of 5–6% for the growth of unorganized sector EPA, the share of total agricultural output that is processed (to the secondary processing level) in 2011/12 is thus estimated to be between 13 and 14%.

The main conclusion that emerges from these estimates is that the extent of food that is being processed in India has grown rapidly post 2000/01. This is consistent with the trends in both consumption, with rapid growth in processed foods, and that processing industry does not show rising dependence on imported products. With transformation this process is likely to continue, as evidence suggests that the EPA for India remains substantially below the estimates for other major agriculture producers.

Appendix 2.1: Agro Processing Industries/Enterprises (Under Manufacturing Sector)

NIC 2008	Description
016	Post-harvest crop activities
101	Processing and preserving of meat
102	Processing and preserving of fish, crustaceans and molluscs and products thereof
103	Processing and preserving of fruit and vegetables
104	Manufacture of vegetable and animal oils and fats
105	Manufacture of dairy products
106	Manufacture of grain mill products, starches and starch products
107	Manufacture of other food products
108	Manufacture of prepared animal feeds
110	Manufacture of beverages
120	Manufacture of tobacco products
131 revised	Spinning, weaving and finishing of textiles (after deducting non-agro-industries)
139	Manufacture of other textiles
141	Manufacture of wearing apparel, except fur apparel
142	Manufacture of articles of fur
143	Manufacture of knitted and crocheted apparel
151	Tanning and dressing of leather; manufacture of luggage, handbags, saddler and harness; dressing and dyeing of fur

(continued)

(continued)

NIC 2008	Description
152	Manufacture of footwear
161	Saw milling and planning of wood
162	Manufacture of products of wood, cork, straw and plaiting materials
170	Manufacture of paper and paper products
0893	Extraction of salt
2012	Manufacturing of fertilizers
2021	Manufacturing of pesticides
2821	Manufacturing of special purpose agricultural machinery
2825	Manufacturing of food, beverage and tobacco processing machinery
2826	Manufacturing of textile, apparel and leather production machinery
25,932	Manufacturing of agriculture hand tools
28,132	Manufacturing of pumps—how much agriculture not known
31,001	Wood and cane furniture manufacturing
33,122	Repair of agriculture, forestry and beverage/tobacco processing equipment
33,124	Repair of textile apparel, leather production and paper machinery
33,126	Repair of textile apparel, leather production and paper machinery
33,127	Washing, cleaning of textile and fur

Agro-wholesale and retail activities under tertiary sector as per NSS 57th round:

NIC 2008	Description
561	Hotels and motels
562	Restaurants, bars and canteens activities
750	Veterinary activities
52,102	Warehousing of agricultural products without refrigeration
52,101	Warehousing of agricultural products with refrigeration (i.e. cold storage)

Agro-wholesale and retail activities under tertiary as per NSS 67th round:

561	Restaurants and mobile food service activities
562	Event catering and other food services activities
563	Beverage serving activities
750	Veterinary activities
4620	Wholesale trade in livestock
4630	Wholesale trade in food, beverages and tobacco
4653	Wholesale trade in agriculture machinery

(continued)

(continued)

4711	Retail trade in food, beverage and tobacco—non-specialized stores
4721	Retail trade in food—specialized stores
4722	Retail trade in beverages—specialized stores
4723	Retail trade in tobacco specialized stores
4781	Retail trade in food, beverage and tobacco—other formats
46,101	Wholesale commission agents and brokers in agriculture and livestock
46,692	Wholesale of fertilizer and agrochemicals
46,695	Wholesale of textile fibres, etc.
52,102	Warehousing of agricultural products without refrigeration
52,101	Warehousing of agricultural products with refrigeration (i.e. cold storage)

Note NSS 57th round excludes wholesale and retail trade. Concordance is done between NIC 2004 and NIC 2008

Appendix 2.2: Data Limitations

The estimates for organized (large units) and unorganized (small units) sectors are arrived at using nationally representative surveys (noted above). Currently there are no comparable surveys for the manufacturing units in between these two segments, creating a potential "missing middle" problem, which may be a source of underestimation. To assess the likely magnitude of such underestimation, the fourth Census on Micro, Small and Medium Enterprises (MSMEs) for 2006–07 is useful. This MSME census provides an alternative estimate of the processing sector, and can help identify the likely size of the micro, small and medium enterprise sectors. The population for this census overlaps with that of both the organized and unorganized segments of manufacturing. The MSME Census gives an estimate of nearly 60 lakh registered and unregistered agro enterprises, employing 125 lakh workers. However, more than 90% of the agro and food enterprises fall under the category of micro-enterprises, which are covered by the NSS on unorganized manufacturing. As per Census MSME, micro-enterprises are ones that have fixed investment in plant &machinery up to Rs. 2.5 million, small enterprises above Rs. 2.5 million & up to Rs. 50 million; medium enterprises above Rs. 50 million & up to Rs. 100 million. To avoid duplication, and maintain consistency with the formal sector, the NSS data are used for analysis. The implication is that while the estimates derived in this paper are likely underestimated due to the "missing middle," the downward bias is expected to be relatively small. Second, data on organized wholesale and retail trade in agricultural and food products are not available, which restricts accounting for the totality of the agro-related service sector. For the unorganized (or informal) service sector, the quinquennial NSS rounds

(57th and 67th) are available for 2000/01 and 2010/11, respectively. These data also have their limitation, as there are no data on wholesale and retail trade activities for 2000/01, but they are available for the 67th round (along with data on restaurant, catering and food service activities, veterinary services, and warehousing). Thus, only a snapshot of the informal service sector is possible for 2010/11. In terms of the scope of the service sector represented by the NSS 67th round, a comparison with the national accounts statistics reveals that the available data account for about 40% of the gross value added of the entire (agro and non-agro-related) activities of the trade, hotels and restaurants, and storage sub-sectors of the economy. This estimate of the scope of coverage of the data in hand is used to arrive at an estimate of the size of the food services sector below. Third, the estimates for EPA are affected by the fact that while the 57th round collected detailed information on individual inputs used by each enterprise, the 67th round (by design) collected information only on the five "main inputs" used by each enterprise. The survey does not provide any details on the type of input that each of the five input categories represent. To avoid guessing what each of the "main" inputs used by individual enterprises might be, these inputs are not considered for analysis in this study. The consequence of these data shortcomings is that the EPA and the extent of linkages between the agriculture and the unorganized industry and tertiary sectors are underestimated.

Appendix 2.3: Classification of Food Items According to the Level of Processing

S. no.	Unprocessed agriculture commodities	Primary processing products	Low secondary processing	Medium secondary processing	High secondary processing
1	Eggs	Rice PDS	Liquid Milk	Bread; baked goods	Tea (prepared)
2	Potato	Rice others	Curd	Baby food	Coffee (prepared)
3	Onion	Chira	Butter	Milk: condensed powder	Prepared/cooked meals
4	Radish	Khoi, lawa	Mustard oil	Ghee	
5	Carrot	Muri	Ground nut oil	Ice cream	
6	Turnip	Other rice products	Coconut oil	Other milk products	
7	Beet	Wheat atta-PDS	Edible oil: other	Vanaspati, margarine	
8	Sweet potato	Wheat atta-other sources	Fish, prawn	Candy, misri	

(continued)

(continued)

S. no.	Unprocessed agriculture commodities	Primary processing products	Low secondary processing	Medium secondary processing	High secondary processing
9	Arum	Maida	Goat meat/mutton	Curry powder	
10	Pumpkin	Suji, rawa	Buffalo meat	Cold beverages: bottles/canned	
11	Gourd	Sewai noodles	Pork	Fruit juice and shake	
12	Bitter gourd	Other wheat products	Chicken	Other beverages: cocoa, choc, etc.	
13	Cucumber	Jowar and products	Others: birds, crabs, oyster	Biscuits	
14	Parwal	Bajra and products	Sugar (PDS)	Salted refreshments	
15	Jhinga; torai	Maize and products	Sugar-other sources	Prepared sweets	
16	Snake gourd	Barley and products	Gur	Cake, pastry	
17	Papaya;green	Small millets and products	Honey	Pickles	
18	Cauliflower	Ragi and products	Tea: Leaf	Sauce	
19	Cabbage	Other cereals	Coffee: powder	Jam, jelly	
20	Brinjal	Cereal substitutes (tapioca,jackfruit)		Other processed food	
21	Lady's finger	Arhar, tur			
22	Palak/leafy vegetables	Gram, split			
23	French beans	Gram, whole			
24	Tomato	Moong			
25	Peas	Masur			
26	Chillies, green	Urd			
27	Capsicum	Peas			
28	Plantain: green	Soybean			
29	Jackfruit: green	Khesari			
30	Lemon	Other peas			

(continued)

(continued)

S. no.	Unprocessed agriculture commodities	Primary processing products	Low secondary processing	Medium secondary processing	High secondary processing
31	Other vegetables	Gram products			
32	Banana	Besan			
33	Watermelon	Other pulse products			
34	Pineapple	Coconut copra			
35	Coconut	Groundnut			
36	Guava	Dates			
37	Singara	Cashewnut			
38	Orange, mausami	Walnut			
39	Papaya;green	Other nuts			
40	Mango	Raisin, etc.			
41	Melon	Other dry fruits			
42	Pears	Salt			
43	Berries	Turmeric			
44	Litchi	Black pepper			
45	Apple	Dry chillies			
46	Grapes	Tamarind			
47	Other fresh fruits	Oilseeds			
48	Garlic	Other spices			
49	Ginger	Ice			
50	Coconut: green				

Source Adapted from Morriset and Kumar (2011)

Appendix 2.4

See Tables 2.5, 2.6 and 2.7.

Appendix 2.5

See Tables 2.8 and 2.9.

Table 2.5 Structure and size of agro-processing industry (base 2004–05)

	Organized agro-processing		Unorganized agro-processing		Annual rate of growth in	
	2000–01	2011–12	2000–01	2010–11	Organized	Unorganized
Factories/enterprises (No. thousand)	58	91	14,050	14,030	4.12	−0.01
Employment (No. thousand)	3992	5447	27,897	25,007	2.87	−1.09
Fixed assets (Rs. million)	1,286,181	26,595,763	687,455	1,177,244	6.83	5.53
Output (Rs. million)	3,913,677	8,948,691	1,205,372	1,623,245	6.82	3.02
Input (Rs. million)	3,280,456	8,087,151	742,933	968,445	9.55	2.69
GVA (Rs. million)	681,889	1,511,575	459,173	649,734	7.51	3.53
%age share in total manufacturing						
Factories/units	44.40	41.76	82.53	81.30		
Employment	49.98	40.56	75.23	71.49		
Fixed assets	28.16	18.28	58.43	60.39		
Output	35.09	24.17	53.51	54.90		
Input	36.42	26.30	48.85	52.17		
GVA	31.77	24.10	63.39	59.82		

Note NSS 57th Rounds (2001–02) and NSS 67th round (2010–11) are not comparable as the former did not cover retail trade. Employment refers to persons engaged

Source GOI-ASI and GOI-NSSO, MOSPI, CSO

Table 2.6 Structure and size of food processing industry (base 2004–05)

	Organized food processing		Unorganized food processing		Annual rate of growth in	
	2000–01	2011–12	2000–01	2010–11	Organized	Unorganized
Factories/enterprises (No. thousand)	27	41	3018	2247	3.75	−2.91
Employment (No. thousand)	1456	1889	6855	4806	2.40	−3.49
Fixed assets (Rs. million)	371,201	1,487,482	219,693	346,359	10.47	4.66
Output (Rs. million)	1,866,745	7,943,965	535,509	675,066	8.43	2.34
Input (Rs. million)	1,636,303	7,095,851	405,750	518,374	10.87	2.48
GVA (Rs. million)	230,442	848,114	128,103	154,774	8.12	1.91
%age share in total manufacturing						
Factories/units	20.87	18.88	17.73	13.02		
Employment	18.22	14.06	18.49	13.74		
Fixed assets	8.13	7.63	18.67	17.77		
Output	16.74	13.75	23.77	22.83		
Input	18.17	14.79	26.68	27.92		
GVA	10.74	8.67	17.69	14.25		

Note NSS 57th Rounds (2001–02) and NSS 67th round (2010–11) are not comparable as the former did not cover retail trade. Employment refers to persons engaged
Source GOI-ASI and GOI-NSSO, MOSPI, CSO

Table 2.7 Structure and size of unorganized agro wholesale and retail trade (base 2004–05)

	Agro services (selected) 2001–02	Agro services (selected) 2010–11	Annual growth in agro services (selected)	Agro-wholesale and retail 2010–11	% share of agro-services (selected) 2010–11
Factories/Enterprises (No. thousand)	2188	2805	2.80	14,353	19.54
Employment (No. thousand)	5130	6231	2.19	23,631	26.37
Fixed assets (Rs. million)	484,278	381,309	−2.62	1,418,372	26.88
Output (Rs. million)	499,685	731,829	4.33	5,120,836	14.29
Input (Rs. million)	342,773	503,282	4.36	4,253,079	11.83
GVA (Rs. million)	155,863	225,713	4.20	856,984	26.34
%age share in total					
Factories/units	15.12	n.a	n.a	35.51	n.a
Employment	19.32	n.a	n.a	32.37	n.a

(continued)

Table 2.7 (continued)

	Agro services (selected) 2001–02	Agro services (selected) 2010–11	Annual growth in agro services (selected)	Agro-wholesale and retail 2010–11	% share of agro-services (selected) 2010–11
Fixed assets	19.66	n.a	n.a	19.66	n.a
Output	26.88	n.a	n.a	30.47	n.a
Input	34.78	n.a	n.a	31.65	n.a
GVA	17.92	n.a	n.a	25.89	n.a

Note GOI-NSSO 57th rounds (2001–02) and NSSO 67th round (2010–11) are not comparable as the former did not cover wholesale and retail trade activities. Agro retail trade (selected) is made comparable by taking restaurant-bars and other services activities, veterinary and warehousing services

Table 2.8 Extent of processing in unorganized and organized manufacturing (%) (based on value): primary products

Commodity	Unorganized 2000–01	Organized 2001–02	Organized 2011–12	Organized 2011–12			
	Food grains			Other commodities			
Paddy	13	–	34.71	Linseed	7.13	Banana	0.19
Wheat	3.3	–	18.37	Sesame	15.11	Mango	2.58
Jowar	0.01	–	3.12	Groundnut	7.05	Grapes	2.75
Bajra	0.1	–	7.2	R&M[a]	1.74	Papaya	0.42
Maize	0.1	–	43.04	Safflower	33.13	Apple	0.06
Gram	12.7	–	–	Sunflower	49.04	Lemon	2.07
Arhar	7	–	–	Soybean	100	Orange	0.01
Moong	4.2	–	–	Sugarcane	0.04	Pine Apple	0.32
Masoor	3.7	–	–	Gur	0.03	Potato	2.17
Oth. pulses	32.2	–	–	Kapas	2.04	Onion	0.23
All pulses	–	–	18	Jute	60.78	Tomato	0.16
				Coffee	38.01	Peas	
				Black pepper	18.95	Other Fruits	
				Dry ginger	1.16	Oth. Veg.	2.26
				Garlic	0.93	Cocoa, beans[c]	54.54
				N&C[b]	0.33	Coffee	38.01

(continued)

Table 2.8 (continued)

Commodity	Unorganized	Organized	Organized	Organized			
	2000–01	2001–02	2011–12	2011–12			
	Food grains			Other commodities			
				Walnut	46.55	Peas, dry[c]	81.2
				Cashew nut	57.06	Cucumber[c]	64.4
				Chillies/pepper, dry[c]	35.4	Peaches and nectarines[c]	26.2
				Beans dry[c]	31.84	Watermelon[c]	0.3
Group weighted average	**6.1**	**9.65**	**26.96**	**15.64**		**2.65**	
Overall weighted average	**14.14**						

Notes Allowance is made for feed, seed and wastage
Source Estimations based on value of input and output in GOI-NSSO 56th round and ASI 2011–12
[a]R&M stands for rapeseed and mustard
[b]N&C stands for nutmeg and cardamom
[c]Based on quantity. Value of output of agriculture is taken from CSO. All crops for which inputs are reported in ASI or NSS data are included for EPA estimation
Scope of coverage: these crops account for 96% of all food grains, 72% of all horticultural crops, and 71.4% of other crops (oilseeds, spices and fibre crops)

Table 2.9 Extent of processing in unorganized and organized manufacturing (%) (based on value): milled/processed products

Commodity	Unorganized	Organized	Organized
	2000–01	2001–02	2011–12
Rice	1.09	0.31	3.8
Wheat	2.96	1.64	3.1[a]
Maize	1.05	0.07	–
Gram	5.38	0.05	9.41
Other pulses	5.47	3.26	10.1
Other food products	0.01	0.05	0.02

Source Estimates based on GOI-NSSO and ASI
[a]Includes maize also

References

Balassa, B. (1965). Trade liberalization and "revealed" comparative advantage. *The Manchester School, 33*(2), 99–123.
GOI, National Accounts Statistics (NAS). (2000 to 2014). *Ministry of Statistics and Programme implementation*. India: Central Statistical Organisation.
GOI-National Sample Survey Organisation (NSSO) (2000–01, 2001–02 and 2010–11). Unorganised Manufacturing 56th, 57th and 67th Rounds, Ministry of Statistics and Programme implementation. India: Central Statistical Organisation.

GOI-National Sample Survey Organisation (NSSO) (1993–94, 2004–05 and 2011–12). Consumer expenditure in India, NSS 50th Round, NSS 60th Round and NSS 66th Round. New Delhi: Government of India.

GOI-Annual Survey of Industry (ASI) (2000 to 2014). Annual Survey of Industry, Ministry of Statistics and Programme implementation. India: Central Statistical Organisation.

Gollin, D., & Probst, L. T. (2015). Food and agriculture: Shifting landscapes for policy. *Oxford Review of Economic Policy, 31*(1), 8–25.

Morisset, M., & Kumar, P. (2011). *Trends and pattern of consumption of value added foods in India.* Paper Presented at the 7th Annual Conference on Economic Growth and Development held at Indian Statistical Institute, New Delhi During December 15–17.

Ghosh, N,. (2014). An assessment of the extent of food processing in various food sub-sectors. Report submitted to the Ministry of Agriculture and Farmers Welfare, GOI.

World Bank. (2014). *India: Accelerating agricultural productivity growth.* Washington, DC.

Chapter 3
Output and Employment Linkages of the Primary, Secondary and Tertiary Sectors in the Indian Economy: A Computable General Equilibrium (CGE) Analysis

Nitin Arora and Rahul Arora

3.1 Introduction

During the turn of the twentieth century, India's traditional agro-based economy was reallocated to the manufacturing and services sectors, and their shares in gross domestic product (GDP) and employment changed drastically. The rate of growth in manufacturing was not adequate to absorb the surplus labour, the share of the services sector in both GDP and employment rose, and the structural shift from agriculture to services lowered the rate of growth in agriculture, perhaps because the backward linkage of services to agriculture is weak. Services-based growth is demand-oriented and, hence, termed less sustainable. In most of the services in India, growth and employment are followed by a growth in GDP—rather than leading it (Zalk 2014). Growth in the services sector pumps additional demand—for capital-intensive secondary sector products such as fast-moving consumer goods (FMCG) and electronics—and it seldom augments the supply of goods in an economy or guarantees substantial employment linkages to the secondary and primary sectors. If the supply oriented primary and secondary sectors remain underdeveloped, the excess demand resulting from a demand–supply mismatch may generate unending inflationary tendencies and cause heavy dependence on foreign markets to satisfy an

A version of the Global Trade Analysis Project (GTAP version 9) licensed to the second author (Rahul Arora) has been used for analysis.

N. Arora (✉)
Department of Economics, Panjab University, Chandigarh, Punjab, India
e-mail: nitineco@pu.ac.in

R. Arora
Department of Economics and Finance, Birla Institute of Technology and Science,
Pilani, Rajasthan, India
e-mail: rahul.arora@pilani.bits-pilani.ac.in

economy's consumption needs. The primary and secondary sectors, along with the services sector, must grow in a sustained manner if the Indian economy is to meet its supply-side challenges. To optimize the twin objectives of growth and employment in a labour-surplus economy like India, it is important to identify the sectors that have high output and employment linkages, as promoting high-linkage sectors is one of the most important ways to sustain a high growth path in the Indian economy. Therefore, we must investigate intersectoral and intra-sectoral linkages to analyse the structural relationships among the sectors and understand not only the evolution and progression of such relationships but also the intersectoral adjustments over time. A clear perspective of the intersectoral dynamics could be useful in devising an appropriate strategy for the growth of the Indian economy, but the literature on output and employment linkages in India using a computable general equilibrium (CGE) approach is scant, and the computations of sectoral linkages based on the social accounting matrix (SAM) make various unrealistic assumptions. This chapter attempts a comparative elaboration of the output and employment linkages in India, and it takes up aggregate and disaggregate sectoral analysis to develop a more nuanced approach towards various sectors with respect to their interlinkages with other economic sectors.

3.2   Literature on Intersectoral and Intra-sectoral Linkages

In his book *Strategy of Economic Development*, Hirschman (1958) contends that deliberately unbalancing the economy in accordance with a predesigned strategy is the best way to achieve economic growth. In an underdeveloped economy, simultaneous investment in all the sectors is hindered by the lack of resources and the inability to utilize the existing ones efficiently. Hirschman points out that the pattern of investment should induce investment in other sectors, implying that the robust sector of the economy pulls the linked sectors and distinguishes between substitution and postponement, the two types of investment choice; deciding which project to undertake, A or B, is a substitution choice, and deciding how to sequence projects is a postponement choice (Thirlwall 1983). Postponement choices initiate the sequence of projects (Hirschman 1958), and the decision to concentrate on a sector depends on the strength of progress that it induces in the other sector(s). The strength can be measured through the magnitude of the linkages of one sector to another. The theory of linkages stresses that when certain industries are developed first, their interconnections or linkages with other sectors will induce or, at least, facilitate the development of new industries. Backward linkages raise the demand for an activity while forward linkages lower the costs of using an industry's output. Forward linkages refer to investments that encourage investment in the subsequent stages of production, which works by easing the supply of another product. Backward linkages refer to investments that encourage investment in the earlier stages of production (Todaro and Smith 2012). The concept of linkages is the fulcrum of the unbalanced growth doctrine. To create effective imbalance in an economy, efforts should be laid on projects with the greatest linkages. With a knowledge of input-output (I-O) analysis or inter-industry flows in an economy, one can easily discern the foremost sectors by the degree of their combined linkage effects.

There are a few analyses of the intersectoral and intra-sectoral linkages in India. Using the Rasmussen (1957) indices of backward and forward linkages, Hansda (2003) checks the sustainability of services-led growth in the long run. The linkages emanated from the input-output transaction tables (IOTT) for 1993–1994 at both the disaggregated and aggregated levels. Since forward linkages are inherently less effective than backward linkages, the inducing impact of services on the rest of the economy could be limited. The study concludes that industrial activities such as manufacturing are the major pace-setters for services growth. Sastry et al. (2003) examine the sectoral linkages of growth using both an I-O framework and a simultaneous equation framework and conclude that although the share of the services sector in GDP increased substantially over the years, agriculture plays an important role in determining the overall growth rate of the economy through demand linkages with other sectors. Saikia (2011) uses an I-O framework and observes structural changes in the intersectoral linkages before and after the period of reform. The agriculture–industry linkage has not only been deteriorating over the years but it has also undergone directional changes; both the production and demand linkages, primarily industry-to-agriculture in the pre-reform period, changed to agriculture-to-industry in the post-reform period. No significant interdependence is noticed between agriculture and services, but the interdependence between industry and services is strong, and it improved during the post-reform period.

Several other studies incorporate the I-O and SAM-based model to investigate employment and output linkages (Raihan and Khondker 2010; Bhatt and Munjal 2013; Bhattacharya and Rajeev 2016). Raihan and Khondker (2010) estimate the backward and forward linkages of textile and clothing sectors in India, Bangladesh and Pakistan. The study constructs and updates the SAM of these three South Asian countries and uses them in the SAM multiplier model to estimate the linkages. Bhatt and Munjal (2013) place the tourism sector into the IOTT framework to analyse the sector's interlinkages with the other sectors of the economy. The IOTT is elaborated with SAM tables. The SAM-based multiplier analyses demonstrate that the tourism sector has strong backward linkages with other economic sectors, while it would be affected positively through forward linkages from other sectors.

Bhattacharya and Rajeev (2016) evaluate the intersectoral output and employment linkages with the help of I-O tables from 2003 to 2004 and 2007 to 2008. The backward, forward and employment linkages were used to identify the key employment generating sectors with high output linkage capabilities. The agriculture, textiles, and wood and wood products sectors generate the most employment, and they possess high employment with low output linkage during both periods. On the other hand, the petroleum products, chemicals and metals sectors affect other sectors in terms of their high output linkages accompanied with low employment linkages. The assumptions that apply to the key sectors apply also to the four remaining potential sectors: mining and quarrying, food and beverages, tobacco and non-metallic mineral products. These sectors have a reasonably good output and employment linkage for both periods.

Many studies analyse the linkages of various sectors using the I-O or SAM-based methodology, but only a few studies compare employment linkages with backward and forward output linkages. The biggest gap in the literature is of the computation of linkages based on a CGE framework.

3.3 Database and Methodology

The CGE-based linkages are examined to observe the key, potential and weak sectors that can ensure sustained growth to the Indian economy. The SAM-based linkages can be computed using the methodology suggested by Bhatt and Munjal (2013), but some of its assumptions—all goods and inputs are tradable, and supplies are perfectly elastic—are unrealistic. The nonlinear nature of equations is added to the CGE approach, and CGE model linkages are based on the optimizing behaviour of all economic agents such as regional household and firms; therefore, CGE model-based linkages are considered more real and are preferred (Nganou et al. 2009). In a CGE model, too, the basic input is the SAM data. A SAM is not a model in itself; it is simply a representation of a set of data for an economy. Suitably designed and supported by survey data and other information, it does suggest some important and useful features about the socio-economic structure in general and the relationship between the structure of production and the distribution of income in particular (Round 2003). A SAM is thus a particular representation of the macroeconomic accounts of a socio-economic system that captures the transactions and transfers among all economic agents in the system (Pyatt and Round 1985; Reinert and Roland-Holst 1997).

3.3.1 Structure of the CGE Model

The Global Trade Analysis Project (GTAP) was started in 1992 to facilitate the quantitative analysis of international trade. The fully documented GTAP database gives economy-wide data of all 140 defined regions of the world. The GTAP model (see Brockmeier 2001; Hertel 1997) is a static multi-region general equilibrium model that divides the entire economy into various agents dependent on each other. It is a general equilibrium model in that it takes care of the feedback and linkage effects in the entire economy. It is static in that it provides a comparison of the state of the economy before and after changing the value of shock variable(s). Under the GTAP model framework, each separate region assumes common domestic structure and linked through trade and investment flows between them. The domestic structure consists of one regional household, specified over private consumption, government consumption and saving activities; production behaviour in the region; and two global sectors through which all the regions of the world are linked with each other. The GTAP-based CGE model is used to compute the linkages of various sectors of the

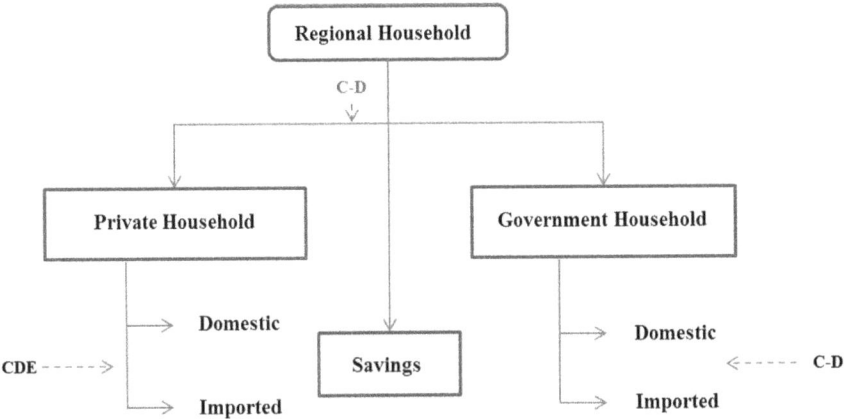

Fig. 3.1 Representation of regional household behaviour. *Source* Arora (2016)

Indian economy under the Rasmussen-Hirschman framework. The framework of this model is provided under the GTAP.

The GTAP model structure can be explained with the help of accounting relationships that are defined for each region such that the entire economy is in balance. These relationships remain the same for each region[1] with common producer and consumer behaviour (briefly explained in the following sub-section). In the GTAP model, each separate region assumes common domestic structure. The pictorial representation of these relationships provides the circular flow for any GTAP region (see Fig. 6 in Brockmeier 2001). It is mandatory that each relationship should hold to satisfy the conditions of Walras's law [for details on accounting relationships, see Hertel and Tsigas (1997)]. In the GTAP model, the behavioural equations for the economy or region specify the behaviour of optimizing agents such as the demand functions in consumer behaviour and the production function in producer behaviour.

3.3.1.1 Regional Household Behaviour

A regional household allocates the expenditure across private consumption expenditure, government consumption expenditure and savings activities. A private household further allocates the given expenditure over domestic and imported goods through the constant difference elasticity (CDE) implicit expenditure function. However, the government household allocates the given expenditure among domestic and imported goods following a Cobb-Douglas (CD) utility function, in which saving is assumed as a single commodity and fully exhausted by investment demand (Fig. 3.1).

---

[1]Here, the term region is used for the individual country or collection of countries in one region. The number of regions in any study may vary as per the study's requirement. The GTAP 9 database clubbed almost all the countries of the world into 140 regions.

3.3.1.2 Production Structure and Firm Behaviour

In the GTAP model, producers try to minimize the cost of production, and their behaviour is specified by the nested constant elasticity of substitution (CES) function (Gohin and Hertel 2003). In the case of more than two inputs, Sato (1967) proposed a nested CES function with less restrictive conditions on elasticity of substitution, which is a good approximation for empirical applications. In the GTAP model, the same nested structure is used to specify the substitution possibilities between various inputs. At the upper level, the CES function is defined to indicate the substitution possibility between intermediate inputs and value added, and at the lower level, the CES function is defined to show the substitution between primary factors in the value-added nest. The basic idea behind the nested CES structure is to accommodate the substitution possibilities within the aggregated input category, which is composed of other individual inputs.

In the first stage, the inputs required to produce an output are divided into intermediate goods and factor inputs (Fig. 3.2). Factor inputs are clubbed under the endowment category (land, labour and capital), and two sources of intermediate goods are mentioned. The source of intermediate inputs can be domestic industry and/or the industry of another country, and intermediate imports may come from different exporters, depending on the unit cost of production. Producers sell consumption goods to private and government households; investment goods to the savings

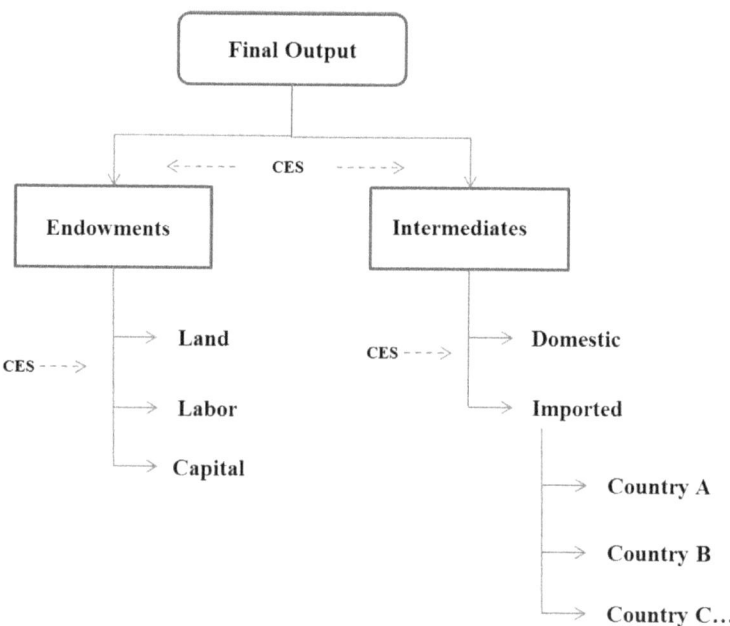

Fig. 3.2 Representation of production structure in the Global Trade Analysis Project (GTAP) Model. *Source* Arora (2016)

sector; and intermediate goods to other producers and receive income. The income from these sales is exhausted on the purchase of intermediate goods and primary inputs.

The primary factors in this model are divided into perfectly mobile and sluggish. In the case of mobile factors, the reward is the same regardless of the employed sector, but in the case of sluggish factors, the reward changes with the position of its employment. The estimation of this model using the GTAP database provides a new equilibrium solution that contains the updated value of each variable in the model. From those results, one can meaningfully calculate the number of effects through which a comparison can be made in pre- and post-simulation values.

3.3.2 Modelling CGE Linkages

We used version 9 of the GTAP database (GTAP 9) to compute the linkage effect based on the CGE model. We made different types of aggregations with respect to countries, sectors and factors of production. Keeping the Indian economy in the main lead, we categorized the remaining countries as *rest of the world* (*row*). Under sectoral aggregations, we classified all the sectors into primary, secondary and tertiary. However, for disaggregated analysis, we used the 34-sector-economy SAM under the GTAP 9 framework. For the factors of production, we aggregated all the factors into labour and capital.

To compute the linkages, the CGE (GTAP model) modelling-based effects under the Rasmussen-Hirschman framework are used. The Rasmussen linkage indices are accepted as being the method mostly used to identify the key sectors of the economy. Under this framework, the backward and forward production linkage coefficients represent the amount of output generated by the sector both within itself and in other sectors through their linkage effect. The backward linkage of a sector j quantifies the change in economy-wide income relative to an average change in the economy caused by a unitary injection in the final demand of that sector j. These linkages are known as production linkages or output multipliers because these measure the changes in the output or production with unitary injections. On the other hand, the forward linkage (in percentage terms) of sector j quantifies the change in income in sector j relative to the average change in the economy caused by a unitary injection in the final demand of all sectors (Parra and Wodon 2010). These linkages are known as input multipliers. If the forward linkage for sector j is greater than unity (100%), the change in sector j's income is higher than the average income changes in the economy after a unitary injection in all sectors. A key sector is usually defined as one with both backward and forward linkages greater than 1. A sector with backward linkages greater than 1 is termed backward-oriented, and a sector with forward linkages above 1 is termed forward-oriented.

Assume there are n endogenous accounts. Let A_{nxn} denote the matrix of technical coefficients, the matrix resulting from dividing every cell T_{ij} in T_{nxn} by the respective column sum Y_j. Let Y_{nx1}, N_{nx1} and X_{nx1} denote column vectors with, respectively, output, the sum's total expenditures and the exogenous component. Then, by construction, the following two equations hold:

$$Y = N + X \tag{3.1}$$

$$N = AY \tag{3.2}$$

Combining these equations gives

$$Y = AY + X \tag{3.3}$$

which can be rewritten as

$$Y = \begin{bmatrix} y_1 & y_2 & \dots & y_n \end{bmatrix}' \text{ endogeneous accounts}$$
$$X = \begin{bmatrix} x_1 & x_2 & \dots & x_p \end{bmatrix}' \text{ exogeneous accounts}$$
$$\text{and } A = \begin{bmatrix} a_{ij} \end{bmatrix}_{n \times p} \text{ matrix of technology coefficients}$$

The technology coefficients represent change in intermediate demand due to a unit change in the output of jth sector or activity. Since Y is endogenous, Eq. 3.3 can be adjusted to represent Y as a function of X to model the effect of exogenous shock on the output of each sector:

$$Y = (I - A)^{-1} X \tag{3.4}$$

where I is the $n \times n$ identity matrix. Using a_{ij}, the matrix $M = (I - A)^{-1}$ is known as the accounting multiplier matrix, the Leontief (1936) inverse matrix, or simply the inverse matrix. Each cell m_{ij} of M quantifies the change in total income account i as a result of a unitary increase in the exogenous component of account j. Let us define m_{ij} as a typical element of the Leontief inverse matrix M and V as the sum of all cells of the inverse matrix:

$$V = \sum_i \sum_j m_{ij} \tag{3.5}$$

Let M_i denote the sum of the ith row of the inverse matrix and $M_{.j}$ denote the sum of the jth column of the inverse matrix:

$$M_{i.} = \sum_k M_{ik} \tag{3.6}$$

$$M_{.j} = \sum_k M_{kj} \tag{3.7}$$

Then, the Hirschman-Rasmussen indices may be developed as a backward linkage (BL_i) index of sector i as

$$BL_i = \frac{nM_{.i}}{V} \tag{3.8}$$

and, the forward linkage index is given by

$$FL_i = \frac{nM_{i.}}{V} \tag{3.9}$$

To compute the employment multipliers, we used the method suggested by (Ali Bekhet 2011):

$$\text{Let} \quad w = e\hat{X}^{-1} \tag{3.10}$$

where w represents the rupee value of labour inputs to each of the n sector per rupee worth of sectoral output, $\hat{X}$ represents the diagonalized matrix of total outputs, and e is the number of workers employed and is defined as the employment vector. The simple employment multipliers can be obtained as:

$$l = w'(I - A)^{-1} \tag{3.11}$$

These multipliers would represent the number of new jobs created expressed as total employment for every new employee to meet increased final demand for new output. In all the above matrices, the household sector has been treated as the exogenous sector.

Under the GTAP framework, the matrix A can be generated and the coefficients m_{ij} are constructed to build matrix $M = (I - A)^{-1}$. The matrix M is constructed for a one per cent shock in each qo of the jth commodity of region r. In the GTAP model, qo is an endogenous variable and shock on endogenous variable is not possible. Model closure statements define which variables adjust (endogenous) and which are fixed (exogenous), and model closure is the next crucial step in the model simulations under the RunGTAP environment. The "swap" option has been used to modify the model's standard closure statements, i.e. an exogenous variable for an endogenous variable. This swap preserves the number of endogenous variables that were originally in the GTAP model. As the qo (the total output of jth commodity/sector) is an endogenous account within the GTAP model, it has been swapped with an exogenous account po (the total profits out of jth commodity/sector) to compute the results. The remaining model is the same as given in the GTAP methodology. Swapping qo with po and defining a shock of one per cent to qo of the jth commodity provides the percentage changes in output levels of all 34 commodities for region r. Using 34 shocks (one shock for each commodity in one simulation) in 34 simulations provides a 34 × 34 matrix equivalent to matrix A given above. Using this matrix A obtained under the CGE (based on the GTAP model) framework, we construct the $M = (I - A)^{-1}$, and we use Eqs. 3.5–3.11 to compute backward and forward production linkages along with employment linkages.

3.4   Empirical Analysis and Results

We bifurcated the linkage analysis of production and employment into two subsections: an aggregated analysis of production and employment linkages, computed using a 3 × 3 sector economy, and a disaggregated analysis of production and employment linkages, computed using a 34 × 34 sector economy. We computed the CGE-based linkages using the RunGTAP package and the GTAP 9 database. We conducted the aggregations for the two regions and the 34 sectors. The aggregated analysis represents the relative situation of the primary, secondary and tertiary sectors for the production and employment linkages, while the disaggregated analysis helps to gauge a better picture of the entire economy through the lenses of production and employment linkages. The key sectors are dependent sectors strongly connected to other industries along with their input demand and the output supply chains and thus have relative backward and forward linkages greater than 1 (Temursho 2016). The potential sectors are the budding ones that can become key sectors and usually have values close to 1 or above the mean level. The weak sectors are the most laggard sectors with weak production and employment linkages to other sectors. These can be considered as independent sectors that have low input and output linkages with other sectors of the economy.

3.4.1   Aggregated Analysis of Linkages

We use the CGE approach to compute the aggregate backward and forward production linkages and the employment linkages for the agriculture and allied activities-based primary sector; industry-based secondary sector; and the services-based tertiary sector. Some CGE linkages are negative. A negative backward (forward) production linkage implies that the allocation of resources in one sector shall adversely affect the output of vertically (horizontally) linked sectors; the negative figure is therefore a sort of opportunity cost of developing the ith sector in terms of production loss in the j backwardly (forwardly) linked sectors in the economy. A CGE is designed with the assumption of Pareto optimum behaviour of all economic agents; therefore, any reallocation will improve one sector at the cost of another. A negative employment linkage of the ith sector represents that a positive shock in the output of that sector shall cause a loss in the total employment of the linked sectors because of the reallocating behaviour of the CGE model (Nganou 2005, 156); higher inputs in the form of labour and capital are required in the sector where output shock is given (output is increased by one per cent). This reallocation of labour in the jth sector will cause the withdrawal of labour from some other sectors as the supply of workers is fixed under CGE framework. Under the SAM multiplier framework, the supply of resources is perfectly elastic, but under the CGE framework, the supply is fixed; hence, the negative employment linkages to other sectors have been noticed.

In the first instance, the primary and secondary sectors appear to be forward-looking sectors with a linkage coefficient above 1, while the tertiary sector is backward-looking (Table 3.1). The primary sector does not offer positive backward linkages while the services sector's forward linkages are negative. It may be inferred that the industry-based secondary sector is offering positive production linkages of both types, but the sector is designated as forward-looking in nature, as the backward linkage coefficient is below 1. Thus, in the case of all economic agents behaving optimally, the secondary sector is an ideal sector that can offer positive backward and forward production linkages. The other two sectors are ineffectual in offering positive production linkages to the horizontally or vertically linked sectors of the Indian economy.

However, the major concern is the negative employment linkages of the primary sector—so big that any reallocation of employment (with fixed supply of labour) due to a one per cent increase in output will cause a huge withdrawal of labour from the secondary and tertiary sectors. The primary sector contributes nearly 17% of the GDP at current prices, while the share of this sector in total employment is around 53% (Singh 2020); hence, a one per cent increase in output requires reallocation of (53/17) 3.12% of labour force to this sector. A reallocation of 3.12% in agriculture with a fixed supply of labour means an equal withdrawal of labour (-3.12%) from other sectors of the economy. The CGE-based linkage coefficient is -3.29, a value close to this raw observation of -3.12%. The CGE figure is more authentic as it considers the behaviour of all economic agents. The secondary and tertiary sectors have been noticed to have positive employment linkages. Any reallocation of employment to these two sectors because of a one per cent output shock will not cause a big withdrawal of labour from other linked sectors; therefore, these two sectors' employment linkages are positive.

In sum, the aggregated analysis reveals that the industry-based secondary sector is the key sector with a combination of positive backward and forward production linkages and positive employment linkages; the other two sectors have either a negative backward production linkage or a forward production linkage in an optimum situation. An economy though needs to develop a sector with high employment linkages, but the output linkages must be taken care of while designing a policy. The

Table 3.1 A summary of production and employment linkages—an aggregated picture

Sectors	Forward linkages	Backward linkages	Employment linkages
Primary	3.00	−0.65	−3.29
Secondary	1.36	0.60	1.45
Tertiary	−1.36	2.10	1.50

Source Authors' calculations using the GTAP 9 database

sectors those guarantee both output and employment linkages to entire economy are surely the key sectors and must be given priority while resource allocation.

3.4.2 Disaggregated Analysis of Linkages

We used CGE approaches to compute employment and production (backward and forward) linkages for 34 sectors of the economy (Table 3.2). We plotted the three types of linkage (Figs. 3.3, 3.4 and 3.5): Panel A represents CGE linkages for the first 10 primary subsectors (coded $S1$–$S10$); Panel B offers the same linkages for the 14 subsectors ($S11$–$S24$) of the secondary sector; and Panel C plots the CGE linkages computed for 10 subsectors ($S25$–$S34$) of the tertiary sector. The backward linkages (Fig. 3.3) of the agriculture-based *Other Crops (S4)* classification have the highest CGE linkage coefficient in the primary sector. The other key sectors with backward CGE linkages above unity within the primary category are *Animal Husbandry (S5)*, *Food Crops (S1)* and *Cash Crops (S2)*. Only one sector *Food Products Manufacturing (S11)* appears with above-unity CGE backward linkages. The remaining 13 affiliates ($S12$–$S24$) of the manufacturing-based secondary sector cannot be included in key sectors. Seven of the 10 subsectors of the services sector appear with the CGE backward linkages above unity. The *Trade (S30)* related services sector appears with highest backward linkages followed by the *Electricity (S26)* and *Other Transport Services (S28)* sectors at second and third places. The *Construction (S25)*, *Public Administration (S34)*, *Banking and Insurance (S31)* and *Ownership of Dwellings (S32)* are the remaining four sectors in ascending order of CGE backward linkages above unity.

Next, we analysed the forward production linkages to identify the forward-looking sectors of an economy (Fig. 3.4), and we find that only three primary sectors—*Crude Petrol, Natural Gas (S9)*, *Coal and Lignite (S8)* and *Plantation Crops (S3)*—are forward-looking and have CGE forward linkage coefficients above unity. However, of the fourteen secondary sectors, eight are forward-looking (see Fig. 3.4, Panel B). In the services sector, only two subsectors are forward-looking: *Gas and Water supply (S27)* and *Banking and Insurance (S31)*.

An analysis of the third dimension, employment linkages, presents a gloomy picture of the secondary sector (Fig. 3.5): only one, *S11 (Food Products)*, of fourteen sectors has employment linkages above unity. Hence, the primary and services sectors play a major role in employment generation. Some hope of employment generation exists in the agriculture and animal husbandry sectors. Six out of ten subsectors of tertiary sectors have employment linkages above unity, along with the three agriculture-oriented sectors—*Other Crops (S4)*, *Food Cops (S1)* and *Cash Crops (S2)*.

The Indian economy is reeling under the pressure to generate substantial employment opportunities; therefore, we analysed the relationship of employment linkages with the two types of production linkages (Fig. 3.6). From the scatter plot of employment linkages against the backward linkages in Panel A and against forward linkages

Table 3.2 Sectoral production and employment linkages using CGE approach

Aggregated sector classification	Sector code	Sector classification	CGE multipliers		
			BL	FL	EL
Primary sector	S1	Food crops	1.4395	−0.4265	1.4325
	S2	Cash crops	1.1187	−0.5578	1.0669
	S3	Plantation crops	−0.0214	2.5757	−0.0416
	S4	Other crops	3.5121	−0.3030	3.7044
	S5	Animal husbandry	1.6848	−0.4700	1.8791
	S6	Forestry and logging	−0.0406	0.2549	−0.1218
	S7	Fishing	0.1888	−0.9924	0.0920
	S8	Coal and lignite	−0.1485	3.6709	−0.2139
	S9	Crude petrol, natural gas	−0.0529	7.7137	−0.1749
	S10	Other minerals	0.2275	0.7258	0.1237
Secondary sector	S11	Food products	1.2406	−0.4215	1.1604
	S12	Beverages and tobacco	0.1735	−1.0204	0.2051
	S13	Textile and textile products	0.2817	2.2212	0.2182
	S14	Wood and furniture	−0.1674	1.3377	−0.1091
	S15	Paper and printing	−0.0911	0.4779	−0.0335
	S16	Leather and leather products	−0.1926	4.8312	−0.1091
	S17	Rubber, petrol, plastic, cola	0.5340	−0.0193	0.4220
	S18	Chemical	0.5927	1.7508	0.4773
	S19	Metals	0.6122	0.6832	0.4832
	S20	Metal product expect machinery	−0.1675	2.4354	−0.0922
	S21	Tractors, agricultural implements, etc.	0.3829	1.1024	0.3139
	S22	Electrical, electronic machinery appliances	−0.1275	2.0867	−0.0541
	S23	Transport equipment	0.2063	0.7914	0.1893
	S24	Misc. manufacturing Industries	0.2951	3.3748	0.2166
Tertiary sector	S25	Construction	2.7788	−1.1272	2.4003
	S26	Electricity	3.5342	0.0316	3.8320
	S27	Gas and water supply	−0.0980	3.5121	−0.0923
	S28	Other transport services	3.4509	−0.2854	3.4549

(continued)

Table 3.2 (continued)

Aggregated sector classification	Sector code	Sector classification	CGE multipliers		
			BL	FL	EL
	S29	Communication	0.2869	0.5256	0.3339
	S30	Trade	7.3607	−0.5663	6.3434
	S31	Banking and insurance	1.6513	1.6709	2.0053
	S32	Ownership of dwellings	1.1831	−1.6134	0.9205
	S33	Other services	−0.1687	0.7144	−0.1209
	S34	Public administration	2.5397	−0.6850	3.8885
		Mean values	**1.0000**	**1.0000**	**1.0000**

Note (i) The CGE multipliers have been calculated using GTAP 9 database and RunGTAP program coupled with GEMPACK software; the GTAP 9 and GEMPACK are licensed with the second author
Source Authors' calculations

in Panel B, we may infer that the employment linkages are positively associated with backward linkages with high coefficient of multiple determinants to the tune of 0.9587. However, the same are negatively associated with forward linkages with coefficient of multiple determinants to the tune of 0.2086.

3.5 Summary, Conclusions and Policy Implications

The analysis reveals that most of the services sectors in India are backward-oriented; only a few sectors are forward-looking. Most services sectors use the products of secondary or primary sectors as inputs to ensure substantial backward linkages; the horizontal linkages of services are missing. The backward linkages of industry-based secondary sectors are low enough; only one sector, *Food Products Manufacturing (S11)*, is a key sector. The production linkages of industry-to-agriculture in India are low, as evidenced in Ghosh (2014) and Bathla (2018). The secondary sector is forward-looking; more than 50% of the sectors have a forward production linkage above unity. Four of the ten primary sectors are vertically linked to other sectors of the economy, i.e. they use the output of other sectors as their inputs. The count of forward-looking primary sectors is also low; three sectors have CGE forward linkages above unity. The employment linkages are high in either the subsectors of the services (tertiary) category or in the primary classification-based animal husbandry and agriculture areas. The industry-based secondary sector is weak in terms of employment linkages. About 35% of industries (five of fourteen) do not appear in the list of backward- or forward-looking sectors. The scatter plot analysis reveals that the backward-looking sectors must be given priority and resources allocated to the various sectors of the economy to generate substantial employment opportunities. Allocation with any other priority will not satisfy the dual objective of output

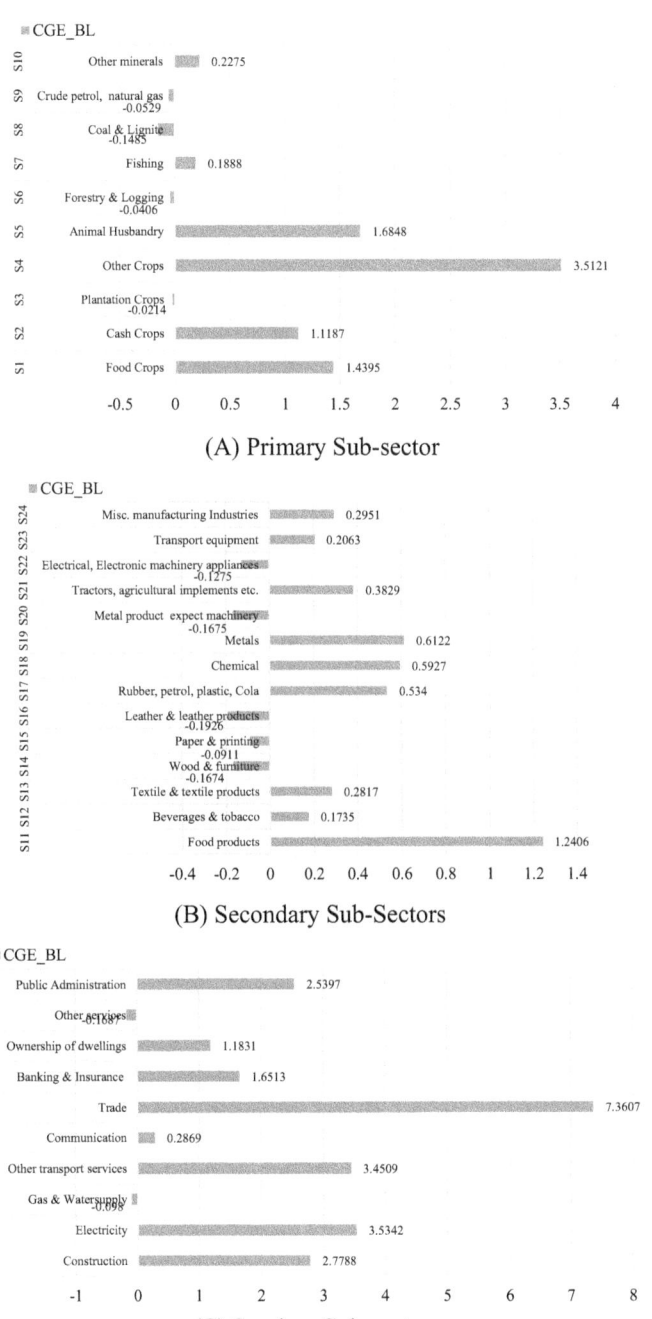

Fig. 3.3 Backward linkages for 34 sector economy. *Source* Authors' Elaborations in MS Excel

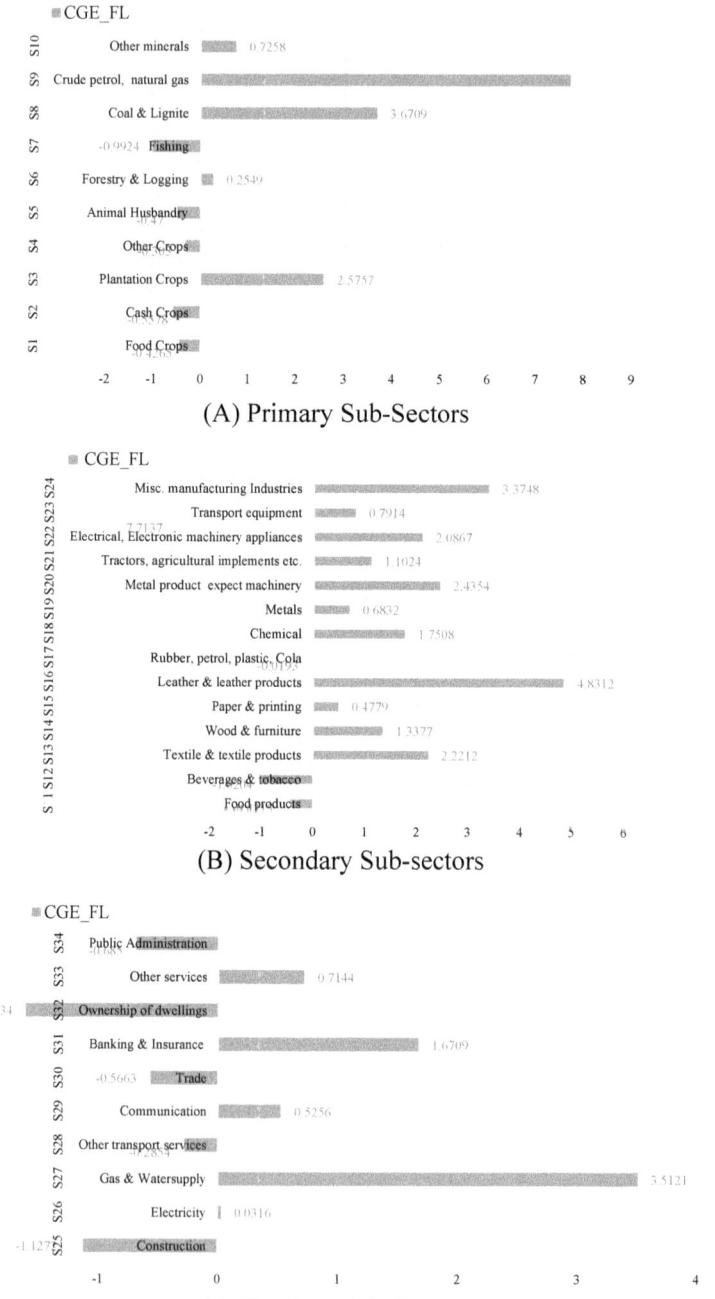

(A) Primary Sub-Sectors

(B) Secondary Sub-sectors

(C) Services Sub-Sectors

Fig. 3.4 Forward linkages for 34 sector economy. *Source* Authors' Elaborations in MS Excel

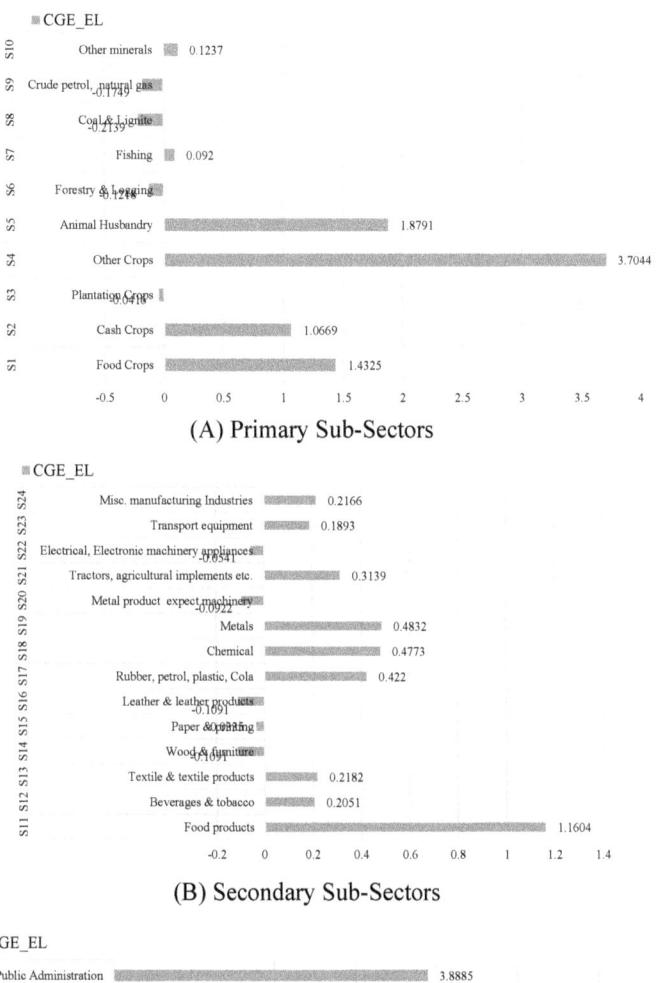

(A) Primary Sub-Sectors

(B) Secondary Sub-Sectors

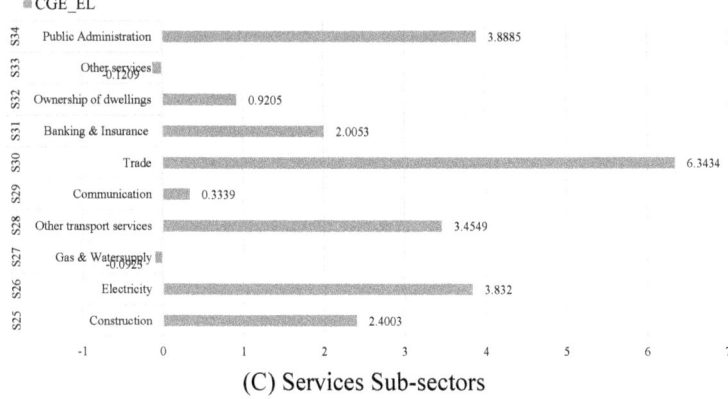

(C) Services Sub-sectors

Fig. 3.5 Employment linkages for 34 sector economy. *Source* Authors' Elaborations in MS Excel

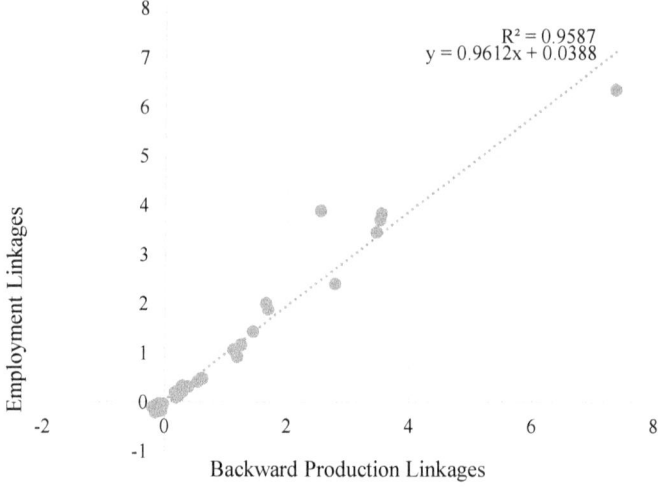

(A) Backward Production and Employment Linkages Plot

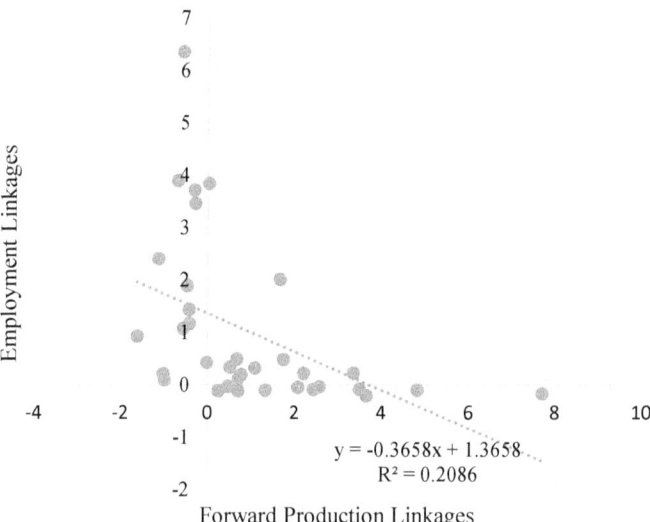

(B) Forward Production and Employment Linkages Plot

Fig. 3.6 Employment linkages' association with production linkages. *Source* Authors' Elaborations in MS Excel

and employment growth and will, hence, constrain the economy from yielding the potential demographic dividend.

References

Ali Bekhet, H. (2011). Output, income and employment multipliers in Malaysian economy: Input-output approach. *International Business Research, 4*(1), 208–223.

Arora, R. (2016). *Mega regional trade deals in the Asia-Pacific region and their impact on Indian economy: Partial and general equilibrium analysis.* An unpublished Ph.D. thesis submitted to the Department of Economic Sciences. Indian Institute of Technology Kanpur, India.

Bathla, S. (2018). *Post-harvest food management, extent of processing and inter-sectoral linkages in India.* Report submitted to the World Bank, Washington D.C. (unpublished).

Bhatt, M. S., & Munjal, P. (2013). Social Accounting Matrix to study the socio-economic linkages of tourism sector—A case study of India. *Indian Economic Review, 48*(2), 381–408.

Bhattacharya, T., & Rajeev, M. (2016). *Measuring linkages to identify key sectors of the Indian economy: An application of input-output analysis.* Institute for social and economic change. Available at http://203.200.22.249:8080/jspui/handle/123456789/13427.

Brockmeier, M. (2001). A graphical exposition of the GTAP model (GTAP Technical Paper No. 3-1-2001). IN, USA: Center for Global Trade Analysis, Purdue University.

Ghosh, N. (2014). *An assessment of the extent of food processing in various food sub-sectors.* Report submitted to the Ministry of Agriculture and Farmers Welfare, GOI.

Gohin, A., & Hertel, T. W. (2003). A note on the CES functional form and its use in the GTAP model (GTAP Research Memorandum No. 2). IN, USA: Center for Global Trade Analysis, Purdue University.

Hansda, K. S. (2003). *Sustainability of service-led growth: An input-output analysis of Indian economy.* RBI occasional papers.

Hertel, T. W. (Ed.). (1997). *Global trade analysis: Modeling and applications.* NY, USA: Cambridge University Press.

Hertel, T. W., & Tsigas, M. E. (1997). Structure of GTAP. In T. W. Hertel (Ed.), *Global trade analysis: Modeling and applications* (pp. 13–73). New York, USA: Cambridge University Press.

Hirschman, A. O. (1958). *The strategy of economic development.* New Haven, USA: Yale University Press.

Leontief, W. (1936). Quantitative input-output relations in the economic system of the United States. *Review of Economics and Statistics, 18*(1), 105–125.

Nganou, J. P. (2005). *A multisectoral analysis of growth prospects for Lesotho: SAM-multiplier decomposition and computable general equilibrium perspectives.* Unpublished Ph.D. Thesis, Faculty of the College of Arts and Sciences of American University, American University, Washington, D.C.

Nganou, J. P., Parra, J. C., & Wodon, Q. (2009). Oil price shocks, poverty and gender: A social accounting matrix analysis for Kenya. In M. Bussolo & R. de Hoyos (Eds.), *Gender aspects of the trade and poverty Nexus.* London: Palgrave Macmillan.

Parra, J. C., & Wodon, Q. (2010). Gender, time use, and labor income in Guinea: Micro and macro analysis. In J. Arbache, E. Filipiak, & A. Kolev (Eds.), *Gender disparities in Africa's labor markets.* Washington, DC: Agencies Française de Development and the World Bank.

Pyatt G., & Round, J. I. (1985). *Social accounting matrices: A basis for planning.* The World Bank, Washington D. C.

Raihan, S., & Khondker, B. H. (2010). *Backward and forward linkages of the textile and clothing industry in India, Bangladesh and Pakistan.* MPRA WP No. 41231, Munich Personal RePEc Archive.

Rasmussen, P. N. (1957). *Studies in inter-sectoral relations.* Amsterdam: North-Holland.

Reinert, K. A., & Roland-Holst, D. W. (1997). *Social accounting matrices.* In J. F. Francois & K. A. Reinert (Eds.), *Applied methods for trade policy analysis: A handbook* (pp. 94–121). Cambridge University Press, Cambridge.

Round, J. I. (2003). Constructing SAMs for development policy analysis: Lessons learned and challenges ahead. *Economic Systems Research, 15*(2), 161–183.

Saikia, D. (2011). Analyzing inter-sectoral linkages in India. *African Journal of Agricultural Research, 6*(33), 6766–6775.

Sastry, D. V. S., Singh, B., Bhattacharya, K., & Unnikrishnan, N. K. (2003). Sectoral linkages and growth prospects: Reflections on the Indian economy. *Economic and Political Weekly, 38*(24), 2390–2397.

Sato, K. (1967). A two-level constant-elasticity-of-substitution production function. *The Review of Economic Studies, 34*(2), 201–218.

Singh, H. (2020). What is the sector-wise contribution of GDP in India? Information. Accessed from https://www.jagranjosh.com/general-knowledge/what-is-the-sectorwise-contri bution-in-gdp-of-india-1519797705-1 dated 06-02-2020 at 10.01 am.

Temursho, U. (2016). *Backward and forward linkages and key sectors in the Kazakhstan economy.* Report on Services Sector in Kazakhstan as an Engine for Diversified Economic Growth by Joint Government of Kazakhstan and Asian Development Bank Knowledge and Experience Exchange Program.

Thirlwall, A. P. (1983). A plain man's guide to Kaldor's growth laws. *Journal of Post Keynesian Economics, 5*(1), 345–358.

Todaro, M. P., & Smith, S. C. (2012). *Economic development (10th eds.).* Pearson Education Ltd.

Zalk, N. (2014). What is the role of manufacturing in boosting economic growth and employment in South Africa? Industrial Development Policy and Strategic Advisor https://www.econ3x3. org/sites/default/files/articles/Zalk%202014%20Industrialisaton%20and%20Employment%20F INAL.pdf.

Chapter 4
The Food Processing Industry in India: Regional Spread, Linkages and Space for Farmer Producer Organisations

K. J. S. Satyasai and Aparajita Singh

4.1 Introduction

The linkages between agriculture and industry have attracted the attention of academicians and policymakers alike. The role of agriculture and its linkages with industry is part of the main discourse in the two-sector growth models in Kuznets' (1961) elucidation of agriculture's contribution to the economy. According to Bhattacharya and Rao (1986), sectoral linkages in India weakened during the green revolution (1967–1978) compared to the previous period. Since the result seemed counterintuitive, Satyasai and Viswanathan (1997, 1999) analysed the intersectoral linkages and found that these strengthened over time, though the magnitude of the relation weakened in later years. Irrespective of the metrics, agriculture and the other sectors are interrelated; none of the sectors can be sustainable in isolation. Using the by-products of one (sub)sector as the inputs for the others is the key to reaping economies of scale.

To develop a vibrant non-farm sector, the economy requires a strong agricultural sector. Promoting agriculture–industry linkages would cater to the employment needs of local rural households. Development planning can be effective if all the sectors are viewed as part of the entire economy rather than as silos. In India, the shift of workers away from agriculture to the secondary and tertiary sectors has been rather slow, unlike the development path taken in several other countries; a reckonable shift occurred only in recent decades, and nearly half the workforce still depends on agriculture for livelihood. The changes in the rural and agricultural landscape, too,

K. J. S. Satyasai (✉)
DEAR, NABARD, Mumbai, India
e-mail: satyasaik@outlook.com

A. Singh
FPOs, Research & Consulting, Dvara E-Registry, Hyderabad, India
e-mail: aparajita.singh101@gmail.com

have certain specificities that compel us to focus on the linkages between agriculture and industry.

First, agriculture has increasingly been smallholder-oriented; the average farm size declined from 1.33 hectares (ha) in 2000–2001 to 1.08 ha in 2015–2016 (Agriculture Census 2015–16). Small and marginal holdings account for 86% of the total holdings, and they have limited marketable surplus and weak bargaining power in the market. This has led to the realisation that farming by individuals may no longer be sustainable, and hence, innovations such as contract farming and Farmer Producer Organisations (FPOs) are needed. Second, product-factor market linkages often compel individual farmers to sell at suboptimal prices (Negi et al. 2018)—they cannot choose the right marketing channel—and rising agriculture costs have reduced profitability (Srivastava et al. 2017; Satyasai and Balanarayana 2018). Third, farmers are often forced to pursue multiple livelihood options to sustain themselves. It is therefore important to forge linkages across the sectors to generate enough employment opportunities. Fourth, consumption patterns have changed in urban and rural areas, and consumers now demand greater convenience and products that are processed and prepared to a higher degree (McKinsey and Company & CII 2013).

Fifth, the country is experiencing a horticulture revolution. The production of horticulture products in 2018–19 was 314.87 million tonnes—greater than the food grain production (*Hindu Businessline* 2019). There are ample scope and need for processing and value addition of such high volumes of perishable produce. This is an opportunity waiting to be monetised, as processing and value addition would minimise the handling cost and wastage and improve the return to farmers. A concerted focus on developing FPOs will change the production landscape in agriculture and its interface with other sectors of the economy.[1]

In this light, in Sect. 4.2, we begin with a discussion on the size and direction of the food processing industry in the country, and on the number and geographical spread of processing units across the states and their correlates with agriculture and infrastructure. We discuss the food processing industry's access to credit and financing arrangements—especially the Scheme for Agro-Marine Processing and Development of Agro-Processing Clusters (SAMPADA). In Sect. 4.3, we examine the scope of FPOs in strengthening the agriculture–industry linkages and enhancing the access of food processing units to finance. This section covers the organisation and integration of unorganised processing units through FPOs. Food processing units are concentrated in a few states, and while some states have the potential, they do not have a processing industry. The North-Eastern states are taken as an example. The scope for food processing in the North-Eastern states and avenues for involving FPOs are discussed. Section 4.4 presents the conclusions and the way forward. The data and information for the study are collected from documents published by the Ministry of Food Processing Industries, the National Accounts Statistics of the Central Statistics Office, Ministry of Statistics and Programme Implementation

---

[1]India has about 5000 FPOs, and the Union Budget 2019–20 announced that 10,000 new FPOs would be formed over the next five years. The policy measures announced in May 2020 have confirmed that FPOs will be the convergence point for all agricultural reforms.

and National Sample Survey Office (NSSO) Reports No. 581 and 582 (73rd round) on Unincorporated Non-Agricultural Enterprises (excluding construction).

4.2 The Landscape of the Food Processing Industry in India

India is the largest producer of several agricultural commodities, and it has the advantage of being one of the fastest-growing economies in the world. The demand for branded and packaged food has expanded significantly in the wake of population growth, rapid urbanisation and the shift of women from unpaid care work to participation in the labour workforce. Large investments have been directed to building world-class ports, logistics and supply chain infrastructure.

In India, the food processing sector ranks first in terms of employment and the number of factories in operation and third in terms of output. The food processing industry was expected to employ nine million persons in 2020 (Grant Thornton and ASSOCHAM 2017), and it was estimated to grow from US\$258 billion (Rs. 18.06 trillion) in 2015 to US\$482 billion (Rs. 29.96 trillion) in 2020. Table 4.1 shows that in 2015–16, 13 major agriculture processing sectors had an industry size (sales) of Rs. 12.66 trillion (NABARD 2018). The meat industry was at the top, at Rs. 4.5 trillion. The growth rates in industry size vary across sectors, with the weighted average growth being 12%.

The food industry has a lot of potential—irrespective of the various, divergent estimates of its size—as evidenced by the trends in the economy: changing consumer tastes, the entry of international companies, rising export demand, higher consumption of horticultural products, enhanced safety and health consciousness, preference for packed and branded food, consumer preference for processed food, modern snacking habits, opportunities for farmer-firm linkages and so on. These trends demand product and process innovations and heavy investments in logistics and in safety and quality control infrastructure.

To promote food processing, several schemes and programmes are being implemented by the Ministry of Food Processing Industries, GoI. The industry's gross value added (GVA) has grown at 7.68% during 2017–2018 compared to the 4.98% for agriculture, forestry and fishing. In constant prices (2011–2012), the GVA of food products and beverages stood at Rs. 1.75 trillion (Table 4.2). Food, beverages and tobacco accounted for 8.5% of the GVA in manufacturing in 2016–2017, about half the share in 1950–1951. The share of the food processing sector in the GVA of agriculture and allied sectors has increased from 2.5% in 1950–1951 to 10.2%. Since 2006–2007, its share has hovered around 10–11%. The growth in the sector peaked at 11.61% from 2000–2001 to 2010–2011, but later, it declined to 2.28%.

The trends in the 15-year moving period growth rates of the food processing sector show that growth in constant terms peaked at 10% in 2009–2010 (Fig. 4.1). Growth oscillated around a negligible 4% until 1974–1975, and it hovered at around 10% in the recent periods before touching 6% during the last period. The trends in the growth rate in the GVA of food processing industries in current prices were

Table 4.1 Industry size and growth for key food processing and related sectors in India (FY 2015–16)

Financials	(INR crore)			CAGR (%) FY 2012–2016	PBIDTA to sales (%)	PAT to sales (%)	ROCE (%)	Employment (million households)
	Industry size (sales)	Export value	Import value					
Edible oil	163,998	65,325	2728	10	3	1	12.24	
Fruits and vegetables	144,000	9103	5960	21	24	4		
Dairy	105,000	755	322	14	5	2	15.29	76
Spices	75,000	16,238	4466	14	14	5	18.1	
Poultry	57,028	769	26	16	8	3	15.37	0.4
Basmati rice	53,740	26,870	0	1	6	−3	35.47	
Meat processing and export	42,660	42,660	0	2	3	0.9	26.1	50
Cold chain	27,200	0	0	14				
Shrimp	26,895	24,320	0	9	8	6	33	14.50
Beverages	23,173	9664	973	7	14	7	13.07	1.6
Hybrid seed	19,500	0	0	11	19	13.4	20.83	
Warehouse	8500	0	0	29	9	3	6.61	
Shrimp feed	7000	0	0	17	8	3		
Maize starch	7000	458	17	14	11	3	10.07	
Total	12,66,139		14,492	12				

Source NABARD (2018)

Note PBIDTA stands for profit before interest, depreciation, tax and amortisation; PAT stands for profit after tax; and ROCE stands for return on capital employed

similar. The growth rate overall has been lower than the avowed potential because of several challenges: infrastructure, innovation, skill, branding and access to credit (Grant Thorton and ASSOCHAM, India 2017). These are generic challenges, apart from the many sector-specific challenges.

To address a few of these challenges, a recent umbrella programme, SAMPADA, brings together a host of old and new interventions catering to the various needs of the industry. The outlay for the programme is Rs. 6000 crore; its duration is coterminous with the period of the 14th Finance Commission. The scheme has seven components—mega food parks; integrated cold chain and value addition infrastructure;

Table 4.2 GVA from food products, beverages and tobacco (FPBT) and share in GVA from manufacturing and agriculture (organised and unorganised sectors)

Year	GVA in constant prices			
	GVA food products, beverages and tobacco (FPBT) (Rs. crore)	FPBT GVA to manufacturing (%)	FPBT GVA to agriculture (%)	CAGR (%)
1950–51	7420.72	16.9	2.5	
1960–61	11,918.20	15.1	3.0	5.03
1970–71	13,539.80	10.3	2.7	1.62
1980–81	14,693.30	7.5	2.5	3.48
1990–91	33,938.80	9.5	4.2	8.42
2000–01	61,880.40	9.7	5.8	6.69
2010–11	143,177.90	10.5	10.1	11.61
2016–17	174,619.00	8.5	10.2	2.28

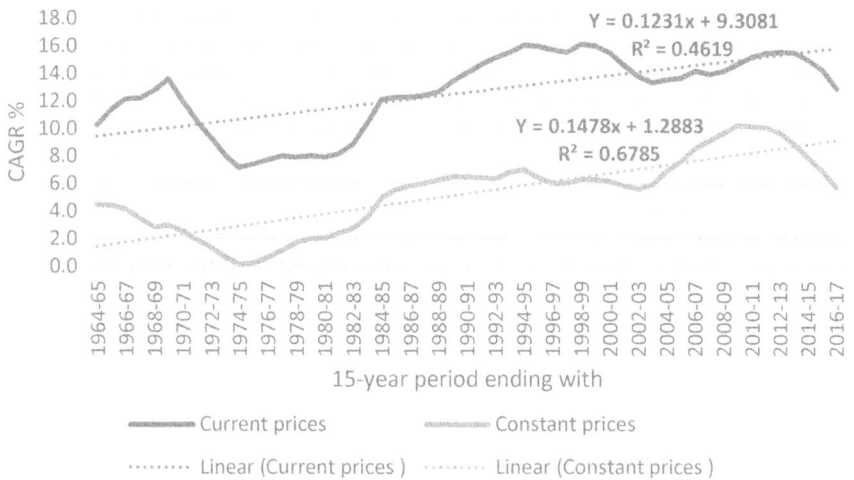

Fig. 4.1 Fifteen-year moving period exponential growth rates in GVA from food processing industries

creation/expansion of food processing and preservation capacities; infrastructure for agro-processing clusters; creation of backward and forward linkages; food safety and quality assurance infrastructure; and human resource and institutions.[2]

---

[2]SAMPADA intends to identify agricultural clusters and grant them subsidies and enable the seamless transfer of food products from producing centres to markets. It aims to complete the linkage by plugging gaps in the supply chain, modernising or expanding existing food processing units and building processing and preservation capacity. The scheme will also benefit farmers by increasing their income, generating employment opportunities, stimulating the export of processed food and reducing food wastage.

The MOFPI has approved the establishment of 263 designated food parks—including 54 mega food parks and 236 integrated cold chains—to create modern infrastructure for the processing industry along the farm-to-market value chain. Steps are being taken to boost this sector and help it fulfil the objective of completely eliminating post-harvest wastages and losses. Other measures to boost the food processing sector include 100% foreign direct investment (FDI) in trading including through e-commerce in respect of food products manufactured in India. A mega food park scheme launched in 2008–2009 revealed value addition, improved price realisation, reduced wastage and benefitted all stakeholders in one way or the other (ICRIER 2015). The mega food parks and cold chains are estimated to have benefited 520,000 farmers and created 677,000 jobs (Government of India 2018c).

There are 39,741 registered food processing factories in India, accounting for 16.9% of the 234,865 registered factories (Government of India 2019). Andhra Pradesh accounts for 15% of the registered food processing units, Tamil Nadu 13%, Telangana 10%, Maharashtra 7% and Punjab 7.3% (Table 4.3). However, most units are not registered. The National Sample Survey Reports No. 581 (73rd round, 2015–16) on Unincorporated Non-Agricultural Enterprises (excluding construction) gives an idea of the number of food processing units operating in the unorganised sector not covered by the Annual Survey of Industries. Uttar Pradesh tops the list with a share of 14.3% of UNAEs, followed by West Bengal (13.1%) and Maharashtra (9.3%). Tamil Nadu and Andhra Pradesh occupy the next two positions.

The number of food and beverage processing enterprises—organised and unorganised—varies widely by state. The correlation coefficients reveal that in states with many factories, agricultural output is higher, the electricity supply is better, the ease of doing business (EODB) scores are better, the bank branch density and tele-density are greater, the density of railway lines (per 1000 ha of area) is higher, and a larger proportion of the population lives in urban areas (Table 4.4). The first four factors correlate strongly with the number of UNAEs in a state, and population density is found to be an additional correlate. Road density can be an important factor of the spread of manufacturing units across states—as revealed by the positive correlation—but it did not show a stronger coefficient. However, it seems to be working through its significant relation with bank branch density.

There are 2.46 million unorganised food processing and beverage units in the country, which account for 12.5% of the 19.7 million UNAEs (other than construction). Rural UNAEs constitute 58% of all the UNAEs in the country (Table 4.5). Rural food processing UNAE accounts for 66% of the food processing UNAEs in the country. Interestingly, 31% of UNAE food production units have been expanding over the past three years, but 40% have been stagnating. Relatively more of beverage processing units, and UNAEs as a whole, are stagnating.

On average, food processing UNAEs have a higher operating expenses-to-receipts ratio and a lower GVA-to-receipts ratio (Table 4.6). This trend is true for both rural and urban units. Operating expenses account for about 60% of the receipts overall and a little over 71% for processing units. Rural units other than for beverages are somewhat more cost-effective than their urban counterparts; the GVA is less than 30%. The ASI data (Government of India 2019) shows that organised (registered)

Table 4.3 State-wise number of food and beverage processing industries and enterprises

State/UT	Food and beverage registered (organised) factories, 2016–2017		Unincorporated non-agricultural enterprises, 2015–2016 (unorganised)	
	Number	Share in total (%)	Number	Share in total (%)
Andhra Pradesh	5861	14.7	154,330	6.3
Arunachal Pradesh	30	0.1	145	0.0
Assam	1409	3.5	65,997	2.7
Bihar	881	2.2	145,300	5.9
Chhattisgarh	1309	3.3	26,957	1.1
Gujarat	2240	5.6	94,066	3.8
Haryana	918	2.3	24,577	1.0
Himachal Pradesh	193	0.5	21,885	0.9
Jammu & Kashmir	176	0.4	28,089	1.1
Jharkhand	228	0.6	116,536	4.7
Karnataka	2251	5.7	127,458	5.2
Kerala	1629	4.1	77,167	3.1
Madhya Pradesh	876	2.2	102,808	4.2
Maharashtra	2808	7.1	229,372	9.3
Manipur	28	0.1	6038	0.2
Meghalaya	26	0.1	3268	0.1
Mizoram	0	0.0	1538	0.1
Nagaland	21	0.1	3642	0.1
Odisha	1127	2.8	77,781	3.2
Punjab	2906	7.3	63,626	2.6
Rajasthan	883	2.2	101,666	4.1
Sikkim	19	0.0	101	0.0
Tamil Nadu	5077	12.8	178,527	7.3
Telangana	3969	10.0	80,392	3.3
Tripura	95	0.2	13,998	0.6
Uttar Pradesh	2068	5.2	350,883	14.3
Uttarakhand	372	0.9	18,116	0.7
West Bengal	1960	4.9	322,590	13.1
All-India	39,741	100.0	2459,929	100.0

Source GoI (2018a, b and 2019)

Table 4.4 Correlates for the number of food processing units across states (critical value of $r = 0.39$)

Indicator	Unit	Organised factories	Unorganised units	Agriculture output	Power	Road density	Railway density	Population density	Urbanisation	EODB Score	Tele-density 2015	Bank branch density
Organised factories	No. 2016–2017	1.00										
Unorganised units	No. 2015–2016	0.53	1.00									
Agriculture output	Rs.billion TE 2015	0.56	0.87	1.00								
Power (electricity)	Mn units 2016	0.65	0.69	0.86	1.00							
Road density	Km/1000 ha 2016	0.15	0.28	0.10	0.02	1.00						
Railway density	Km/1000 ha 2016	0.56	0.14	0.17	0.07	−0.09	1.00					
Population density	Per sq km 2011	0.33	0.69	0.51	0.32	0.60	−0.03	1.00				
Urbanisation	percent	0.42	0.12	0.19	0.45	0.09	−0.01	0.06	1.00			
EODB Score	Score	0.48	0.52	0.60	0.57	−0.08	0.15	0.32	−0.14	1.00		
Tele-density	Percent 2015	0.39	−0.14	−0.01	0.27	0.00	0.07	−0.15	0.47	−0.09	1.00	
Bank branch density	No/1000 ha 2017	0.39	0.39	0.35	0.29	0.62	−0.01	0.82	0.33	0.21	0.25	1.00

Table 4.5 Unorganised manufacturing (UNAE) units as per their growth status over last 3 years

Sector	Activity category	Percentage of enterprises by growth status (over a period of last 3 years)					
		Expanding	Stagnant	Contracting	Not applicable	Not reported	All
Rural	Food products	30.8	38.4	11.4	14	5.4	100
	Beverages	22.8	62.1	5.9	5.3	3.9	100
	Total manufacturing	23.6	48.4	14.7	9	4.3	100
Urban	Food products	31.4	42.1	8.3	14.2	4.1	100
	Beverages	17.2	32.7	9.6	34.5	6	100
	Total manufacturing	26.5	43.7	12.7	12	5.1	100
Rural + Urban	Food products	31	39.7	10.3	14.1	4.9	100
	Beverages	21.7	56.3	6.6	11	4.3	100
	Total manufacturing	24.9	46.5	13.8	10.3	4.6	100

Source NSS 73rd round (GoI)

food factories have an input-to-output ratio of 90%, higher than the average of all categories of factories (81%) and beverages (75%). Further, profits are very thin in food factories and margins are thin in both registered and informal processing units alike (Table 4.7). These units need support.

About 99% of food processing UNAEs do not have access to loans, subsidy, machinery or equipment, skills development, marketing, raw material or any form of support. Only 0.9% have access to loans, and 0.4% have access to subsidies. Rural units are a shade better off here (Table 4.8).

On average, the fixed capital of a food processing UNAE is Rs. 2.53 lakh. The fixed capital of urban processing unit is Rs. 4.37 lakh, almost three times that of a rural processing unit. The outstanding loan of each UNAE is hardly 7–9% of the fixed assets reported (Table 4.9). The loan intensity is, thus, very low. The loan-to-fixed capital ratio is 62% for registered food processing units and 36% for registered beverage processing units and 43% for all units.

So far, we have seen firm-level information on credit aspects. The macro-level assessment reveals that the debt-to-equity ratio is minimum at 0.39 for hybrid seeds and maximum 2.21 for basmati rice (Table 4.10). This demonstrates that agro-industries are under-leveraged. The total estimated debt for the 2015–16 financial year was Rs 1.18 trillion, and the additional debt needed by 2022–23 was estimated at Rs. 0.27 trillion.

From the financing point of view, subsidies are offered under the SAMPADA scheme during 2014, and a Food Processing Fund of Rs. 2000 crore was created by NABARD. NABARD can finance them directly or through consortium financing with other banks. The entities eligible for such loans are state governments, entities

Table 4.6 Performance of unorganised (UNAEs) food processing enterprises (per unit)

Sector	Activity category	No. of workers	Total receipts (Rs)	Total op exp (Rs)	GVA (Rs)	Operating expenses-to-receipts (%)	GVA-to-receipts (%)
Rural	Food products	1.9	349,697	239,612	108,665	68.5	31.1
	Beverages	1.6	143,428	76,875	65,591	53.6	45.7
	Total manufacturing	1.6	178,549	99,235	78,698	55.6	44.1
Urban	Food products	2.5	980,930	718,814	259,418	73.3	26.4
	Beverages	2.9	516,359	254,102	256,859	49.2	49.7
	Total manufacturing	2.1	579,924	360,172	216,035	62.1	37.3
Rural + urban	Food products	2.1	572,158	408,494	161,794	71.4	28.3
	Beverages	1.9	216,405	111,556	103,019	51.5	47.6
	Total manufacturing	1.8	346,944	208,710	136,317	60.2	39.3

Table 4.7 Characteristics of food processing factories (registered)

Characteristics	Food products	Beverages	All categories
Number	37,468	2272	234,865
Fixed capital	518	1412	1358
Total output	2733	3130	3093
Total input	2455	2361	2511
Gross value added	277	769	582
Outstanding loan Rs.	321	513	582
Income	183	569	414
Profit	91	372	230
Input-to-output ratio	90	75	81
Loan-to-fixed asset ratio	62	36	43

promoted by state governments or the Government of India (GoI), joint ventures and special purpose vehicles, cooperatives and federations of cooperatives, FPOs, corporates, companies and entrepreneurs (Annex 4.13 and 4.14). A sum of Rs. 543 crores had been sanctioned for 15 projects across 13 states as in June 2019.

However, many ventures cannot produce adequate security cover or collateral, or arrange for the permissions and clearances needed to acquire land, or experience delays in getting government guarantees. Some potential entrepreneurs have a poor credit rating or lack the skill set required (Rais et al. 2013; Grant Thornton and CII 2014). Most of the policies seem to have been drafted keeping bigger states in mind (Rais et al. 2014); the reality is different in smaller states, and the necessary flexibility needs to be introduced into the policies. The agro-cluster scheme needs a minimum plot of 10 acres, for instance, but that is difficult to find in hilly terrains. States should put in place an entrepreneur-centric policy to suit the local context. For the successful implementation of such schemes, three pillars—entrepreneurs, project fundamentals and the ecosystem—are crucial.

The foregoing discussion points to the weak financial status of unorganised food processing units and the low penetration of loans. The organised sector, though somewhat better off in terms of loan intensity, has a higher proportion of input to output. Here we witness that infrastructure, skill and branding constitute hurdles. The absence of support—loans, subsidies, machinery or equipment, skills development, marketing and raw material—is a cause of great concern, particularly for UNAEs.

Table 4.8 Status of assistance received by unincorporated manufacturing units

Sector	Activity category	Proportion of enterprises received assistance by type of assistance (%)								Total
		Not received any assistance	Financial loan	Subsidy	Machinery/equipment	Skill development	Marketing	Raw material	Others	
Rural	Food products	98.1	1.3	0.4	0	0	0	0	0.1	100
	Beverages	99.4	0.4	0.2	0	0.1	0	0	0.1	100
	Total	99.0	0.4	0.3	0.1	0.1	0	0	0.1	100
Urban	Food products	99.5	0.2	0.3	0	0	0	0	0	100
	Beverages	99.5	0.3	0	0	0	0	0	0.2	100
	Total	98.9	0.4	0.4	0.1	0.1	0	0	0.3	100
Overall	Food products	98.6	0.9	0.4	0	0	0	0	0.1	100
	Beverages	99.4	0.4	0.1	0	0.1	0	0	0.1	100
	Total	98.9	0.4	0.4	0.1	0.1	0	0	0.2	100

Source GoI (2018a, b)

Table 4.9 Outstanding loans, fixed capital of unincorporated food processing enterprises (per unit)

Sector	Activity category	Market value (Rs.) of fixed assets	Loans outstanding and interest (Rs.)		Loan-to-fixed asset ratio (%)
			Amount	Annual interest	
Rural	Food products	152,571	13,664	2214	8.96
	Beverages	81,959	7473	1064	9.12
	Total	90,063	7207	1065	8.00
Urban	Food products	436,865	25,449	3729	5.83
	Beverages	748,941	56,589	8318	7.56
	Total	425,230	32,229	4264	7.58
Rural + Urban	Food products	252,763	17,817	2748	7.05
	Beverages	212,477	17,084	2484	8.04
	Total	230,683	17,705	2407	7.68

Table 4.10 Financial requirements of food proceeding sector (Rs Crore)

Sector	Debt-to-equity ratio	Total debt (FY 2015–16)	Projected debt (FY 2022–23)	Additional debt required by 2022–23
Dairy	1.35	16,800	23,343	3543
Shrimp	0.89	2675	3859	1184
Shrimp feed		525	730	205
Maize starch	1.89	2741	3808	1067
Warehouse	1.52	4389	6099	1710
Hybrid seed	0.39	2138	2971	833
Meat processing and export	1.30	4266	4737	471
Fruit and vegetables		37,761	39,714	1953
Basmati rice	2.21	37,761	39,714	1953
Spices	1.76	2174	3020	846
Poultry	1.64	14,829	17,772	2943
Edible oil	1.73	19,567	25,396	5829
Beverages	1.92	8530	11,740	3210
Total		117,971	145,379	27,408

Source NABARD (2018)

4.3 Organisation and Integration of Unorganised Processing Units Through FPOs

The solution lies in a twofold strategy: to integrate production and processing activities and adopt aggregation as a philosophy. This will assure firms of supply of raw material while mitigating price risks. A prevalent model here is contract farming (FAO 2013). The processors can stand guarantor to help their suppliers obtain bank loans. Since transaction and risk costs will decline for all players, banks would gain confidence to lend to these producers. In fact, one of the suggested strategies to mitigate price and availability risk is opting for contract farming with FPOs (NABARD 2019).

The preliminary step towards adopting aggregation as a philosophy requires firms to form a cooperative or company and pool their produce. This gives them bargaining power in input and output markets. These farmer aggregates can employ the contract farming model to integrate production and processing activities.[3] Technology adoption and innovation are catching on, but currently, farmers hardly sell their produce directly to processors. They sell to various agencies, mostly to local traders, at non-remunerative prices, which raise handling costs and expands timelines and leads to wastage, especially of perishable produce. Processers buy raw material at very high prices, which is possibly reflected in the higher proportion of input costs in output value as elicited above.

This twofold strategy can optimally be realised with the help of FPOs; FPOs registered as Farmer Producer Companies (FPCs[4]) can enter into contracts with processors. This would give buyers a single point for procuring produce from numerous farmers and reduce operational expenses. An FPC would also raise the bargaining power of farmers. This requires the large-scale participation of FPCs in processing and value addition to create a win-win-win situation for farmers, processing units and consumers.

4.3.1 Objectives of Farmer Producer Organisations (FPOs)

Farmer Producer Organisations (FPOs) constitute an institutional intervention introduced in 2002. The objective was to improve value addition, market linkages and access to better machinery; remove the constraints that arise from the small size of landholdings; and eliminate intermediaries. The goal was that, eventually, farmers would graduate from the primary sector to the secondary sector. In the current context, FPOs can be used to organise food processing units and help them achieve economies of scale (Leitch 2014).

---

[3]The contract farming model can be an appropriate model for UNAEs, which are mostly (80%) own account enterprises and have limited bargaining power in input or output markets.

[4]Here, "FPO" refers to trusts, societies, cooperatives and companies, and "FPC" to FPOs registered under the Companies Act.

An FPO can be registered under various acts as a trust, cooperative, non-profit society or Section 8 Company. It can also be registered as a company as specified in Part IX-A of the Companies Act 1956 and Reference Section 465(1) of the Companies Act, 2013. In its company form, the FPO model aims to achieve competitiveness and improve smallholder welfare. As all sectors experience the effects of privatisation and globalisation, the FPC model is being argued as being the most apt solution for farmers (SFAC 2013; World Bank 2016; RBI 2019). The FPC model accommodates principles of mutual assistance, cooperation and welfare practices, and it adopts a corporate-like approach in functioning. It assures minimal political interference and provides room to earn profits like any other private company.

To aid FPOs, in 2011 NABARD set up the Producer Organisation Development Fund (PODF) to support through capacity building and by enabling access to credit and market linkages. The PODF provides for funding up to 90% of the total project outlay with a flexible repayment schedule. Similarly, NABARD's Producers Development and Upliftment Corpus (PRODUCE) also supports the FPOs. The Small Farmers' Agribusiness Consortium (SFAC), an autonomous body set up by the Ministry of Agriculture, has set up schemes such as the Credit Guarantee Fund and the Equity Grant Fund.[5]

4.3.2 Farmer Producer Organisations (FPO) in the Food Processing Industry

Ideally, an FPC has three stages of development or a three stage graduation model (Rani n.d.). The initial stage is of an aggregator, input provider and knowledge provider. In the second stage, there is some intermediation with corporate entities, in the form of contract farming or selling produce to corporate entities for further sale. The third and the final stage is when the FPC has its own processing facility, brands and market channels. At this stage, the whole value chain has been acquired by its rightful owner, the farmer, and the entire profit margin goes to them.

There is ample scope for FPCs to bring value to every stage of the food processing cycle.[6] Currently, only 12% of NABARD FPOs, which consist of 84% of the total FPOs in the country promoted by NABARD and SFAC,[7] are engaged in value

---

[5]Additionally, they facilitate the preparation of Detailed Project Reports for FPCs. Several organisations like Hivos, Rabobank Foundation, Sir Ratan Tata Trust, Ford Foundation and Axis Bank Foundation are investing in FPOs (Tagat 2016).

[6]Section 581B(1) of the Companies Act elaborates the mandate of FPCs to include, among other things, production, harvesting, procurement, grading, pooling, handling, marketing, selling, export of primary produce of members or import of goods or services for their benefit; and processing, including preserving, drying, distilling, brewing, venting, canning and packaging of produce of its members.

[7]We restrict ourselves to the data provided by NABARD and SFAC, the major promoters of FPOs in India—although other, reputed non-government organisations promote FPOs—because we do not have a comprehensive database.

addition. At least, 45% of the FPOs—which currently limit themselves to aggregation, providing inputs or procurement—have the potential to graduate to their own processing facility or marketing related activities. NABARD FPOs are engaged in various activities such as aggregation (8%), agri-inputs (25%), procurement (12%), value addition (12%), marketing (30%) and others activities (13%) (Chatterjee et al. 2019). Annex 4.15 summarises the status of all FPOs promoted by NABARD and SFAC in the country as of August 2019.

FPOs enable agriculture–industry linkages in several ways. They help aggregate landholdings to use machinery efficiently at the input level. At the output level, they assist in aggregating produce. Since the quantum of produce is large and it is represented by a farmer agglomerate, the bargaining power improves and, in turn, better prices are offered to the farmer. The food processing industry requires heavy investments in logistics like safety and quality control infrastructure, value addition equipment and maintenance. A legal entity like an FPO offers the economies of scale and modes of financing needed to fulfil these requirements. Most UNAEs are registered in rural areas, and it is convenient for them to register as an FPO or go through an FPO to access the benefits they have been hitherto deprived of.

Many farmers are women, and they also head 45% of proprietary enterprises in India (NSSO and MOFPI 2018). Collectives can empower them in a traditionally male-dominated value chain. Farmer collectives can also help reduce transaction costs like information, negotiation, monitoring and enforcement costs. These tasks, when performed through a collective rather than as individuals, would cost less. The market for perishables waiting to be tapped in India can be fathomed from the fact that the USA processes 65% of its total perishable produce, the Philippines 78% and China 23%, but India processes only 7% of its total perishable produce. Processing would help reduce wastage, which currently stands at 25–30% (Grant Thorton and ASSOCHAM India 2017). FPOs can benefit from this untapped market for processing.

Unregistered enterprises cannot access formal sources of credit, and accessing credit from informal sources raises their cost of capital. Formalisation and registration, as a study observed for organisations registered with VAT departments, are associated with an increase in financial and non-financial assistance (Mukherjee and Rao 2017). Unorganised processing units do not have the scale or equipment to expand into as many activities as the organised sector. The organised sector is engaged in over 12 activities—including fruits, vegetables, milled coarse cereals, edible oils and soybean—but the unorganised sector operates in only half as many such as eggs, sugar, milled wheat, rice and pulses (Ghosh 2014). An FPC would provide a stepping stone to the unorganised sector to expand their business in these activities. These UNAEs can also register as an FPC and reap the same benefits as their counterparts in the organised sector.

Trebbin (2014) studied the importance of forging stronger relations between FPCs and modern retailers. Kakati and Roy (2018) backed the arguments made by the three-stage graduation model discussed earlier. Retailers and FPCs need to develop a relationship to eliminate middlemen and other third parties and improve profit margins for both farmers and processing units.

4.3.3 Financing Food Processing Via the FPO Model

The Government of India accords the food processing industry "high priority" and offers it a lot of policy support; it has allowed 100% FDI under the automatic route and rationalised tariff and duties (Grant Thorton and ASSOCHAM, India 2017). Both food processing and FPC are a part of the priority sector lending mandated by the Reserve Bank of India (RBI). And the GoI has announced a full tax holiday for FPOs with a turnover below Rs. 100 crores for up to five years (Kumar et al. 2018).

Alternative financing options can be explored where lenders could provide back-end integration through funding FPOs and farmer groups, and the processing company can be the guarantor. FPOs provide a fertile ground for garnering funds and services via e-negotiable warehouse receipts, agri-specific loan products and nurturing partnerships with agri-fintechs (Singh and Shah 2019). Financing cold storage infrastructure and common packhouses through FPOs can be explored (NABARD 2019); the improved productivity would help increase farm income. Additionally, loans can also be given under Micro, Small, and Medium Enterprises (MSME) Act 2006 (Singh and Shah 2019).

Compared to unregistered businesses, registered businesses provide for the formal protection of the rights of employees and businesses. Registration is associated with lower risk, and transaction costs go down considerably, and we witness improved access to credit, government support and other forms of assistance. Unregistered entities, especially Own Account Enterprises (OAEs), face a major roadblock in recovering financial dues; registering as an FPC would improve their recourse (NSSO and MOFPI 2018). Registration enables businesses to expand beyond their vicinity and tap into larger regional and global markets. From a development and research lens, data from registered entities like FPCs is easier to access and can help map growth trends better (Dayan and Bolislis 2017).

4.3.4 The Triple Win for Farmers, Processing Units and Consumers

The FPO-FP alliance benefits farmers, processing units and consumers. FPOs make it easier for farmers to access machinery and input material at competitive (sometimes lower) rates than the market. An FPO is large and, usually, dominant in the area, and helps farmers bargain for better prices. It is difficult to attract investment in infrastructure at an individual level, and farmers are usually at the mercy of the state. FPOs can lobby for investment in rural infrastructure facilities—collection centres, soil testing laboratories, packhouses, distribution centres, packing infrastructure, cold storage units, roads and electricity. Erratic power supply is one of the biggest hurdles for food manufacturing enterprises (NSSO and MOFPI 2018). Such investment would create employment opportunities, especially for the large unorganised workforce.

To fathom the size of this market, consider that 98% of the fruits and vegetable market is unorganised. Simple modular training initiatives can help employ people in the processing industry (Grant Thorton & ASSOCHAM, India 2017). The dispersed food products sector employs the maximum number of people, especially women, among MSMEs in India. Registering as a formal entity like FPCs would make it easier for units to monitor and improve employment conditions, conduct training sessions and provide employees social security benefits. Registration also improves the compliance of MSMEs with labour laws (ILO 2014).

Processing units help aggregate produce and ensure quality control through a single channel. Improved product-factor linkages would reduce their input cost and, thereby, increase profit margins. In Madhya Pradesh, "to fulfil the buyer's require-ments such as assured quantity, good quality, procedural expertise (like seed or organic certification), easy operation, reliability and sustainability and enable small and marginal farmers to get a good price, farmers were needed to be organised into a formal business institution like Farmer Producer Companies" (Dwivedi and Joshi 2007; Kakati and Roy 2018). Enterprises need to see the tangible benefits of aggre-gation (Dayan and Bolislis 2017), and the government should make it easy for them to verify documents and pay registration fees by setting up one-stop points.

It is necessary to shift from traditional techniques and crops that revolve around the individual farmer to economies of scale and scope (Trebbin and Hassler 2012; Kumar et al. 2018). At the national level, 25–30% of agricultural produce is wasted. Food processing FPOs would help eliminate post-harvest wastage entirely and reduce food inflation (NABARD 2019).

Farmer Producer Organisations offer several options for funding via various schemes and tax incentives. In May 2020, the government announced agricultural reforms. All farmer welfare and agri-industry growth schemes will be based on FPOs, and micro-food enterprises will be formalised at the cost of Rs. 10,000 crore. Now, FPOs can add value to commodities in addition to aggregating them, and they will be supported in processing and manufacturing agri-products that can be marketed directly to consumers. That will ensure that a larger share of the amount spent by end consumers on agri-products reaches farmers. If FPOs take the initiative of manu-facturing products, farmers will then familiarise themselves with the norms of the Food Safety and Standards Authority of India (FSSAI) and their implications, and the initiative will encourage the practice of health and safety standards.

FPOs can also help farmers onboard e-spot markets. The National Agriculture Market (eNAM) is a pan-India electronic trading portal for agricultural commodities. It obviates the physical mobility barrier, ensures transactions at scale on digital platforms and makes it easier for FPOs to procure produce.[8] On the eNAM, FPO collection centres can trade in commodities, and these centres have been declared as "deemed market" or "sub-market yards". The government has also increased the licensed areas for trade. As 10,000 FPOs spring up across the country, the market yard density in the country will increase manifold even if only 50% of the FPOs register

---

[8]The eNAM has been in existence for only four years, and already 1012 FPOs have registered as users and traded 3053 million tons of agri-produce worth Rs. 8.11 crore.

on the eNAM. To access market yards, farmers forgo at least a day's labour and incur travel and other transaction costs or pay intermediaries hefty prices. Electronic procurement would be a huge relief. The government has earmarked one lakh crore rupees for creating farm gate infrastructure and aggregation points, and FPOs will be able to build their own financially viable post-harvest management infrastructure—warehouses, packhouses and machinery for cleaning, sorting, grading and packaging of commodities—to integrate procurement, processing and sale at one place.

4.4 The North East and Food Processing Opportunities

We take the case of the North-Eastern states to demonstrate how FPOs can improve growth in the agriculture and processing industries. The North-Eastern states—Arunachal Pradesh, Assam, Manipur, Meghalaya, Mizoram, Nagaland, Tripura and Sikkim—account for less than 6% of the total geographical area of the country.

The growth in the number of UNAE food processing manufacturing units (including beverages) between 2010–2011 and 2015–2016 was modest; in certain states, it was negative (Table 4.11). Manipur stands out, with a compound annual growth rate (CAGR) of 27.4% followed by Nagaland (21.4%) and Sikkim (15.6%, on a low base). Arunachal Pradesh, Tripura and Meghalaya registered substantial negative growth. The food processing and beverage UNAE units grew at less than 2% at the country-level, but the North-Eastern states recorded a decline of 1.5%. Manufacturing enterprises in the North Eastern states—except for Mizoram and Tripura to some extent—have no access to financial loans or subsidies, machinery or equipment, skills development or any type of assistance in any form (NSS & MOFPI 2018).

Table 4.11 Number of food processing and beverage units among UNAE manufacturing units

NE state	UNAE FP 2010–11	UNAE FP 2015–16	CAGR (%)
Arunachal Pradesh	383	145	−17.66
Assam	61,068	65,997	1.56
Manipur	1800	6038	27.39
Meghalaya	6857	3268	−13.78
Mizoram	1398	1538	1.93
Nagaland	1380	3642	21.42
Sikkim	49	101	15.56
Tripura	29,328	13,998	−13.75
NER total	102,263	94,727	−1.52
All-India	2,241,195	2,459,929	1.88

Source NSSO surveys 67th and 73rd rounds

A variety of agro-horticultural indigenous crops can grow in this climate, having enough potential for processing (Rais et al. 2014). The quality of some of these crops is superior to those in other parts of the country. Of late, the region has started growing several fruit crops, such as kiwi and litchi, that were never grown before. The product range and potential vary by state. In Manipur, apart from fruits, black rice is a premium product known for its nutraceutical value. Pineapple, citrus, banana and passion fruit are the major fruits, and the ginger and turmeric are of high quality.

The Ministry of Agriculture and Farmers' Welfare set up the Mission Organic Value Chain Development for North-East Region (MOVCD-NER) to develop certified organic production in value chains. The mission supports integrated processing units as part of its assistance for post-harvest infrastructure, and its implementation structure is based on FPCs and Farmer Interest Groups. There are 33 clusters in Manipur under the MOVCD-NER; of these, 10 are FPCs under various clusters (Table 4.12).

Kakati and Roy (2018) discuss the scope for entrepreneurship in FPCs with special reference to Assam. Keeping in mind the similar topography and climate in the North East, it is argued that FPCs will help overcome the problem of consolidation of produce from fragmented landholdings (Dash 2016). If we observe the geographical spread of FPOs in the country, the North-Eastern states combined houses 3.2% of all, and Assam accounts for 1.4%, much like bigger states such as Chhattisgarh, Haryana, Kerala and Punjab. In Assam, FPOs are constrained mainly because finance and management capabilities are not available and agricultural produce cannot be marketed online. India's Act East policy proposes to reach Thailand and Indonesian markets through a India-South-East-Asia Corridor. Foreign trade through land routes with Bangladesh, Bhutan, Nepal and Myanmar can expand the demand for food products and the investment in food processing. Using FPCs to spur the food processing industry in the North East would help generate multifold returns.

4.5   Conclusion

India has 39,731 registered food processing factories (including beverage units) and 24.6 lakh Unincorporated Non-Agricultural Enterprises (UNAEs) engaged in food products and beverages. About 79% of all food manufacturing enterprises operate as family-based own account enterprises (OAEs) on uneconomical scales and thin margins—even formal sector units have low margins—aggregation holds immense scope for improving returns.

Several food processing FPCs have enhanced income and livelihoods, and the FPC-FP alliance across the country should learn from these models and benefit. In supporting these FPOs, NABARD has been instrumental. If FPOs integrate with processing units, they can help growers generate higher incomes. Especially in the North-Eastern states, FPOs can tap the food processing potential and improve the economics of production and processing. In combination with contract farming, FPOs can reduce the transaction costs, and the benefits of aggregation and scale can bring

Table 4.12 FPCs registered with MOVCD-NER for cluster based organic production in Manipur

FPC	Commodity/cluster	Production (MT/year)	Processing technology
Phou-Oibee Organic Producer Company Ltd., Bishnupur	Paddy	500—black rice	Modern rubber roller sheller rice milling
Chak-Hao Poireiton Organic Producer Company Ltd., Imphal West			
Chingarel Organic Producer Company Ltd., Imphal East			
Apunba Louba Organic Producer Company Ltd., Thoubal			
Reangluang Organic Farmers Producer Company Limited, Noney, (Operating area: Tamenglong)	Tamenglong Orange (local)	Gestation period	Juice concentrate
	King Chilli	260	Sauce, dry powder
	Turmeric (Lakadong)	200	Dry powder
Thayong Organic Producer Company Ltd., (operating area: Kangpokpi Sadar Hills & Thoubal)	Pineapple	4000	Juice concentrate
	Tamenglong Orange (Kangpokpi)	Gestation period	-Do-
	Ginger (Nadia)	100	Dry powder
	Turmeric (Lakadong)	200	Dry powder
Loulhoumi Organic Producer Company Ltd. Sagolban Meino Leirak, Imphal West, Manipur	Pineapple (Kew)	2000	Canning, candy, concentrate
	King Chilli	350	Sauce, dry powder
	Ginger(Nadia)	400	Dry powder
	Turmeric (Lakadong)	400	Dry powder
Rimrumlang Organic Producer Company Ltd. Imphal West, Manipur, (Area of Operation-Ukhrul)	King Chilli	350	Sauce, dry powder
	Ginger(Nadia)	400	Dry powder
	Turmeric (Lakadong)	400	Dry powder
Ruwmee Organic Producer Company Ltd. Imphal West, Manipur, Area of Operation—Chandel	Ginger(Nadia)	1000	Dry powder
	Turmeric (Lakadong)	1000	Dry powder

(continued)

Table 4.12 (continued)

FPC	Commodity/cluster	Production (MT/year)	Processing technology
Progressive Farmer Organic Producer Company Ltd. Imphal West, Manipur Area of Operation–Senapati	King Chilli	1137	Sauce, dry powder
	Ginger(Nadia)	500	Dry powder
	Turmeric (Lakadong)	200	Dry powder

Source MOVCD-NER, Manipur

about a triple-win situation for farmers, processing units and consumers. Multiple financing avenues would open up and help consolidate produce from small landholdings and ease access to inputs and, thereby, reduce the production cost and improve product-factor linkages. The employment generated would enable livelihoods for many people, especially those employed in the unorganised sector or unregistered entities. Integrating production and processing activities, along with adopting aggregation as a philosophy, would catalyse successful agri-industry linkages and the benefits therefrom.

Annex

See Annexes 4.13, 4.14 and 4.15.

Annex 4.13 Types of raw material and stages of processing

Type of raw material	Primary processing	Secondary processing	Tertiary processing
Seeds and grains	Cleaning, sorting and grading	Milling, flour, puffing, malting, etc.	Biscuits and bakery products, flakes, noodles, etc.
Oil seeds	Cleaning, sorting and grading	Oil cakes	Extraction, refinement, fortification of oils, value added products such as spreadable fats
Fruits and vegetables	Washing, cleaning, grading, waxing	Slicing, dicing (normal or frozen), pulps, pastes, juices, drying, etc.	Jams, jellies, ketchups, sauces, candies, pickles, etc.
Milk	Chilling, pasteurisation	Cream, cottage cheese, simmered milk, milk powder, etc.	Spreadable milk fats (Butter, cheese), ghee, yoghurt, ice cream
Meat	Cleaning, removing bones, chilling, etc.	Cut, fried and frozen	Ready-to-eat products

Source Mukherjee et al. (2013)

Annex 4.14 Terms of lending under the Food Processing Fund

Particulars	State Govt.	State promoted entities		Private parties
		With guarantee	w/o guarantee	
Maximum term loan (of TFO) (%)	95	95	95	75
Rate of interest	BR—1.50%	BR—1.50%	PLR + Risk Premium	PLR + Risk Premium
Evaluation fee	–	0.25% of TFO	0.25% of TFO	0.25% of TFO, max Rs. 30 lakh
Total repayment period	7 years (incl 2 years of grace period	7 years (incl 2 years of grace period	Up to 7 years (incl 2 years of grace period	Not exceeding 7 years (2 years moratorium)
Servicing of interest	Quarterly	Quarterly	Quarterly	Quarterly
Instalment of loan repayment	05 annual inst.	Qtrly/HY/Annual	Qtrly/HY/Annual	Qtrly/HY/Annual
Primary security	Undertaking by the State Government that the repayments will be made from budgetary provisions	Yes	Yes	Yes
Collateral security		DSRA	DSRA Tangible Collateral	DSRA Tangible Collateral
Guarantees		State Government Guarantee	–	Personal Guarantees Corporate Guarantee

Note: *DSRA* Debt Service Reserve Amount for one quarter Interest and one quarter Principal); *BR* bank rate; *PLR* prime lending rate; *TFO* total financial outlay

Annex 4.15 Status of FPOs promoted by NABARD and SFAC as in August, 2019

States/UT	NABARD (Produce + Promotional)		SFAC		Total		
	Registered members	FPOs	Registered members	FPOs	Registered members	FPOs	Percentage as of grand total (%)
Andaman & Nicobar	187	5	0	0	187	5	0.1
Andhra Pradesh	80,616	282	6852	7	87,468	289	5.7
Arunachal Pradesh	255	2	1850	2	2105	4	0.1
Assam	13,952	59	7147	12	21,099	71	1.4
Bihar	38,989	273	34,609	29	73,598	302	6.0

(continued)

Annex 4.15 (continued)

States/UT	NABARD (Produce + Promotional)		SFAC		Total		
	Registered members	FPOs	Registered members	FPOs	Registered members	FPOs	Percentage as of grand total (%)
Chhattisgarh	24,123	69	29,436	26	53,559	95	1.9
New Delhi	0	1	3535	4	3535	5	0.1
Goa	104	2	1810	2	1914	4	0.1
Gujarat	46,013	171	19,484	21	65,497	192	3.8
Haryana	24,678	75	14,049	23	38,727	98	1.9
Himachal Pradesh	9468	79	6007	6	15,475	85	1.7
Jammu & Kashmir	1340	23	6814	2	8154	25	0.5
Jharkhand	27,228	190	11,009	10	38,237	200	4.0
Karnataka	69,900	263	121,467	119	191,367	382	7.6
Kerala	48,232	121	0	0	48,232	121	2.4
Madhya Pradesh	69,313	361	138,346	143	207,659	504	10.0
Maharashtra	33,517	239	97,596	99	131,113	338	6.7
Manipur	1833	5	5671	6	7504	11	0.2
Meghalaya	1353	9	2990	3	4343	12	0.2
Mizoram	3016	19	1700	1	4716	20	0.4
Nagaland	0	5	1750	2	1750	7	0.1
Odisha	40,511	325	38,622	41	79,133	366	7.2
Punjab	4601	94	6288	7	10,889	101	2.0
Rajasthan	47,314	296	54,292	48	101,606	344	6.8
Sikkim	692	4	16,279	30	16,971	34	0.7
Tamil Nadu	122,643	214	12,199	11	134,842	225	4.5
Telangana	36,572	300	25,328	20	61,900	320	6.3
Tripura	80	1	2874	4	2954	5	0.1
Uttar Pradesh	44,500	362	54,079	51	98,579	413	8.2
Uttarakhand	16,153	83	6004	7	22,157	90	1.8
West Bengal	109,113	303	88,801	83	197,914	386	7.6
Total	916,296	4235	816,888	819	1733,184	5054	100.0

Source Compiled from data from SFAC and NABARD

References

Bhattacharya, B. B., & Rao, C. H. H. (1986). *Agriculture-industry interrelations: Issues of relative prices and growth in the context of public investment.* Theme 18. Eighth World Economic Congress of International Economic Association, New Delhi.

Chatterjee, T., Raghunathan, R., & Gulati, A. (2019). *Linking farmers to futures market in India.* Working paper No 383, August 2019, Indian Council for Research on International Economic Relations, New Delhi.

Confederation of India Industry (CII) and Grant Thornton. (2014). Indian Food & Beverage Sector— The new wave, New Delhi.

Dash, S. K. (2016). Producer companies and small holder' inclusion in the market system; Emerging issues, opportunities and challenges in India. *Journal of Research Innovation and Management Science, II*(1), 35–40.

Dayan, Z., & Bolislis, W. (2017). *Business registration pillars: Good regulatory practice for ASEAN.* OECD Regulatory Policy Working Papers, No. 9, OECD Publishing, Paris.

Dwivedi, Y. K., & Joshi, A. R. (2007). *Producer company—A new generation farmers institution.* LEISA INDIA.

FAO. (2013). *Contract farming for inclusive market access.* Rome.

Ghosh, N. (2014). *An assessment of the extent of food processing in various food sub-sectors.* Institute of Economic Growth, Delhi: Submitted to Ministry of Agriculture.

Government of India. (2018a). *Operational characteristics of unincorporated non-agricultural enterprises (excl construction) in India.* NSS report No 581 (73rd round), Ministry of Statistics and Programme Implementation, National Sample Survey Office, New Delhi.

Government of India. (2018b). *Economic characteristics of unincorporated non-agricultural enterprises (excl construction) in India.* NSS report No 582 (73rd round), Ministry of Statistics and Programme Implementation, National Sample Survey Office, New Delhi.

Government of India. (2018c). State-wise Details of Employment Created under the Scheme Pradhan Mantri Kisan SAMPADA Yojana for Integrated Cold Chain and Mega Food Parks (in reply to Unstarred question on 27 July 2018) (From: Ministry of Food Processing Industries), Answers Data of Rajya Sabha Questions for Session 246. Accessed on December 1, 2019.

Government of India. (2019). Annual survey of industries (factory sector), 2016–2017, volume— I. Ministry of Statistics and Programme Implementation, National Sample Survey Office, Data Processing Division, Industrial Statistics Wing, Kolkata.

Grant Thorton and ASSOCHAM, India. (2017). *Food processing sector-challenges and growth enablers.* Unpublished report.

ICRIER. (2015). Report on evaluation of the impact of the scheme for Mega Food Park of the Ministry of Food Processing Industries, Submitted to Ministry of Food Processing Industries Government of India on July 31, 2015, New Delhi.

International Labour Organisation. (2014). *Labour laws and growth of micro and small enterprises.* India: Country Report/K.P. Kannan; International Labour Organization, ILO DWT for South Asia and Country Office for India, New Delhi.

Kakati, S., & Roy, A. (2018). *The scope of entrepreneurship in Farmer Producer Companies: With special reference to the state of Assam.* Presented in the National Conference for "Agribusiness potentials of Assam" during 30–31 January 2018 organised by Department of Agriculture Economics, Assam Agriculture University, Assam, India and Indian Society of Agriculture Marketing, Hyderabad, India.

Kumar, A., Perumal, A., & Jha, G. (2018). States in promotion of Farmer Producer Organisations in India. *Indian Journal of Extension Education, 54*(2), 108–113.

Kuznets, S. (1961). Economic growth and the contribution of agriculture: Notes on Measurement, Proceedings of the Eleventh International Conference Of Agricultural Economists on "The Role Of Agriculture In Economic Development: Held At The Hotel Casino De La Selva Cuernavaca, Morelos Mexico on 19 August–30 August 1961.

Leitch, H. (2014). *Producer companies in India: Potential to support increased productivity and profitability of poor smallholder farmers.* IFC smart lessons brief; World Bank Group, Washington, DC. © World Bank.

Mukherjee, S., & Rao, K. (2017). *Determinants of registration of unincorporated enterprises under state value added tax Act in India.* MPRA Paper No. 81236.

Mukherjee, D., Bajaj, H., Garg, N., & Abraham, J. (2013). *Feeding a billion: Role of the food processing industry, September.* New Delhi: A.T.Kearney and FICCI.

NABARD. (2018 & 2019). Study on agro-processing sectors in India, Head Office, Mumbai, India.

Negi, D. S., Birthal, P. S., Roy, D., Khan, M. T. (2018, December). Farmers' choice of market channels and producer prices in India: Role of transportation and communication networks. *Food Policy, 81,* 106–121.

NSSO and MOFPI. (2018). Report on operational characteristics of unincorporated non-agricultural enterprises (Excluding Construction) in India, NSS 73rd round, Government of India.

Rais, M., Acharya, S., & Sharma, N. (2013). Food processing industry in India: S&t capability, skills and employment opportunities. *Journal of Rural Development, 32* (4), 451–478. NIRD, Hyderabad.

Rais, M., Acharya, S., & Vanloon, G. W. (2014). Food processing industry: Opportunities in north east region of India. *The NEHU Journal, XII* (1), 37–51.

Rani, R. (n.d.). *Training programme on formation and management of producers groups and federations.* National Institute of Agricultural Extension Management, Hyderabad.

Reserve Bank of India. (2019). Report of the Internal Working Group to Review Agricultural Credit, GoI.

Satyasai, K.J. S., & Balanarayana, M. (2018). Can mechanization in agriculture help achieving sustainable development goals? *Agricultural Economics Research Review, 31* (Conference Number), 147–156.

Satyasai, K. J. S., & Viswanathan, K. U. (1997). Agricultural transformation and implications for agriculture-industry linkage. *Agricultural Economics Research Review, 10*(2), 205–213.

Satyasai, K. J. S., & Viswanathan, K. U. (1999). Dynamics of agriculture-industry linkages. *Indian Journal of Agricultural Economics, 54*(3), 394–401.

SFAC. (2013). *Krishi Sutra 2—Success stories of Farmer Producer Organisations.* Unpublished.

Singh, A., & Shah, S. (2019, June 20). *The road ahead for farmer producer organisations in India* [Dvara Research Blog].

Srivastava, S. K., Chand, R., & Singh, J. (2017). Changing crop production cost in India: Input prices, substitution and technology effects. *Agricultural Economics Research Review, 30* (Conference Number), 171–182.

Tagat, V., (2016). *Financing for Farmer Producer Organisations—Focus on transforming agricultural lending.* NABARD Knowledge Series-3.

The Hindu BusinessLine. (2019). Horticulture output marginally up at 314.87 mt in 2018–19. The Hindu BusinessLine, May 31st. https://www.thehindubusinessline.com/economy/agri-business/horticulture-production-marginally-up-at-31487-mt-in-2018-19/article27379179.ece. Accessed on December 1, 2019.

Trebbin, A. (2014). Linking small farmers to modern retail through producer organizations—Experiences with producer companies in India. *Food Policy, 45,* 35–44.

Trebbin, A., & Hassler, M. (2012). Farmers' producer companies in India: A new concept for collective action? *Environment and Planning A, 44*(2), 411–427.

World Bank Group. (2016). *Linking farmers to markets through productive alliances: An assessment of the World Bank experience in Latin America.* Washington, DC: World Bank.

Chapter 5
Forging Linkages to Promote Agriculture Exports Through Contract Farming: A Case Study of Okra Cultivation

Anjani Kumar and Gaurav Tripathi

5.1 Introduction

In India, significant policy initiatives and institutional changes have transformed the agricultural sector. In this process of agricultural transformation, contract farming has emerged as an institutional innovation that facilitates direct firm-to-farm linkages. Contract farming benefits farmers, especially smallholders, by enabling access to credit, inputs and extension services and by raising productivity, profitability and income. By organising the production of high-value food crops, contract farming can create links between input markets and producers, and international markets.

The evidence of the impact of contract farming in the Indian context has been mixed, however. Some studies show that contract producers in India enjoy higher yields and assured output prices, and their profits are almost three times higher than those of independent producers (Dev and Rao 2005; Nagaraj et al. 2008; Kumar and Kumar 2008; Ramaswami et al. 2006; Tripathi et al. 2005; Birthal et al. 2005; Kalamkar 2012; Kumar 2006; Dileep et al. 2002). But other studies indicate that contract farming negatively impacts the environment and farmers' welfare and upsets the power structure between contractors and farmers (Singh 2002; Opondo 2000). And there is little evidence on the impact of contract farming on vegetable cultivation in the context of leveraging exports.

Contract farming can play a significant role in connecting vegetable growers, who are primarily small and marginal farmers, with lucrative export markets such as Europe. The demand for fresh and safe food products, including vegetables, in developed countries is vast. There are instances in India of corporate firms contracting with smallholders for producing fresh fruits and vegetables for export; the firms provide farmers the inputs, including biopesticides, and training so that the residual

A. Kumar (✉) · G. Tripathi
International Food Policy Research Institute, South Asia Office, New Delhi, India
e-mail: anjani.kumar@cgiar.org

© The Author(s), under exclusive license to Springer Nature Singapore Pte Ltd. 2021
S. Bathla and E. Kannan (eds.), *Agro and Food Processing Industry in India*, India Studies in Business and Economics, https://doi.org/10.1007/978-981-15-9468-7_5

levels in the produce are minimal and these levels meet the requirements of the destination markets.

We present here a case study of such linkages between firms and farmers. We aim to identify the factors that motivate farmers' participation in the contract farming of okra, a key vegetable crop in India, in an overwhelmingly smallholder-dominated context. The study also assesses the impact on farmers' economic welfare. In doing so, it contributes to the ongoing debate on contract farming in India. The study and debate are important because the government has developed a new model law to promote contract farming domestically, and it is also in the process of reforming the agriculture marketing system.

The paper is organised as follows. Section 5.2 describes the production of okra in India and presents the details of the survey data. Section 5.3 deals with the methodological approach. Section 5.4 presents and discusses the estimation results, and Sect. 5.5 concludes and provides some policy implications.

5.2   The Commodity and the Contexts

India is the world's largest okra producer (6.1 million tonnes); in 2018, its share of global production was 62% (9.9 million tonnes) (FAO 2020). Maharashtra is known for its success in the contract farming of fruits and vegetables like grapes, onion and okra.

This study is based on data from a survey of 141 okra farmers (84 contract farmers and 57 independent farmers) conducted in Maharashtra during March and April 2016. The list of contracting farmers for the year of the survey was obtained from one contracting firm (hereafter, the sample firm). We collected data on farm and farmer characteristics such as cropping patterns, cultivation economics, marketing channels, good agricultural practices, assets and social networks.

Kay Bee Exports, a firm established in 1989, exports fresh fruits and vegetables. It contracts with okra farmers in Baramati block of Pune district and Faltan block of Satara district. The contracts are formal and renewable annually. The farmers we surveyed had been contracting with the firm for four years on average. The firm's purchase price for okra is dynamic and based on weekly or fortnightly changes in its export market price. To ensure that the residual levels of inputs in okra are minimal and meet the requirements for exports to Europe, the company supplies its own inputs (pesticides, insecticides and biofertilisers) free to farmers.

It is mandatory for farmers to register with the State Horticulture Department for certification by the Agricultural and Processed Food Products Export Development Authority (APEDA) under Hortinet. Hortinet is a risk tracing and mitigation and phytosanitary certification system for export farmers; laboratory tests and residue analysis of the consignments are conducted under Hortinet. If the consignments pass muster, the APEDA issues the phytosanitary certificate to the exporter.

We surveyed most of the contract okra farmers from eight villages in sample districts. The independent farmers were surveyed randomly from the Solapur, Pune and Satara districts in western Maharashtra. Few independent farmers grow okra, and we could survey only 57 farmers scattered over 21 villages in the Solapur, Pune and Satara districts.

5.3 Methodology

We worked out descriptive statistics to understand the characteristics of sample households, and we conducted a partial budget analysis to estimate the costs and returns for each commodity for both contract and independent farmers.

A farmer's profit is the difference between revenue generated and cost incurred. We conducted an econometric analysis to assess the impacts of contract farming on profitability, a proxy for economic welfare. To identify the factors that motivate farmers to participate in contract farming, we employed the probit model (Greene 2012):

$$p_i = \Phi(X_i\beta + \beta_0) = \int_{-\infty}^{X_i\beta+\beta_0} \varphi(t)\mathrm{d}t \tag{1}$$

where Φ is the cumulative standard distribution, while φ represents the standard normal density function. We estimated the marginal effect of independent variables in the probit model (McNelis 2005):

$$\frac{\partial p_i}{\partial x_{i,k}} = \varphi(X_i\beta + \beta_0)\beta_k \tag{2}$$

We also developed a farm-level food safety index (FSI) to assess compliance with food safety practices. The survey gathered information from farmers on 45 distinct good agricultural practices, including record keeping and site management, propagation material, nutrition management, water management, plant protection and post-harvest management. We sought an objective response from farmers on whether they follow each of the 45 practices and summed up all responses by a farm household to create an aggregate score of good practices. This serves as a proxy for compliance with food safety measures (FSM). The aggregate score for adoption of good practices for the kth household is given as

$$S = \sum_{j=1}^{45} F_{jk} \tag{3}$$

where F_{jk} represents jth good agricultural practice followed by the kth household. Then, we standardised the scores and calculated the FSI:

$$\text{FSI} = \left(\frac{S_A - S_L}{S_M - S_L} \right) \times 100 \tag{4}$$

where, S_A is the household's actual score, S_L is the minimum score and S_M is the maximum score among surveyed households.

An FSI-like index has been used to assess compliance with milk production FSMs (Kumar et al. 2011, 2017). We used a two-stage least squares (2SLS) model with instrumental variables to assess the impact of participation in contract farming on profitability (the second stage of regression). The equation for 2SLS regression is

$$\pi_i = \alpha + \delta d_i + \gamma X_i + \varepsilon_i \tag{5}$$

where π_i is the net profit per kilogram (kg) or FSI for a farm household cultivating okra, d_i is a dummy variable that equals 1 if a farmer is under contract and 0 if not under contract, X_i is a vector of farmer characteristics and ε_i is the error term.

A farmer's decision to participate in contract farming is influenced by socio-demographic and economic characteristics such as age, education, social caste group, farm size, migration, primary occupation and access to institutional credit. In the first stage of 2SLS regression, the dependent variable was a binary variable (farmer's participation in contract farming = 1, otherwise = 0); the independent variables were a mix of qualitative and quantitative factors representing farmer characteristics.

A farmer's decision to participate in contract farming is not random; if ordinary least squares (OLS) regression is used to estimate Eq. 5.5, the results may be biased. Farmers choose to participate in contract farming or a contractor selects them. A farmer's entry into contract farming is guided by observed and unobserved factors. The variable representing participation in contract farming (d_i) can be endogenous, and it can correlate with the error term ε_i. We use the 2SLS model with instrumental variables to address the unobserved factors and minimise the bias in estimating the impact of contract farming on a farmer's profit. An ideal instrumental variable should not correlate with the dependent variable in Eq. 5.5 or be a variable from the vector of a farmer's characteristics, X_i; it should correlate with d_i, the variable representing participation in contract farming. Accordingly, suitable instrumental variables for the profit equation of okra are found.

We identified the instrumental variable "farmers perceived risk of infestation of crop by pests and diseases" (yes = 1, 0 otherwise). A farmer who perceives particular production, sale or delivery risks is more likely to participate in contract farming; for instance, farmers concerned about the risk of pest and disease infestation are more likely to participate in contract farming to mitigate the risk. For the FSI, we identify a specification comprising two instrumental variables: "lack of crop insurance facility" (yes = 1, 0 otherwise) and "risk of price crash" (yes = 1, 0 otherwise). Farmers typically lack crop insurance, and prices fluctuate; farmers are likely to participate in contract farming to overcome these risks. Although the instrumental variables are strongly related to d_i, they are not systematically related with the dependent variable—profit or FSI—in Eq. 5.5.

We conducted the Hausman test for endogeneity for the profit and FSI equations. The result indicated endogeneity; therefore, the 2SLS result should be preferred over the OLS.

5.4 Results and Discussions

5.4.1 Characteristics of Contract and Independent Farmers

We compute the average values of the key household (HH) characteristics of the okra farmers in our sample (Table 5.1). The average age of farmers is around 44 years.

Table 5.1 Household characteristics of farmers

Household characteristics	All	Contract	Independent	Difference	t-test value
Age of HH head (years)	43.9	44.1	43.6	0.5	0.2522
Social caste (%)					
Scheduled caste	5.7	2.4	10.5	−8.1**	2.0683
OBC	18.4	19.0	17.5	1.5	0.2244
General	75.9	78.6	71.9	6.6	0.9009
Education of HH head (years)	9.9	10.2	9.5	0.7	1.1364
Number of economically active household members	1.8	1.7	1.9	-0.2	0.7875
% farmers with farming as main occupation	99.3	100.0	98.2	1.8	1.2160
Operational land (ha)	1.9	1.8	2.0	−0.3	0.7999
% of farmers having access to institutional credit (%)	48.9	36.9	66.7	−29.8***	3.6019
% of farmers with migration of any family member in last five years (%)	3.5	0.0	8.8	−8.8***	2.8218
Visits by government extension officials per year	1.6	2.1	0.9	1.2***	2.7573
No. of yearly visits by private extension officials	1.2	1.0	1.5	−0.5	1.1348
No. of yearly visits by farmers to extension officials	2.0	2.4	1.5	0.9	1.3159
Own means of personal transport (%)	67.4	78.6	50.9	27.7***	3.5710
% of farmer who perceive risk of infestation by pests and diseases	9.2	13.1	3.5	9.6*	1.9431

Source Field survey (2016)
Notes ***, ** and * represent 1%, 5% and 10% significance, respectively

Table 5.2 Economics of okra cultivation for contract and independent farmers in India

Economics of cultivation	All	Contract	Independent	Difference
Yield (quintal per hectare)	180.8	200.6	151.5	49.1***
	(71.9)	(68.3)	(67.6)	
Price (INR per quintal)	2871.6	2700.0	3124.6	−424.6***
	(359.6)	(0.0)	(462.6)	
Production cost (INR per quintal)	2028.4	1469.4	2852.2	−1382.9***
	(1153.3)	(775.7)	(1128.5)	
Profit (INR per quintal)	843.2	1,230.6	272.3	958.3***
	(1022.5)	(775.7)	(1079.3)	

Source Field survey (2016)

Notes ***, ** and * represent 1%, 5% and 10% significance, respectively. Figures in brackets represent standard deviation

Over 75% of the farmers fall in the General category[1]; Other Backward Classes (OBC) make up 18.4%, and Scheduled Castes (SC) make up 5.7%. The household head has 9.9 years of education on average. The average number of economically active household members is 1.8. Farming is the main occupation of around 99% of farmers. The average farm size is 1.9 hectare. Around 49% of farmers have access to institutional credit. A household member migrated in the past five years for around 3.5% of the households. Government extension officials visited farmers 1.6 times a year on average, and private extension officials visited around 1.2 times. Farmers visit extension officials two times a year on average. About 67% of farmers own their own means of personal transport. Around 9% of farmers perceive that pest and disease infestation is a risk to crop cultivation and marketing.

Contract and independent farmers differ significantly in some characteristics: caste, access to institutional credit, migration, number of annual visits by government extension officials, ownership of personal transport and risk perception of pests and diseases. Scheduled Caste farmers comprise 2.4% of contract growers and 10.5% of independent cultivators. Around 37% of contract farmers and 67% of independent growers have access to institutional credit. There is no migration among the households of contract farmers, while 8.8% of independent farmers observe the migration of family members. Government extension officials visit contract farmers 2.1 times a year and independent cultivators 0.9 times a year. Around 79% of contract growers and 51% of independent farmers have their own means of personal transport.

Contract and independent farming households differ in yield, production cost, output prices and profits (Tables 5.2, 5.3 and 5.4). The yield for contract cultivators is about 201 quintal per hectare, significantly more than the 152 quintal per hectare for independent producers. Prices and production costs are lower for contract farmers than for independent farmers. The open market prices that independent farmers

---

[1]In India, the government groups socio-economically disadvantaged castes into Scheduled Castes (SCs), Scheduled Tribes (STs), and OBCs. The socio-economically privileged castes are grouped into the General category.

Table 5.3 Components of cultivation cost (INR per hectare)

Component	Contract	Independent	Difference
Labour	99,707	116,404	−16,697
	(59,339)	(80,800)	
Seed	24,926	22,167	2579*
	(8563)	(8865)	
Fertilisers	28,818	56,123	−27,304***
	(25,623)	(28,815)	
Irrigation	63,844	73,220	−9376
	(44,699)	65,579	
Farmyard manure (FYM)	17,372	18,143	−1941
	(17,852)	(12,706)	
Pesticides	1486	51,744	−50,258***
	(7825)	(52,581)	
Other costs	6195	4413	1781
	(15,833)	(10,448)	
Rent for bullock pair/machinery	17,919	19,825	−1906
	(11,829)	(20,557)	
Marketing costs	1691	27,181	−25,489***
	(9674)	(26,511)	
Total cost of cultivation	261,959	389,220	−127,262***
	(116,246)	(171,796)	

Source Field survey (2016)

Notes ***, ** and * represent 1%, 5% and 10% significance, respectively. Figures in brackets represent standard deviation

receive are higher (INR 3124.60 per quintal) than the fixed prices (INR 2700.00 per quintal) received by contract farmers. But support (subsidy) for input costs, particularly for plant protection material and bio-fertilisers, reduces the production cost of contract farmers to INR 1469 per quintal; the cost for independent farmers is INR 2852 per quintal. Therefore, the profit (INR 1231 per quintal) is significantly higher for contract farmers.

A number of studies have reported significant positive impact on gross margins, crop income or total household income of contract farmers in developing countries; these include studies on Kenya (Wainaina et al. 2012), India (Singh 2002; Birthal et al. 2005; Tripathi et al. 2005; Ramaswami et al. 2006; Kalamkar 2012), Senegal (Warning and Key 2002), Laos (Leung et al. 2008), Madagascar (Bellemare 2012), Nicaragua (Michelson 2013), China (Zhu 2007; Miyata et al. 2009; Xu and Wang 2009) and Indonesia (Simmons et al. 2005).

Empirically, contract farming appears to have a positive impact on the adoption of FSMs (Fig. 5.1); adoption is better among contract farmers (55.1%) than among independent farmers (48.8%).

Table 5.4 Components of cultivation cost (percentage distribution)

Head of costs	% share in total cost of cultivation	
	Contract	Independent
Labour cost		
Land preparation	0.55	1.69
Sowing	1.12	2.67
Irrigation	0.87	5.05
Weeding	5.98	3.34
Spraying	1.94	9.90
Harvesting	27.11	6.06
Input costs		
Seed	9.91	6.01
Fertilisers	10.15	15.20
Irrigation	25.77	18.97
FYM	6.54	4.68
Pesticides	0.65	13.01
Costs for hiring bullocks and equipment	6.47	5.33
Other costs	2.39	1.10
Marketing costs		
Labour	0.35	3.72
Transport and others	0.19	3.28

Source Field survey (2016)

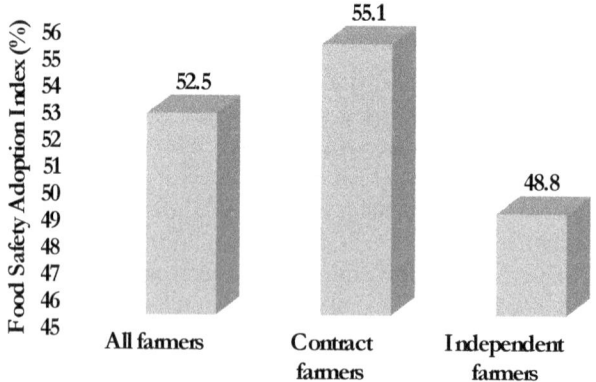

Fig. 5.1 Status of adoption of food safety practices in okra cultivation in Maharashtra, India (%). *Source* Authors' analysis based on field survey (2016)

Table 5.5 Compliance with food safety measures (FSM)

Food safety index (FSI)	Farmers		
	All (%)	Contract (%)	Independent (%)
<30 (low)	21.3	15.5	29.8
30–60 (medium)	37.6	41.7	31.6
≥60 (high)	41.1	42.9	38.6

Source Authors' analysis based on field survey (2016)

But average FSI scores may mask the exact status of compliance with FSM; therefore, we calculate the frequency distribution of farmers by compliance (Table 5.5), and we find that adoption is low among 15.5% of contract farmers and 29.8% of independent farmers.

5.4.2 Determinants of Farmers' Participation in Contract Farming

We use the probit model to establish the determinants of participation in contract farming, and the marginal effect of independent variables is given in Table 5.6. Participation in contract farming is significantly influenced by several variables: caste, education of household head, number of visits by government extension officials, number of visits by private extension officials and the number of extension visits by farmers.

The probability of participation in contract farming is higher for farmers of the General and OBC categories than for SC/ST farmers (the base category). Participation is significantly and positively influenced by the household head's education; educated and privileged-caste farmers are likely to know about new institutional arrangements like contract farming. Participation is inversely related to visits by public and private extension officials and positively related with extension visits by farmers (Table 5.6). Farmers of high-value crops like okra need expert advice and guidance promptly and frequently. If extension support is not available, farmers may not cultivate these crops or consider institutional arrangements like contract farming, as it fills the gap in extension services. Frequent visits to extension officials indicate that farmers want prompt extension support. Such farmers are more likely to participate in contract farming.

5.4.3 Impact of Contract Farming on Farmers' Profit

Table 5.7 depicts the impact of contract farming on profits from okra cultivation and gives the outcomes of the second stage of 2SLS regression along with OLS regression. Unlike OLS regression, the 2SLS regression takes care of the unobserved factors in

Table 5.6 Determinants of participation in contract farming (probit model)

Dependent variable: participation in contract farming (yes = 1/no = 0)

Variable	Coefficient	Marginal effect
Contract farming (yes = 1, 0 otherwise)		
Socio-demographic variables		
ln(Age of HH head) (years)	0.188	0.0195
	(0.275)	(0.0288)
Caste (base: scheduled caste/scheduled tribe)		
OBC (yes = 1, 0 otherwise)	1.988**	0.2064**
	(0.951)	(0.0959)
General (yes = 1, 0 otherwise)	1.860***	0.1931***
	(0.428)	(0.0418)
ln(years of education of HH head)	0.0528**	0.0054*
	(0.0263)	(0.0028)
ln(number of economically active family members)	−0.310	−0.0321
	(0.852)	(0.0888)
Ln(operational land) (Ha)	0.467	0.0484
	(0.333)	(0.0339)
Own personal transport (yes = 1, 0 otherwise)	−0.0818	−0.0084
	(0.514)	(0.0535)
Economic variables		
Access to institutional credit (yes = 1, 0 otherwise)	−0.546	−0.0566
	(0.354)	(0.0375)
ln(No. of visits by government extension officials)	−0.365***	−0.0378***
	(0.126)	(0.0125)
ln(No. of visits by private extension officials)	−0.574**	−0.0595**
	(0.258)	(0.0275)
ln(number of visits by farmer for extension)	1.153***	0.1197***
	(0.144)	(0.0165)
Constant	−0.854***	
	(0.158)	
No. of observations	96	
Pseudo R2	0.3435	
Log pseudolikelihood	−23.744017	
District Fixed Effect	Yes	Yes

Source Authors' analysis based on field survey (2016)

Notes Standard errors in parentheses; ***, ** and * represent 1%, 5% and 10% significance, respectively. Standard errors are clustered at the district level

Table 5.7 Impact of contract farming on profit

Dependent variable: ln(unit profit in production of okra (Rs/kg))

Variable	OLS	2SLS	
		1st stage	2nd stage
Contract farming (yes = 1, 0 otherwise)	0.00135		0.288*
	(0.0137)		(0.0818)
Socio-demographic variables			
ln(age of HH head) (years)	0.0207	0.0700	0.000338
	(0.0196)	(0.0683)	(0.0241)
Caste (base: scheduled caste/scheduled tribe)			
OBC (yes = 1, 0 otherwise)	0.0162	0.537**	−0.139
	(0.0189)	(0.222)	(0.126)
General (yes = 1, 0 otherwise)	0.0339	0.499**	−0.110
	(0.0162)	(0.198)	(0.104)
ln(years of education of HH head)	0.0126	0.0176	0.00746
	(0.0117)	(0.0297)	(0.0185)
ln(number of economically active family members)	0.00973	−0.0191	0.0149
	(0.0136)	(0.0586)	(0.0400)
ln(operational land) (Ha)	−0.00193	0.0470	−0.0156
	(0.00797)	(0.0449)	(0.0102)
Own personal transport (yes = 1, 0 otherwise)	−0.0104	−0.00411	−0.0102
	(0.0166)	(0.0312)	(0.0204)
Migration of household members in last five years (yes = 1, 0 otherwise)	−0.0266*	0.0979	−0.0551*
	(0.00849)	(0.0798)	(0.0137)
Economic variables			
Main occupation (farming = 1, other = 0)	−0.00293	0.00104	−0.00386
	(0.0133)	(0.0780)	(0.0447)
Access to institutional credit (yes = 1, 0 otherwise)	−0.0121**	−0.0568	0.00485
	(0.00263)	(0.0447)	(0.0127)
ln(No. of visits by government extension officials)	−0.00902	−0.00924	-0.00783
	(0.0123)	(0.0610)	(0.00578)
ln(No. of visits by private extension officials)	−0.00127	−0.0321	0.00888
	(0.00420)	(0.0416)	(0.00752)
ln(Number of visits by farmer for extension)	−0.0161	0.0391	−0.0273*
	(0.0124)	(0.0432)	(0.00883)
Instrumental variables			
Farmer perceives risk of pests and diseases (yes = 1, 0 otherwise)		0.0491	
		(0.0322)	

(continued)

Table 5.7 (continued)

Dependent variable: ln(unit profit in production of okra (Rs/kg))

Variable	OLS	2SLS	
		1st stage	2nd stage
Constant	5.010***	−0.785*	5.238***
	(0.130)	(0.398)	(0.291)
No. of observations	141	141	141
R-squared	0.448	0.776	
Root MSE	0.04696	0.2478	0.08517
District fixed effect	Yes	Yes	Yes

Source Authors' analysis based on field survey (2016)

Notes Standard errors in parentheses; ***, ** and * represent 1%, 5% and 10% significance, respectively. Standard errors are clustered at the district level

regression and gives the true impact of contract farming on farmers' profit. The instrumental variable used in the 2SLS model is "farmer perceives risk of infestation by pests and diseases" (yes = 1, 0 otherwise). The Hausman test shows endogeneity in the profit equation (Table 5.9); therefore, the estimates of the 2SLS regression should be preferred over that of OLS regression, and participation in contract farming significantly and positively impacts profits—by around 29%.

5.4.4 Impact of Contract Farming on the Adoption of Farm-Level FSMs

Contract farming impacts the adoption of farm-level FSM (Table 5.8); the 2SLS regression shows the true impact by accounting for the unobserved factors in regression. Two instrumental variables are used in the 2SLS regression: "lack of crop insurance facility" (yes = 1, 0 otherwise); and "risk of price crash" (yes = 1, 0 otherwise). We use Sargan's test to determine the validity of the instrumental variables, and we find them valid (Sargan (score) chi2(1) = 0.230744, p = 0.6310).

The result of Hausman's test shows endogeneity in the food safety equation (Table 5.9); therefore, the estimates of 2SLS regression should be preferred over that of OLS regression. The results in Table 5.8 show that contract farming has a significant and positive impact on the adoption of farm-level FSMs; it is higher among contract farmers by about 104.2%. The contracting firm needs that the fresh okra has minimal chemical residuals so that it meets the quality requirements for export; therefore, farmers follow farm-level FSM. Access to institutional credit is also positively related with the adoption of FSM.

Table 5.8 Impact of contract farming on adoption of food safety practices (FSI) by okra cultivators in India

Dependent variable: Food Safety Adoption Index			
Variable	OLS	2SLS	
		1st stage	2nd stage
Contract farming (yes = 1, 0 otherwise)	27.23**		104.2*
	(3.766)		(30.17)
Socio-demographic variables			
ln(age of HH head) (years)	−1.849	0.0886	−7.336
	(9.534)	(0.0723)	(10.11)
Caste (base: scheduled caste/scheduled tribe)			
OBC (yes = 1, 0 otherwise)	−0.0912	0.509**	−41.73
	(10.67)	(0.202)	(23.22)
General (yes = 1, 0 otherwise)	1.139	0.497***	-37.70
	(3.480)	(0.188)	(17.82)
ln(years of education of HH head)	1.876	0.0206	0.490
	(7.746)	(0.0332)	(9.539)
ln(number of economically active family members)	−4.901	−0.00819	−3.512
	(3.689)	(0.0581)	(4.876)
ln(operational land) (Ha)	0.703	0.0531	−2.974
	(1.859)	(0.0448)	(4.200)
Own personal transport (yes = 1, 0 otherwise)	−6.459	−0.0193	−6.406
	(4.805)	(0.0365)	(5.842)
Migration of household members in last five years (yes = 1, 0 otherwise)	16.73*	0.103	9.064
	(5.569)	(0.0701)	(7.920)
Economic variables			
Main occupation (farming = 1, other = 0)	−16.07**	0.0546	−16.32
	(2.042)	(0.0898)	(9.889)
Access to institutional credit (yes = 1, 0 otherwise)	1.653	−0.0707	6.213**
	(2.418)	(0.0456)	(0.786)
ln(No. of visits by government extension officials)	18.64	−0.0101	18.96
	(9.019)	(0.0573)	(7.845)
ln(No. of visits by private extension officials)	1.793	−0.0287	4.522
	(4.317)	(0.0407)	(4.444)
ln(number of visits by farmer for extension)	−8.603	0.0262	−11.62
	(8.262)	(0.0351)	(7.499)
Instrumental variables			
Lack of crop insurance facility (yes = 1, 0 otherwise)		0.0752	

(continued)

Table 5.8 (continued)

Dependent variable: Food Safety Adoption Index

		(0.0491)	
Risk of price crash (yes = 1, 0 otherwise)		0.115*	
		(0.0616)	
Constant	74.29	−0.927**	135.6
	(35.24)	(0.439)	(79.54)
No. of observations	141	141	141
R-squared	0.343	0.784	
Root MSE	19.938	0.2443	27.62
District fixed effect	Yes	Yes	Yes

Source Authors' analysis based on field survey (2016)

Notes Standard errors in parentheses; ***, ** and * represent 1%, 5% and 10% significance, respectively. Standard errors are clustered at the district level

5.5 Conclusion and Policy Implications

Contract farming plays an important role in connecting smallholders to high-end international markets. Conditional on participation, contract farmers earn relatively higher profits, stemming mainly from higher yields and lower production costs. Participation in contract significantly enhances their adoption of farm-level FSMs, which is essential for accessing high-end global markets and desirable in domestic markets.

It is incorrect to look at only one side of the market, since the integrator operates on both sides. The integrator supplies inputs and also buys the output, and it is optimal to under-price both input and output. By paying a similar or even lower price for output, the integrator can subsidise inputs, and the net effect for farmers is higher or more stable profits.

These findings have several important policy implications. The benefits of contract farming are context-specific; therefore, appropriate policy strategies and mechanisms—and not a one-size-fits-all solution for agricultural production—need to be designed to promote the contract farming of several agricultural commodities, especially in high-value crops. Attention needs to be paid to both sides of the market—technological inputs and risk mitigation—in assessing the impacts on small farmers.

Table 5.9 Hausman test for endogeneity in the profit and FSI equations for okra

Dependent variable:	ln(unit profit in production of okra (Rs/kg))	Food safety adoption index
Variable	**IV**: Farmers perceived risk of pests and diseases (yes = 1, 0 otherwise)	**IVs**: 1. Lack of crop insurance facility (yes = 1, 0 otherwise); 2. Risk of price crash (yes = 1, 0 otherwise)
Contract farming (yes = 1, 0 otherwise)	0.0515*	55.62**
	(0.0156)	(9.894)
Socio-demographic variables		
ln(age of HH head) (years)	0.0204	−0.224
	(0.0183)	(8.256)
Caste (base: scheduled caste/scheduled tribe)		
OBC (yes = 1, 0 otherwise)	0.0157	−0.961
	(0.0183)	(11.14)
General (yes = 1, 0 otherwise)	0.0329	1.499
	(0.0164)	(4.284)
ln(years of education of HH head)	0.0125	1.988
	(0.0119)	(7.599)
ln(number of economically active family members)	0.00940	−4.604
	(0.0144)	(4.007)
ln(operational land) (Ha)	−0.00209	0.626
	(0.00808)	(1.638)
Own personal transport (yes = 1, 0 otherwise)	−0.0114	−6.610
	(0.0172)	(5.835)
Migration of household members in last five years (yes = 1, 0 otherwise)	−0.0270*	17.83*
	(0.00849)	(5.441)
Economic variables		
Main occupation (farming = 1, other = 0)	−0.00356	−17.41**
	(0.0133)	(2.176)
Access to institutional credit (yes = 1, 0 otherwise)	−0.0115*	1.728
	(0.00330)	(2.668)
ln(No. of visits by government extension officials)	−0.0105	18.67
	(0.0123)	(8.463)
ln(No. of visits by private extension officials)	−0.000337	2.570
	(0.00439)	(4.186)
ln(number of visits by farmer for extension)	−0.0161	−10.86
	(0.0121)	(7.722)
Ehat	**−0.0511****	**−29.72***

(continued)

Table 5.9 (continued)

Dependent variable:	ln(unit profit in production of okra (Rs/kg))	Food safety adoption index
	(0.00882)	(8.168)
Constant	4.983***	52.94
	(0.127)	(28.31)
No. of observations	141	141
R-squared	0.452	0.358
Root MSE	0.04697	19.787
District fixed effect	Yes	Yes

Source Authors' analysis based on field survey (2016)

Notes Standard errors in parentheses; ***, ** and * represent 1%, 5% and 10% significance, respectively. Standard errors are clustered at the district level

References

Bellemare, M. F. (2012). As you sow, so shall you reap: The welfare impacts of contract farming. *World Development, 40*(7), 1418–1434. https://doi.org/10.1016/j.worlddev.2011.12.008.

Birthal, P. S., Joshi, P. K., & Gulati, A. (2005). *Vertical coordination in high value food commodities: Implication for small holders*. MTID Discussion Paper No 85. Washington, DC: IFPRI.

Dev, S. M., & Rao, N. C. (2005). Food processing and contract farming in Andhra Pradesh: A small farmer perspective. *Economic and Political Weekly, 40*(26), 2705–2713.

Dileep, B. K., Grover, R. K., & Rai, K. N. (2002). Contract farming in tomato: An economic analysis. *Indian Journal of Agricultural Economics, 57*(2), 197–210.

FAO (Food and Agriculture Organization of the United Nations). (2020). FAOSTAT database. Accessed April 10, 2020. https://faostat.fao.org/.

Greene, W. H. (2012). *Econometric analysis* (7th ed.). Princeton Hall: New York University.

Kalamkar, S. S. (2012). Inputs and services delivery system under contract farming: A case of broiler farming. *Agricultural Economics Research Review, 25*(Conf), 515–521. https://www.aer aindia.in/publication/Contents_Vol%2025_conf..pdf.

Kumar, J., & Kumar, P. K. (2008). Contract farming: Problems, prospects and its effects on income and employment. *Agricultural Economics Research Review, 21*, 243–250. https://www.aeraindia. in/publication/Contents-%20Vol%2021%20No.%202.pdf.

Kumar, P. (2006). Contract farming through agribusiness firms and state corporation: A case study in Punjab. *Economic and Political Weekly, 41*(52), 5367–5375.

Kumar, A., Wright, I. A., & Singh, D. K. (2011). Adoption of food safety practices in milk production: Implications for dairy farmers in India. *Journal of International Food and Agribusiness Marketing, 23*(4), 330–344.

Kumar, A., Thapa, G., Joshi, P. K., & Roy, D. (2017). Adoption of food safety measures on milk production in Nepal: Impact on smallholders' farm-gate prices and profitability. *Food Policy, 70*, 13–26.

Leung, P., Sethboonsarng, S., & Stefan, A. (2008). *Rice contract farming in Lao PDR: Moving from subsistence to commercial agriculture*. ADB Institute Discussion Paper No. 90. Tokyo: Asian Development Bank Institute.

McNelis, P. D. (2005). *Neural networks in finance: Gaining predictive edge in the market* (pp. 13– 58). Elsevier Academic Press. https://doi.org/10.1016/B978-012485967-8.50002-6.

Michelson, H. C. (2013). Small farmers, NGOs, and a Walmart world: Welfare effects of supermarkets operating in Nicaragua. *American Journal of Agricultural Economics, 95*(3), 628–649. https://doi.org/10.1093/ajae/aas139.

Miyata, S., Minot, N., & Hu, D. (2009). Impact of contract farming on income: Linking small farmers, packers, and supermarkets in China. *World Development, 37*(11), 1728–1741. https://doi.org/10.1016/j.worlddev.2008.08.025.

Nagaraj, N., Chandrakanth, M. G., Chengappa, P. G., Roopa, H. S., & Chandakavate, P. M. (2008). Contract farming and its implications for input-supply, linkages between markets and farmers in Karnataka. *Agricultural Economics Research Review, 21*(Conf), 307–316. https://www.aeraindia.in/publication/Contents-%20Vol%2021%20Conf..pdf.

Opondo, M. M. (2000). The socio-economic and ecological impacts of the agro-industrial food chain on the rural economy in Kenya. *Ambio, 29*(1), 35–41.

Ramaswami, B., Birthal, P. S., & Joshi, P. K. (2006). *Efficiency and distribution in contract farming: The case of Indian poultry growers*. MTID Discussion Paper No. 91. Washington, DC: IFPRI.

Simmons, P., Winters, P., & Patrick, I. (2005). An analysis of contract farming in East Java, Bali, and Lombok, Indonesia. *Agricultural Economics, 33*(s3), 513–525. https://doi.org/10.1111/j.1574-0864.2005.00096.x.

Singh, S. (2002). Contracting out solutions: Political economy of contract farming in the Indian Punjab. *World Development, 30*(9), 1621–1638. https://doi.org/10.1016/S0305-750X(02)00059-1.

Tripathi R. S., Singh, R., & Singh, S. (2005). Contract farming in potato production: An alternative for managing risk and uncertainty. *Agricultural Economics Research Review, 18*(Dec), 47–60.

Wainaina, P. W., Okello, J. J., & Nzuma, J. (2012). Impact of contract farming on smallholder poultry farmers' income in Kenya. Paper presented at the 2012 Triennial Conference of International Association of Agricultural Economists, Foz do Iguaçu, Brazil, August 18–24.

Warning, M., & Key, N. (2002). The social performance and distributional consequences of contract farming: An equilibrium analysis of the *Arachide de bouche* program in Senegal. *World Development, 30*(2), 255–263. https://doi.org/10.1016/S0305-750X(01)00104-8.

Xu, J., & Wang, X. (2009). An empirical analysis of the impact of contract farming and its organization models on farmers' income [in Chinese]. *Chinese Rural Economy, 2009*(4), 39–47.

Zhu, H. (2007). An assessment of the effects of adopting contract farming structure in the tomato industry in Xinjiang [in Chinese]. *Journal of Agrotechnical Economics, 3*, 89–95.

Part II
Employment, Investment and Productivity Growth

Chapter 6
Temporal and Spatial Patterns in Employment and Productivity Growth in the Organised Food Industry

Seema Bathla and Shiv Jee

6.1 Introduction

In the recent decades in India, the improvement in infrastructure and fiscal incentives has led to a favourable business environment, readily available markets, the availability of sufficient raw material for value addition and rising per capita income. These developments have, in turn, led to a change in food habits and rise in the demand for organised foods and beverages and caused the industry, and its share in the gross domestic product (GDP), to grow continually.

The analysis in the 1980s and 1990s indicated scaling-up and consolidation at the factory level with the active involvement of multinational companies (MNCs) in food processing (Bhavani et al. 2006). However, technical progress was identified only in few industries—dairy, grain mill, confectionery, distillery and blending of spirits—that too in a small magnitude. Increasing returns to scale were found in fish products, vegetable and animal oils, animal feeds, sugar and starch products from 1984–85 to 2001–02 (Ali et al. 2007).

The foremost concern was a deceleration in the employment growth rate and total factor productivity (TFP), though these improved in the 2000s (Mitra 1999; Sidhu 2005; Mitra et al. 2002; Hashim et al. 2009). In most manufacturing industries, the annual growth rate of TFP was higher between 2003–04 and 2014–15 than between 1980–81 and 2002–03 (Goldar 2017).

The TFP of the food products and beverages segment grew at 1.42% per annum in the first period (1980–81 to 2002–03) and at 0.95% in the second period (2003–04 to 2014–15). The performance varied by state. In the 2000s, the TFP growth of the segment was higher in India's low-income agriculturally dominant states—Odisha, Madhya Pradesh and Chhattisgarh—and it may indicate that the increase in demand for processed food and the easy availability of raw material (agriculture produce)

S. Bathla (✉) · Shiv Jee
Centre for the Study of Regional Development, Jawaharlal Nehru University, New Delhi, India
e-mail: seema.bathla@gmail.com

raised its growth potential (World Bank 2014). The industry operated well below the optimal level in each state, however, implying considerable scope to improve the scale and technical efficiency. Large intra-industry variations in performance have also been identified.[1]

Several industries tend to operate at low efficiency—capacity utilisation is merely 50% on average (Ali et al. 2007). Of the 31 "labour-intensive industries" at the four-digit level, three are food processing industries: manufacture of macaroni, noodles and similar farinaceous products; manufacture of bakery and other food products; manufacture of prepared animal feeds (Das et al. 2009). The elasticity of output for the food industry overall was higher for capital than for labour. The study found that labour intensity (labour/gross fixed capital stock) declined for capital-intensive and labour-intensive industries from 0.72 in 1990–91 to 0.30 in 2003–04; the output increased, but it did not generate enough employment growth, and employment elasticity declined significantly. These findings defy the repeated claims that the agricultural and food industries are highly labour-intensive.

In the tobacco sector, the growth rate was negative throughout (Goldar 2017); the slow pace of employment and productivity can be explained by the increasing capital intensity, labour productivity and wage rates. The organised food industry faces other challenges: production and packaging are expensive; safety and quality management procedures are inappropriate; access to regular finance is poor; the investment in transport and cold chain infrastructure for perishables is inadequate; technology adoption is poor; and the produce is not competitive in world markets (Sidhu 2005; EPW 2005).

This chapter focuses on the temporal and spatial patterns in employment and partial productivity growth in the organised food and beverage industry in India and its relative position with respect to organised manufacturing overall from 1980–81 to 2014–15. Such an analysis helps to assess the status of organised food processing and draw implications about the key performance indicators under varying trade regimes.

6.2 Sources of Data

To identify the changes over time, we work out the decadal averages for the key variables for 1980–89 (the pre-reforms period), 1990–1999, 2000–09 and 2010–2014 (the post-reform period). We extract data for the foods and beverages industry at the National Industrial Classification (NIC) 2004 two-digit level from the Annual Survey of Industries (ASI) and Economic and Political Weekly Research Foundation (EPWRF) database. We base our investigation on the data in the ASI published by the Ministry of Statistics and Programme Implementation (MOS&PI), Government

---

[1]The food industry comprises meat and meat products; fish and fish products; fruits and vegetables; vegetable oils and fats; milk and milk products; cereals; pulses and value-added products; animal feeds; confectionery products; bakery products; raw and processed sugar; beverages; and distillery and blending of spirits.

of India (GoI), 1980 to 2015. We select 17 major states for analysis of food products and beverages (NIC 15) at the NIC two-digit level. We draw the data for the organised sector from the data disc of the ASI provided by the EPWRF (1976–77 to 1997–98) and thereafter by the MOS&PI. We prepare a comparable time series data on different variables in food and beverage industry based on a concordance matrix between three-digit classes of NIC-1998, NIC-2004 and NIC-2008. The three-digit NIC-1998 and NIC-2004 codes industries included the following.

- production, processing and preservation of meat, fish, fruit, vegetables, oils and fats (151);
- manufacture of dairy products (152);
- manufacture of grain mill products, starches and starch products and prepared animal feeds (153);
- manufacture of bakery and other food products (154); and
- manufacture of beverages including water and liquor (155).

The NIC-2008 three-digit codes group industries into

- processing and preserving of meat (101);
- processing and preserving of fish, molluscs and crustaceans (102);
- processing of fruits and vegetables (103);
- manufacturing of animal and vegetable fats and oils (104);
- manufacturing of dairy products (105);
- manufacturing of grain mills products, starch products (106);
- manufacturing of other food products (107);
- manufacturing of prepared animal feeds (108); and
- manufacturing of beverages, including spirits and liquor (110).

The selected performance indicators of the industries at the two-digit level are gross value-added (GVA); output; workers (persons engaged); and TFP. We also use three partial productivity measures: labour productivity (GVA per worker); capital intensity (capital per worker); and capital productivity (GVA per capital). We use the perpetual inventory method to estimate the series on capital stock. The selected indicators are converted into 2004–05 prices using the wholesale price index (WPI), consumer price index (CPI) and gross state domestic product (GSDP) deflator.

6.2.1 Trends in Employment and Partial Productivity Measures

The absolute number of factories and persons engaged (employment) in the organised food industry increased since the 1980s, as did the GVA (Table 6.1). The average number of factories almost doubled—from 17,925 to 32,731. The number of factories and people employed in food industry fell in the 2000s in Assam, Bihar, Haryana, Madhya Pradesh and Uttar Pradesh, but the industry remained a major

Table 6.1 Average number of factories, workers and output in organised food industry (2004–05 price)

State	Factories (No.)				Employment (No.)				Gross value-added (GVA) (INR lakh)			
	1980–89	1990–99	2000–09	2010–14	1980–89	1990–99	2000–09	2010–14	1980–89	1990–99	2000–09	2010–14
Andhra Pradesh	3567	5218	6107	7147	74,378	220,765	540,755	857,124	68,221	160,532	277,024	323,236
Assam	801	769	900	1251	42,789	99,249	135,336	250,294	76,917	88,319	66,223	103,046
Bihar	475	293	190	723	14,370	34,315	53,896	185,905	18,155	22,780	22,688	38,633
Gujarat	1092	1134	1301	1941	68,086	157,475	298,719	655,573	58,357	100,916	168,255	273,010
Haryana	384	593	530	682	15,619	61,312	152,218	434,980	22,609	57,490	100,380	165,982
Himachal Pradesh	21	45	96	168	1173	8577	31,983	144,233	1,316	3,671	15,686	59,130
Jammu & Kashmir	50	69	100	150	2090	4724	16,412	31,162	1,644	4,316	6,069	17,862
Karnataka	1138	1171	1429	2005	58,990	149,999	430,441	1,065,774	52,675	101,819	241,913	365,657
Kerala	575	753	1095	1463	12,552	55,997	104,297	200,086	36,158	76,499	85,909	111,816
Madhya Pradesh	794	859	530	741	21,669	148,469	194,684	358,894	21,020	82,619	119,373	157,766
Maharashtra	1454	1927	2184	3038	189,145	433,069	965,363	1,907,519	150,688	329,530	449,743	592,242
Odisha	327	365	552	905	5086	27,438	63,105	120,386	4,856	13,626	21,953	53,825
Punjab	961	1280	1762	2798	45,981	142,657	260,642	391,566	57,631	137,960	230,920	173,189
Rajasthan	354	445	533	800	17,285	56,574	93,261	270,945	10,172	34,698	79,978	143,459
Tamil Nadu	2824	3599	3654	5182	66,929	228,337	460,438	923,086	94,050	179,165	228,415	289,778
Uttar Pradesh	2172	2338	1709	2075	120,282	368,697	920,157	1,620,010	140,202	249,735	305,200	334,255
West Bengal	938	998	1183	1662	30,076	76,321	189,259	533,348	38,723	56,501	76,263	152,347

(continued)

Table 6.1 (continued)

State	Factories (No.)				Employment (No.)				Gross value-added (GVA) (INR lakh)			
	1980–89	1990–99	2000–09	2010–14	1980–89	1990–99	2000–09	2010–14	1980–89	1990–99	2000–09	2010–14
17 States	17,925	21,855	23,856	32,731	1,122,678	1,278,372	1,354,713	1,605,813	853,393	1,700,176	2,495,990	3,355,235

Source GOI-MOS&PI

provider of employment—average employment increased from 786,499 in the 1980s to 9,950,883 in 2014. The GVA grew almost four times over four decades—from INR 853,393 lakh to INR 3,355,235 lakh (at 2004–05 prices) (Annex Table 6.8). At the all-India level (the average based on 17 states), the number of factories grew at 1.17% per annum between 1980 and 1989; 1.43% between 1990 and 1999; 1.76% between 1999–2000 and 2009–10; and −1.88% between 2010 and 2015 (Table 6.2). The average employment growth rose from −2.54% in the 1980s to 2.27% per annum in the 2000–09 period and fell to 0.50% in the 2010–14 period.

The growth rate of the organised food industry was negative in Andhra Pradesh, Tamil Nadu and Uttar Pradesh and positive in other states—the highest being in Bihar, Haryana, Rajasthan and West Bengal. Employment grew more than 4% per annum in Bihar, Jammu and Kashmir, Madhya Pradesh, Gujarat and Uttar Pradesh. The growth rate in GVA per enterprise (factory) was positive except in Assam, Gujarat, Haryana, Himachal Pradesh, Karnataka, Madhya Pradesh, Odisha, Uttar Pradesh and West Bengal.

The annual growth rate in capital stock per factory was positive and impressive throughout the study period (1980–89 to 2010–2014). The capital in processed food increased primarily due to an increase in the scale of operation (output per factory). The number of factories grew at a much slower pace. The employment per factory was not impressive, but the number of factories increased and that raised total employment. Capital invested per factory grew more than fourfold after 2000 at the rate of more than 6% per annum. Capital deepening increased in almost all the states, due to possibly the increasing substitution of capital for labour.

Table 6.3 furnishes estimates on labour productivity, capital intensity and capital productivity. Labour productivity in almost every state increased from 1980–89 to 2009–10 and fell later. The labour productivity of all the states taken together increased three times—from INR 77,968 on average in the 1980s to INR 208,839 in 2010–14. Productivity was highest in Jammu and Kashmir, Kerala, Rajasthan, Haryana and Punjab. The growth rate was negative in Kerala and Bihar in the 2000s. Labour productivity grew at a negative rate in Gujarat, Haryana, Himachal Pradesh, Madhya Pradesh and Odisha but at more than 9% per annum in Bihar, Jammu and Kashmir and Punjab.

Table 6.4 shows the estimates of their annual decadal rates of growth. Capital intensity increased sharply in processed foods in almost every state during the pre-reform period; the annual growth in capital intensity exceeded that in labour productivity during the pre-reform period and continued to be higher in each decade. Capital intensity increased from 1980 to 2014 in Andhra Pradesh, Gujarat, Himachal Pradesh, Odisha, Rajasthan and West Bengal. In other states, growth decelerated, which indicates that an effort is required to improve technology. Capital productivity decreased in every state except Jammu and Kashmir, Kerala and Maharashtra. During the 2010–14 period, capital productivity growth was negative, at 0.51. The capital output ratio, a measure of capacity utilisation, is high; it indicates that the capacity utilisation was low.

Overall, the analysis indicates that employment and GVA per factory increased, albeit both grew at a low rate in some states. Seen through partial productivity

Table 6.2 Annual rate of growth in factories, employment, GVA/factory and capital/factory in organised food industry (2004–05 prices)

State	Factories (%)				Employment (%)				GVA/factory (%)				Capital/factory (%)			
	1980–89	1990–99	2000–09	2010–14	1980–89	1990–99	2000–09	2010–14	1980–89	1990–99	2000–09	2010–14	1980–89	1990–99	2000–09	2010–14
Andhra Pradesh	4.8	1.4	1.1	−12.8	−2.4	2.0	3.3	−14.4	3.8	5.1	6.0	3.1	1.5	10.6	6.6	9.0
Assam	−1.1	1.9	2.0	3.1	−1.0	1.3	0.4	1.1	11.7	−1.2	1.3	−0.5	10.0	4.6	1.2	5.7
Bihar	−6.6	−5.1	0.6	10.8	−11.8	−6.3	0.7	17.0	12.1	10.6	−0.3	24.4	16.9	11.7	3.1	9.0
Gujarat	−3.6	3.7	2.8	0.3	−2.5	2.4	4.8	0.2	10.4	2.1	6.7	−3.8	9.0	5.5	4.4	10.8
Haryana	5.7	0.7	−2.3	6.2	3.2	0.7	0.6	3.3	8.5	7.7	12.3	−28.5	3.8	12.3	14.0	1.1
Himachal Pradesh	5.1	10.6	5.3	0.2	4.6	16.8	9.7	2.3	4.9	15.2	6.9	−6.5	0.1	16.2	4.8	6.6
Jammu & Kashmir	5.4	6.6	6.0	3.1	4.9	6.8	6.5	11.3	9.8	2.9	7.9	21.7	10.9	4.4	0.0	14.3
Karnataka	1.6	0.9	2.4	2.3	−2.9	2.5	1.9	2.0	9.2	8.5	8.1	−2.5	5.5	9.6	6.2	3.0
Kerala	1.0	1.1	1.0	1.0	0.9	1.0	1.0	1.0	1.1	1.0	1.0	1.1	1.1	1.1	1.0	1.1
Madhya Pradesh	−1.6	−5.4	1.2	1.2	−1.5	−3.9	4.3	4.6	17.6	7.2	12.4	−18.9	20.0	18.1	6.3	2.5
Maharashtra	−0.5	4.1	0.9	0.2	−2.6	3.3	0.3	3.2	12.4	5.9	2.3	9.9	7.9	4.4	5.3	8.0
Odisha	−4.1	2.3	4.1	4.0	−2.0	6.7	2.7	−0.7	5.7	7.2	6.7	−18.4	10.4	15.7	6.2	5.0
Punjab	6.7	2.9	6.2	0.4	6.8	3.7	2.4	−0.5	4.5	4.7	−0.2	8.1	5.6	6.4	1.2	4.1
Rajasthan	−0.4	2.0	2.0	4.8	−0.9	3.6	6.2	1.7	7.9	8.9	13.9	2.7	5.0	10.0	4.3	6.2
Tamil Nadu	1.6	1.5	1.7	−0.2	−2.9	2.2	3.1	3.9	6.7	3.0	6.0	7.1	4.7	7.2	6.9	8.7
Uttar Pradesh	2.4	−1.6	−1.2	−0.5	−3.4	−2.5	1.3	0.6	6.4	7.4	5.7	−3.0	7.2	10.4	11.8	4.2
West Bengal	−3.3	2.1	2.2	4.2	−3.0	0.6	3.8	1.5	10.6	−0.3	12.4	−6.1	8.8	6.6	6.5	7.7
17 States	1.17	1.43	1.76	−1.88	−2.54	1.53	2.27	−0.50	8.29	5.33	5.54	1.36	6.54	8.15	6.08	8.15

Source GOI-MOS&PI

Table 6.3 Estimates on partial productivity in foods and beverages manufacturing: decadal averages (INR 2004–05 price)

State	Labour productivity (INR)				Capital intensity (INR)				Capital productivity (INR)			
	1980–89	1990–99	2000–09	2010–14	1980–89	1990–99	2000–09	2010–14	1980–89	1990–99	2000–09	2010–14
Andhra Pradesh	91,722	72,716	51,229	37,712	214,471	183,680	167,546	178,327	42,767	39,588	30,576	21,148
Assam	179,760	88,987	48,932	41,170	219,938	211,523	212,326	182,373	81,732	42,070	23,046	22,575
Bihar	126,339	66,386	42,096	20,781	218,932	208,021	191,920	147,049	57,707	31,913	21,934	14,132
Gujarat	85,710	64,084	56,325	41,645	237,690	206,073	188,166	166,107	36,060	31,098	29,934	25,071
Haryana	144,750	93,766	65,945	38,159	222,084	182,127	171,543	153,065	65,178	51,484	38,442	24,930
Himachal Pradesh	112,196	42,804	49,044	40,996	231,459	148,635	154,728	138,110	48,473	28,798	31,697	29,684
Jammu & Kashmir	78,647	91,360	36,980	57,321	193,109	214,640	173,460	178,882	40,727	42,564	21,319	32,044
Karnataka	89,295	67,880	56,201	34,309	225,805	197,862	167,624	154,750	39,545	34,307	33,528	22,171
Kerala	288,059	136,611	82,369	55,884	238,249	173,522	187,112	175,751	120,907	78,729	44,021	31,797
Madhya Pradesh	97,007	55,647	61,316	43,959	178,249	151,326	172,790	167,740	54,422	36,773	35,486	26,207
Maharashtra	79,668	76,092	46,588	31,048	209,762	196,547	175,026	161,802	37,980	38,714	26,618	19,189
Odisha	95,476	49,660	34,788	44,711	228,924	160,518	163,704	169,711	41,707	30,937	21,251	26,345
Punjab	125,336	96,708	88,596	44,230	205,870	191,985	180,015	184,530	60,881	50,373	49,216	23,969
Rajasthan	58,850	61,331	85,757	52,948	228,055	176,653	183,875	154,655	25,805	34,719	46,639	34,236
Tamil Nadu	140,523	78,465	49,608	31,392	243,642	190,340	175,038	168,743	57,676	41,224	28,341	18,604
Uttar Pradesh	116,561	67,734	33,168	20,633	228,459	196,538	161,668	163,243	51,020	34,464	20,516	12,639
West Bengal	128,750	74,031	40,296	28,564	231,018	203,350	178,487	156,567	55,731	36,406	22,576	18,244

(continued)

Table 6.3 (continued)

State	Labour productivity (INR)				Capital intensity (INR)				Capital productivity (INR)			
	1980–89	1990–99	2000–09	2010–14	1980–89	1990–99	2000–09	2010–14	1980–89	1990–99	2000–09	2010–14
17 States	77,968	132,356	182,358	208,839	158,722	337,394	621,651	1,019,278	48,494	39,901	29,535	20,671

Source GOI-MOS&PI

Table 6.4 Annual rate of growth in partial productivity measures in organised food manufacturing at 2004–05 prices

State	Labour productivity (%)				Capital intensity (%)				Capital productivity (%)			
	1980–89	1990–99	2000–09	2010–14	1980–89	1990–99	2000–09	2010–14	1980–89	1990–99	2000–09	2010–14
Andhra Pradesh	11.4	4.5	3.7	4.9	8.9	10.0	4.3	11.0	2.3	−5.0	−0.6	−5.5
Assam	11.6	−0.6	2.9	1.5	9.9	5.2	2.8	7.8	1.6	−5.5	0.1	−5.9
Bihar	18.6	12.0	−0.4	17.8	23.8	13.1	3.0	3.3	−4.1	−1.0	−3.4	14.0
Gujarat	9.1	3.4	4.6	−3.6	7.8	6.9	2.3	10.9	1.3	−3.2	2.2	−13.1
Haryana	11.0	7.6	9.1	−26.5	6.3	12.2	10.7	3.9	4.5	−4.1	−1.5	−29.3
Himachal Pradesh	5.4	9.1	2.7	−8.5	0.5	10.0	0.6	4.4	4.8	−0.9	2.0	−12.3
Jammu & Kashmir	10.3	2.7	7.3	12.8	11.4	4.2	−0.5	6.0	−1.0	−1.5	7.9	6.5
Karnataka	14.2	6.8	8.5	−2.2	10.3	8.0	6.6	3.3	3.5	−1.0	1.8	−5.4
Kerala	1.1	1.0	1.0	1.2	1.1	1.1	1.0	1.1	1.0	1.0	1.0	1.1
Madhya Pradesh	17.4	5.5	9.1	−21.6	19.8	16.2	3.2	−0.8	−2.0	−9.2	5.8	−20.9
Maharashtra	14.8	6.7	3.0	6.7	10.2	5.3	5.9	4.8	4.2	1.4	−2.8	1.8
Odisha	3.5	2.8	8.1	−14.5	8.0	10.9	7.6	10.0	−4.2	−7.4	0.5	−22.3
Punjab	4.4	4.0	3.5	9.0	5.5	5.6	5.0	5.0	−1.0	−1.6	−1.4	3.8
Rajasthan	8.4	7.2	9.3	5.8	5.5	8.2	0.1	9.4	2.7	−1.0	9.2	−3.3
Tamil Nadu	11.6	2.3	4.6	2.8	9.5	6.4	5.4	4.4	1.9	−3.9	−0.8	−1.5
Uttar Pradesh	12.7	8.4	3.2	−4.1	13.6	11.3	9.1	3.0	−0.8	−2.7	−5.4	−6.9
West Bengal	10.3	1.2	10.6	−3.7	8.4	8.2	4.9	10.5	1.7	−6.5	5.5	−12.8

(continued)

Table 6.4 (continued)

State	Labour productivity (%)				Capital intensity (%)				Capital productivity (%)			
	1980–89	1990–99	2000–09	2010–14	1980–89	1990–99	2000–09	2010–14	1980–89	1990–99	2000–09	2010–14
17 States	12.41	5.24	5.02	−0.04	10.59	8.06	5.55	6.65	1.64	−2.61	−0.51	−6.27

Source GOI-MOS&PI

measures, the performance indicates a phenomenal increase in capital intensity and labour productivity. The capital productivity growth rate decelerated, which may indicate that capacity utilisation was low. The processed food sector performed better in the low per capita income states—Bihar, Madhya Pradesh and Jammu and Kashmir. The much higher rate of growth in capital intensity and labour productivity in the processed food sector suggests that this segment of manufacturing has been growing rapidly—due to an increase in demand for processed commodities, owing to rising per capita income and urbanisation.

Capital intensity grew at a higher rate than labour productivity in the pre-reform period, but the growth rate of both fell in the post-reform period. The average growth rate of labour productivity decreased almost 2% from 1990 to 2014 in some states. The growth rate of capital intensity continues to be higher than labour productivity in each decade. The growth rate of capital productivity increased from 1980 to 2014 only in a few states—Andhra Pradesh, Gujarat, Himachal Pradesh, Odisha, Rajasthan and West Bengal—and fell in other states.

The main concern, however, is a consistent fall in the labour intensity—from an average 0.68 in the 1980s to less than 0.50 in the 1990s to 0.10 in 2014–15. The decline in labour intensity in the organised food and beverage segment is not as sharp or steep as in manufacturing overall (Fig. 6.1). It may imply that the segment has the potential to absorb people, though at a slower pace. The labour intensity has declined rapidly except in Assam, Jammu and Kashmir and Tamil Nadu, where the decline less sharp. Clearly, capital is substituted for labour, and the faster increase in capital intensity explains the increase in labour productivity in every state (Table 6.5).

The correlation coefficient between workers per factory (employment) and capital intensity is estimated at −0.68, statistically significant at 1% level for all states together. The scale of operations (captured through GVA per factory) is positively correlated with employment. Employment is negatively correlated with the wage

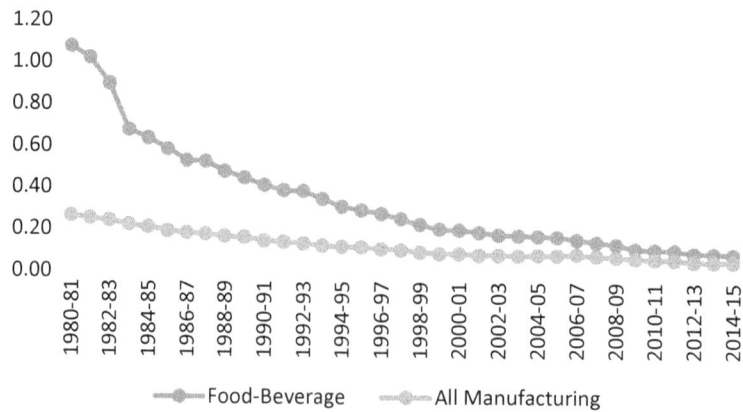

Fig. 6.1 Labour intensity in food and overall manufacturing: 1980–81 to 2014–15

Table 6.5 Labour intensity in the organised foods and beverages industry (decadal averages)

State	Labour intensity			
	1980–89	1990–99	2000–09	2010–14
Andhra Pradesh	0.85	0.44	0.21	0.12
Assam	0.80	0.36	0.25	0.19
Bihar	1.17	0.28	0.12	0.09
Gujarat	0.44	0.25	0.14	0.09
Haryana	0.75	0.40	0.17	0.07
Himachal Pradesh	0.45	0.25	0.10	0.06
Jammu & Kashmir	0.76	0.38	0.18	0.13
Karnataka	0.50	0.24	0.12	0.07
Kerala	3.02	1.43	0.80	0.48
Madhya Pradesh	1.19	0.22	0.09	0.07
Maharashtra	0.34	0.19	0.11	0.07
Odisha	0.79	0.41	0.22	0.14
Punjab	0.62	0.28	0.21	0.14
Rajasthan	0.37	0.19	0.14	0.10
Tamil Nadu	0.80	0.34	0.19	0.12
Uttar Pradesh	0.88	0.29	0.11	0.06
West Bengal	0.94	0.42	0.19	0.10
17 States	0.68	0.31	0.17	0.10

Source GOI-MOS&PI

rate, indicating that increasing capital intensity and wage rate adversely affected labour demand. These findings affirm the findings in earlier studies, including in World Bank (2014), on the factors associated with a slow growth in employment in the organised food industry.

6.2.2   Relative Position of States in Key Industry Indicators

Many state governments encourage private investment, and ranking states helps disaggregate the growth prospects by state. The relative size of food manufacturing varies by state, and little changed each decade. Table 6.6 provides the details on each state's share in employment, investment and output. The share of factories increased in Andhra Pradesh, Himachal Pradesh, Jammu and Kashmir, Kerala, Maharashtra, Odisha, Punjab and Rajasthan. The employment share increased in some states from 1980 to 2014. In the 2010–14 period, the highest employment share was in Maharashtra (19.2%), Uttar Pradesh (16.3%) and Karnataka (10.7%). The share of employment in organised food manufacturing increased only in Karnataka—from 7.5% in

Table 6.6 States' share in factories, employment, investment and output in organised food manufacturing

State	Factories (%)				Employment (%)				Capital stock (%)				Gross value-added (GVA) (%)			
	1980–89	1990–99	2000–09	2010–14	1980–89	1990–99	2000–09	2010–14	1980–89	1990–99	2000–09	2010–14	1980–89	1990–99	2000–09	2010–14
Andhra Pradesh	19.9	23.9	25.6	21.8	9.5	9.7	11.0	8.6	9.2	9.3	10.6	9.4	8.0	9.4	11.1	9.6
Assam	4.5	3.5	3.8	3.8	5.4	4.4	2.8	2.5	5.4	4.8	3.4	2.8	9.0	5.2	2.7	3.1
Bihar	2.6	1.3	0.8	2.2	1.8	1.5	1.1	1.9	1.8	1.6	1.2	1.7	2.1	1.3	0.9	1.2
Gujarat	6.1	5.2	5.5	5.9	8.7	6.9	6.1	6.6	9.3	7.5	6.6	6.7	6.8	5.9	6.7	8.1
Haryana	2.1	2.7	2.2	2.1	2.0	2.7	3.1	4.4	2.0	2.6	3.1	4.1	2.6	3.4	4.0	4.9
Himachal Pradesh	0.1	0.2	0.4	0.5	0.1	0.4	0.7	1.4	0.2	0.3	0.6	1.2	0.2	0.2	0.6	1.8
Jammu & Kashmir	0.3	0.3	0.4	0.5	0.3	0.2	0.3	0.3	0.2	0.2	0.3	0.3	0.2	0.3	0.2	0.5
Karnataka	6.3	5.4	6.0	6.1	7.5	6.6	8.8	10.7	7.7	6.8	8.5	10.1	6.2	6.0	9.7	10.9
Kerala	3.2	3.4	4.6	4.5	1.6	2.5	2.1	2.0	1.7	2.2	2.3	2.2	4.2	4.5	3.4	3.3
Madhya Pradesh	4.4	3.9	2.2	2.3	2.8	6.5	4.0	3.6	2.2	5.2	4.0	3.7	2.5	4.9	4.8	4.7
Maharashtra	8.1	8.8	9.2	9.3	24.0	19.0	19.7	19.2	22.8	19.6	19.8	18.9	17.7	19.4	18.0	17.7
Odisha	1.8	1.7	2.3	2.8	0.6	1.2	1.3	1.2	0.7	1.0	1.2	1.3	0.6	0.8	0.9	1.6
Punjab	5.4	5.9	7.4	8.5	5.8	6.3	5.3	3.9	5.4	6.3	5.5	4.4	6.8	8.1	9.3	5.2
Rajasthan	2.0	2.0	2.2	2.4	2.2	2.5	1.9	2.7	2.3	2.3	2.0	2.6	1.2	2.0	3.2	4.3
Tamil Nadu	15.8	16.5	15.3	15.8	8.5	10.0	9.4	9.3	9.4	10.0	9.5	9.5	11.0	10.5	9.2	8.6
Uttar Pradesh	12.1	10.7	7.2	6.3	15.3	16.2	18.7	16.3	15.8	16.7	17.5	16.2	16.4	14.7	12.2	10.0
West Bengal	5.2	4.6	5.0	5.1	3.8	3.4	3.9	5.4	4.0	3.6	4.0	5.1	4.5	3.3	3.1	4.5
India	100	100	100	100	100	100	100	100	100	100	100	100	100	100	100	100

Source GOI-MOS&PI

the 1980s to 11% in 2014. An oddity can be seen in the case of Assam—its share in employment decreased significantly from 5.4% in the 1980s to 2.5% in 2014.

The food industry is growing at a much faster rate in the less developed states—Odisha, Rajasthan and West Bengal. This is a promising sign in view of the surplus labour force in agriculture and the high incidence of rural poverty in these states. The processed food sector is growing in these poorer states although these states account for a much lower share in the number of factories, workers and output. The growth rate in factories and employment in some of these states has not been impressive. The share of food processing in investment and output in lagging states (Bihar, and Madhya Pradesh) and some agriculturally advanced states (Punjab and Andhra Pradesh) have increased; few show discernible trends, however.

6.3 Relative Position of Organised Food in Overall Organised Manufacturing

We examine the position of the processed food industry vis-à-vis the overall industry to gauge whether the reforms initiated by the states have helped it grow and upgrade its share in employment, investment and output.

In the past, the central government had announced several reform measures to encourage private investment in processed food. The ongoing fiscal incentives are supplemented with a policy change to allow 100% foreign direct investment (FDI) in retail business in food products, ease of doing business through fast clearance and the creation of the necessary infrastructure. The National Mission on Food Processing would scale up these efforts at the state level, with technological and logistical support from the centre. The centrally sponsored schemes have a three-tier structure—national, state and district level—and aim at improving outreach by offering states and union territories greater flexibility in supervision and monitoring. In tandem with concerted efforts to boost agricultural growth under the Rashtriya Krishi Vikas Yojana, National Food Security Mission and National Horticulture Mission, these reforms are expected to accelerate investment and productivity in food processing in the states.

Figures 6.2, 6.3, 6.4 and 6.5 depict the relative position of the processed food manufacturing sector in terms of its share in total organised segment's factories, employment, output and investment. The status of these and some other indicators are furnished in Annex Tables 6.9 and 6.10. At the national level, the processed food share continues to be almost the same in factories (18%), employment (14%), investment (8%) and GVA (8%). Only in the case of employment, there is a change—a slight downward trend during the second phase of the post-reform period, from early 2000. The average decadal share of employment increased from 10% in the 1980s to 26% in the 1990s, but it fell drastically to 13.85% in the 2000s and in the 2010–14 period. But there were large variations in each of these indicators at the state level.

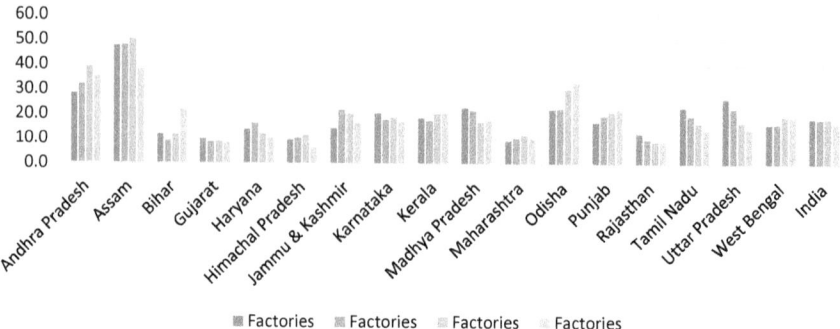

Fig. 6.2 Number of organised food–beverage factories as a percentage of total factories in organised manufacturing

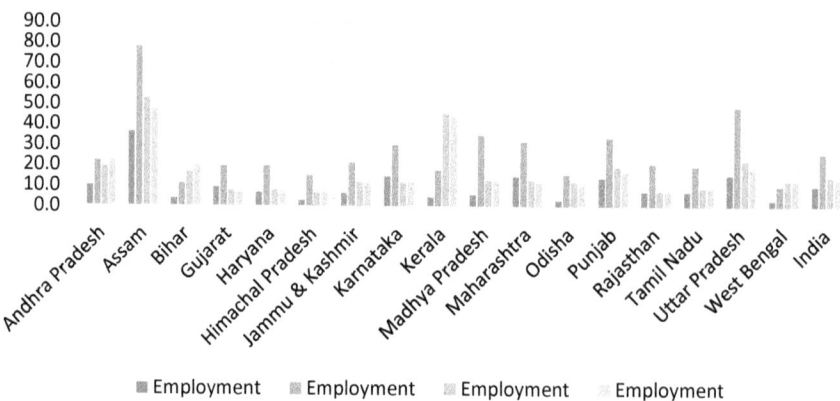

Fig. 6.3 Food industry employment as a percentage of total organised industry employment

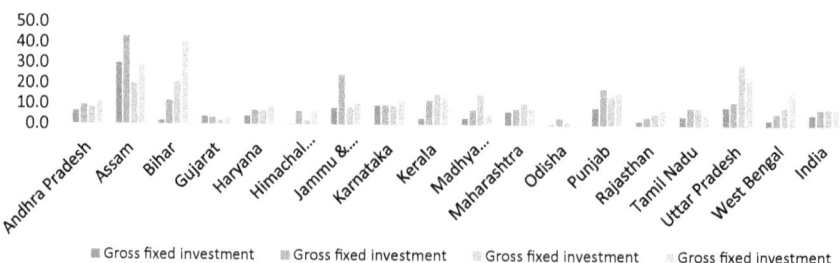

Fig. 6.4 Investment in food manufacturing as a percentage of total organised manufacturing investment

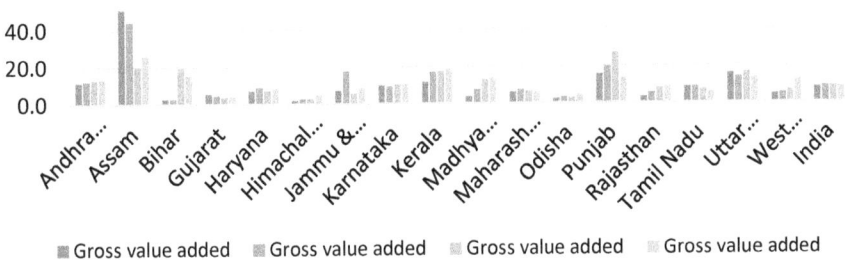

Fig. 6.5   Food industry gross value-added (GVA) as a percentage of total organised industry GVA

The food industry in Andhra Pradesh, Assam and Odisha occupies the highest share in factories (over 30%), followed by Uttar Pradesh, Tamil Nadu, Madhya Pradesh and Kerala. Andhra Pradesh, Assam, Uttar Pradesh and Kerala have a higher share in employment (over 20%). The share of workers in total workers fell in the post-reform period in all the states except Bihar and Kerala, but there was a revival in the 2010–14 period in Andhra Pradesh, Bihar, Himachal Pradesh, Karnataka and Rajasthan.

As shown in Fig. 6.4, Assam, Bihar, Jammu and Kashmir and Uttar Pradesh stand out in the share of fixed investment in organised food manufacturing in total organised manufacturing. In Bihar, the share increased from 2% in the 1980s to 41% in 2014; its share of factories, employment and output in total organised manufacturing escalated in the past four decades. Uttar Pradesh's share in investment grew from 9.3% in 1980 to 22.5% in 2014. Assam attracted the next highest share in investment, and it tops in the share of highest employment in the organised food manufacturing out of total organised manufacturing. Assam is followed by Kerala, which accounts for 43% of the share of employment in 2014; it rose from 4.9% in the 1980s.

Assam, Andhra Pradesh, Bihar, Kerala and Uttar Pradesh have a 10–20% share in the share of GVA in food in total manufacturing. Punjab also shows a high share (over 10%). The share of GVA in total GVA has either gone up in most states or stayed the same (Fig. 6.5). The food industry is much behind the manufacturing industry overall in capital intensity and labour productivity. The relative position of key indicators (ratios of food to overall manufacturing) is less than 1, indicating that productivity is much lower in the food industry than in overall manufacturing in the states. The ratio is close to 1 for the wage rate and over 1 for labour intensity (Annex Tables 6.9 and 6.10).

We compare the annual growth rate from 2000–01 to 2014–15 in the key indicators of the organised foods and beverages sector with that in the manufacturing industry overall (Table 6.7). The number of food processing factories grew at 3.33% for all the states together, and the number of manufacturing industry factories grew at 4.61%, but the growth rate was higher in food processing factories in West Bengal, Punjab, Odisha and Bihar than in manufacturing industry factories. The number of workers in the processed food sector grew at a higher rate in West Bengal, Rajasthan, Madhya Pradesh and Bihar than in the rest of the states. The only anomaly is seen in the case of Andhra Pradesh—the growth rate in the number of workers in aggregate industry was negative. From 2000 to 2014, overall employment grew in both food (2.20% per annum) and overall manufacturing (4.41% per annum). Labour intensity was negative in every state in the case of foods and beverages and overall manufacturing, but labour productivity growth was positive in almost every state, 1–9.7% per annum. Labour productivity growth was negative in Punjab and Bihar, though capital intensity grew at above 4% per annum.

The growth rate in capital intensity and labour productivity was high and positive; it indicates that the growth rate in capital productivity was negative. The growth rate in labour productivity was much higher in the food industry than in overall manufacturing, but it lags much behind the non-food segment. Labour productivity rose faster in the non-food-processing sector, but wages increased more rapidly in the food sector. Labour productivity declined sharply in Gujarat, Haryana, Himachal Pradesh, Karnataka, Madhya Pradesh, Odisha, Uttar Pradesh and West Bengal. Worryingly, the food and non-food segments' labour absorption capacity has fallen. A reduction in the absorptive capacity of labour in food and non-food segments is worrisome and can be explained by an increasing capital intensity and wage rate. Literature has also highlighted the role of stringent labour regulations, seen as causing significant inflexibilities in the labour market but this issue remains controversial in explaining a slow pace of employment growth (Bhattacharjea 2019).

6.4 Conclusions

The organised foods and beverages industry grew steadily since 1980–81, but large temporal and spatial differences exist in the number of factories, persons engaged, investment and GVA. The food industry grew significantly in the 1980s, but the growth rate in factories and employment slowed in the 1990s, coinciding with the first phase of the post-reform period, and revived in the 2000s. By 2014–15, nearly 96,367 enterprises provided employment to 1.8 million people, growing at a rate of 2.20% in the 2000–15 period; much of the progress was realised in the 2000s, during the second phase of the post-reform period. Capital invested per factory grew more

Table 6.7 Annual rate of growth in key performance indicators in organised food–beverage vis-à-vis total manufacturing (2000–01 to 2014–15)

State	Factories (No.)		Workers (No.)		GVA/factory		Labour productivity		Capital productivity		Capital intensity	
	FoodBev (%)	All (%)	FoodBev (%)	All (%)	FoodBev (%)	All (%)	FoodBev (%)	All (%)	FoodBev (%)	All (%)	FoodBev (%)	All (%)
Andhra Pradesh	1.00	2.19	0.30	−2.57	1.99	0.26	2.71	5.16	−3.82	−6.63	6.79	12.63
Assam	3.72	7.60	1.67	4.48	1.56	−3.06	3.61	−0.16	−0.19	−0.79	3.80	0.63
Bihar	13.19	7.52	7.13	6.90	−7.12	2.35	−1.87	2.95	−5.04	11.43	3.34	−7.61
Gujarat	4.52	4.76	3.72	6.05	2.28	2.80	3.07	1.55	−1.77	−1.46	4.93	3.05
Haryana	1.74	3.81	0.84	6.99	3.86	3.40	4.79	0.33	−6.43	−2.07	11.99	2.46
Himachal Pradesh	6.84	16.22	12.25	16.22	9.19	2.40	3.93	2.40	−0.62	1.01	4.57	1.37
Jammu & Kashmir	5.73	9.00	5.43	8.77	9.39	11.30	9.70	11.54	6.72	5.82	2.79	5.41
Karnataka	3.90	4.84	3.14	5.82	3.40	2.73	4.15	1.78	−3.06	−2.12	7.44	3.99
Kerala	3.62	3.33	1.04	2.04	−0.44	−0.54	2.09	0.72	−3.78	−1.89	6.11	2.66
Madhya Pradesh	3.44	2.99	4.27	3.38	2.66	1.19	1.85	0.82	−1.68	−2.72	3.59	3.64
Maharashtra	3.27	4.28	2.21	4.38	0.53	2.84	1.57	2.73	−3.76	−0.40	5.54	3.15
Odisha	5.97	4.48	3.42	7.54	4.93	6.30	7.51	3.28	0.89	−6.11	6.57	9.99
Punjab	6.25	5.28	1.23	4.93	−5.63	0.50	−0.95	0.84	−5.89	−0.43	5.25	1.28
Rajasthan	4.48	4.59	6.72	6.34	5.89	3.62	3.66	1.91	0.02	0.09	3.64	1.82
Tamil Nadu	3.68	5.95	3.34	5.45	1.14	1.34	1.47	1.82	−4.11	−2.03	5.83	3.93
Uttar Pradesh	1.39	4.02	0.63	4.38	0.59	0.65	1.34	0.31	−6.43	−0.15	8.31	0.45
West Bengal	3.91	3.36	3.72	1.65	7.31	−0.60	7.51	1.08	−0.31	−3.39	7.83	4.63

(continued)

Table 6.7 (continued)

State	Factories (No.)		Workers (No.)		GVA/factory		Labour productivity		Capital productivity		Capital intensity	
	FoodBev (%)	All (%)	FoodBev (%)	All (%)	FoodBev (%)	All (%)	FoodBev (%)	All (%)	FoodBev (%)	All (%)	FoodBev (%)	All (%)
17 States	3.33	4.61	2.20	4.41	1.67	2.23	2.80	2.42	−3.50	−1.62	6.52	4.11

than fourfold after 2000, when investment grew by almost 20% per year. Employment also grew rapidly in some states in the preceding decade. The food processing industry expanded in each state, but its growth was fast mainly in low per capita income states that are significantly dependent on agriculture.

The performance of the food processing sector seen through partial productivity measures—capital intensity, labour productivity and capital productivity—suggests that both capital intensity and labour productivity have increased phenomenally, whereas the rate of growth in capital productivity has decelerated and turned negative. An increase in capital deepening seems to have taken place because of an increasing substitution of capital for labour. Labour productivity has increased at an annual rate of 2.80%, which can be explained by the high growth rate in capital intensity (6.52%). However, labour productivity in the food industry lags that of the non-food segment. Labour productivity has risen faster in the non-food-processing sector, but wages have increased more rapidly in the food sector. Further, capital productivity has almost converged, but significant gaps remain in wage rates and labour productivity in favour of the non-food industry.

Underlying these trends, however, is a rapid decline in labour intensity (L/K)—from a decadal average of 0.68 in the 1980s to 0.10 in the 2010–15 period, which may be explained by the rising wage rate apart from the growing capital intensity. This may imply that the increase in food industry output has not generated adequate growth in employment and, hence, reduced the employment elasticity. Consistent with this trend, labour productivity has increased, while capital productivity (GVA/capital) has declined.

A negative rate of growth in capital productivity (GVA per Capital) indicates a lower capacity utilisation in this industry. The capacity utilisation, captured through capital per GVA, was higher in the 2010–14 period (average value 4.89) than in the 1980–89 period (average value 2.07). The scenario was similar across the states though the estimated value differed widely. Overall, the growth rate in capacity utilisation, negative at 1.61% in the 1980s, rose to 2.68% in the 1990s, slowed down to 0.51 in the 2000s and jumped to 6.69% in the 2010–14 period. Labour productivity and capital intensity in the processed food sector were higher in Bihar, Gujarat, Himachal Pradesh, Karnataka, Madhya Pradesh, Maharashtra, Punjab, Rajasthan and Uttar Pradesh. The food industry's labour absorption capacity fell in all the states; it may be explained by a rapid increase in the capital intensity and wage rate or by stringent labour laws and regulations, but it is a matter of concern.

Annex

See Tables 6.8, 6.9 and 6.10.

Table 6.8 Employment, GVA and capital stock in organised food manufacturing (2004–05 price)

State	Factories (INR lakh)				Employment (INR lakh)				Gross value-added (GVA) (INR lakh)				Capital stock (INR lakh)			
	1980–89	1990–99	2000–09	2010–14	1980–89	1990–99	2000–09	2010–14	1980–89	1990–99	2000–09	2010–14	1980–89	1990–99	2000–09	2010–14
Andhra Pradesh	3567	5218	6107	7147	74,378	220,765	540,755	857,124	68,221	160,532	277,024	323,236	159,519	405,501	906,011	1,528,482
Assam	801	769	900	1251	42,789	99,249	135,336	250,294	76,917	88,319	66,223	103,046	94,109	209,936	287,354	456,468
Bihar	475	293	190	723	14,370	34,315	53,896	185,905	18,155	22,780	22,688	38,633	31,461	71,382	103,438	273,372
Gujarat	1092	1134	1301	1941	68,086	157,475	298,719	655,573	58,357	100,916	168,255	273,010	161,833	324,514	562,089	1,088,955
Haryana	384	593	530	682	15,619	61,312	152,218	434,980	22,609	57,490	100,380	165,982	34,688	111,666	261,120	665,801
Himachal Pradesh	21	45	96	168	1173	8577	31,983	144,233	1316	3671	15,686	59,130	2715	12,749	49,487	199,201
Jammu & Kashmir	50	69	100	150	2090	4724	16,412	31,162	1644	4316	6069	17,862	4036	10,140	28,469	55,742
Karnataka	1138	1171	1429	2005	58,990	149,999	430,441	1,065,774	52,675	101,819	241,913	365,657	133,202	296,790	721,523	1,649,284
Kerala	575	753	1095	1463	12,552	55,997	104,297	200,086	36,158	76,499	85,909	111,816	29,906	97,168	195,153	351,654
Madhya Pradesh	794	859	530	741	21,669	148,469	194,684	358,894	21,020	82,619	119,373	157,766	38,624	224,674	336,393	602,009
Maharashtra	1454	1927	2184	3038	189,145	433,069	965,363	1,907,519	150,688	329,530	449,743	592,242	396,754	851,186	1,689,637	3,086,408
Odisha	327	365	552	905	5,086	27,438	63,105	120,386	4,856	13,626	21,953	53,825	11,642	44,043	103,305	204,309
Punjab	961	1280	1762	2798	45,981	142,657	260,642	391,566	57,631	137,960	230,920	173,189	94,661	273,880	469,196	722,557
Rajasthan	354	445	533	800	17,285	56,574	93,261	270,945	10,172	34,698	79,978	143,459	39,420	99,940	171,484	419,031
Tamil Nadu	2824	3599	3654	5182	66,929	228,337	460,438	923,086	94,050	179,165	228,415	289,778	163,066	434,618	805,940	1,557,642
Uttar Pradesh	2172	2338	1709	2075	120,282	368,697	920,157	1,620,010	140,202	249,735	305,200	334,255	274,795	724,630	1,487,597	2,644,557
West Bengal	938	998	1183	1662	30,076	76,321	189,259	533,348	38,723	56,501	76,263	152,347	69,481	155,199	337,802	835,044
17 States	17,925	21,855	23,856	32,731	1,122,678	1,278,372	1,354,713	1,605,813	853,393	1,700,176	2,495,990	3,355,235	1,739,912	4,348,014	8,515,998	16,340,515

Table 6.9 Ratio of key performance indicators of food–beverage manufacturing in total organised manufacturing at 2004–05 price

State	GVA/factory				Capital stock/factory				Labour productivity				Capital intensity			
	1980–89	1990–99	2000–09	2010–14	1980–89	1990–99	2000–09	2010–14	1980–89	1990–99	2000–09	2010–14	1980–89	1990–99	2000–09	2010–14
Andhra Pradesh	0.40	0.38	0.34	0.44	0.24	0.20	0.28	0.24	0.66	0.73	0.71	0.63	0.39	0.39	0.58	0.36
Assam	1.08	0.92	0.46	0.68	0.54	0.65	0.48	0.69	0.86	0.75	0.41	0.55	0.43	0.54	0.43	0.56
Bihar	0.22	0.50	2.08	0.78	0.08	0.20	0.44	0.62	0.36	0.53	1.32	0.85	0.13	0.26	0.29	0.69
Gujarat	0.55	0.52	0.41	0.49	0.45	0.40	0.32	0.33	0.57	0.47	0.44	0.61	0.47	0.37	0.35	0.41
Haryana	0.49	0.54	0.62	0.83	0.21	0.31	0.54	0.78	0.62	0.67	0.72	1.16	0.26	0.38	0.64	1.11
Himachal Pradesh	0.19	0.23	0.30	0.72	0.09	0.19	0.32	0.74	0.49	0.51	0.46	0.66	0.25	0.45	0.48	0.68
Jammu & Kashmir	0.52	0.82	0.42	0.52	0.20	0.40	0.72	0.63	0.79	1.05	0.61	0.70	0.33	0.50	1.04	0.89
Karnataka	0.47	0.51	0.58	0.66	0.40	0.46	0.52	0.63	0.63	0.70	0.80	0.93	0.53	0.63	0.72	0.88
Kerala	0.63	0.98	0.87	0.90	0.17	0.37	0.55	0.65	0.36	0.43	0.38	0.43	0.09	0.16	0.24	0.31
Madhya Pradesh	0.15	0.41	0.72	0.77	0.06	0.22	0.44	0.41	0.36	0.81	0.97	1.04	0.13	0.45	0.60	0.56
Maharashtra	0.65	0.71	0.61	0.58	0.66	0.61	0.72	0.82	0.63	0.64	0.50	0.50	0.63	0.55	0.60	0.70
Odisha	0.12	0.14	0.11	0.14	0.05	0.07	0.09	0.04	0.45	0.36	0.23	0.45	0.18	0.17	0.19	0.13
Punjab	0.94	1.01	1.26	0.66	0.31	0.47	0.69	0.63	0.92	1.13	1.19	0.86	0.31	0.52	0.66	0.83
Rajasthan	0.27	0.54	0.87	0.92	0.19	0.34	0.50	0.62	0.52	0.83	0.99	1.01	0.38	0.52	0.57	0.68
Tamil Nadu	0.37	0.45	0.46	0.44	0.24	0.33	0.42	0.49	0.61	0.70	0.72	0.64	0.39	0.51	0.67	0.73
Uttar Pradesh	0.60	0.62	0.96	0.93	0.25	0.39	1.00	1.43	0.57	0.52	0.66	0.72	0.24	0.33	0.68	1.11
West Bengal	0.29	0.34	0.33	0.64	0.16	0.21	0.33	0.49	0.63	0.67	0.54	0.95	0.36	0.42	0.54	0.74
17 states	0.47	0.57	0.67	0.65	0.25	0.34	0.49	0.60	0.59	0.68	0.68	0.75	0.32	0.42	0.54	0.67

Table 6.10 Ratio of key performance indicators of food–beverage manufacturing in total organised manufacturing at 2004–05 price

State	Capital productivity				Labour intensity				Wage rate			
	1980–89	1990–99	2000–09	2010–14	1980–89	1990–99	2000–09	2010–14	1980–89	1990–99	2000–09	2010–14
Andhra Pradesh	1.72	1.97	1.25	1.86	2.64	2.72	1.78	2.94	0.66	0.78	0.80	0.68
Assam	2.01	1.42	0.95	0.99	2.34	1.88	2.37	1.82	0.73	0.56	0.51	0.52
Bihar	3.33	2.30	5.10	1.20	11.70	4.05	3.80	1.47	0.45	0.70	1.40	1.46
Gujarat	1.21	1.28	1.27	1.51	2.14	2.75	2.90	2.46	0.61	0.71	0.78	0.81
Haryana	2.36	1.83	1.18	1.05	3.89	2.78	1.75	0.91	0.50	0.56	0.66	0.79
Himachal Pradesh	2.09	1.23	0.95	0.99	4.23	2.40	2.15	1.49	0.83	0.82	0.87	0.85
Jammu & Kashmir	2.52	2.16	0.57	0.79	3.22	2.23	0.98	1.13	0.59	0.75	0.79	0.85
Karnataka	1.18	1.11	1.12	1.07	1.95	1.59	1.43	1.15	0.50	0.73	0.78	0.81
Kerala	3.82	2.75	1.60	1.38	10.94	6.50	4.24	3.29	0.30	0.36	0.47	0.52
Madhya Pradesh	2.84	1.84	1.66	1.96	8.90	2.52	1.73	1.90	0.33	0.60	0.73	0.78
Maharashtra	0.99	1.17	0.84	0.71	1.61	1.82	1.69	1.42	0.65	0.73	0.68	0.74
Odisha	2.51	2.14	1.25	3.34	5.73	5.96	5.47	7.77	0.33	0.39	0.34	0.40
Punjab	3.05	2.19	1.81	1.03	3.35	1.95	1.56	1.21	0.66	0.78	0.81	0.90
Rajasthan	1.39	1.57	1.74	1.47	2.71	1.93	1.75	1.51	0.51	0.78	1.01	0.99
Tamil Nadu	1.56	1.40	1.09	0.89	2.60	2.00	1.52	1.38	0.44	0.63	0.72	0.69
Uttar Pradesh	2.46	1.59	1.04	0.65	4.44	3.07	1.58	0.91	0.58	0.71	0.82	0.97
West Bengal	1.78	1.69	1.01	1.30	2.83	2.52	1.88	1.36	0.52	0.54	0.53	0.63

(continued)

Table 6.10 (continued)

State	Capital productivity				Labour intensity				Wage rate			
	1980–89	1990–99	2000–09	2010–14	1980–89	1990–99	2000–09	2010–14	1980–89	1990–99	2000–09	2010–14
17 states	2.17	1.74	1.44	1.31	4.43	2.86	2.27	2.01	0.54	0.66	0.75	0.79

References

Ali, J., Singh, S. P., & Ekanem, E. (2007). *Efficiency and productivity changes in Indian food processing industry: Determinants and policy implications.* Presentation at 17th Annual World Food and Agribusiness Forum and Symposium on "Food Culture: Tradition, Innovation and Trust—A Positive Force for Modern Agribusiness" organized by the International Food and Agribusiness Management Association (IAMA) during June 23–26, 2007 at Parma, Italy.

Bathla, S. (2018). Productivity in food processing industry under varying trade regimes: Analysis across the Indian States. In A. Mitra (Ed.), *Economic growth in India: Its various dimensions* (Essays in Honour of Prof. B. B. Bhattacharya). Hyderabad: Orient BlackSwan.

Bhattacharjea, A. (2019). *Labour market flexibility in Indian industry: A critical survey of the literature.* Working papers 296, Centre for Development Economics, Delhi School of Economics.

Bhavani, T. A., Gulati, A., & Roy, D. (2006). Structure of the Indian food processing industry: Have reforms made a difference? In plate to plough: Agricultural diversification and its implications for the smallholders in India. Report Submitted to Ford Foundation by the International Food Policy Research Institute. Washington, DC.

Das, D. K., Wadhwa, D., & Kalita, G. (2009). *The employment potential of labor intensive industries in India's organized manufacturing.* Working Paper No. 236, Indian Council for Research on International Economic Relations (ICRIER).

EPW. (2005). Food processing—More recommendations. In *Economic and political weekly* (pp. 164).

GOI-MOS&PI. (1980 to 2015). Annual Survey of Industries, Centre Statistical Organisation, Ministry of Statistics and Programme Implementation, New Delhi.

Goldar, B. (2017), Growth, productivity and job creation in Indian manufacturing. In U. Kapila (Ed.), *India's economy pre-liberalisation to GST: Essays in honour of Raj Kapila* (pp. 619–652). New Delhi: Academic Foundation.

Hashim, D. A., Kumar, A., & Virmani, A. (2009). *Impact of major liberalization on productivity: The J curve hypothesis.* Working Paper No 5/2009, Department of Economic Affairs, Ministry of Finance.

Mitra, A. (1999). Total factor productivity growth and technical efficiency in Indian industries. *Economic and Political Weekly, 34*(31), M98–M105.

Mitra, A., Varoufakis, A., & Veganzones, M. A. (2002). Productivity and technical efficiency in Indian States' manufacturing: The role of infrastructure. *Economic Development and Cultural Change, 50*(2), 395–426.

Sidhu, M. S. (2005), Fruits and vegetable processing industry in India: An appraisal of the post-reform period. *Economic and Political Weekly,* 3056–3061.

World Bank. (2014). *India: Accelerating agricultural productivity growth.* Washington DC.

Chapter 7
Unorganised Food Processing Enterprises in India: Key Performance Indicators

N. Padmavathi and Parmod Kumar

7.1 Introduction

The agro-processing industry, particularly the food processing industry, plays a major role in rural development as it facilitates commercialization of agriculture and enhancement of factor income. It bridges gap between agriculture and manufacturing sector by processing agricultural produce and offering employment opportunities. The industry has the potential to enhance real income and mitigate rural outward migration. The value of India's food processing industry rose from USD 121 billion in 2012 to USD 194 billion in 2015 (ASSOCHAM 2017). The industry contributes around 8.80% of the gross value added (GVA) to the manufacturing sector and employs around 18% of its total labour force. The food processing industry is enormously important, and the Government of India accorded it high priority status in its National Manufacturing Policy, 2011, and extended to it several fiscal incentives (Rao 2009).

Like any other manufacturing industry, the food processing industry has two segments: organised and unorganised. The unorganised segment is much larger, and it has a sizeable number of highly labour-intensive enterprises, mostly located in rural areas. Unorganized food enterprises across the country generate substantial employment opportunities and relieve the pressure on agriculture. However, the efficiency of unorganised enterprises is low because they are not using employment and creating output to their full capacity (Bathla and Sharma 2012; Goldar 2014). The

This chapter is a part of ongoing Ph.D. research work titled "Performance of Unorganised Food Processing Industries in India" at ISEC, Bangalore.

N. Padmavathi (✉) · P. Kumar
Agricultural Development and Rural Transformation Centre, Institute for Social and Economic Change, Bangalore, Karnataka, India
e-mail: padmavathi@isec.ac.in

P. Kumar
e-mail: pkumar@isec.ac.in

153

uneven composition of organised and unorganised segments within manufacturing sector in different states lead to large inter-state variations in their performance due to varying quality of industrial activities (Papola et al. 2011).

The existing studies of unorganised manufacturing sector in India do not focus on its segments or changes within these segments (Trivedi 2004; Burange and Ranadive 2014; Goldar and Sadhukhan 2015). The unorganized food processing sector is the most labour-intensive sector in the Indian economy and the third largest employment provider. An understanding of the role of labour in the unorganized food processing sector and the factors determining labour productivity will be useful for making policy relating to this sector. Labour is the most important factor of production, and it is measured more easily than inputs such as capital, energy and raw materials.

Labour productivity is closely linked to economic growth, competitiveness and living standards in an economy, and therefore, it is an important economic indicator (International Labour Organisation (ILO)). Labour productivity is influenced mainly by capital intensity, firm size, skilled manpower, capacity utilisation and the real wage rate (Rath 2006). Compared to capital-intensive enterprises, labour-intensive enterprises offer greater earning stability but a lower remuneration package (Islam and Shazali 2011).

The determinants of labour productivity provide general information about the efficiency and quality of human capital in the production process in an economic and social context, including other complementary inputs and innovations used in production. Labour productivity is most likely to rise if the number of machines increases or if there is technical change that enhances the quality of capital (Balakrishnan 2004). Investing capital in enterprises and upgrading their technology will help increase labour productivity, raise employment and prevent under-employment.

Food, tobacco and textiles enterprises employed a large number of workers in both rural and urban locations (Banga, Bathla and Sharma 2008). However, these agro-enterprises lagged behind non-agro enterprises on labour productivity and capital intensity; an implication may be that the unorganized food processing sector is unprepared to adopt new innovations and technological advancements in a free trade regime.

In the short run, profit-maximizing firms continue to employ labour until the marginal labour productivity is equal to the real wage rate (Lal 1979); however, the profit-maximising scenario exists only in the long run where both capital and labour can change (Paul 2015). Comparing the performance of states would help to identify successful practices that states can adapt or replicate and induce healthy competition (Bhandari and Ray 2012).

This chapter aims to assess the performance of unorganized food processing enterprises across states, based on the key performance indicators: number of enterprises, employment, gross value added (GVA), capital investment and capital intensity. Further, the chapter also tries to examine the determinants of labour productivity using enterprises level data. Precisely, it attempts to answer the following questions.

1. Has the dualistic structure of food processing industry changed in the recent period?

2. What is the structure and composition of the unorganised food processing sector? How does it differ across states?
3. Which states and enterprises have experienced improvement on the key performance indicators?
4. What determines labour productivity in unorganised food enterprises?

Section 7.2 discusses the data sources and methodology. Section 7.3 describes the size and structure of India's food processing sector (organised and unorganised) based on select indicators between 2010–11 and 2015–16. It also examines the composition of unorganised food processing enterprises at the state level. Section 7.4 analyses the inter-linkages of selected performance indicators to understand the inter-temporal dynamics of enterprises across states. It also provides empirical estimates of the determinants of labour productivity based on data from the 73rd round (2015–16) of the National Sample Survey (NSS). Section 7.5 provides the conclusion.

7.2   Data and Methodology

We use unit-level records of the 67th (2010–11) and 73rd (2015–16) rounds of the NSSO titled "Unincorporated Non-agricultural Enterprises (Excluding Construction) in India". These rounds follow the NIC code 2008; food products belong to division 10 and beverages to division 11. The data for Telangana is presented separately from that for Andhra Pradesh in the 73rd round, but we club the data to enable comparison of the states and time periods. In all, 18,254 unorganised food processing enterprises were covered in the 67th round and 15,865 enterprises in the 73rd round; the survey covered 18 sub-sectors in the industry for all states and union territories. We have confined analysis to 15 major states covering more than 80% of the total sample. The data on organised manufacturing industry is extracted from the Annual Survey of Industries (ASI) for the period 2010–11 and 2015–16.

We use both descriptive and inferential statistics in this study, and we estimate the determinants of labour productivity using a linear regression model with robust standard errors. We identify the determinants of labour productivity in unorganised food enterprises based on the existing literature. We use the data on the gross state domestic product (GSDP) in agriculture and the GVA in manufacturing from the State Finances Database of the Reserve Bank of India (RBI). GVA in nominal terms was converted into real terms using the wholesale price index (WPI) of processed food products, beverages and tobacco at 2015–16 prices. The conversion was based on the single deflation method, due to data constraints, despite the relevance of the double deflation method (Balakrishnan and Pushpagandan 1994).

Fixed assets include various components (i.e. land and building, plant and machinery, transportation, others), which was adjusted for inflation using the appropriate price indices for each component. The land and building components were adjusted for inflation, using construction price index of price and quantum indices published by National Account Statistics (NAS), Government of India (GoI). WPI of food and beverage machinery index was used to account for the inflation with respect to plant and machinery. Transportation component has been adjusted for inflation with the help of WPI of auto and tempo. Finally, WPI of non-food articles was used to account for inflation with respect of other components of fixed assets. We obtained data on the Human Development Index (HDI) from the Ministry of Statistics and Programme Implementation (MOSPI), Government of India.

7.3   Structure and Size onf Food Processing Industry in India

The food processing industry accounts for 32% of India's food market. It contributes nearly 8.8% to the GVA of the manufacturing sector, 8.39% to the GVA of agriculture and allied sector, 13% to India's exports and 6% to total industrial investment (IBEF 2017). The food sector, including the tobacco sector, accounted for 1.6% of the national income in 2015–16, as per National Accounts Statistics. The processed food industry employs around 7 million people; it has the potential to attract $33 billion in investment by 2024 and generate employment for 9 million people (ASSOCHAM 2017).

Prevalence of both organised and unorganised sectors is termed as 'manufacturing dualism'. Persistence of duality has greater implications for efficiency and productivity, and it may cause income inequality in the economy (Kathuria et al. 2013). A few capital-intensive enterprises make up the small organised segment, and many labour-intensive enterprises located mostly in rural areas, make up the large unorganised segment. The organised food processing sector comprises less than 2% of enterprises, but it employs almost 26% of the industry's labour force and generates a whopping 72% of the GVA of the food processing industry (2015–16) (Table 7.1). The share of organised enterprises in the food processing industry increased marginally from 1.58% to 1.60% in the total food processing industry between 2010–11 and 2015–16. The shares of employment and GVA declined, though the GVA in absolute terms has increased nominally.

Unorganised food processing sector comprises 98.41% of enterprises. It employs 74.24% of the labour force and generates only 28% of the GVA. Rao and Dasgupta (2009) argue that the significance of the unorganised segment in terms of employment creation could be understood by the fact that 1% increase in employment in this segment creates 60,000 jobs as compared to mere 13,000 jobs created by the organised segment. Although, there is an increase in the number of unorganised enterprises and employment, their respective shares in the total food processing industry have remained more or less constant overtime. However, the GVA increased from 25.43% in from 2010–11 to 28% in 2015–16. The unorganised sector's share of GVA has grown more than that of the organised sector due to the more efficient use of resources, technological upgradation and positive spillover effects from the organised sector.

Table 7.1 Broad structure of food processing industry in India

Food processing industry	Year	Enterprises	Employment	GVA
		Number in lakh (%)	Number in lakh (%)	INR (crore)
Unorganised sector	2010–11	22.41 (98.46)	47.84 (74.23)	29,300 (25.44)
	2015–16	24.64 (98.43)	52.08 (74.69)	39,720 (27.66)
Organised sector	2010–11	0.35 (1.54)	16.61 (25.77)	85,861 (74.56)
	2015–16	0.39 (1.57)	17.65 (25.31)	103,878 (72.34)
Total	**2010–11**	**22.76 (100)**	**64.45 (100)**	**1,15,161.24 (100)**
	2015–16	**25.03 (100)**	**69.73 (100)**	**1,43,598 (100)**

Source Authors' computation using NSS 73rd and 67th rounds unit-level records and ASI. *Note* figures in parentheses are percentages to the total

The organised sector's share in employment has grown up, and therefore, the gap between the organised and unorganised sectors has shrunk gradually.

7.3.1 The Unorganised Food Processing Sector

About 65.88% of the unorganised food processing enterprises were located in rural areas in 2015–16, but a comparison of 2010–11 and 2015–16 reveals that enterprises are gradually moving from rural to urban areas. The food processing industry is dominated by own account enterprises[1]. In 2010–11, 80% of all enterprises all over India in rural and urban areas were own account enterprises, and this percentage has grown over time. In 2010–11, establishment enterprises made up 21.06% of all enterprises and the same fell to 20.22% in 2015–16 (Table 7.2).

Around 59% of this workforce is in rural areas, but a comparison of 2010–11 and 2015–16 shows that the rural part of India is gradually losing its dominance with respect to the share of enterprises, workforce and GVA. The data suggests that there is a shift in the share of enterprises, workforce and value addition (GVA) to the tune of three (3), six (6) and five (5) percent, respectively, from rural to urban enterprises over the period from 2010–11 to 2015–16. In 2015–16, around 60% of all workers worked for own account enterprises, and workers of OAEs in rural India alone constitute 40%

---

[1]The unorganised food processing sector includes Own Account Enterprises (OAEs) and establishment type of enterprises wherein OAEs are the enterprises which are run without any hired worker employed on a fairly regular basis. The establishments are the enterprise which employ at least one hired worker on a fairly regular basis with paid or unpaid apprentices. Paid household member/servant/resident workers in an enterprise are considered as hired workers.

Table 7.2 Structure of unorganised food processing enterprises

Indicator	Year	Rural			Urban			Combined		
		Own account enterprise (OAE)	Est	Total	OAE	Est	Total	OAE	Est	Total
Enterprises (no. in lakhs)	2010–11	13.02 (84.22)	2.45 (15.79)	15.46 (68.98)	4.68 (67.24)	2.28 (32.77)	6.96 (31.03)	17.7 (78.95)	4.72 (21.06)	22.42 (100)
	2015–16	13.93 (85.79)	2.31 (14.22)	16.24 (65.88)	5.74 (68.21)	2.68 (31.8)	8.41 (34.13)	19.66 (79.79)	4.99 (20.22)	24.65 (100)
Workers (no. in lakhs)	2010–11	20.3 (65.83)	10.54 (34.18)	30.83 (64.43)	7.86 (46.15)	9.17 (53.86)	17.03 (35.58)	28.15 (58.83)	19.71 (41.18)	47.85 (100)
	2015–16	21.16 (69.13)	9.45 (30.88)	30.61 (58.76)	10 (46.52)	11.5 (53.49)	21.49 (41.25)	31.15 (59.8)	20.95 (40.21)	52.09 (100)
GVA (INR in crore)	2010–11	7,780 (55.26)	6,300 (44.74)	14,080 (48.05)	5,250 (34.47)	9,980 (65.53)	15,230 (51.98)	13,000 (44.37)	16,300 (55.63)	29,300 (100)
	2015–16	10,000 (58.45)	7,110 (41.56)	17,110 (43.08)	7,510 (33.22)	15,100 (66.79)	22,610 (56.93)	17,510 (44.09)	22,210 (55.92)	39,720 (100)
Capital (INR in crore)	2010–11	13,927 (50.83)	13,472 (49.17)	27,400 (40.77)	13,100 (32.59)	27,100 (67.41)	40,200 (59.82)	26,800 (39.88)	40,400 (60.12)	67,200 (100)
	2015–16	14,600 (60.99)	9,340 (39.02)	23,940 (38.22)	13,400 (34.63)	25,300 (65.38)	38,700 (61.79)	28,000 (44.7)	34,640 (55.31)	62,640 (100)

Source Authors' computation using NSS 73rd and 67th rounds unit-level records
Note Figures in parentheses are percentage shares to their respective totals

of the total workforce for 2015–16. The share in total employment of own account enterprises has grown more in rural areas than in urban areas, and own account food processing enterprises are increasing more rapidly in urban areas than in rural areas. These findings are in line with the finding that people in rural areas who work in agriculture and allied activities during the cropping season set up own account enterprises to tide over seasonal unemployment (Bathla and Sharma 2009). Usually, the food processing accommodates illiterate and landless labourers, especially from rural areas, and the grip of own account enterprises over the industry continues to tighten, though their falling share in the GVA certainly accentuates concerns over their productivity (Rao and Dasgupta 2009).

About 67% of the workforce composed of males, and females make up slightly higher share of the workforce in rural areas than in urban. Only 10% of the total workforce works part time as of 2015–16; around 90% of the workforce work full time. A mere 23% of full-time workers, but 43% of part-time workers are female. Around 74.52% of the part-time workforce is engaged in rural enterprises. Females are more likely to be part-timers in rural areas than urban areas. The industry provides more employment to rural women.

The share of urban areas in the total GVA is larger than that of rural areas. Moreover, the GVA share of rural enterprises fell from 47.97% in from 2010–11 to 43.08% in 2015–16. On the contrary, share of urban enterprises in the total GVA rose from 52.04 to 58.93%. On the other hand, the share of own account enterprises in the total GVA is significantly lesser than establishment enterprises, and this has marginally decreased despite the increase in the share of enterprises and employment. A diametrically opposite pattern is observed in the case of establishment enterprises. Establishment enterprises have a larger share in the total GVA than own account enterprise, but the later generates more GVA than establishments in rural areas.

At the national level, establishment enterprises account for a maximum share in total capital, though it has decreased from 60.12% in 2010–11 to 55.31% in 2015–16. In rural areas, own account enterprises have a larger share in capital than establishment enterprises, and this share has increased from 50.83% to 60.99% over time—because the number of establishment enterprises in rural areas are gradually decreasing, and own account enterprises in rural areas are increasingly becoming capital-oriented. Similarly, the disparity in the share of fixed capital between OAEs and establishment enterprises is shrinking in urban areas overtime. Although urban area consists of larger number of OAEs than establishment enterprises, a large share of value addition and fixed assets comes mainly from establishment enterprises. Thus, establishment enterprises are performing better than OAEs both in urban and rural areas, probably due to the influence of organised enterprises and better infrastructure facilities.

7.3.2 Spatial Disparities in Unorganised Food Processing Enterprises

This section analyses the key performance indicators of the unorganised food processing industry such as spread of enterprises, employment pattern, value addition, capital investment, GVA per worker and capital-to-labour ratio across major states of the country. We selected 15 states: Andhra Pradesh, Assam, Bihar, Gujarat, Haryana, Karnataka, Kerala, Madhya Pradesh, Maharashtra, Odisha, Punjab, Rajasthan, Tamil Nadu, Uttar Pradesh and West Bengal. These states represent around 90% of the enterprises, 90.72% of employment and 91.18% of the GVA of all unorganised food processing enterprises. We segregated the data by location (rural, urban and combined), and we attempted disaggregation with respect to rural or urban areas by enterprise type.

Table 7.3 Shares of enterprises in unorganised food processing enterprises (UFPI) across the states (%): 2015–16

State	Rural			Urban			Combined			UFPI in UMS
	OAE	Est	Total[a]	OAE	Est	Total[a]	OAE	Est	Total	
AP	59.13	40.87	52.45	79.58	20.42	47.55	68.85	31.15	9.53	10.85
ASM	84.10	15.90	87.52	65.98	34.02	12.48	81.84	18.16	2.68	32.48
BHR	88.81	11.19	87.60	56.09	43.91	12.40	84.75	15.25	5.90	18.91
GUJ	88.82	11.18	49.85	61.21	38.79	50.15	74.97	25.03	3.90	7.73
HAR	82.02	17.98	45.27	55.31	44.69	54.73	67.40	32.60	1.00	13.45
KAR	84.48	15.52	50.35	66.60	33.40	49.65	75.61	24.39	5.17	10.21
KRL	63.12	36.88	51.69	59.17	40.83	48.31	61.21	38.79	3.13	14.14
MP	95.47	4.53	72.61	73.43	26.57	27.39	89.43	10.57	4.17	12.34
MAH	95.50	4.50	63.46	68.76	31.24	36.54	85.73	14.27	9.33	18.48
ODH	89.56	10.44	83.86	74.16	25.84	16.14	87.07	12.93	3.16	15.99
PNB	84.18	15.82	69.87	58.04	41.96	30.13	76.31	23.69	2.58	16.59
RAJ	94.76	5.24	56.92	82.37	17.63	43.08	89.42	10.58	4.13	13.54
TN	69.37	30.63	34.51	62.01	37.99	65.49	64.55	35.45	7.31	10.32
UP	86.67	13.33	72.11	77.50	22.50	27.89	84.12	15.88	14.24	15.88
WB	87.55	12.45	76.88	66.46	33.54	23.12	82.67	17.33	13.09	7.72
IND	**85.78**	**14.22**	**65.87**	**68.20**	**31.80**	**34.13**	**79.78**	**20.22**	**100**	**12.53**

Source Authors' computation using NSS 73rd round unit-level records

Notes UMS—Unorganised Manufacturing Sector;

[a]Percentage to combined total

AP—Andhra Pradesh, ASM—Assam, BHR—Bihar, GUJ—Gujarat, HAR—Haryana, KAR—Karnataka, KRL—Kerala, MP—Madhya Pradesh, MAH—Maharashtra, ODH—Odisha, PNB—Punjab, RAJ—Rajasthan, TN—Tamil Nadu, UP—Uttar Pradesh, WB—West Bengal, IND—All India

As shown in Table 7.3, Uttar Pradesh accounts for 14.24% of all enterprises, West Bengal 13.09% and Andhra Pradesh 9.53%. Haryana, Assam and Kerala have fewer enterprises. Most of the enterprises in Tamil Nadu, Haryana, Maharashtra, Gujarat and Karnataka are located in urban areas. Uttar Pradesh employs 13.62% of the workforce, Andhra Pradesh 12.67% and West Bengal 12.58%. Tamil Nadu and Maharashtra occupy the next two places. Punjab, Haryana, Assam and Odisha account for a smaller percentage. More than 50% of the workforce in Punjab, Madhya Pradesh, Kerala, Haryana and Andhra Pradesh work for urban enterprises. More than 50% of the workforce in Haryana, Madhya Pradesh, Maharashtra, Karnataka and Kerala work for establishments.

States that have a larger share of the working-age population account for a higher share in the total workforce and vice versa. The percentage of workers in the unorganised food processing sector in Andhra Pradesh, West Bengal, Tamil Nadu and Karnataka is higher than their percentage share in the working-age population (Table 7.4). Employment opportunities are better in these states, and therefore, the labour supply is greater (Trivedi 2004). Poor people make up a high proportion of the population of Assam, Bihar, Madhya Pradesh and Odisha (RBI 2011–2012). These states have few non-farm employment opportunities and only a small percentage of the workers work in the unorganised food processing sector. Non-farm employment opportunities are critical in reducing poverty as these tighten the labour market (especially rural) and serve as a safety net for people. Policy measures are needed urgently to improve the quality of employment in the unorganised food processing sector.

Tamil Nadu generates 12.73% of the total GVA, Uttar Pradesh 10.76%, Maharashtra 9.98% and West Bengal 9.91% (Table 7.5). Odisha, Haryana and Assam contribute a meagre percentage of the GVA. Enterprises are spread evenly across rural and urban areas in Gujarat, but urban enterprises, mainly establishments, contribute 80% to the GVA. Uttar Pradesh has the largest share of enterprises and the workforce; it ranked 10th with respect of contribution to the GVA per enterprise because the state has many own account enterprises and these generate less value per capita. States derive their major share of the GVA from rural areas, and own account enterprises account for the least share in the GVA of all enterprises. Rural enterprises contributed 75% of the GVA in Assam, Bihar and Odisha, and urban enterprises contributed 70% of the GVA in Gujarat, Rajasthan and Maharashtra.

We further assessed the regional disparities in capital investment by assets per enterprise (Table 7.6). The all-India value is INR 2.54 lakh, more than the value of assets in West Bengal, Odisha, Assam, Bihar, Andhra Pradesh, Madhya Pradesh and Uttar Pradesh, but less than in Gujarat (INR 7.18 lakh), Haryana (INR 5.80 lakh), Maharashtra (INR 4.34 lakh) and Tamil Nadu (INR 3.70 lakh). The asset value of enterprises in rural Maharashtra was less than the national average. The states (except Uttar Pradesh) that had an asset value below the national average also underperformed in rural India. The per-enterprise asset value was less than the national average in urban areas in many states; it was higher only in Haryana, Gujarat, Maharashtra and Karnataka. Capital assets are concentrated in a few states in urban India, and these states determine the mean value of assets.

Table 7.4 Share of workers in unorganised food processing enterprises across the states during 2015–16 (%)

State	Rural			Urban			Combined			UFPI in UMS
	OAE	Est	Total[a]	OAE	Est	Total[a]	OAE	Est	Total	
AP	28.44	71.56	61.08	65.55	34.45	38.92	42.88	57.12	12.67	19.17
ASM	75.65	24.35	85.92	38.06	61.94	14.08	70.36	29.64	2.05	27.66
BHR	82.37	17.63	84.04	39.94	60.06	15.96	75.60	24.40	4.55	19.46
GUJ	76.91	23.09	29.84	26.98	73.02	70.16	41.88	58.12	4.88	9.44
HAR	54.39	45.61	36.45	27.75	72.25	63.55	37.46	62.54	1.18	14.69
KAR	62.93	37.07	41.68	55.89	44.11	58.32	58.82	41.18	5.71	13.68
KRL	44.53	55.47	52.57	34.48	65.52	47.43	39.76	60.24	3.98	20.49
MP	91.35	8.65	62.56	53.59	46.41	37.44	77.21	22.79	3.10	11.12
MAH	87.51	12.49	52.06	42.41	57.59	47.94	65.89	34.11	8.43	17.53
ODH	78.47	21.53	78.95	61.45	38.55	21.05	74.89	25.11	2.75	16.89
PNB	68.89	31.11	55.66	39.76	60.24	44.34	55.98	44.02	2.12	16.09
RAJ	90.16	9.84	45.93	64.83	35.17	54.07	76.47	23.53	3.55	13.82
TN	36.98	63.02	38.01	36.13	63.87	61.99	36.45	63.55	9.56	14.47
UP	77.90	22.10	68.73	62.57	37.43	31.27	73.11	26.89	13.62	15.06
WB	77.23	22.77	72.05	42.00	58.00	27.95	67.39	32.61	12.58	9.42
IND	**69.12**	**30.88**	**58.75**	**46.51**	**53.49**	**41.25**	**59.80**	**40.20**	**100**	**14.42**

Source Authors' computation using NSS 73rd round unit-level records
Notes UMS—Unorganised Manufacturing Sector;
[a]Percentage to combined total
AP—Andhra Pradesh, ASM—Assam, BHR—Bihar, GUJ—Gujarat, HAR—Haryana, KAR—Karnataka, KRL—Kerala, MP—Madhya Pradesh, MAH—Maharashtra, ODH—Odisha, PNB—Punjab, RAJ—Rajasthan, TN—Tamil Nadu, UP—Uttar Pradesh, WB—West Bengal, IND—All India

Establishment enterprises had a higher asset value than own account enterprises. The asset value of own account enterprises was less than the national value in Assam, West Bengal, Odisha, Andhra Pradesh, Bihar and Madhya Pradesh, and the asset value of establishments was less than the national value in Bihar, West Bengal, Andhra Pradesh, Odisha, Assam, Uttar Pradesh, Punjab, Kerala and Tamil Nadu. The asset value was less than the national average on location and enterprise type in Bihar, Assam, West Bengal, Odisha and Andhra Pradesh. Thus, the enterprises in these states were less capital intensive, and capital assets were concentrated in most industrially developed states and in urban establishments and enterprises.

We compared the performance of the food processing industry (unorgnised) in states with that of the entire unorganised manufacturing sector. In Assam, the food processing industry makes up 32.48% of the total enterprises in the unorganised manufacturing sector and more than 25% of workers and GVA. But its role was negligible in the case of Gujarat because the share of unorganised food processing industry with respect to enterprises, workers and GVA is lesser than 10% in the entire

Table 7.5 Share of GVA in unorganised food processing enterprises across the states (%)

State	Rural			Urban			Combined			UFPI in UMS
	OAE	Est	Total[a]	OAE	Est	Total[a]	OAE	Est	Total	
AP	34.10	65.90	43.77	45.30	54.70	56.23	40.40	59.60	7.76	15.90
ASM	64.90	35.10	80.04	42.63	57.37	19.96	60.46	39.54	1.90	24.26
BHR	80.18	19.82	76.24	29.37	70.63	23.76	68.11	31.89	4.37	18.65
GUJ	69.56	30.44	20.18	17.23	82.77	79.82	27.79	72.21	7.05	7.99
HAR	48.25	51.75	35.21	27.48	72.52	64.79	34.79	65.21	1.84	14.75
KAR	38.01	61.99	39.04	41.05	58.95	60.96	39.86	60.14	7.64	15.69
KRL	22.61	77.39	49.72	18.54	81.46	50.28	20.56	79.44	5.89	22.64
MP	88.92	11.08	40.07	27.97	72.03	59.93	52.40	47.60	3.11	17.47
MAH	75.55	24.45	31.15	28.94	71.06	68.85	43.46	56.54	9.98	14.59
ODH	61.83	38.17	76.16	41.56	58.44	23.84	57.00	43.00	1.80	22.69
PNB	66.40	33.60	49.68	36.52	63.48	50.32	51.36	48.64	3.14	17.33
RAJ	79.53	20.47	29.62	50.79	49.21	70.38	59.30	40.70	3.61	11.84
TN	30.93	69.07	32.94	30.97	69.03	67.06	30.96	69.04	12.73	17.18
UP	68.90	31.10	51.60	55.58	44.42	48.40	62.46	37.54	10.76	16.13
WB	64.30	35.70	55.40	31.88	68.12	44.60	49.84	50.16	9.61	13.64
IND	**58.45**	**41.55**	**43.08**	**33.22**	**66.78**	**56.92**	**44.08**	**55.92**	**100**	**14.77**

Source Authors' computation using NSS 73rd round unit-level records
Notes UMS—Unorganised Manufacturing Sector;
[a]Percentage to grand total
AP—Andhra Pradesh, ASM—Assam, BHR—Bihar, GUJ—Gujarat, HAR—Haryana, KAR—Karnataka, KRL—Kerala, MP-Madhya Pradesh, MAH-Maharashtra, ODH—Odisha, PNB—Punjab, RAJ—Rajasthan, TN-Tamil Nadu, UP—Uttar Pradesh, WB—West Bengal, IND—All India

unorganised manufacturing sector. Interestingly, the food processing enterprises in Kerala and Tamil Nadu accounted for smaller share; however, their share of workforce and GVA were relatively higher in the unorganised manufacturing sector.

7.3.2.1 GVA Per Worker

The GVA of the states alone cannot be considered as a good measure of the sector's performance; therefore, we computed the GVA per worker for each state. Table 7.7 shows GVA per worker to be highest in Haryana, Kerala and Punjab and lowest in Andhra Pradesh, Odisha and West Bengal. The GVA per worker was below the national average in Assam, Bihar and Uttar Pradesh. Although states like Uttar Pradesh and West Bengal accounted for higher share in the total GVA generation, GVA per worker in these states is below the national average. Higher shares of workforce of these states brought down their per worker GVA generation.

Table 7.6 Capital per enterprise in unorganised food processing across the states during 2015–16 (INR in lakh)

State	Rural			Urban			Combined		
	OAE	Est	Total	OAE	Est	Total	OAE	Est	Total
AP	0.71	1.63	1.16	1.34	7.38	2.37	1.04	2.68	1.64
ASM	0.44	4.57	1.10	0.71	3.33	1.60	0.47	4.28	1.16
BHR	1.04	1.54	1.10	1.57	2.30	1.89	1.09	1.81	1.20
GUJ	1.76	5.83	2.21	5.02	23.29	12.11	3.09	19.40	7.18
HAR	3.30	10.09	4.52	3.41	11.13	6.86	3.35	10.87	5.80
KAR	1.57	6.21	2.29	2.51	8.85	4.63	1.98	8.00	3.45
KRL	1.48	6.26	3.24	1.68	6.49	3.64	1.57	6.38	3.44
MP	1.09	3.08	1.18	2.36	10.46	4.52	1.38	8.16	2.09
MAH	1.03	9.58	1.41	3.48	22.52	9.43	1.75	19.93	4.34
ODH	0.56	3.89	0.91	0.65	2.92	1.24	0.58	3.58	0.96
PNB	1.75	4.10	2.12	2.86	7.01	4.60	2.00	5.65	2.87
RAJ	1.18	6.36	1.45	2.49	14.11	4.54	1.70	11.93	2.78
TN	2.05	8.72	4.09	1.97	5.98	3.49	2.00	6.80	3.70
UP	1.40	3.50	1.68	2.79	7.45	3.84	1.76	5.06	2.28
WB	0.45	2.45	0.70	0.64	3.54	1.61	0.48	2.93	0.91
IND	**1.05**	**4.05**	**1.47**	**2.34**	**9.46**	**4.60**	**1.42**	**6.95**	**2.54**

Source Authors' computation using NSS 73rd round unit-level records
AP—Andhra Pradesh, ASM—Assam, BHR—Bihar, GUJ—Gujarat, HAR—Haryana, KAR—Karnataka, KRL—Kerala, MP—Madhya Pradesh, MAH—Maharashtra, ODH—Odisha, PNB—Punjab, RAJ—Rajasthan, TN—Tamil Nadu, UP—Uttar Pradesh, WB—West Bengal, IND-All India

The enterprises belonging to rural areas demonstrated the same pattern as that of all India with respect to per worker GVA in the ranking of states, but urban enterprises' order of ranking deviates minutely from that of the all-India pattern: Maharashtra, Punjab and Gujarat are the three best-performing states. The GVA per worker of own account enterprises was mostly identical to the all-India pattern, barring Kerala. Establishment enterprises performed best in Madhya Pradesh, Maharashtra and Karnataka. The data segregation based on sector (rural or urban) and enterprise type (OAE or establishment) show that rural enterprises and own account enterprises determined the overall position of states on GVA per worker.

7.3.2.2 Capital-to-Labour Ratio

The capital-to-labour ratio is considered as a proxy for technological upgradation. It is a crucial determinant of an enterprise's productivity (Majumder 2004). We obtained

Table 7.7 GVA per worker in unorganised food processing across the states during 2015–16 (INR in lakh)

State	Rural			Urban			Combined		
	OAE	Est	Total	OAE	Est	Total	OAE	Est	Total
AP	0.40	0.31	0.33	0.47	1.07	0.67	0.44	0.49	0.47
ASM	0.56	0.95	0.66	1.12	0.93	1.00	0.61	0.94	0.71
BHR	0.65	0.75	0.66	0.80	1.28	1.09	0.66	0.96	0.73
GUJ	0.67	0.98	0.75	0.80	1.42	1.25	0.73	1.37	1.10
HAR	1.02	1.30	1.15	1.20	1.22	1.21	1.11	1.24	1.19
KAR	0.58	1.60	0.96	0.78	1.42	1.07	0.69	1.49	1.02
KRL	0.54	1.49	1.07	0.64	1.49	1.20	0.58	1.49	1.13
MP	0.48	0.63	0.49	0.64	1.90	1.22	0.52	1.60	0.76
MAH	0.47	1.06	0.54	0.89	1.60	1.30	0.60	1.50	0.90
ODH	0.38	0.86	0.48	0.38	0.86	0.57	0.38	0.86	0.50
PNB	0.97	1.09	1.01	1.18	1.35	1.28	1.04	1.25	1.13
RAJ	0.44	1.04	0.50	0.79	1.41	1.01	0.60	1.34	0.78
TN	0.74	0.96	0.88	0.94	1.19	1.10	0.86	1.10	1.01
UP	0.40	0.64	0.45	0.83	1.11	0.93	0.51	0.84	0.60
WB	0.37	0.70	0.45	0.71	1.09	0.93	0.43	0.90	0.58
IND	**0.47**	**0.75**	**0.56**	**0.75**	**1.31**	**1.05**	**0.56**	**1.06**	**0.76**

Source Authors' computation using NSS 73rd round unit-level records
AP—Andhra Pradesh, ASM—Assam, BHR—Bihar, GUJ—Gujarat, HAR—Haryana, KAR—Karnataka, KRL—Kerala, MP—Madhya Pradesh, MAH—Maharashtra, ODH—Odisha, PNB—Punjab, RAJ—Rajasthan, TN—Tamil Nadu, UP—Uttar Pradesh, WB-West Bengal, IND—All India

the capital-to-labour ratio by dividing the total fixed assets of an enterprise by its total workforce.

Gujarat, Haryana and Maharashtra performed the best, and West Bengal, Odisha and Assam performed the worst. States like West Bengal, Odisha, Assam, Andhra Pradesh, Bihar, Madhya Pradesh and Uttar Pradesh fell below the all-India figures (Table 7.8).

The availability of capital per worker was lowest in West Bengal, and it was significantly less than the national average in respect of every disaggregation considered. Gujarat was highly capital intensive; its per worker availability of capital was the highest, and it was significantly larger than the national average. There is a wide gap in capital possession by enterprise type and location. Urban establishments led all the best-performing states to achieve higher capital intensity. This indicates that capital is highly concentrated in urban establishments, and that rural and own account enterprises are less capital intensive.

Table 7.8 Capital-to-labour ratio in unorganised food processing enterprises across the states during 2015–16 (INR in lakh)

State	Rural			Urban			Combined		
	OAE	Est	Total	OAE	Est	Total	OAE	Est	Total
AP	0.75	2.11	1.30	1.95	6.44	2.87	1.07	3.46	2.05
ASM	0.44	4.57	1.10	0.71	3.33	1.60	0.47	4.28	1.16
BHR	1.04	1.54	1.10	1.57	2.30	1.89	1.09	1.81	1.20
GUJ	1.76	5.83	2.21	5.02	23.29	12.11	3.09	19.40	7.18
HAR	3.30	10.09	4.52	3.41	11.13	6.86	3.35	10.87	5.80
KAR	1.57	6.21	2.29	2.51	8.85	4.63	1.98	8.00	3.45
KRL	1.48	6.26	3.24	1.68	6.49	3.64	1.57	6.38	3.44
MP	1.09	3.08	1.18	2.36	10.46	4.52	1.38	8.16	2.09
MHA	1.03	9.58	1.41	3.48	22.52	9.43	1.75	19.93	4.34
ODH	0.56	3.89	0.91	0.65	2.92	1.24	0.58	3.58	0.96
PNB	1.75	4.10	2.12	2.86	7.01	4.60	2.00	5.65	2.87
RAJ	1.18	6.36	1.45	2.49	14.11	4.54	1.70	11.93	2.78
TN	2.05	8.72	4.09	1.97	5.98	3.49	2.00	6.80	3.70
UP	1.40	3.50	1.68	2.79	7.45	3.84	1.76	5.06	2.28
WB	0.45	2.45	0.70	0.64	3.54	1.61	0.48	2.93	0.91
IND	**1.05**	**4.05**	**1.47**	**2.34**	**9.46**	**4.60**	**1.42**	**6.95**	**2.54**

Source Authors' computation using NSS 73rd unit-level records
AP— Andhra Pradesh, ASM—Assam, BHR—Bihar, GUJ—Gujarat, HAR—Haryana, KAR—Karnataka, KRL—Kerala, MP-Madhya Pradesh, MAH—Maharashtra, ODH—-Odisha, PNB—Punjab, RAJ—Rajasthan, TN—Tamil Nadu, UP—Uttar Pradesh, WB—West Bengal, IND—All India

7.4   Inter-linkages Between the Key Performance Indicators and Determinants of Labour Productivity

We used correlation coefficients to verify the interaction between GVA per worker, capital productivity and the capital-to-labour ratio at the all-India level (Table 7.9). The GVA per worker was positively and significantly associated with the capital-to-labour ratio, and capital productivity was negatively associated with the capital-to-labour ratio; a capital-intensive production process enhances the contribution per worker to GVA (Sharma and Dash 2006). Although a similar pattern of association is observed between the select indicators when we consider rural and urban enterprises separately, positive association between per worker GVA and the capital-to-labour ratio was more prominent in respect of rural and own account enterprises, and a negative association between capital productivity and the capital-to-labour ratio was more visible for urban enterprises and establishments.

We assessed the inter-linkages of these factors at the state level by cross-tabulating the performance indicators. States that had a better per-worker GVA than the national

Table 7.9 Correlation coefficients between performance indicators

Indicators	All India			Rural India			Urban India		
	GPW	CP	CI	GPW	CP	CI	GPW	CP	CI
GVA per worker	1	….	….	1	….	….	1	….	….
Capital productivity	0.312	1	….	0.329	1	….	0.31	1	….
Capital-to-labour ratio	0.35	−0.724	1	0.348	−0.714	1	0.287	−0.769	1
	Rural OAE			*Rural Est.*			*OAE*		
GVA per worker	1	….	….	1	….	….	1	….	….
Capital productivity	0.346	1	….	0.27	1	….	0.331	1	….
Capital-to-labour ratio	0.339	−0.705	1	0.333	−0.771	1	0.353	−0.707	1
	Urban OAE			*Urban Est.*			*Est.*		
GVA per worker	1	….	….	1	….	….	1	….	….
Capital productivity	0.326	1	….	0.274	1	….	0.262	1	….
Capital-to-labour ratio	0.325	−0.734	1	0.239	−0.827	1	0.309	−0.792	1

Source Authors' computation using NSS 73rd round unit-level records
Note All the coefficients are significant @ 0.05 level

average also had a better capital-to-labour ratio than the national average (Table 7.10). The per-worker GVA was about the national average in nine states; capital productivity was below the average in five of these states. The per-worker GVA had a positive relationship with the capital-to-labour ratio but no clear association with capital productivity. The per-worker GVA and capital productivity were equal and better in Karnataka, Kerala, Punjab and Tamil Nadu, and their association implied the substitution of labour for capital. These findings are consistent with those of Sharma and Dash (2006): in the small-scale industry sector, states with a higher capital-to-labour ratio tend to have a higher per-worker GVA.

Table 7.10 Interaction between selected performance indicators

Criterion	GVA per worker	Capital-to-labour ratio	Capital productivity
Above Average	Gujarat, Haryana, Karnataka, Kerala, Madhya Pradesh, Maharashtra, Rajasthan, Punjab, Tamil Nadu	Gujarat, Haryana, Karnataka, Kerala, Madhya Pradesh, Maharashtra, Rajasthan, Punjab, Tamil Nadu	Andhra Pradesh, Assam, Bihar, Karnataka, Kerala, Odisha, Punjab, Tamil Nadu and West Bengal
Below Average	Andhra Pradesh, Assam, Bihar, Odisha, Uttar Pradesh, West Bengal	Andhra Pradesh, Assam, Bihar, Odisha, Uttar Pradesh, West Bengal	Gujarat, Haryana, Madhya Pradesh, Maharashtra, Rajasthan and Uttar Pradesh

Source Authors' computation using NSS 73rd unit-level records

7.4.1   Disparities Across the States: Comparison of 67th and 73rd NSS Rounds

In 2010–11, the unorganised food processing sector had 22 lakh enterprises and employed more than 47 lakh workers. It generated INR 27,000 crore of value addition to the economy with the help of INR 51,887 crore of fixed assets. In 2015–16, the number of enterprises increased to 24 lakh, and the sector employed 52 lakh workers; value addition increased to INR 39,720 crore and fixed assets to INR 62,000 crore. To understand the changing structure of this sector, we compared the spread of enterprises, employment composition, gross value addition and fixed assets separately for rural and urban areas and the basic performance indicators (such as per-worker GVA and the capital-to-labour ratio) for major states.

We used the coefficient of variation to assess the dynamics of regional disparities. The disparities in the spread of enterprises and workers increased, and these disparities are consistent across enterprise types. The disparity in the spread of enterprises across the selected states rose from 63.47 to 66.49%, and disparity in employment increased from 67.61 to 69.99%; establishments induced these inter-state disparities. The variation in the spread of enterprises increased from 63.28 to 71.56% for establishments, and it remained the same for own account enterprises. The inter-state difference in the workforce ranged from 81.68% to 83.40% for establishments, while a meagre change was observed in the case of own account enterprises.

In the GVA per worker, however, the inter-state disparities declined from 37.36% in 2010–11–29.13% in 2015–16. Both enterprise types contributed to this decline, but establishments were primarily responsible for the 11.69 percentage-point decline from 2010–11 to 2015–16. The market value of fixed assets per worker and the capital-to-labour ratio, decreased in the inter-state variation across enterprises. Establishments induced this decline too, although own account enterprises contributed significantly. The increase in disparity was higher among establishments than among own account enterprises.

The increased coefficient of variation indicates that both the enterprises and workers were concentrated only in a few states. Hence, the industry is becoming lesser representative over time with increasing regional disparities. A fall in the disparity in per-worker GVA and the capital-to-labour ratio signals a competitive environment.

We captured inter-state disparities by computing the compound annual growth rate (CAGR) of enterprises, workers, per-worker GVA and capital-to-labour ratio (Table 7.11). There are considerable variations in growth rates of indicators; to capture the time dynamics, we grouped states into four broad categories of growth rates—negative, 0–5%, 5–10% and above 10%. The growth in the number of enterprises was negative in Haryana, Madhya Pradesh and Odisha. The number of enterprises grew more than 10% per year in West Bengal, at 0–5% in most states and at 5–10% in Karnataka and Punjab.

Despite a fall in the number of rural enterprises, the total number of enterprises increased in Andhra Pradesh, Gujarat, Kerala and Rajasthan; the increase in the

Table 7.11 Classification of states based on CAGR (nominal terms) of selected indicators

Enterprises					
CAGR (%)	All	Rural	Urban	OAE	EST
Negative	HAR, MP, ODH	AP, GUJ, KRL, HAR, ODH, RAJ	HAR,MP,MAH, PNJ,UP	GUJ, HAR, ODH, UP	ASM, MP, MAH, ODH, RAJ
0-5	AP, ASM, BHR, GUJ, KRL, MAH, RAJ, TN, UP	ASM, BHR, MP, MAH, TN, UP	BHR, GUJ, ODH, WB	AP, ASM, BHR, KRL, MP, MAH, RAJ, TN	AP, GUJ, HAR, KAR, KRL, PNJ, UP, WB
5–10	KAR,PNJ	KAR	AP,KAR,KRL,RAJ,TN	KAR,PNJ	TN
> 10	WB	PNB, WB	ASM	WB	BHR
Workers					
Negative	ASM, HAR, MP, MAH, ODH, UP	AP, ASM, GUJ, KRL, MP, ODH, RAJ	HAR, MP, MAH, PNJ, UP	GUJ, HAR, MP, MAH, ODH,UP	AP, ASM, MP, MAH, ODH, PNB, RAJ, UP
0-5	AP, BHR, GUJ, KRL, PNJ, RAJ	BHR, HAR, KAR, MAH, UP	ASM, BHR, ODH	AP, ASM, BHR, KRL, TN, RAJ	KAR, KRL, WB
5 to 10	KAR, TN, WB	RAJ, TN	AP, GUJ, KAR, RAJ, TN, WB	KAR, PNB	BHR, HAR
> 10	–	WB	KRL	WB	GUJ, TN
Per Worker GVA					
Negative	AP, HAR, KRL, TN	AP, RAJ	AP,KAR,ODH	KAR, KRL	–

(continued)

Table 7.11 (continued)

Enterprises

CAGR (%)	All	Rural	Urban	OAE	EST
0–5	MAH, PNB, RAJ	ASM,HAR,KRL, MAH,TN,WB	BHR,HAR,KRL,MAH,PNB,TN	AP, BHR, HAR, MP, MAH, PNB, RAJ, TN,	AP,HAR, KAR,MAH, TN,UP,WB
5 to 10	GUJ, KAR, WB	BHR,GUJ,KAR, MP,ODH,PNB, UP	RAJ,UP,WB	ASM,GUJ,MP, ODH, UP,WB	GUJ,KRL, PNB,RAJ
>10	ASM, BHR, MP, ODH,UP	–	ASM,GUJ,MP	–	ASM,BHR, MP,ODH

Capital-to-Labour Ratio

	All	Rural	Urban	OAE	EST
Negative	AP,HAR,KRL, PNB, RAJ,TN	AP,ASM,BHR, KRL,MAH,PNB, RAJ,WB	AP, ASM, BHR, HAR, MP MAH, KAR,KRL, ODH, PNB, RAJ, TN, UP, WB	AP, ASM, BHR, KAR, KRL, MAH, MP, PNB, RAJ, TN, WB	AP,BHR,HA,KRL,ODH, PNB,RAJ, TN,UP,WB
0–5	MP,GUJ,KAR, MAH, WB	HAR,MP,ODH, TN,UP	–	HAR, UP	ASM, KAR, MAH
5 to 10	BHR,ODH	GUJ, KAR	–	ODH	GUJ
>10	ASM,UP	–	GUJ	GUJ	MP

Source Authors' computation using NSS 67th and 73rd unit-level records
AP-Andhra Pradesh, ASM-Assam, BHR-Bihar, GUJ-Gujarat, HAR-Haryana, KAR-Karnataka, KRL-Kerala, MP-Madhya Pradesh, MAH-Maharashtra, ODH-Odisha, PNB-Punjab, RAJ-Rajasthan, TN-Tamil Nadu, UP-Uttar Pradesh, WB-West Bengal, IND-All India

growth of urban enterprises highly influenced the overall growth rates. The growth in number of own account enterprises was negative in Gujarat and Uttar Pradesh, though the overall growth of enterprises increased. The number of establishments in Assam, Maharashtra and Rajasthan fell despite the positive growth of enterprises overall. The rate of growth was the highest for West Bengal with respect to rural enterprises. The growth in urban enterprises was highest in Assam and in the case of establishments in Bihar.

Employment seems to have grown apace with enterprises. The states that experienced negative growth in enterprises also witnessed a decline in employment growth in respect of almost all the disaggregation considered. Enterprises and employment grew at more than 5% in Karnataka and West Bengal. Employment grew at 5–10% in Rajasthan, despite the negative growth in enterprises in rural areas, and the food processing sector enhanced employment opportunities for the rural population. The analogy between enterprises and employment growth also suggests that reduction in workforce is more rapid in most of the states than the cutback in the number of enterprises.

Per worker GVA at all-India level accounted to INR 57,840 per annum for the year 2010–11, that further increased to INR 76,256 by 2015–16, an increase of around 32% in real terms. The per worker GVA ranged from INR 31,727 to INR 97,350 for 2010–11 and that increased to INR 46,718 to INR 1,18,976 for the year 2015–16. This increase was in congruence with overall increase in the average per worker GVA. On the contrary, per capita availability of capital in real terms actually decreased. It was INR 1,28,064 per worker in 2010–11, that marginally reduced to INR 1,20,259 in the year 2015–16 for all India. Hence, on average, the unorganised food processing industry did not make any addition to its fixed capital stock from 2010–11 to 2015–16. On the other hand, one can observe greater dynamics with respect to inter-state disparity in per worker GVA for the same duration. In 2010–11, Kerala reported highest GVA per worker while Odisha registered the least followed by Madhya Pradesh. These positions completely altered, as Madhya Pradesh secured second highest position and Kerala figured in the 4th place form the bottom in 2015–16. The real per worker GVA absolutely decreased only in the state of Andhra Pradesh.

Further, CAGR for the period from 2010–11 to 2015–16 indicates that the growth of per worker GVA was found negative in very few states, across the location and enterprises type except the establishments. Enterprises belonging to own account enterprises and rural did not possess more than 10% growth, whereas the urban establishments in Assam, Gujarat and MP did possess more than 10% growth. Maharashtra performed moderately well by falling 0–5% growth slab while the Gujarat performed better with 5 to 10 and more than 10% growth all across the location and enterprise types.

Growth rates with respect to capital-to-labour ratio were negative for many of the states indicating that the industry did not significantly add to the existing stocks in fixed assets instead there was a depreciation of fixed assets in many states. This pattern is consistent across location and types of enterprises. The growth in the capital-to-labour ratio was negative in most states, but the per-worker GVA growth in nominal terms was not negative in any state. A positive growth was not evident in the case of capital-to-labour ratio for many states, as the capital has a longer gestation period and the time comparison here is confined to only for 5 years. Therefore, an appreciation if any, in the capital accumulation of the industry across states was not observed.

7.4.2 Labour Productivity and Its Determinants During 2015–16

As elicited above, labour productivity is an important measure to gauge competitiveness of firms in producing goods and services (Heshmati 2003). Labour is by far the most common factor of production used in measuring productivity. A wide spread disparity with respect to availability of technology, resource availability both material and human, other forms specific factors across enterprises, have greater practical significance in determining labour productivity. In this section, an attempt is being made to contribute to the empirical literature by exploring the determinants of labour productivity in unorganised food enterprises.

Labour productivity indicates the quantity of production obtained per unit of labour, while labour can be represented by the number of hours worked or the number of workers or number of employed persons. In general number of hours worked is the most used denomination in determining labour productivity, as mere presence of workers may not necessarily ensure productivity. However, in this study we have also discussed inter-state disparities with reference to per worker GVA, and hence, there is a clear distinction between labour productivity and per worker GVA for that purpose in this study. We made use of annual labour days as the denominator in estimating labour productivity. It is calculated by multiplying number of working hours of enterprises with total numbers of days (annual) operated divided by one labour day, i.e. 8 h in a day. Notationally,

$$\text{Annual Labor Days}(L)_i = \frac{(\text{Working Hours}_i) * (\text{Days Operated}_i)}{8} \tag{7.1}$$

Then,

$$\text{Labor Productivity}_i = \frac{\text{Total Annual GVA}_i}{\text{Total Annual Labor Days}_i} \tag{7.2}$$

Table 7.12 reports mean labour productivity value for enterprises level data for 2015–16. According to the estimates, a labour day of unorganised food processing produced on an average INR 565 of GVA during 2015–16 and the productivity was higher for urban enterprises compared to rural, and the same was true with respect to establishments compared to own account enterprises. The labour productivity of enterprises in Kerala was highest while the state of Assam registered the least productivity. It may be noted that Assam registered highest per worker GVA and the

Table 7.12 Mean labour productivity (LP) across states, location and enterprise type (in INR)

S.No.	State	LP	S.No.	State/Location/Type	LP
1	Andhra Pradesh	658	11	Punjab	477
2	Assam	366	12	Rajasthan	431
3	Bihar	399	13	Tamil Nadu	906
4	Gujarat	959	14	Uttar Pradesh	470
5	Haryana	904	15	West Bengal	385
6	Karnataka	691	**16**	**All India**	**565**
7	Kerala	1,165	**17**	**Rural**	**430**
8	Madhya Pradesh	347	**18**	**Urban**	**827**
9	Maharashtra	697	**19**	**OAE**	**328**
10	Odisha	408	**20**	**EST**	**1,501**

Source Authors' computation using NSS 73rd unit-level records

performance of Kerala with this respect was not so impressive. Hence, it is proven from the above analysis that mere presence of worker is not sufficient to augment the production but their active engagement does play an important role. Inter-state analysis also reveals that most of backward states, such as Assam, Bihar, Madhya Pradesh, Rajasthan and Uttar Pradesh had witnessed labour productivity below the national average.

The initial point of model building for labour productivity determinants is the general production function for food processing, that is

$$Y = f(K, L, M, E) \tag{7.3}$$

where Y represents output/GVA of an enterprise, K, L, M and E are capital, labour, material and energy inputs, respectively. Dividing Eq. (7.3) both the sides by labour (L) adding technology (T) and other control variable (Z) provide the following relationship.

$$\frac{Y}{L} = f\left[\frac{K}{L}, \frac{M}{L}, \frac{E}{L}, T, Z\right] \tag{7.4}$$

While $\frac{Y}{L}$ measures labour productivity, $\frac{K}{L}, \frac{M}{L}, \frac{E}{L}$ indicate intensity of capital, material and energy with respect to labour, respectively. T captures the state of technology, and Z indicates the vector of firm specific factors that influence labour productivity.

Improvement in labour productivity depends on a range of factors such as increased quality and efficiency of human capital factors that include worker's training, education, experience, age, etc. Also includes factor intensities such as per capita availability of capital, energy, material, etc., and other controlled factors or enterprises' specific factors. The empirical model has pooled the determinants of

LP in three different categories following the classification used by Heshmati and Rashidghalam (2016). The model in vector form is written as

$$\ln LP_i = \alpha + \sum_j \beta_j \ln \text{Main}_{ji} + \sum_k \beta_k \ln \text{Labor}_{ki} + \sum_m \beta_m \ln \text{Firm}_{mi} + \varepsilon_i \quad (7.5)$$

A brief summary of all the variables is explained in Annex 1. A good number of studies have tried to identify the determining factors of LP on similar lines, for example, Heshmati and Rashidghalam (2016), Xiaodong et al. (2016), Nagler and Naude (2014), Heshmati and Su (2010), Afrooz et al. (2010), Sala and Silva (2011), Rijkers et al. (2010), Dearden et al. (2006), etc. The empirical model is written as follows.

$$\ln LP_i = \alpha + \beta_1 \ln CI_i + \beta_2 \ln EI_i + \beta_3 \ln \text{Wage}_i + \beta_4 \ln \text{Female}_i$$
$$+ \beta_5 \ln \text{Hired}_i + \beta_6 \ln \text{Age}_i + \beta_5 \text{Rural}_i + \beta_6 \text{Credit}_i + \beta_7 \text{Problem}_i$$
$$+ \beta_8 \text{Registered}_i + \beta_9 \text{Medium}_i + \beta_{10} \text{High}_i + \varepsilon_i \quad (7.6)$$

The model is estimated with log linear least square method. The relevant post-estimation diagnostic tests have been conducted such as Ramsey RESET for specification error bias, variance inflation factor (VIF) for multicollinearity and Breusch–Pagan test for heteroscedasticity. The estimates of Breusch–Pagan test for heteroscedasticity indicates rejection of the null hypothesis of homoscedasticity at 5% level of significance. Hence, Eq. (7.6) is estimated with robust standard errors that are consistent with heteroscedasticity. The estimation is done at enterprise level and type, i.e. OAE and establishments (EST).

The R^2 value of the model shows that 30% of variation in the dependent variable is explained by model selected for enterprise-level estimation and 12 and 31% for OAE and establishments, respectively. The results of the model are presented in Table 7.13. Looking at the explanatory factors of LP with respect to main determinants, the estimates reveal that capital intensity (ln CI) is positive and significant at 1% level across the models estimated except for establishments, which is negative. That in turn indicates that investment in technology in terms of machines and other innovations should be a priority to motivate workers (Kipene et al. 2013). Although other main variables, such as energy intensity (lnEI) and Wage (lnWage) were positive and significant in determining LP, capital had the strongest effect when compared to others. These findings are consistent with theory, expectations and other empirical studies.

Share of female work force (ln Female) and share of hired workers in total workers (ln Hired) were the two variables which come under second category as determinants. Although, the unorganised food enterprises in India over-represented by male workers in general, the sector provided considerable job opportunities to women in rural areas, especially on the part-time basis. However, the coefficient of female share of worker indicated negative impact on LP in case of all enterprises as well as own account enterprises. While it was not the case with establishments as the female

Table 7.13 Regression estimates of determinants of labour productivity

Variables	All enterprises		OAE		Establishments	
	Coefficients	Robust SE	Coefficients	Robust SE	Coefficients	Robust SE
lnCI	0.048	0.001	0.06	0.001	−0.009	0.001
lnEI	0.044	0.000	0.047	0.001	0.019	0.001
lnWage	0.027	0.000	0.018	0.000	0.318	0.003
lnFemale	−0.014	0.000	−0.038	0.000	0.113	0.001
lnHired	0.233	0.002	0.259	0.002	0.137	0.005
lnAge	−0.013	0.001	0.005	0.001	−0.077	0.001
Rural	−0.207	0.001	−0.273	0.002	−0.099	0.003
Credit	0.22	0.003	0.198	0.004	0.239	0.003
Problem	−0.11	0.001	−0.125	0.002	−0.067	0.002
Registered	0.268	0.001	0.338	0.002	0.119	0.003
Medium_HDI	0.022	0.002	−0.118	0.002	0.216	0.003
High_HDI	0.117	0.002	0.058	0.002	0.088	0.004
Constant	4.16	0.009	3.986	0.010	2.905	0.038
R2	0.3065		0.1286		0.3196	
No. of Observations	2,424,476		1,932,499		491,977	

Source Authors' estimation

Note All the coefficient values are significant at 1% level; list of states covered

workforce was largely concentrated in the rural areas (62%) and their share was only 23% in the total full-time employment (NSS 2015–16). In other words, female workforce mostly worked on part-time basis especially during the agricultural off-season, and hence, this might perhaps had served as a reason for their insignificant role in augmenting labour productivity. The sector consisted of hired workers and own workers. The hired employment is characterised by stipulated working hours, fixed emoluments and disciplinary regulations. Based on these characteristics, a higher labour productivity is expected from the hired workers than working owners, and the coefficient value indicated that for every per cent increase in the share of hired workers, there was an increase in labour productivity.

The unorganised enterprises are highly heterogeneous in nature. They differed with reference to age, location type, credit facilities, etc. Accordingly, five important enterprise specific variables were included in the third category of determinants. The enterprises 'age is expected to have a positive impact on labour productivity as the older enterprises may have an easier access to labour markets and may employ superior quality of labour. In addition, they may enjoy greater economies of scale through their quality organisation and managerial skills. Nevertheless, coefficient value related to age variable was significant and had a negative sign. That concludes that per labour-day value generation in older enterprises was far lesser than that of newer enterprises.

To capture the impact of location of enterprises, the rural dummy was included which showed a negative sign and was significantly different from zero. Many studies have argued that the credit constraints substantially diminish the potential growth and investment of enterprises (Tybout 1983; Nabi 1989). This in turn reduces per capita availability of capital. Incidentally, findings with respect to credit dummy also confirm that labour productivity in enterprises which had access to credit was higher than the ones who did not have access.

The coefficient related to problem dummy suggests that the unorganised food processing enterprises faced various problems like erratic power supply, lack of raw materials, non-recovery of financial dues, etc. These problems in return seemed to have adverse effect on labour productivity of enterprises. The sector consists of registered and unregistered enterprises. An enterprise is considered as registered if it is registered under any act or the authority. On the other hand, an unregistered enterprise is the one which is not registered under any act and authority. These unregistered enterprises are characterised by less productive small-sized units, non-hired labour base, typical household units, use of outdated technology, inability to integrate with formal economy and shortage of capital (Chandrasekhar and Ghosh 2003). Hence, the present study also tries to understand the impact of status of registration of the enterprises on their performance. Empirical findings on this account suggest that labour productivity of registered enterprises was relatively higher unlike their counterparts.

To apprehend the state-specific character effect on labour productivity, HDI values were used to categorise the states into high, medium and low. This variable is used to capture the development of state, i.e. in terms of income growth, education and education of labours on the labour productivity. The states with high HDI (Punjab, Kerala and Tamil Nadu) and medium HDI (AP, Haryana, Gujarat, Maharashtra and

Karnataka) had positive and significant effect on labour productivity unlike their counterpart low HDI (Assam, Bihar, MP, Odisha, Rajasthan, UP and WB). However, in case of own account enterprises, the states belonged to medium HDI had a negative effect on the productivity when compared to their counterpart, which implies that the own account enterprises in states with low HDI performed better than the medium HDI states.

7.5 Conclusions

The food processing industry is termed as a sunrise industry in India's manufacturing given the synergy between agriculture and manufacturing sectors. It helps generate a larger employment both as a share of total unorganised manufacturing and total food processing industry. However, the value generation of the industry is quite negligible. It mainly caters to the employment needs of the rural population, especially unskilled and illiterate population. Interestingly, in the context of jobless manufacturing growth, the unorganised food processing industry has succeeded whereas the manufacturing sector has failed. Therefore, our findings reiterate that it is one of the highly labour-intensive industries.

The manufacturing dualism is also evident in the food processing industry. However, the inter-temporal observations indicate shrinkage of duality. The unorganised food processing is dominated by own account enterprises in terms of enterprises and workers. The dominance is persistent, as the own account enterprises are increasing in urban areas as well. However, their contribution towards value generation is less than the establishments and is even declining. Whereas, the establishments have improved their share in value generation, though, their share in enterprises and worker force are declining. Therefore, the duality in the industry is highly representative from the perspective of type of enterprise.

Gender disparity is also evident in the workforce with establishment enterprises employing more of male workers than female workers. Given their accountability towards household and agricultural commitments, womenfolk in the rural areas tend to take up mostly part-time employment. The urban enterprises are more capital-oriented than the rural enterprises as the share of fixed capital of urban enterprises are increasing overtime. This calls for proper policy and programme incentives focusing specially on rural enterprises to ensure credit and infrastructure facilities as part of improving the capital and technological upgradation.

Bigger states like UP, WB, AP and MP have a larger share in enterprises and work force. However, their performance with respect to labour productivity and capital-to-labour ratio is not significant, implying that it is not proportionate to the share they hold in enterprises and workers. However, poorer states such as Assam, Bihar and Odisha do not account for a considerable share in the workforce which may erode the non-farm employment opportunities, critical to poverty reduction. Hence, these states should focus on startup policies for opening up of more food processing enterprises. The prevalence of self-owned enterprises also contributes to inter-state disparities, as the states that derive their major share of GVA from these enterprises, especially from rural areas have a relatively lower share in the total segments value generation. This signifies that the own account enterprises are less remunerative than their counterparts. Therefore, own account enterprises should focus more on improving their productivity and an efficient use of resources.

There exists a positive correlation between capital-to-labour ratio and GVA per worker, while the opposite is evident with respect to capital productivity and capital-to-labour ratio. This implies that a capital-intensive production process leads to a higher per worker GVA. The unorganised food processing segment is also undergoing a structural transformation, moving away from own account enterprises to establishments, and this has helped attaining a more rapid per worker availability of GVA. The temporal analysis reveals that most of the states have performed above the national average with respect to labour productivity and capital-to-labour ratio during the year 2015–16, as compared to 2010–11. This implies that the processed food enterprises are becoming more competitive over the years.

We estimated the determinants of labour productivity for the recent NSS data (2015–16) for all food processing enterprises and enterprise types. The analyses revealed that capital intensity, energy intensity and per worker emoluments have positive and strong association with labour productivity. The female workers have negative association while the hired workers have positive association. The result also revealed that the younger enterprises are better than the older ones as the younger enterprises may use new technologies in the production process. The firms with registration under Act or the authority possess better labour productivity and enterprises which have availed credit facility also attributed for productivity.

Hence, an urgent need for policy intervention and programme incentives like scheme for technology upgradation, establishment and modernisation of food processing enterprises, credit flow to rural enterprises, infrastructure, etc. Food processing provides avenues for diversification away from farm, especially in the agricultural off-season. These non-farm jobs can help tighten the rural labour market and act as a safety net in preventing workers from falling into a poverty trap or migrate despite the residual nature of work. Further, increased employment opportunities in processed food can significantly enhance the prospects of India's low skilled and unskilled workforce getting suitable jobs.

Annex 1: Notations and Explanations of Variables

S.No.	Variable	Description	Category
1	lnLP	Dependent variable, labour productivity expressed in natural log	Main

(continued)

(continued)

S.No.	Variable	Description	Category
2	lnCI	Capital Per Worker. It is obtained by dividing the total fixed asset by total worker. The total fixed asset includes the market value of enterprises 'own and hired fixed asset net of market value of capital in progress.	
3	lnEI	Refers to energy available per worker. This variable is obtained by adding market value of electricity and fuel consumed by enterprises in a reference period	
4	lnWage	Indicate Per Worker Emoluments that include salary and other allowances	
5	lnFemale	Female worker share in total worker of the enterprises	Labour
6	lnHired	Hired worker share in total worker of the enterprises	
7	lnAge	The survey does not report the age of enterprises directly. However, it provides the information on the initiation year/establishment year of the enterprises. Hence, the age of the enterprises is derived by subtracting the year of establishment from the surveyed year	enterprises
8	Rural	Dummy variable, 1 if the enterprises belong to rural, otherwise 0	
9	Credit	Dummy variable, 1 if the enterprises has credit access from banks, otherwise 0	
10	Problem	Dummy Variable, 1 if the enterprises reported any problem, otherwise zero? not clear? There is no firm that is free of any problem	
11	Registered	Dummy Variable, 1 if the enterprises is registered under any act, authority, etc., otherwise 0	
12	Low_HDI	Dummy Variable,1 if the state's HDI is low, otherwise 0	State
13	Medium_HDI	Dummy Variable,1 if the state's HDI is medium, otherwise 0	
14	High_HDI	Dummy Variable,1 if the state's HDI is high, otherwise 0	

Source Authors' compilation

References

Annual Survey of Industries (ASI). Government of India, Ministry of Statistics and Programme Implementation (MOSPI).

ASSOCHAM. (2017). *Food processing sector in India: Challenges and growth enablers.* New Delhi: Grant Thornton and ASSOCHAM.

Balakrishnan, P. (2004). Measuring productivity in manufacturing sector. *Economic and Political Weekly, 39*(14), 1465–1471.

Balakrishnan, P., & Pushpangadan, K. (1994). Total factor productivity growth in manufacturing industry: A fresh look. *Economic and Political Weekly, 29*, 2028–2035.

Bathla, S., & Sharma, R. (2009). Labour market in rural unorganised manufacturing: Its growth, disparities and determinants during the post-reform period in India. *The Indian Journal of Labour Economics, 52*(2).

Bathla, S., Sharma, R., & Banga, R. (2008). *Impact of trade on employment, wages and labour productivity in unorganized manufacturing in India. How the poor are affected by trade.* New Delhi: UNCTAD-DFID.

Bhandari, A. K., & Ray, S. C. (2012). Technical efficiency in the Indian textiles industry: A non-parametric analysis of firm-level data. *Bulletin of Economic Research, 64*, 109–124.

Burange, L., & Ranadive, R.R. (2014). *Inter-state analysis of the organised manufacturing sector in India.* Working Paper, ISFIRE.

Chandrasekhar, C.P., & Ghosh, J. (2003). Regulating labour markets for more employment. *Business Line*, June 17, 2003.

Goldar, B. (2014). *Globalisation, growth and employment in the organised sector of the Indian economy.* Working Paper, Institute for Human Development.

Goldar, B., & Sadhukhan, A. (2015). *Employment and wages in Indian manufacturing: Post- reform performance.* Working Paper, International Labour Office, Employment Policy Department Employment, Geneva.

Heshmati, A. (2003). Productivity growth, efficiency and outsourcing in manufacturing and service industries. *Journal of Economic Survey, 17*(1), 79–112.

India Brand Equity Foundation (IBEF). (2017). *Food processing.* https://www.ibef.org/download/Food-Processing-June-2017.pdf.

Islam, S. & Shazali, S. T. S. (2011). Determinants of manufacturing productivity: Pilot study on labor-intensive industries. *International Journal of Productivity and Performance Management 60*(6), 567–582.

Kathuria, V., Raj, S. R., & Sen, K. (2013). The effects of economic reforms on manufacturing dualism: Evidence from India. *Journal of Comparative Economics, 41*, 1240–1262.

Kipene, V., Lazaro, E., & Isinika, A. C. (2013). Labour productivity performance of small agro-processing firms in Mbeya and Morogoro, Tanzania. *Journal of Economics and Sustainable Development, 4*(3).

Lal, D. (1979). Theories of industrial wage structures: A review. *Indian Journal of Industrial Relations, 15*(2), 167–195.

Majumder, R. (2004). Productivity gowth in small enterprises-role of inputs, technological progress and learning by doing. *India Journal of Labour Economis, 47*(4).

Nabi, I. (1989). Investment in segmented capital markets. *Quarterly Journal of Economics, 104*, 453–462.

National Sample Survey Organisation (NSSO). Government of India, Ministry of Statistics and Programme Implementation (MOSPI).

Papola, T., Maurya, N., & Jena, N. (2011). *Inter-regional disparities in industrial growth and structure.* New Delhi: Institute for Studies in Industrial Development.

Paul, B. (2015). *Wages and labour productivity in Indian manufacturing.* http://www.esocialscien ces.org/eSS_essay/Manufacturing/Wages%20and%20Labour%20Productivity.pdf.

Rao, C.N. (2009). *Growth and productive employment linkages in the food processing sector.* Monograph, Centre for Economic and Social Studies.

Rao, C. N., & Dasgupta, S. (2009). Nature of employment in food processing sector. *Economic and Political Weekly, 44*(17), 109–115.

Rath, B. N. (2006). Labour productivity determinants in Indian manufacturing: A panel data analysis. *Indian Journal of Labour Economics, 49*(1), 113–119.

Reserve Bank of India (RBI). (2011–12). *State finances.* New Delhi: Government of India.

Sharma, R., & Bathla, S. (2012). *Economic and social viability of agro-processing indus-tries in India. African-Asian rural development organisation.* New Delhi: African-Asian Rural Development Organization.

Sharma, R., & Dash, A. (2006). Labour productivity in small scale industries in India: A state-wise analysis. *The Indian Journal of Labour Economics, 49*(3), 407–427.

Trivedi, P. (2004). An inter-state perspective on manufacturing productivity in India: 1980–81 to 2000–01. *Indian Economic Review, 39*(1), 203–237.

Tybout, J. R. (1983). Credit rationing and investment behaviour in a developing country. *Review of Economics and Statistics, 65*, 393–410.

Chapter 8
Dynamics of Competition in Food and Agriculture Inputs Industries in India: A Mobility Analysis

M. L. Nithyashree

8.1 Introduction

Competition is key in enhancing efficiency and productivity in the industry. It is multi-dimensional in nature and difficult to define or measure (Scherer 1973; Lall 2001). Competition may be static or dynamic.[1] Few studies have attempted to study the dynamic nature of domestic competition in the Indian industry, especially at the disaggregate level (Pushpangadan and Shanta 2008). Sector-specific studies show that increased competition leads to mixed results; the telecom sector, once a total monopoly, is now an oligopoly (Jain and Sridhar 2003), and the banking sector underwent major structural change in the early 1990s despite many mergers (Bikker and Haaf 2001: Kaushik and Abhiman 2003). It is envisaged that market reforms help firms accessing specialised inputs—which enhance international competition—and improve production efficiency (Horn et al. 1994). However, competition decreased in the post-liberalisation period in comparison to the pre-liberalisation period (Kambhampati 1995; Glen et al. 2003; Pushpangadan and Shanta 2008).

---

[1] The static view of competition, which emerged from the early work of Adam Smith (1776) and Augustin Cournot (1938), considers the profit maximization behaviour of firms under the free entry and free exit market condition. If a given industry is larger than a firm, profits will be equalised, or profits should converge to zero in a competitive market (Baldwin 1998; Mueller 1990). Stigler tested this concept, and noted that because the stationary state does not exist in the real world, the application of the free market assumptions of the model and its outcomes was limited (Pushpangadan and Shanta 2008). The dynamic measure of competition, which originated from the work of Schumpeter (1942), held that the process of innovation is dynamic and a market can be at disequilibrium at any time. Different forms of innovation create excess profit by creating temporary monopolistic advantages, but these advantages attract imitators and new investors and increase competition, and eventually become the norm. In the post-liberalisation era, the dynamic view of competition seems more realistic than the static view.

M. L. Nithyashree (✉)
Division of Agricultural Economics, ICAR-IARI, New Delhi, India
e-mail: nithya.econ@gmail.com

We study the dynamic nature of competition in the agricultural input and food industries—fertilisers, pesticides, farm machinery and food processing—that have a direct linkage with agriculture, the primary sector. The agriculture and food industries have deep resources and a wide diversity of products, and the demand for high-value food items is growing. To meet the growing demand and capture the market, product development and packaging technologies are emerging fast (Stewart-Knox and Mitchell 2003; Wells et al. 2007). The food-producing sector has vast growth potential, but it lacks the efficient backward and forward supply chain linkages that can add value to food products and the supply of agri-inputs—fertilisers, chemicals and machinery. To improve productivity and competition, the government made several policy changes—it introduced the New Industrial Policy 1991 and the Competition Act 2002; removed entry barriers; and allowed 100% foreign direct investment (FDI) through the automatic route. We analyse their impact on the dynamics of competition of firms. Non-structural approaches use several models to analyse the dynamic nature of competition. The mobility of firms in an industry is perceived to capture the dynamic aspects of competition (Gort 1963; Baldwin 1998), and mobility can be used to measure the intensity of competition in firms of various sizes. A structural shift in the rank of firms can explain mobility and, hence, the dynamics of industrial competition (Hymer and Pashigian 1962; Joskow 1960). Firm-level transition matrices explain the structure and mobility patterns across the size (Hart and Prais 1956; Singh and Whittington 1968).

We follow the methods used in these studies to analyse the dynamics of competition in the processed foods, fertiliser, pesticide and machinery industries from 2004–05 to 2015–16, based on secondary data published by CMIE (2016). We analyse firm size rank and stability in their respective industry and the degree of competition to gauge changes in the competition level over the study period and the dynamics of firm-level competition to draw implications for effective competition. Mobility analysis helps in understanding the dimensions of competition by firm size, and it will also help to see the competitive level of small firms,[2] which is not possible with the usual concentration measures, indicating the market share of bigger firms. Section 8.2 explains the database and methodology, Sect. 8.3 furnishes empirical results and Sect. 8.4 presents the summary and conclusions.

---

[2]The Micro, Small and Medium Enterprises Development Act, 2006 (GoI 2006), provides guidelines for classifying firms by investment in plant and machinery. Small and marginal firms constitute about 61% of the manufacturing industry, 65% of the food manufacturing industry, 71percentof the machinery industry, 68% of the machinery industry and 72% of the fertilizer industry (Annual Survey of Industries unit records, GoI 2015–16).

Table 8.1 Sample size by industry group (from 2004–05 to 2015–16)

Industry	Sample size
Food products	152
Fertilisers and nitrogen compounds	21
Pesticides and other agrochemical products	15
Manufacture of agricultural and food processing machinery	19
All Industries	207

Source CMIE, Prowess

8.2 Data and Methodology

We use the Prowess database of the Centre for Monitoring Indian Economy (CMIE). The period selected, 2004–05 to 2015–16, coincides with the enactment of the Competition Act, 2002 in India[3]. The sample size of this database is not uniform, and we constructed balanced panel data to ensure that the same firms exist throughout the study period (Table 8.1).

The concentration measure captures the market segment served by large firms, and it is commonly used to understand competition. Mobility analysis helps us understand other dimensions of competition in the industry and, hence, market structure. We consider sales data a measure of size. A turnover index presents the relative rank of firms; it tells us that a firm ranks above or below another firm, but not by how much. To overcome this limitation and analyse size rank and stability, we construct a New Turnover Index that uses normalised data through an order-preserving transformation (Hymer and Pashigian 1962; Pushpangadan and Shanta 2006).

Let $N_1, \ldots N_n$ be n firms in a firm or industry that represents their respective size arranged in ascending order of magnitude. Further with transformation, order-preserving ranks are obtained with an interval ranging from 0 to 1 and 0 are replaced by adding the differences between two consecutive values beginning from the highest value of one to obtain the transformed size ranks $(N_1^1, \ldots, N_n^1)$.

$$Zj = \frac{[Nj - \min(N1, \ldots, Nn)]}{[\max(N1, \ldots, Nn) - \min(N1, \ldots, Nn)]}, j = 1, \ldots \ldots, n.$$

To capture the direction and degree of competition, we compute the Ijiri-Simon Index (Ijiri and Simon 1977) using the following formula:

$$\text{Standard deviation } (Q_i) = \frac{R_i}{R_i^*}$$

where,

R_i = Rank of the *i*th firm at the end of a period
R_i^* = Rank at the beginning of the period.
Q_i = Average amount of shifting in rank during the period

We prepare the firm-level transition matrix (Hart and Prais 1956: Singh and Whittington 1968) for each industry to display dynamic competition, an important aspect of a firm's mobility.

8.3 Results and Discussion

We obtain the stability of size ranks from the New Turnover Index. The value of a correlation coefficient can range from 0 (perfect competition) to 1 (imperfect competition). The significance of the correlation coefficients shows that competition is absent. The empirical results of rank correlation show that mobility is absent; the coefficient values of more than 0.90 show that the food processing and pesticide industries are rigid in nature (Table 8.2). The corresponding figure estimated for the food industry is 0.73 (Pushpangadan and Shanta 2006). Therefore, with the larger sample size, our results show that the immobility of the processed food firms increased during the recent period.

We analysed stability using the Ijiri-Simon Index of relative ranks for two consecutive initial years, 2003–04 and 2004–05, and two later years, 2014–15 and 2015–16 (Table 8.3). The pace of competition has decreased in processed food (79.71%), fertilizer and pesticide (38.83%) and other agro chemical products (11.72%) respectively, except in the machinery industry, where the level of competition increased by 1.67% from 2003–04 to 2015–16. These figures show that the food, pesticide and fertiliser industries are less competitive. The Ijiri-Simon Index and the stability rank analysis show consistent results and provide better insights into the direction and the magnitude of mobility.

We used a transition matrix to compute the mobility of firms and the dynamics of competition for each industry. We classified firms into decile groups and grouped two consecutive deciles for symmetry across the industry. The distribution of firms by size class is shown in the transition matrix (Tables 8.4, 8.5, 8.6 and 8.7). The diagonal

Table 8.2 Industry-wise rank correlation from new transformed size (from 2004–05 to 2015–16)

Industry	Rank correlation of size
Food products	0.93**
Fertilisers and nitrogen compounds	0.89**
Pesticides and other agrochemical products	0.95**
Manufacture of agricultural and food processing machinery	0.89**

Note ** significant at 5% level
Source CMIE, Prowess

Table 8.3 Degree of competition of relative ranks

Industry	Ijiri-Simon index of relative ranks		Change (%)
	2003–04/ 2004–05	2014–15/ 2015–16	
Food products	0.21	1.02	−79.71
Fertilisers and nitrogen compounds	0.17	0.28	−38.83
Pesticides and other agrochemical products	0.31	0.35	−11.72
Manufacture of agricultural and food processing machinery	0.31	0.30	1.67

Source CMIE, Prowess

Table 8.4 Firm-level transition matrix (food processing industry, from 2004–05 to 2015–16)

Size class (Decile-wise)	1–2	3–4	5–6	7–8	9–10	No. of firms in 2004–05
1–2	29	–	–	–	–	29
3–4	–	30	–	–	–	30
5–6	–	1	29	1	–	31
7–8	–	–	1	30	–	31
9–10	–	–	–	–	31	31
No. of firms in 2015–16	29	31	30	31	31	152

Source CMIE, Prowess

Table 8.5 Firm-level transition matrix (fertiliser industry, from 2004–05 to 2015–16)

Size class (Decile-wise)	1–2	3–4	5–6	7–8	9–10	No. of firms in 2004–05
1–2	3	–	–	1	–	4
3–4	–	3	1	–	1	5
5–6	–	–	2	1	–	3
7–8	–	1	1	3	1	6
9–10	–	–	–	1	2	3
No. of firms in 2015–16	3	4	4	6	4	21

Source CMIE, Prowess

elements indicate the frequency of firms without inter-class mobility. The frequency numbers above the diagonal elements are indicative of the number of firms moved upward and frequency numbers with below the diagonal elements are indicative of the number of firms moved downward. Mobility in the food processing industry was very low—one firm moved upward and two downward—with only 2% inter-class mobility. The rigidity of the remaining 98% of the firms is strong in the smaller (1–2

Table 8.6 Firm-level transition matrix (pesticide industry, from 2004–05 to 2015–16)

Size class (Decile-wise)	1–2	3–4	5–6	7–8	9–10	No. of firms in 2004–05
1–2	3	–	–	–	–	3
3–4	–	3	–	–	–	3
5–6	–	–	3	–	–	3
7–8	–	–	–	3	–	3
9–10	–	–	–	–	3	3
No. of firms in 2015–16	3	3	3	3	3	15

Source CMIE, Prowess

Table 8.7 Firm-level transition matrix (agri-machinery industry, from 2004–05 to 2015–16)

Size class (Decile-wise)	1–2	3–4	5–6	7–8	9–10	No. of firms in 2004–05
1–2	3	–	–	–	–	3
3–4	–	2	1	–	–	3
5–6	–	–	2	1	1	4
7–8	–	1		3	–	4
9–10	–	–	1	1	3	5
No. of Firms in 2015–16	3	3	4	5	4	19

Source CMIE, Prowess

decile) and larger (7–8 and 9–10 decile) firms. It is evident to say that food products industries lack in competition (Table 8.4).

Firms in the fertiliser industry are mobile as compared to the food industry, but the upward mobility exceeds the downward movement, where in three firms moved downstream and five firms moved to upward having the orientation towards going as bigger firms (Table 8.5). India has reoriented fertiliser application: farmers use nutrient based and neem-coated urea, and schemes such as the Soil Health Card help farmers use better nutrients. That has led fertiliser-producing firms to change their production orientation and higher scale that change may have increased the concentration of bigger firms in the short term. Direction of mobility further supports that their exists competition in the fertiliser industry, but skewness is more upward (24%) than downward (14%) implying big firms tend to concentrate in the market, create barriers for small firms, and affect the overall competitiveness of industry. Contrarily firms in the pesticides industry shows perfect rigidity and zero mobility, where there is no single firm considered under the study shifted their position in either direction during 2004–05–2015–16 (Table 8.6) is in line with its high correlation coefficient of 0.95.

From Table 8.7, it is evident that the firms in the machinery industry are mobile, both upward and downward (three firms each); scale efficiency might have enabled

Table 8.8 Mobility of firms by industry (2004–05 to 2015–16)

Industry	No mobility (%)	Upward mobility (%)	Downward mobility (%)
Food products	149 (98.03)	1 (0.66)	2 (1.32)
Fertilisers and nitrogen compounds	13 (61.90)	5 (23.81)	3 (14.29)
Pesticides and other agrochemical products	15 (100.00)	0 (0.00)	0 (0.00)
Manufacture of agricultural and food processing machinery	13 (68.42)	3 (15.79)	3 (15.79)

Notes Figures in parentheses are in percentage
Source CMIE, Prowess

their competitiveness. Small and marginal farmers need farm machinery and implements, and the government has launched the Sub-Mission on Agricultural Mechanization to promote farm mechanisation and set up Custom Hiring Centres to rent
out farm machinery and implements. These initiatives may have provided incentives
to stakeholders and stimulated the industry. Also, the transition matrix captures the
identity of firms even when their frequency remains the same. In the size class 3rd i.e.
5–6 deciles group frequency number is four for both the periods. Among them, two
firms remained in the same class and one firm moved from 7–8 deciles to 3–4 deciles
between 2004–05 and 2015–16 and remaining one positioned in 9–10 deciles.

Based on the direction of mobility, firms were grouped into three categories viz.
no mobility, upward mobility and downward mobility and their proportion across
the industry is presented in Table 8.8. It shows that 98% of the firms in the processed
food industry remained static indicating a weak competition in the industry. Firms
in the fertilizer industry seems to have better competitive advantage as compared
with firms in the food industry, where 38% of the firms reveal mobility; however,
the concentration of the bigger firms is relatively more exhibited by relatively more
upward mobility (23.81%) than downward mobility (14.29%). Contrarily, firms indicate severe adverse competitive environment in the pesticide industry, where there
exists almost zero upward and downward mobility leading to high rigidity. On the
other hand, firms showed mobility in either direction (upward and downward, 15.79%
each) in the machinery industry. It witnessed the presence of scale efficiency which is
required for the competition to be more effective, which also supports the increased
level of competition indicated by the Ijiri-Simon Index.

8.4 Summary and Conclusions

The processed foods, fertilisers, pesticides and machinery industries drive the agricultural value chain. We used mobility analysis as a dynamic dimension, and firm-level

data from the Prowess database CMIE from 2004–2005 to 2015–2016, to assess the level of competition in these industries. Competition was weak and rigidity high in the processed food and pesticides industries (the values of the correlation coefficients exceeded 0.90). The extent to which this stability influenced competition was examined by the pace of competition. During the study period, the level of competition decreased in all industries except in machinery where it increased by 1.67%.

Mobility of the firms within the industry when exists indicates the competitive environment which is crucial for the firms to operate. Dynamics of firm's mobility captured for each industry in the form of transition matrix emphasize the need and further efforts to bring effective competition. The processed food and pesticides industry has been noted with low firms' mobility. In general, the industries are dominated by the small firms and also, they exhibit low mobility indicated by their static positioning in the matrix. The transition matrix for the mobility of firms indicated perfect rigidity in the case of pesticides industry, which is in line with a high correlation coefficient of the size ranks. Mobility was better in the fertiliser industry, but the existing competition was skewed towards bigger firms, resulting in market concentration. Persisting scale efficiency in the machinery industry, due to firms' mobility in either direction, indicated that firms must be dynamic for market competition to be effective.

Since mobility can be closely linked to the market structure, it has long term implications for market concentration and their adverse effect in the industry. This can be noticed in the fertilizer industry, where mobility showed more skewness towards upward direction. Factors that encourage the firms to be more dynamic in the industry are imperative to bring the scale efficiency. Recent policy initiatives viz. upward revision in the definition of Micro, Small and Medium Enterprises, collateral-free automatic loans, and disallowing global tenders in procurement to create more opportunities for domestic players may help the small units to achieve a competitive edge. However, such policy initiatives in firms, dominant in the unorganized and/or unregistered sector are key to bring effective competition and improve industry's performance on the whole.

References

Baldwin, R. J. (1998). *The dynamics of industrial competition. A North American perspective.* UK: Cambridge University Press. https://doi.org/10.1017/cbo9780511664700.

Bikker, J. A., & Haaf, K. (2001). *Measures of competition and concentration: A review of literature.* Amsterdam: De Nederlandsche Bank. Available at: https://www.dnb.nl/en/binaries/ot027_tcm47-146045.pdf.

CMIE. (2016). Prowess, Bombay (https://prowessdx.cmie.com/).

Cournot, A. (1838). *Researches into the mathematical principles of the theory of wealth.* New York: Macmillan. Available at:http://bibliotecadigital.econ.uba.ar/download/Pe/181738.pdf.

Glen, J., Lee, K., & Singh, A., (2003). Corporate profitability and the dynamics of competition in emerging Markets: A time series analysis. *The Economic Journal, 113*, 465–484. doi/abs/https://doi.org/10.1046/j.0013-0133.2003.00165.x.

Gort, M., (1963, February). Analysis of stability and change in market share. *Journal of Political Economy, 71,* 51–63. Available at:https://www.jstor.org/stable/1828375.

Government of India. (2006). *Development commissioner, ministry of micro, small and medium enterprises.* Available at: http://www.dcmsme.gov.in/ssiindia/defination_msme.htm.

Government of India. (2015–16). *Annual survey of industries, unit records.* Ministry of Statistics and Programme Implementation, New Delhi. Available at: http://mospi.nic.in/.

Government of India. (2002). Ministry of corporate affairs, The Competition Act, 2002 Available at:http://www.mca.gov.in/Ministry/actsbills/pdf/The_competition_Act_2002.pdf.

Hart, P. E., & Prais, S. J. (1956). The analysis of business concentration. *Journal of the Royal Statistical Society, 99*(2), 150–181. https://doi.org/10.2307/2342882.

Horn, H., Lang, H., & Lundgren, S. (1994). Managerial effort incentives, X-inefficiency and international trade. *European Economic Review, 38*(2), 213–233. https://doi.org/10.1016/0014-292 1(94)90056-6.

Hymer, S., & Pashigian, P. (1962). Turnover of firms as a measure of market behavior. *Review of Economics and Statistics, 44,* 82–87. https://doi.org/10.2307/1926627.

Ijiri, Y., & Simon, H.A. (1977). *Skewed distributions and the size of business firms.* Amsterdam: North Holland Publishing Co. https://doi.org/10.1016/S0954-349X(97)00040-4.

Jain, P., & Sridhar, V. (2003). Analysis of competition and market structure of basic telecommunication services in India, *Communication and Strategies, 52*(4), 271–293. Available at: https://www.researchgate.net/publication/251995896_Analysis_of_Competition_and_Market_Structure_of_Basic_Telecommunication_Services_in_India.

Joskow, J. (1960). Structural indicia: Rank-shift analysis as a supplement to concentration ratios. *Review of Economics and Statistics, 42,* 113–116. https://doi.org/10.2307/1926106.

Kambhampati, U. S., (1995). The persistence of profit differentials in Indian industry. *Applied Economics, 27,* 353–361. doi/abs/https://doi.org/10.1080/00036849500000119.

Kaushik, B., & Abhiman, D. (2003). Dynamics of market structure and competitiveness of the banking sector in India and its impact on output and prices of banking services. *Reserve Bank of India Occasional Papers, 24*(3), 124–159. Available at: https://rbidocs.rbi.org.in/rdocs/Publicati ons/Pdfs/60614.pdf.

Lall, S. (2001). Competitiveness indices and developing countries: An economic evaluation of the global competitiveness report. *World Development, 29*(9), 1501–1525. https://doi.org/10.1016/ S0305-750X(01)00051-1.

Mueller, D.C. (1990). The persistence of profits in the United States. In D. C. Muller (Ed.), *The dynamics of company profits: An international comparison.* Cambridge, MA: Cambridge University. Press. Available at:https://link.springer.com/chapter/10.1007/978-1-349-11786-4_6).

Pushpangadan, K., & Shanta, N. (2006, Spetember). Competition in Indian manufacturing industries: A mobility analysis. *Economic and Political Weekly, 30,* 4130–4137. Available at: https://www.epw.in/journal/2006/39/review-industry-and-management-review-issues- specials/competition-indian.

Pushpangadan. K., & Shanta, N. (2008). Competition and profitability in Indian manufacturing industries, *Indian Economic Review, 43*(1), 103–123. Available at:https://www.jstor.org/stable/ 29793903.

Scherer, F. M. (1973). *Industrial market structure and economic performance.* Chicago: Rand-Mcnally. https://doi.org/10.2307/3003013.

Schumpeter, J. A. (1942). *Capitalism, socialism, and democracy university of illinois at urbana-champaign's academy for entrepreneurial leadership historical research reference in entrepreneurship.* Available at SSRN: https://ssrn.com/abstract=1496200.

Singh, A. & Whittington, G. (1968). *Growth, profitability and valuation.* London: Cambridge University Press. https://doi.org/10.2307/2296816.

Smith, A. (1776). *An enquiry into the nature and causes of the wealth of nations.* In E. Cannan (Ed.) (1976). Chicago: The University of Chicago Press. (https://press.uchicago.edu/ucp/books/book/ chicago/I/bo3637045.html).

Stewart-Knox, B., & Mitchell, P. (2003). What separates the winners from the losers in new food product *development?. Trends in Food Science and Food Technology, 14*(2), 58–63. https://doi.org/10.1016/s0924-2244(02)00239-x.

Wells, L. E., Farley, H., & Armstrong, G. A. (2007). The importance of packaging design for own-label food brands. *International Journal of Retail and Distribution Management, 35*(9), 677–690. https://doi.org/10.1108/09590550710773237.

Chapter 9
Labour Regulations and Employment Growth in the Organised Food Processing Industry in India

Prateek Kukreja⊙

9.1 Introduction

Industrialisation has always been viewed as an engine of economic growth. The manufacturing sector bears strong bidirectional linkages with agriculture for labour absorption and higher growth. Emphasis has been laid in India on the growth of the manufacturing sector as it can contribute to capital accumulation and technical change. This approach is rooted in a dual-sector growth model (Lewis 1954): in a developing economy, growth can be explained in terms of the labour transition between the "capitalist" sector and the "subsistence" sector. Lewis envisaged that the surplus labour would continually exit the subsistence sector and expand the capitalist sector, but this process of industrialisation remains a challenge in most developing countries, and it has not fully translated into productive jobs in nations where it has occurred (Rodrik 2016; Gollin et al. 2016).

Immediately after independence, India adopted an industry-led growth path of development and initiated wide-ranging reforms in the industrial sector. As a result, output in the organised manufacturing sector[1] has grown impressively, though employment has grown at a sluggish rate. The share of the agriculture and allied sector's income in the total national income has been declining steadily, and it reached 15% in the 2000s, even though the employment share has remained high, at around 55%. In contrast, the share of organised manufacturing output in the national income has been around 25%, as has its share in total employment.

The initiation of economic reforms at the beginning of the 1990s is considered the turning point in India's economic development. The reforms intensified in pace from

---

[1]The Factories Act 1948 statistically defines the formal, or organised, sector as one which covers all factories that run on electricity and employ 10 or more workers and all factories that do not run on electricity and employ 20 or more workers.

P. Kukreja (✉)
Indian Council for Research on International Economic Relations, New Delhi, India
e-mail: prateekkukreja89@gmail.com

© The Author(s), under exclusive license to Springer Nature Singapore Pte Ltd. 2021
S. Bathla and E. Kannan (eds.), *Agro and Food Processing Industry in India*, India Studies in Business and Economics, https://doi.org/10.1007/978-981-15-9468-7_9

1995 and brought in their wake the inflow of foreign capital, gradual dismantling of licensing in intermediate and capital goods and significant reductions in industrial tariffs and non-tariff barriers. These domestic market reforms, complemented with greater openness to external trade, were expected to induce competition and technology transfer and, in turn, raise the rate of growth and productivity which would improve the pace of job creation. Historically, India's comparative advantage has been in unskilled labour-intensive industries, and it seemed likely that economic reforms would allow those industries to yield higher benefits and, thereby, create productive employment. Unfortunately, this has not been the case so far, as employment in the organised manufacturing has slowed down significantly, amidst a consistently high growth rate of output (Singh et al. 2017), and even labour-intensive industries—food processing, textile and clothing—have been experiencing a deceleration in employment growth for quite some time. And if at all labour is hired, it is not deemed productive because informalisation is increasing in the formal (organised) sector.[2]

This issue of informalisation in the labour market has been at the centre stage of discussion for a long time. Goldar (2014) and Sen and Das (2015), among many, find that the capital intensity in organised manufacturing has been growing, and that this capital intensity explains the sluggish growth in employment, higher labour productivity and lowered demand for labour. Trade reforms have reduced the rental rate of capital, and this reduced rate explains the low labour demand in labour-intensive industries. Yet another explanation is that the stringent labour laws cause significant inflexibilities. The focus has largely been on the Industrial Disputes Act, 1947, which forms the basis for the regulation of job security in the organised manufacturing segment. The norms for dismissal are strict; according to Chapter V-B of the Act, "any firm employing 100 or more regular workers has to seek permission from the labour department, with jurisdiction over the firm, before any layoffs or retrenchment". But the concerned labour department rarely gives such permission, even in cases where the unit is unprofitable and on the verge of closure. Such rigidities inhibit the job-creating potential of organised manufacturing and the favourable effects of globalisation (Goldar 2014). The effects of labour regulation have not been felt in India, however, because regulatory compliance and enforcement has been poor or firms have circumvented them (Nagaraj 2002; Dutta 2003; Ramaswamy 2003).

There are two distinct perspectives on the impact of labour market regulations on employment and productivity performance in manufacturing (Freeman 1993). The "distortionists" maintain that regulations upset the functioning of the free market and hinder changes in the labour market in response to economic shocks and, hence, moot for greater flexibility in the labour market (Salvanes 1997; Nickell 1997; Burki and Perry 1997; Blanchard and Wolfers 2000; Forteza and Rama 2002; Besley and Burgess 2004). The "institutionalists" argue that labour institutions facilitate the

---

[2]An informalisation of industrial labour is stated to take place through an increasing share of employment in the unorganised sector in total manufacturing and through subcontracting and use of temporary and contract workers within the organised manufacturing sector (Goldar and Aggarwal 2010).

redistribution of profits between employers and workers, and a wide range of positive effects on economic outcomes; hence, they stress, institutions are important.

The debate between these two distinct perspectives hinges on empirical analysis. Based on a panel of data for more than 70 developing countries, Cesar and Alberto (2003) and Botero et al. (2003) found that industrial growth is distorted by stricter labour regulations, which may result in higher unemployment. In the Indian context, Basu (2005) showed that the labour laws, which are designed to protect the interests of workers, may end up hurting them. A well-known study in this regard is Besley and Burgess (2004),[3] who classified each Indian state as being pro-worker (+1), neutral (0) or pro-employer (−1), based on the amendments made to Chapter V-B of the Industrial Disputes Act, 1947, and cumulated the assigned scores over time to arrive at a "regulatory measure" every year in each state. The economic performance of organised manufacturing varies by state, but it improves significantly in states where labour market flexibility is greater. Hasan et al. (2007)modified the index and derived their measure of labour market rigidity; using it, Kukreja and Bathla (2018) find in case of labour-intensive organised textile and clothing industry that the employment levels in states with flexible labour regulations were on an average 1.20 times higher than in states with relatively rigid regulations. The authors made a case for flexible labour regulations in the case of textile and clothing.

The institutionalists contend that labour laws do not necessarily impede economic development; by upholding standards of pay and working conditions, they may encourage the employer and employee to co-invest in firm-specific skills and complementary productive assets and, in turn, enhance enterprise efficiency and welfare (Freeman 1993; Campbell and Sengenberger 1994; Streeck 2004); and that there is no strong evidence to show that pro-worker legislation impedes employment growth (Baker et al. 2004; Deakin and Sarkar 2011). However, the empirical findings are inconclusive, and fewer studies have been undertaken for the industry-specific effects of labour regulations at the state level.

To gauge the dynamics of employment growth in the context of state-level labour legislation, we take up the case of the organised food and beverages sector (National Industrial Classification 2008; codes 10 and 11) and focus on Chapter V-B of the Industrial Disputes Act, 1947. We choose the organised food and beverages sector because it is a sunrise sector; the demand for processed foods is growing fast, and the potential for generating employment and accelerating agricultural growth is considerable. The government considers this sector a priority sector, and it has extended various fiscal incentives to attract private investment and foreign direct investment (FDI).

Section 9.2 delineates the policy initiatives taken by the government in the processed foods and beverages sector and the employment scenario from 1999–2000

---

[3]This study has been criticised for methodological shortcomings, including the "miscoding of individual amendments and misleading aggregation and cumulation procedures" (Bhattacharjea 2006, 2017, 2019; Anant et al. 2006). But it provides useful insights into the rigidities in India's labour laws, and the index has been used—with and without modification into the impact of labour regulations on employment outcomes (see among others, Hasan et al. 2007; Kukreja and Bathla 2018).

to 2015–14. Section 9.3 investigates the relationship between labour regulations and employment at the state level in 17 major Indian states. We empirically analyse the issue by estimating a modified version of the derived labour demand equation; we use a system generalised method of moments (GMM) for the estimation. Section 9.4 presents the conclusions and implications.

We extracted the data on key indicators—number of persons engaged, contract workers, wages, gross value added (GVA) and fixed capital stock in the organised food processing industry—at NIC-2004 3-digit level from the Annual Survey of Industries, Ministry of Statistics and Programme Implementation, Central Statistical Office (CSO), Government of India (GoI). The time series data is given in nominal prices; we use the appropriate indices to convert these into real prices at the 2004–2005 base. The Consumer Price Index for Industrial Workers (CPI-IW) is used as a deflator for wages. The GVA is deflated by the Wholesale Price Index (WPI) for manufactured goods, and the fixed capital stock is deflated by the WPI for machinery and transport equipment. The information on policy initiatives in the sector is extracted from the secondary literature and from the website of the Ministry of Food Processing Industries, GoI.

9.2 India's Food Processing Industry and Policy Initiatives: An Overview

In the food processing process, the original physical properties of a raw product of agriculture, dairy, animal husbandry, meat, poultry or fishing are transformed such that the transformed product has commercial value, and it is suitable for human and animal consumption. Food processing involves value addition through preservation, addition of food additives, drying, etc. India's food processing sector includes fruit and vegetables; spices; meat and poultry; milk and milk products; alcoholic beverages; fisheries; grain processing; and other consumer product groups such as confectionery, chocolates, cocoa products, soya-based products, mineral water and high-protein foods. Besides having linkages with the agricultural sector, food processing plays a critical role in a country's economic growth. Accounting for around 32% of India's overall food market, the food processing industry contributes significantly to the nation's welfare. The sector is characterised by a dualistic structure, where the organised segment exists alongside a huge unorganised segment that accounts for nearly 28% of gross value added and 75% of employment share in total food processing segment (World Bank 2014). The importance of food processing in any country's economy cannot possibly be overemphasised.

There is a huge, untapped potential in the industry, particularly in the case of fruits and vegetables. India is the world's second largest producer of fruits and vegetables after China, but merely 2.2% of the total produce is processed (Devi 2014). India's food and grocery market is huge, contributing almost 70% to total retail sales, and ranks sixth globally (IBEF 2019). Realising the critical role that the food processing industry plays in economic growth and its prospects of employment generation, the government has undertaken a number of initiatives, from building infrastructure to reducing food wastage and promoting the Ease of Doing Business.

The government has allowed FDI up to 100% under the automatic route. This has resulted in inflows of USD 1.7 billion from April 2014 to December 2016, and of USD 263.71 million from April 2017 to June 2017 (GoI-Ministry of Food Processing Industries).

The government has allowed 100% FDI under the government approval route for trading, including through e-commerce for food products produced and/or manufactured in India. To boost growth in the e-retail segment of the industry, the government has allowed 100% FDI for food processing in e-commerce through the government approval route for products manufactured and/or produced in India. This has not only led to a significant rise in the inflow of foreign investment, but has also given impetus to 'Make in India' programme of the government, creating huge employment opportunities in the sector.

Further, food processing units are now exempt from paying income tax on profits for the first five years of operation; for the next five years, they are exempted from paying income tax on 25% of their profits. The government has reduced excise duty on refrigerated containers from 12.5 to 6%; on food processing and packaging machinery, the excise duty has been reduced from 10 to 6%. The government does not levy excise duty on dairy sector machinery (used for pasteurising, drying or evaporating). The government has reduced the basic customs duty—from 10 to 5%—imposed on project imports for cold storages, cold chambers and cold chains, including pre-cooling units, pack houses, sorting and grading lines and ripening chambers. The government does not levy a service tax on pre-conditioning, pre-cooling, ripening, waxing and retail packing; labelling of fruits and vegetables; or the transport of food grains including rice and pulses, flours, milk and salt by rail, ship and road.

Next, by prioritising infrastructure investment in food processing, the government can provide direct employment in large numbers. To improve infrastructure, the Ministry of Food Processing Industries implemented the Integrated Cold Chain and Value Addition Infrastructure Scheme in 2008 "to provide integrated cold chain and preservation infrastructure facilities, without any break, from the farm gate to the consumer. It covers creation of infrastructure facility along the entire supply chain, viz. pre-cooling, weighing, sorting, grading, waxing facilities at farm level, multi-product/multi-temperature cold storage, controlled atmosphere (CA) storage, packing facility, Individual Quick Freezers (IQF), blast freezing in the distribution hub and Reefer Vans, mobile cooling units for facilitating distribution of horticulture, organic produce, marine, dairy, meat and poultry, etc. The scheme allows flexibility in project planning with special emphasis on creation of cold chain infrastructure at farm level" (GoI—Ministry of Food Processing Industries).

9.3 Employment Scenario in the Organised Food and Beverages Sector and the Share of Contract Workers

In 2016–17, the food processing sector employed around 18.54 lakh people, or 12.43% of the total employment in organised manufacturing (GoI—Annual Survey of Industries, 2016–17), and the unorganised food processing sector employed around 51.11 lakh people, or about 14.18% of the total employment in the unorganised manufacturing sector (GoI—National Sample Survey 2015–16). A major proportion of the employment was generated by units in fruits and vegetable processing, prepared animal feed material, fish processing and meat processing and preserving units.

As has been reported in overall manufacturing, the disaggregate sectors also show growing informalisation in employment. The share of contract workers in overall manufacturing employment rose from 19.73% in 1999–2000 to 33.61% in 2013–14 (GoI—Annual Survey of Industries 1998–2018). Around 31.19% of the workers in the organised food and beverages sector were employed through contractors in 2016–17. Overall employment grew at 2.05% per annum from 1999–2000 to 2013–14, and the employment of contract workers grew at a much higher 5.17% (Table 9.1). In the organised manufacturing sector overall, contract labour employment rose from 1.21 million in 2000–01 to about 3.40 million in 2011–12, and the share of contractual labour in total employment increased from 20.28 to 34.63% (Hoda and Rai 2015).

The employment of contract workers grew in all the selected states, except Haryana, and, in most states, the annual growth rate in hiring contract workers exceeded the annual growth rate of hiring total workers. The highest share of contract workers in total workers (57.79%) is in Haryana, though the rate of growth from 1999 to 2013 was negative. In the formal sector, informalisation is increasing, probably because labour market rigidities, and other factors such as growing capital intensity, raise the labour productivity but lower the demand for labour (Goldar 2014; Sen and Das 2015). Firms may employ temporary or contract workers to escape the strict provisions against firing under Chapter V-B of the Industrial Disputes Act (Goldar and Agarwal 2010). The share of contract workers in total workers has grown significantly in all the sub-sectors of the food and beverage industry (Fig. 9.1); firms may be replacing regular workers with contract workers to avoid the ambit of Chapter V-B of the Industrial Disputes Act. This observation also pertains to the organised cotton and textile industry (Kukreja and Bathla 2018).

9.4 Impact of Labour Regulations on Employment

Based on the labour market flexibility index (Hasan et al. 2007), we partition states to examine the impact of labour regulations on employment. If the state is classified as being pro-employer, its labour market is flexible; if the state is classified as

Table 9.1 Spatial trends in employment in food processing industry and labour market flexibility across states (average 1999–2013)

States	Total Workers (no.)	Contract workers (%)	Total workers (annual growth rate, %)	Contract workers (annual growth rate, %)	Composite measure of labour market flexibility
Andhra Pradesh	146,876	36.08	0.83	1.52	Flexible
Bihar	11,081	45.08	5.82	14.83	Inflexible
Gujarat	60,976	39.28	3.88	7.74	Flexible
Haryana	31,549	57.79	−0.42	−1.06	Inflexible
Karnataka	67,697	25.38	3.30	7.22	Flexible
Kerala	145,267	2.91	1.44	10.13	Inflexible
Madhya Pradesh	28,373	29.15	0.90	7.29	Inflexible
Maharashtra	127,585	28.52	2.45	5.02	Flexible
Orissa	18,351	38.28	4.23	4.06	Inflexible
Punjab	74,590	48.98	1.25	1.29	Inflexible
Rajasthan	20,576	44.95	7.55	11.26	Flexible
Tamil Nadu	127,457	16.28	3.01	11.16	Flexible
Uttar Pradesh	121,176	33.49	0.29	3.35	Inflexible
West Bengal	53,900	19.23	3.34	13.88	Inflexible
All India	1,116,381	26.78	2.05	5.17	

[*]Index of labour market flexibility based on Hasan et al. (2007)
Source Based on the Annual Survey of Industries, CSO, MoSPI

being pro-employee or neutral, its labour market is inflexible. Pro-employee amendments were made to the Industrial Disputes Act in Maharashtra and Gujarat, but Hasan et al. (2007) classify these states as being pro-employer; Kerala, with net pro-employer amendments, is classified pro-employee.[4] The effect of labour regulations is measured using a dummy variable, with value '1' assigned to a state with pro-employer labour regulations, whereas value '0' assigned to a state with pro-employee labour regulations. A modified version of the derived labour demand equation is estimated as follows:

$$L_{ist} = \alpha + \beta_1 W_{ist} + \beta_2 Q_{ist} + \beta_3 \left(\frac{K_{ist}}{L_{ist}} \right) + \varphi \text{FLEX}_s + u_i \tag{1}$$

---

[4]Indian businesses and entrepreneurs perceive Maharashtra and Gujarat to be business-friendly, and they find that labour regulations and over-manning in Kerala are extensive (Dollar et al. 2002; World Bank 2003).

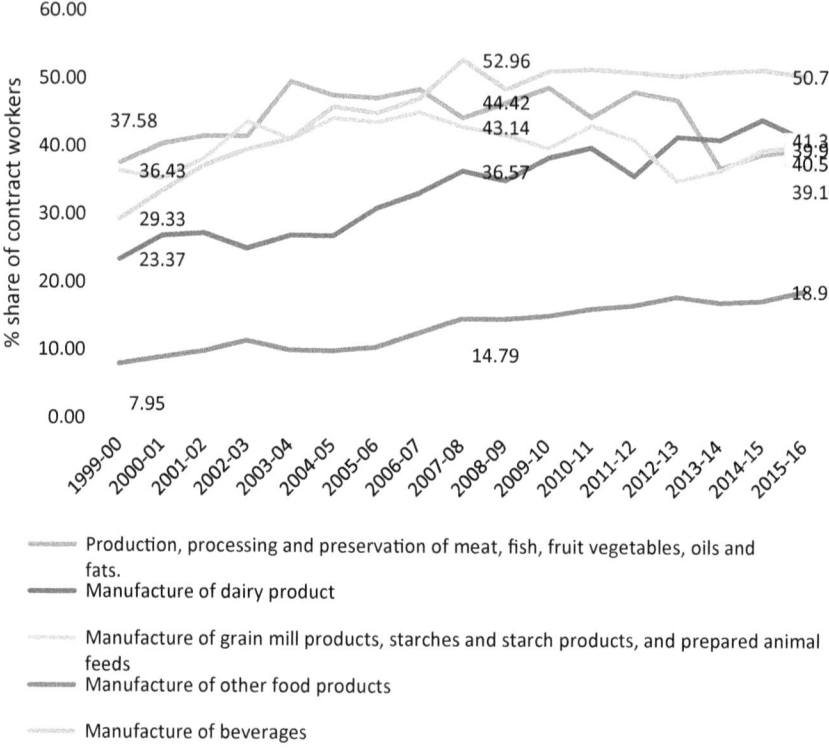

Fig. 9.1 Share of contract workers in the organised food processing industry (%, 1999–2015).
Source Based on Annual Survey of Industries, MoSPI, GoI

where L_{ist} is employment in industry i in state s at time t; W_{ist} real wage rate in industry I in state s at time t; Q_{ist} real GVA in industry i in state s at time t; $(K_{\text{ist}}/L_{\text{ist}})$ capital intensity of industry i in state s at time t; FLEX_s labour market flexibility in state s; and u_i is the error term.

Table 9.2 provides state-wise estimates of these variables averaged from 1999–2000 to 2015–16. The data on wages, GVA and capital stock are given in nominal prices, and we use the appropriate indices to convert them into real prices at the 2004–05 base. We use the Consumer Price Index for Industrial Workers (CPI-IW) as the deflator for wages. To deflate the GVA, we use the WPI for manufactured goods; to deflate the fixed capital stock, we use the WPI for machinery and transport equipment.

From 1999–2000 to 2015–16, on average, employment in the organised food processing sector was high in Maharashtra, Andhra Pradesh and Tamil Nadu and low in Jharkhand, Bihar and Odisha. Maharashtra tops the states in terms of GVA generated, followed by Uttar Pradesh, Karnataka and Andhra Pradesh. Jharkhand recorded the lowest GVA in food processing, followed by Bihar and Odisha. These

Table 9.2 State-wise estimates and annual growth rate of employment, wages, GVA and capital intensity (average 1999–2000 to 2015–16)

States	No. of workers per Industry (growth per annum in %)	Real wage rate per industry (INR) (growth per annum in %)	Real GVA per industry (INR lakh) (growth per annum in %)	Capital Intensity per industry (INR lakh) (growth per annum in %)
Andhra Pradesh	36,473 (−0.36%)	54,595.90 (1.46%)	70,454.32 (5.65%)	5.65 (4.84%)
Assam	15,562 (1.45%)	37,241.22 (2.46%)	21,694.06 (7.27%)	6.83 (2.18%)
Bihar	3,281 (6.16%)	60,119.30 (2.53%)	7,768.44 (9.12%)	9.61 (9.94%)
Gujarat	16,770 (3.23%)	69,978.12 (2.49%)	52,490.74 (9.55%)	8.42 (6.99%)
Haryana	8,580 (0.66%)	75,789.37 (4.25%)	30,428.84 (6.94%)	9.82 (10.62%)
Jharkhand	650 (8.57%)	61,373.78 (1.86%)	2,536.94 (13.62%)	6.66 (4.27%)
Karnataka	18,728 (3.08%)	76,718.57 (3.35%)	72,362.83 (10.23%)	9.58 (5.97%)
Kerala	31,036 (0.36%)	62,839.61 (1.32%)	24,670.28 (6.21%)	5.05 (1.85%)
Madhya Pradesh	6,778 (4.27%)	64,061.06 (1.63%)	32,417.99 (8.37%)	9.11 (6.26%)
Maharashtra	39,344 (2.12%)	79,978.23 (2.34%)	130,094.11 (6.51%)	10.26 (5.71%)
Odisha	4,760 (3.87%)	51,095.17 (2.68%)	8,483.69 (13.83%)	6.64 (4.59%)
Punjab	19,557 (1.29%)	72,641.71 (1.86%)	50,161.67 (3.38%)	6.94 (4.80%)
Rajasthan	5,678 (6.03%)	72,834.88 (2.45%)	25,258.64 (12.81%)	7.15 (6.14%)
Tamil Nadu	32,680 (3.16%)	55,742.29 (2.43%)	62,590.56 (7.79%)	6.37 (4.85%)
Uttar Pradesh	31,788 (0.41%)	72,295.29 (3.48%)	78,707.28 (5.62%)	10.55 (8.62%)
Uttarakhand	3,826 (7.93%)	66,024.89 (1.73%)	20,030.25 (18.99%)	8.67 (6.45%)
West Bengal	14,032 (3.35%)	62,177.46 (0.80%)	27,461.15 (13.55%)	7.72 (6.93%)

Note Figures in parentheses represent annual rate of growth
Source Author's calculation based on the Annual Survey of Industries database

trends in employment and GVA seem to be driven largely by factors such as government incentives, FDI inflow and better infrastructure. The rate of growth in employment is positive, except in Andhra Pradesh, and it is higher (more than 4%) in most of the agriculture-based states—Bihar, Jharkhand, Madhya Pradesh, Uttarakhand and Rajasthan. From 1999–2000 to 2015–16, the rates of growth in GVA per industry and capital intensity are higher, at more than 4% per annum, in all the states except Kerala.

A dynamic panel is estimated, where the lagged-dependent variable (total persons employed) appears as an independent variable. The following double-log functional form is specified.

$$\log L_{\text{ist}} = \beta_0 + \beta_1 \log L_{\text{is}(t-1)} + \beta_2 \log W_{\text{ist}} + \beta_3 \log Q_{\text{ist}}$$
$$+ \beta_4 \log K_{\text{ist}} / L_{\text{ist}} + \beta_5 \text{LABREG}_s + u_{\text{ist}} \tag{2}$$

The analysis pertains to the period from 1999–2000 to 2015–16. Table 9.2 furnishes empirical results with alternate specifications. Specification (1) shows results based on a pooled OLS regression. The OLS estimates may be biased if the lagged independent variable is correlated with the dependent variables. We introduce state fixed effects to control for state-specific and time-invariant factors. The industry fixed effects are also used to control for industry-specific time-invariant factors that influence employment in the organised manufacturing sector. We also introduce year fixed effects to control for state- and industry-invariant but time-variant factors.

The relationship between employment and wages tends to be bidirectional in Indian manufacturing, indicating the possibility of a simultaneity bias. The Hausman endogeneity test confirms the presence of endogeneity; we address this by using a system GMM estimator (GMM-SYS). The GMM-SYS estimator combines time-differencing of the model to get rid of the industry or state fixed effect with instrumenting endogenous covariates with both lagged level and lagged differences of time covariates. This approach allows us to consider the endogeneity arising from unobservable industry-specific or state-specific fixed effects and address the simultaneity bias arising due to the endogeneity of inputs (Van Beveren 2010). The results are presented in Specification (2).

We test the validity of GMM-SYS estimation. We perform the Arellano–Bond test to test for the absence of second-order autocorrelation in the transformed idiosyncratic errors, and we perform the Hansen test to test the validity of the imposed over-identifying moment conditions directly. If the null hypotheses of both these tests cannot be rejected, the GMM-SYS estimation results may be deemed valid.

Table 9.3 shows the results. The equation is well specified, and the coefficients are found to have the expected signs. The coefficient of labour regulations is positive, but it has little effect on employment in the organised food and beverages sector, as indicated by the insignificant sign of the coefficients in Specification (2). This is in contrast with the majority of the extant literature that employed the original index of Besley and Burgess (2004) and concluded that employment growth tends to be higher in states where labour regulations are relatively rigid than in states where

Table 9.3 Estimate of labour demand function in India's organised food processing industry

Variables	(1) OLS	(2) GMM-SYS
Dependent variable: ln L_{ist}		
ln labour$_{is(t-1)}$	0.649^c (0.028)	0.070 (0.073)
ln wage rate$_{ist}$	−0.186^c (0.052)	−0.481^a (0.287)
ln GVA$_{ist}$	0.233^c (0.023)	0.446^c (0.053)
ln capital intensity (K_{ist}/L_{ist})	−0.125^c (0.027)	−0.244^c (0.084)
Labour reglation$_s$	0.083^b (0.033)	0.040 (0.148)
Constant	0.958^c (0.136)	–
Year effects	Yes	Yes
Industry effects	Yes	Yes
State effects	Yes	Yes
AR(1)		Prob > chi2 = 0.000
AR(2)		Prob > chi2 = 0.774
Hansen test		Prob > chi2 = 0.072
No. of observations	1,334	1,334
Overall R-squared	0.972	–

Note
-Figures in parentheses represent robust standard errors
-The asterisks denote statistical significance as follows:
^{a}Statistically significant at 10% level
^{b}Statistically significant at 5% level
^{c}Statistically significant at 1% level
Source Authors' calculations using data from Annual Survey of Industries, GoI

labour regulations are relatively flexible. This contrasting result is expected, however, as with an increased use of contract workers—indicated by their sharply rising share in total employment—employers seem to have circumvented the firing and overall compliance cost of regular workers as stipulated by the Indian labour laws (Sapkal 2016). This is based on the theoretical premise that the employment decisions of firms are a function of firing and compliance costs (Adhvaryu et al. 2013; Bertola 1990).

The coefficients of wage rate (β_2) and capital intensity (β_4) bear the expected signs, indicating a negative relationship with employment growth. A significantly positive value of the coefficient corresponding to lagged employment term (β_1) across all specifications suggests the presence of a significant adjustment cost involved in hiring and firing workers.

9.5   Conclusions and Implications

Based on a derived labour demand equation, we find that the effect of labour regulations on employment in the organised food and beverages industry from 1999–2000 to 2015–16 is insignificant. This finding deviates from the earlier work undertaken for overall manufacturing, based on the original index by Besley and Burgess (2004), which concludes that states with relatively rigid labour regulations tend to exhibit higher employment growth compared to states with relatively flexible labour regulations. This contrasting result is expected, as with an increasing use of contract workers by firms, employers may circumvent the firing and overall compliance cost of regular workers as stipulated by the Indian labour laws.

The government has been making efforts to increase the flexibility in labour regulations. It introduced the Industrial Relations Code, 2019, to ease labour laws for employers by retaining the ceiling on the employee count for a firm to retrench workers without prior approval, while empowering the state government to change the number of employees through a notification. The government has sought to make fixed-term and seasonal employment more attractive for companies, particularly in sectors which typically hire workers for a fixed term. While this provides firms with greater flexibility to shift their workforce depending on market conditions, this form of employment is more often than not deprived of job security safeguards and can, therefore, add to the precarious labour problem. The idea behind these efforts at easing labour regulations stems from the government's sensitivity with respect to the potential adverse effect of labour regulations on employment.

Nevertheless, we find no conclusive evidence of the negative impact of the so-called rigid labour regulations on employment in the case of food manufacturing. The organised manufacturing sector increasingly uses contract workers, and so firms circumvent the "rigidity" caused by labour regulations. Providing additional flexibility by easing labour laws may increase inefficiency overall and lead to welfare losses (Sharma 2006). Instead of attempting to reform labour laws, therefore, policymakers need to look for other factors that may be causing rigidity in the labour market and, in turn, restraining employment. One important factor of labour market rigidity could be a mismatch between industry needs and workers' skills (Solow 1998). The competitiveness of industry may be affected by a shortage of skilled, semi-skilled and unskilled workers. The problem can pervade the entire food value chain and other segments in the manufacturing sector. It is, therefore, essential that industry strengthens its capacity to develop and train human resources efficiently and increase the pace of job creation rather than focusing solely on reforming labour laws by increasing flexibility.

References

Adhvaryu, A., Chari, A. V., & Sharma, S. (2013). Firing costs and flexibility: Evidence from firms' employment responses to shocks in India. *Review of Economics and Statistics, 95*(3), 725–740.

Anant, T. C. A., Hasan, R., Mohapatra, P., Nagaraj, R., & Sasikumar, S. K. (2006). Labour markets in India: Issues and perspectives. In J. Felipe & R. Hasan (Eds.), *Labour markets in Asia: Issues and perspectives* (pp. 205–300). Basingstoke: Palgrave Macmillan.

Baker, D., Glyn, A., Howell, D. R., & Schmitt, J. (2004). Labor market institutions and unemployment: Assessment of the cross-country evidence. In D. R. Howell (Ed.), *Fighting unemployment: The limits of free market orthodoxy* (pp. 72–118).

Basu, K. (2005). Global labour standards and local freedoms. In *Wider perspectives on global development* (pp. 175–200). UK: Palgrave Macmillan.

Bertola, G. (1990). Job security, employment and wages. *European Economic Review, 34*(4), 851–879.

Besley, T., & Burgess, R. (2004). Can labor regulation hinder economic performance? Evidence from India. *The Quarterly Journal of Economics, 119*(1), 91–134.

Bhattacharjea, A. (2006). Labour market regulation and industrial performance in India: A critical review of the empirical evidence. *Indian Journal of Labour Economics, 49*(2), 211–232.

Bhattacharjea, A. (2017). Threshold effects of Indian labour laws: A critical review of some recent research. In U. Kapila (Ed.), *India's economy pre-liberalisation to GST: Essays in honour of Raj Kapila*. New Delhi: Academic Foundation.

Bhattacharjea, A. (2019). *Labour market flexibility in Indian industry: A critical survey of the literature* (Centre for Development Economics Working Paper) (p. 296). New Delhi.

Blanchard, O., & Wolfers, J. (2000). The role of shocks and institutions in the rise of european unemployment: The aggregate evidence. *the Economic Journal, 110*(462), 1–33.

Botero, J. C., Djankov, S., La Porta, R., López de Silanes, F., & Shleifer, A. (2003). *The regulation of labor* (NBER Working Paper (w9756)).

Burki, S. J., & Perry, G. (1997). *The long march: A reform agenda for Latin America and the Caribbean in the next decade*. World Bank Publications.

Campbell, D., & Sengenberger, W. (1994). *International labour standards and economic interdependence*. International Institute for Labour Studies.

Cesar, C., & Alberto, C. (2003). Are labour market regulations an obstacle for long-term growth? In *Seventh Annual Conference of the Central Bank of Chile on Labour Markets and Institutions*.

Deakin, S., & Sarkar, P. (2011). *Indian labour law and its impact on unemployment, 1970–2006: A leximetric study*. Centre for Business Research, University of Cambridge.

Devi, C. U. (2014). Trade performance of Indian processed foods in the international market. *Procedia-Social and Behavioral Sciences, 133*, 84–92.

Dollar, D., Iarossi, G., & Mengistae, T. (2002). *Investment climate and economic performance: Some firm level evidence from India* (Working Paper No. 143). Development Research Group, The World Bank.

Dutta, R. (2003). Labor market, social institutions, economic reforms and social cost. In S. Uchikawa (Ed.), *Labour market and institution in India, 1990s and beyond* (pp. 13–37). New Delhi: Manohar.

Forteza, A., & Rama, M. (2002). *Labor market rigidity and the success of economic reforms across more than one hundred countries*. Mimeo, The World Bank.

Freeman, R. B. (1993). Labor markets and institutions in economic development. *The American Economic Review, 83*(2), 403–408.

GOI. (2016–17). *Economic survey of India-2016–17*.

GOI. (1998–2018). *Annual survey of industries*. Ministry of Statistics and Programme Implementations. Central Statistics Office, Govt. of India.

GOI—Ministry of Food Processing Industries. (n.d.a). *Cold chain*. https://mofpi.nic.in/Schemes/cold-chain.

GOI—Ministry of Food Processing Industries. (n.d.b). *Statement on financial year wise FDI equity inflows (2000–2017): Food processing industries.* https://mofpi.nic.in/sites/default/files/fdi_2_0. pdf.

GOI. (2015–16). *National sample survey—Economic characteristics of unincorporated non-agricultural enterprises.* Ministry of Statistics and Programme Implementation. Central Statistics Office, Govt of India.

Goldar, B. (2014). *Globalisation, growth and employment in the organised sector of the Indian economy* (IHD Working Paper WP 06/2014). New Delhi.

Goldar, B., & Aggarwal, S. C. (2010). *Informalization of industrial labour in India: Are labour market rigidities and growing import competition to blame?*. New Delhi: Institute for Economic Growth.

Gollin, D., Jedwab, R., & Vollrath, D. (2016). Urbanisation with and without industrialisation. *Journal of Economic Growth, 21*(1), 35–70.

Hasan, R., Mitra, D., & Ural, B. P. (2007). Trade liberalization, labor-market institutions and poverty reduction: Evidence from Indian states. In *India policy forum* (Vol. 3, No. 1, pp. 71–122). National Council of Applied Economic Research.

Hoda, A., & Rai, D. K. (2015). *Labour regulations and growth of manufacturing and employment in India: Balancing protection and flexibility* (ICRIER Working Paper 298). New Delhi.

IBEF. (2019). *India food processing industry report.* India Brand Equity Foundation.

Kukreja, P., & Bathla, S. (2018). Labour regulations and informalisation in India's organised manufacturing: A case of textile and clothing. *Indian Journal of Labour Economics, 61*(3), 473–492.

Lewis, W. A. (1954). Economic development with unlimited supplies of labour. *The Manchester School, 22*(2), 139–191.

Nagaraj, R. (2002). *Trade and labour market linkages in India: Evidence and issues* (East-West Center Working Paper No. 50) (pp. 1–24).

Nickell, S. (1997). Unemployment and labor market rigidities: Europe versus North America. *The Journal of Economic Perspectives, 11*(3), 55–74.

Ramaswamy, K. V. (2003). Liberalization, outsourcing and industrial labor markets in India: Some preliminary results. In S. Uchikawa (Ed.), *Labour market and institution in India, 1990s and beyond.* New Delhi: Manohar.

Rodrik, D. (2016). Premature deindustrialisation. *Journal of Economic Growth, 21,* 1–33.

Salvanes, K. G. (1997). Market rigidities and labour market flexibility: An international comparison. *The Scandinavian Journal of Economics,* 315–333.

Sapkal, R. S. (2016). Labour law, enforcement and the rise of temporary contract workers: Empirical evidence from India's organised manufacturing sector. *European Journal of Law and Economics, 42*(1), 157–182.

Sen, K., & Das, D. K. (2015). Where have all the workers gone? Puzzle of declining labour intensity in organised Indian manufacturing. *Economic & Political Weekly, 50*(23), 108–115.

Sharma, A. N. (2006). Flexibility, employment and labour market reforms in India. *Economic and Political Weekly,* 2078–2085.

Singh, J., Das, D. K., Kukreja, P., & Abhishek, K. (2017). Law, skills and the creation of jobs as 'contract' work in India: Exploring survey data to make inferences for labour law reform. *The Indian Journal of Labour Economics, 60*(4), 549–570.

Solow, R. M. (1998). *What is labour market flexibility? What is it good for?* The British Academy

Streeck, W. (2004). Beneficial constraints and economic progress. *Socio-Economic Review, 2*(3), 405ff.

Van Beveren, I. (2010). Total factor productivity estimation: A practical review. *Journal of Economic Surveys, 26*(1), 98–128.

World Bank. (2003) *Doing business in 2004: Understanding regulation.* Oxford University Press for the World Bank.

World Bank Group. (2014). *Republic of India: Accelerating agricultural productivity growth.* Washington, DC: World Bank. https://openknowledge.worldbank.org/handle/10986/21419. License: CC BY 3.0 IGO.

Chapter 10
Beyond the Polemics: Subcontracting in the Unorganised Food Manufacturing Sector in India

Shayequa Zeenat Ali

10.1 Introduction

In India's food manufacturing—as in its manufacturing sector overall—a large number of less productive, small- and medium-sized unorganised units coexists with a few highly productive, large organised units. The complementarity between these two segments is weak, and this is held to adversely affect the development and growth of the unorganised manufacturing sector. Subcontracting[1] can link these unorganised manufacturing units with their organised counterparts and enable their growth,but the literature on this aspect is divided.

The *benign view* is that small dynamic units in the unorganised sector benefit from the trickledown effects of the inputs and technology provided by large, productive units in the organised sector, especially because these small units could not otherwise have afforded these inputs or technology. Unorganised sector units that employ a relatively large number of workers and possess a certain minimum level of capital intensity and dynamism have a static labour–cost advantage, and the ability to increase productivity and purchase intermediate inputs from large units in the organised sector (Marjit 2003). They are more likely to forge links with large units in the organised sector (Basole et al. 2014). When the organised sector expands, the dynamic component of the unorganised sector expands too by drawing labour from

---

[1] According to Ministry of International Trade and Industry (MITI), Government of Japan (GOJ), "A contractual arrangement between a firm and a "parent" firm; typically, the parent firm has more capital and employees. A firm needs production inputs—products, parts, attachments, materials or components—or it needs to produce or repair facilities, equipment or tools used in production. In subcontracting, a parent firm commissions a smaller firm to produce or repair these inputs"- Translated into English by Kimura (2002).

S. Z. Ali (✉)
National Council of Applied Economic Research, New Delhi, India
e-mail: shayequa.z.ali@gmail.com

its own stagnant segment which, in turn, depends on labour from the agricultural sector (Ranis and Stewart 1999).

The contrasting *exploitation view* is that subcontracting hurts small firms because parent units take undue advantage of their low bargaining power. The unfavourable terms of trade result from the asymmetry in bargaining power, mainly from cost-cutting by the larger, organised firms (Mehrotra and Biggeri 2007). The surplus extraction by these firms reinforces stagnation in unorganised units. The larger firms also tend to be exploitative by manipulating the terms of contract and benefits at the expense of growth in subcontracting firms (Moser 1978; Tokman 1978; Portes and Walton 1981; NCEUS 2007).

However, the impact of subcontracting varies across different manufacturing sectors. Delayed payment by the parent firms was cited as one of the most important problems by subcontracting units interviewed in the states of West Bengal, Haryana and Maharashtra (Sahu 2010). There is also evidence that within the unorganised manufacturing, subcontracting linkage plays a very limited role in the transition of some low productivity small units to become medium- and larger-sized high produc-tivity units (Raj and Sen 2016). To delve into this issue, the case of processed food and beverage enterprises in the unorganised segment is taken up. The key hypoth-esis tested is that subcontracting may not be exploitative because affordable inputs would improve the productivity of small units in the unorganised sector. Section 10.2 describes the database and methodology. Section 10.3 is divided into four sections. Sections 10.3.1 and 10.3.2 present the structure of subcontracting units in food manu-facturing and their performance vis-à-vis non-subcontracting units. This is followed by Sect. 10.3.3, which is an analysis of whether subcontracting is a beneficial exer-cise for the workers or not. Finally, Sect. 10.3.4 empirically analyses the factors that influence enterprises to engage in subcontracting,including the role of location and enterprise type. Section 10.4 presents the major findings.

10.2   Database and Methodology

A comparative analysis is conducted across three types[2] of enterprise—own account manufacturing enterprises (OAME), non-directory manufacturing enter-prises (NDME) and directory manufacturing enterprises (DME)—in rural and urban areas. The Government of India (GoI) unit-level data on enterprises from three rounds

---

[2]OAME (own account manufacturing enterprise) is an enterprise, which is run without any hired worker employed on a fairly regular basis.

Establishment: Enterprise which is employing at least one hired worker on a fairly regular basis is termed as establishment. Paid or unpaid apprentices, paid household member/servant/resident worker in an enterprise are considered as hired workers. Establishments are categorised into-

-NDME (non-directory manufacturing enterprise) is a (manufacturing) establishment with 1–5 numbers of workers;

-DME (directory manufacturing enterprise) is a (manufacturing) establishment with number of workers equal to or more than 6 (NSSO 2017).

of the National Sample Survey (NSS) of the National Sample Survey Office (NSSO): 61st (2000–01), 66th (2005–06) and 73rd (2015–16) by enterprise type and location (rural or urban) have been extracted for this study. The GoI-NSS 2010–11 survey data has been excluded from the analysis because the variable "marketing arrangements of enterprise", taken to indicate subcontracting activity, is not clearly defined.[3]

The National Industrial (Activity) Classification (NIC) 2008 groups food manufacturing into meat (101), fish (102), fruits and vegetables (103), oils and fats (104), dairy (105), grain mill and starch (106), other foods (107), animal feed (108) and beverages (110). To compare the performance of subcontracting enterprises with that of non-subcontracting enterprises, the trends in assistance from parent firms, the number of units and workers per unit (firm size); key productivity measures such as labour productivity; and the labour efficiency index[4] (LEI) are analysed. The formula for LEI is:

$$LEI = (Q/L)_d - (Q/L)_a$$

where

$(Q/L)_d$ desired labour productivity.
$(Q/L)_a$ actual labour productivity.

Labour productivity is measured as the Gross Value Added (GVA) per worker and so the actual growth of labour productivity is indicated by the growth in observed values of the GVA per worker. In general accounting practice, the desired growth of labour productivity, is measured as a sum of growth of growth of capital labour ratio (K/L) and growth of GVA per unit of capital (Q/K). Hence, the desired growth of labour productivity (Q/L)d can be expressed as:

$(Q/L)_d$ $GR(K/L) + GR(Q/K)$.
$GR(K/L)$ Compound annual growth rate (GR) of capital intensity (K/L).
$GR(Y/K)$ Compound annual growth rate (GR) of capital productivity (Y/K).
If $LEI = 0$ Labour is as efficient as it should be given technical coefficients of production units.
If $LEI > 0$ Labour is more productive than the expected rate.
If $LEI < 0$ Shows inefficiency in the use of labour inputs given capital-labour ratio and capital productivity in the production unit.

To examine the determinants of subcontracting, a binary logistic regression model has been used.

---

[3]Data for a later year (67th Round Survey data for 2009–10) are available, but has not been used, because the 67th Round yielded results that depart drastically from the previous trend; for example, the incidence of subcontracting for the entire informal sector fell from 30% in the 2000–01 and 2005–06 surveys to around 20% in 2009–10. The results from other NSS surveys (2009–10) show a drastic fall in the female labour force participation rate and almost no growth in the labour force over a five-year period (Basole et al. 2014; Thomas 2014).

[4]As given in Ahmed (1981).

$$SC(\text{subcontracting}) = \beta_0 + \beta_1 \text{Sec}_f + \beta_2 \text{Ent\_type}_f + \beta_3 \text{Premises}_f + \beta_4 \text{Acc}_f$$
$$+ \beta_5 \text{Regis}_f + \beta_6 \text{Status}_f + \beta_7 \text{GVAann}_f + \beta_8 \text{NIC3\_digit}_f$$

Where:

Subcontracting (SC) is the binary dependent variable (Enterprise undertakes work on contract basis = 1; Enterprise does not take work on contract basis = 0).

Ent_Type$_f$	Type of Enterprise (OAME or NDME or DME) with "DME" as the reference category.
Sec$_f$	Sector of enterprise f (Rural or Urban) with Urban as the reference category.
Premise$_f$	Location of enterprise f (within household premises "WHH" or outside household premises "OHH") with OHH as reference category.
Acc$_f$	Maintenance of accounts of enterprise f (Yes or No) with No as reference category.
Regis$_f$	Registration of enterprise f under any authority (Yes or No) with No as reference category.
Status$_f$	Status of enterprise f over the last three years (Yes = increasing or No = not) with No as reference category.
GVAann/worker	Natural log of annual GVA per worker
NIC3_digit$_f$	NIC 3-digit category dummy of enterprise f, with Beverages as reference category.

10.3   Subcontracting in Unorganised Food Manufacturing Units: Structure and Performance

10.3.1   Structure of Subcontracting Food Manufacturing Enterprises

Contractors provide subcontractors with inputs such as raw material, equipment and product designs specifications. The natural conjecture is that these inputs help improve the performance of subcontracting firms, especially if they are OAMEs or located in rural sector, because they could not otherwise have afforded these inputs. In India, the NSSO conducts quinquennial surveys and collects data on subcontracting by unorganised firms and on various other aspects. From 2000–01 to 2015–16, the percentage share and absolute number of subcontracting firms that received equipment from parent firms increased steadily. A substantial share and number of units received raw material from parent firms over the 15 years. However, there was a dip in 2005–06. A large proportion of these units received assistance in the form of product design in 2005–06. The trend for same reversed in 2015–16 (Fig. 10.1).

During the last fifteen years, the number of total unorganised subcontracting enterprises increased from 5.22 million in 2000–01 to 5.41 million in 2005–06 and then to 60.7 million in 2015–16. The share of subcontracting food processing units in total subcontracting units decreased from 2.04% in 2000–01 to 1.87% in 2015–16 (Table 10.1). However, subcontracting in food units grew at a rate of 2.8% per annum from 2005 to 2015. This could be because of the increase in equipment and raw materials provided by the parent units to subcontracting units during the same period.

The share of rural subcontracting units was much higher than that of urban subcontracting units (Figs. 10.2 and 10.3). Irrespective of location and enterprise type, the largest share of units fell under the OAMEs, followed by NDMEs and DMEs. However, these patterns were not specific to just subcontracting units but also to their non-subcontracting counterparts.

The NSS Enterprise Survey data at NIC-3 digit categories indicated that during the early 2000s, more than 50% of the subcontracting units were in the grain mill and starch category, but this concentration shifted to the other foods category since 2005–06. In the year 2015–16, 44.0% of the subcontracting food manufacturing units were found in other foods category, whereas in case of the non-subcontracting units, a major share (48.0%) of the units was in grain mill and starch segment (Figs. 10.4 and 10.5).

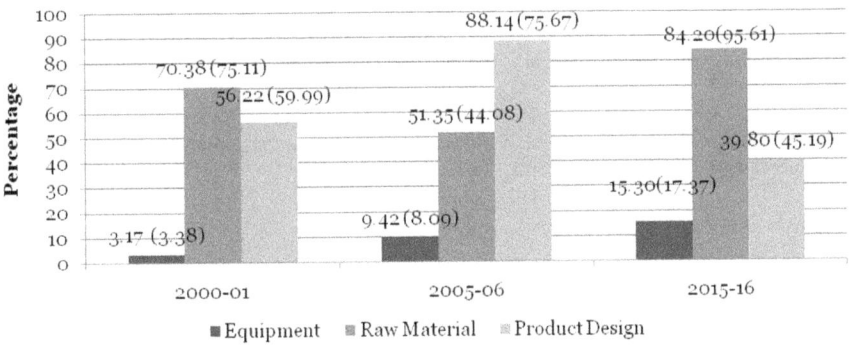

Fig. 10.1 Percentage share of subcontracting units provided with assistance by parents units (2001–2015). Note: Figures in parentheses indicate number of units in thousands. Source: GoI-NSSO (2000–01; 2005–06; 2015–16)

Table 10.1 Subcontracting (SC) in unorganised food manufacturing units

Year	% Share of SC food manufacturing to total SC units	CAGR of SC food manufacturing units (% per annum)
2000–01	2.04	–
2005–06	1.59	−4.3
2015–16	1.87	2.8

Source: GoI-NSSO (2000–01; 2005–06; 2015–16)

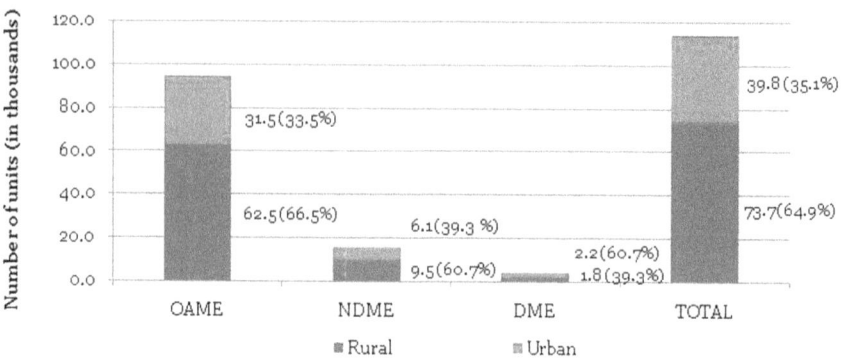

Fig. 10.2 Subcontracting units 2015–16.

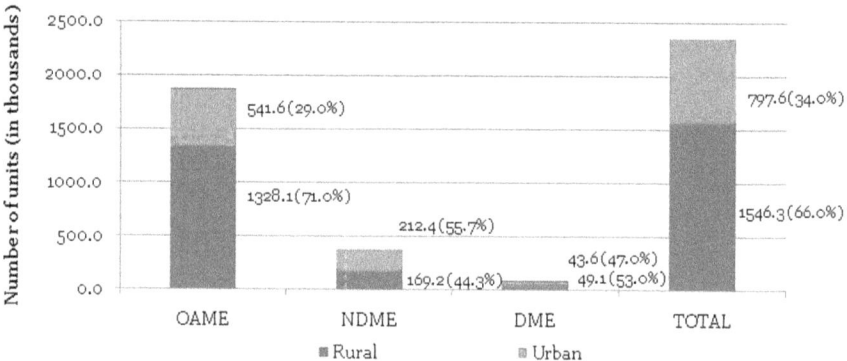

Fig. 10.3 Non-subcontracting units 2015–16. Note: Figures in parentheses indicate percentage share of rural and urban units within each enterprise type. Source: GoI-NSSO 73rd round (2015–16)

Fig. 10.4 Subcontracting units 2015–16 ('000s). Note: F&V-fruits and vegetables; O&F-oils and fats; GMS-grain mill and starch; OF-other foods; AF-animal feed. Source: GoI- NSSO 73rd round (205–16)

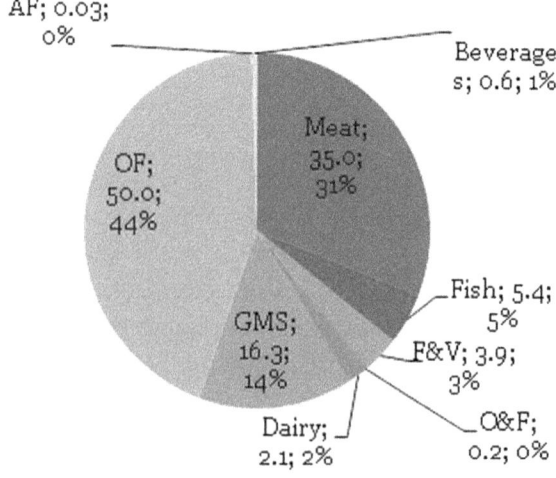

Fig. 10.5 Non-subcontracting units 2015–16 ('000s). Note: F&V-fruits and vegetables; O&F-oils and fats; GMS-grain mill and starch; OF-other foods; AF-animal feed. Source: GoI- NSSO 73rd round (205–16)

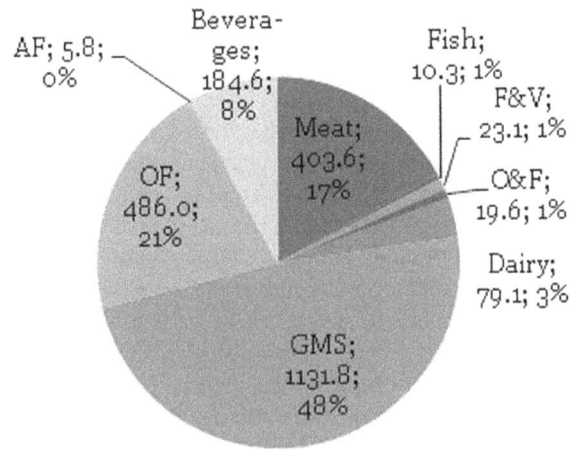

An examination of firm size showed that although both subcontracting and non-subcontracting units were of the same size in total and across locations (two workers per unit), there was some variation across enterprise type (Table 10.2). Subcontracting DMEs had a larger firm size, and in fact, rural DMEs were larger than urban ones. As shown in Fig. 10.4, although most subcontracting units were clustered around other foods and meat, the firm size for the same was not among the largest, implying that 71% of subcontracting units are very small. With four workers per unit, animal feed units were the largest of all subcontracting units, but its percentage share was negligible.

Table 10.2 Firm size of food manufacturing units (2015–16, worker per unit)

	Subcontracting				Non-subcontracting			
	OAME	NDME	DME	Total	OAME	NDME	DME	Total
Total	1	3	11	2	2	3	9	2
Rural	1	2	11	2	2	3	9	2
Urban	2	3	10	2	2	3	9	2
Top three largest units by NIC categories	Animal feed (4), oils and fats, dairy and beverages (all having 3 workers per unit)				Fish, fruits and vegetables and other foods (all having 3 workers per unit)			

Source: GoI-NSSO, 73rd round (2015–16)

10.3.2   Efficiency of Subcontracting Food Manufacturing Units

This section examines the efficiency of subcontracting food manufacturing units vis-à-vis non-subcontracting ones by location, enterprise type and NIC-3 digit categories. From 2005 to 2015, the growth rate in labour productivity was positive in both subcontracting and non-subcontracting units (Table 10.3). Non-subcontracting units were more productive in total. However, in rural areas sub-contracting units fared better than their non-subcontracting counterparts. Among the subcontracting units, Oils and Fats, Beverages and Fish were the most productive units.

Capital intensity on the other hand exhibited positive growth rates for both subcontracting and non-subcontracting units, albeit the rate was higher for the latter (Table 10.4). The growth rate for both categories was the same in rural areas (7.5% per annum). However, in case of urban areas, capital intensity of subcontracting units was lower than that of non-subcontracting units.

Table 10.3 Growth rate of labour productivity of subcontracting versus non-subcontracting units (2005–15) (percent per annum)

	Subcontracting units				Non-subcontracting units			
	OAME	NDME	DME	Total	OAME	NDME	DME	Total
Total	−0.9	0.7	−0.6	1.0	3.3	2.4	−0.3	2.1
Rural	0.8	5.0	−1.7	1.8	2.6	3.2	−3.4	0.9
Urban	−3.8	−2.3	−1.5	−0.2	1.7	0.9	−1.3	0.3
Segments with highest growth rates	Oils and fats (6.6), beverages (6.3) and fish (6.1)				Oils and fats (2.6), other foods (2.2) and beverages (1.6)			

Source: GoI-NSSO, 62nd and 73rd rounds (2005–06 and 2015–16)

Table 10.4 Growth rate of capital intensity of subcontracting vs non-subcontracting units (2005–15) (percent per annum)

	Subcontracting units				Non-subcontracting units			
	OAME	NDME	DME	Total	OAME	NDME	DME	Total
Total	13.3	4.8	−4.1	7.1	10.5	7.9	9.8	9.8
Rural	19.2	4.2	− 12.5	7.5	7.9	6.2	6.9	7.5
Urban	2.0	4.6	5.8	6.6	9.1	7.2	5.0	7.0
3 fastest growing segments	Dairy (10.5), fish (10.4) and other foods (9.0)				Other foods (13.7), fish (12.4) and dairy (12.3)			

Source: GoI-NSSO, 62nd and 73rd rounds (2005–06 and 2015–16)

Table 10.5 Growth rate of capital productivity of subcontracting vs non-subcontracting units (2005–15) (percent per annum)

| | Subcontracting units | | | | Non-subcontracting units | | | |
	OAME	NDME	DME	Total	OAME		NDME	DME	Total
Total	−12.5	−3.9	3.7	−5.7	−6.5		−5.1	−9.2	−7.0
Rural	−15.4	0.7	12.4	−5.3	−5.0		−2.9	−9.6	−6.1
Urban	−5.7	−6.5	−6.9	−6.4	−6.7		−5.9	−6.0	−6.3
3 fastest growing segments	Grain mill and starch (1.8) and fruits and vegetables (0.1). All other segments experienced negative growth rates				All segments experienced negative growth rates				

Source: GoI- NSSO, 62nd and 73rd rounds (2005–06 and 2015–16)

Capital productivity exhibited negative growth rates for both sub-contracting and non-subcontracting units (Table 10.5). In both cases, the annual growth rates for urban units were lower than that of rural units.

Given the performance of the technical coefficients discussed above, a labour efficiency index (LEI) was constructed for the period 2005 to 2015. If labour is as efficient as it should be (based on the technical coefficients of the production units), the index value is 0. The LEI value was 0.4 for subcontracting units, both in rural and urban areas (Fig. 10.6). Barring rural NDMEs, where the LEI value was negative, subcontracting units were found to be performing optimally. The rural non-subcontracting units operated at efficiency levels way below their potential given the respective growths in capital intensity and capital productivity. However, labour in urban non-subcontracting units was more productive than expected, and it increased the overall LEI value to 15.7 and made up for the negative values in rural units.

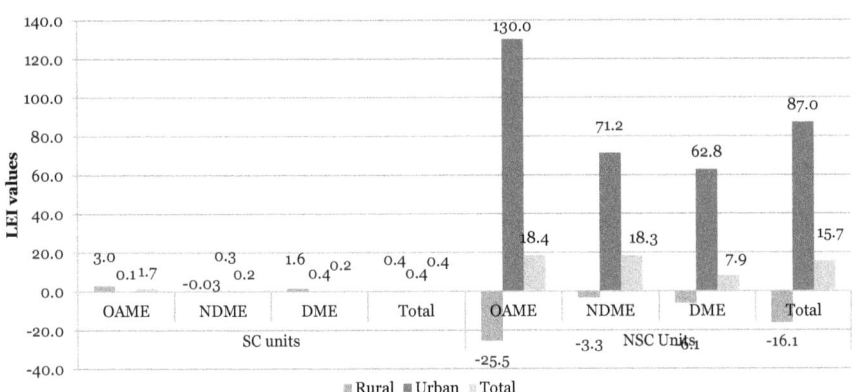

Fig. 10.6 Labour efficiency index (2005–2015). Source: Author's calculations from GoI-NSSO, 62nd and 73rd rounds (2005–06 and 2015–16)

Table 10.6 Labour efficiency index of subcontracting units by NIC 3-digit categories (2005–15)

NIC 3-digit categories	SC total	NSC total	Subcontracting							
			Rural				Urban			
			OAME	NDME	DME	Total	OAME	NDME	DME	Total
Meat	5.1	0.3	5.4	NA	NA	4.5	NA	2.6	NA	2.1
Fish	0.3	2.1	NA	NA	0.7	0.3	−0.1	NA	−2.2	1.3
Fruits and vegetables	0.0	0.3	3.3	NA	1.5	0.1	0.0	9.9	NA	0.3
Oils and fats	0.9	0.5	NA	0.5	NA	−0.1	NA	1.6	NA	1.0
Dairy	5.7	1.3	0.5	NA	−0.1	0.5	0.4	3.7	5.1	8.6
Grain mill and starch	0.0	0.5	0.1	0.2	2.5	0.2	0.0	0.1	0.4	0.0
Other foods	0.2	1.4	0.0	0.0	0.0	0.0	0.2	0.0	1.3	0.4
Animal feed	NA	0.1	NA	NA	NA	NA	NA	NA	NA	NA
Beverages	2.8	0.8	NA	NA	NA	3.3	2.4	−0.2	NA	0.1
Food Manufacturing	0.4	0.7	3.0	0.0	1.6	0.4	0.1	0.3	0.4	0.4

Source: Author's calculations from GoI-NSSO, 62nd and 73rd rounds (2005–06 and 2015–16)

The LEI values (2005-15) for subcontracting units as a whole showed that Fruits and Vegetables and Grain Mill and Starch units operated at the most optimum level given the growth in their technical coefficients. At the NIC three-digit level, one could not compute the LEI for subcontracting animal feed units as data as there were missing values (absence of units) for certain categories at both points of time. Rural-urban location wise data for subcontracting units revealed that in the case of rural beverage units, some categories (enterprise type) had no units in one year, but they did add up to a rational number in total in both years, and the LEI value (3.3) could be computed. From 2005 to 2015, only oils and fats units in rural areas operated below efficiency; meat and beverage units in rural areas operated at a higher efficiency than expected given their technical coefficients; and all the urban units operated at or above efficiency levels (Table 10.6).

10.3.3 Labour Compensation

Labour compensation is a good measure of improvement or deterioration in living standards. While analysing labour compensation for persons engaged in unorganised food units, only working owners and hired workers are considered. Therefore, OAMEs are excluded from this part of the analysis because they do not hire workers whereas NDMEs and DMEs do. In both rural and urban areas, each worker in the subcontracting units earned slightly more (INR 36,500 per annum) than one in non-subcontracting units (INR 34,900 per annum) (Fig. 10.7).

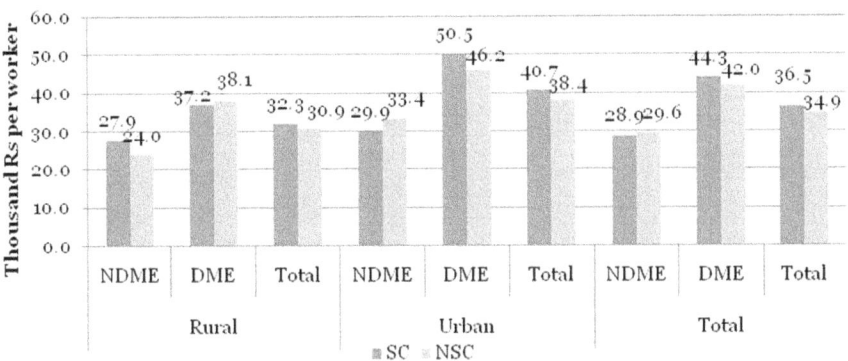

Fig. 10.7 Annual emoluments per worker in unorganised food manufacturing (2015–16). Source: GoI-NSSO, 73rd round (2015–16)

Workers in non-subcontracting NDMEs earned more than those in subcontracting NDMEs. However, subcontracting DMEs gave a higher compensation to their workers (Rs. 44,300 per worker per annum) than their non-subcontracting counterparts (Rs. 42,000 per worker per annum). Again, as in the case of NDMEs, a similar pattern was observed only in urban areas and not in the rural. The DMEs in urban areas outnumber the DMEs in rural areas and raise compensation in subcontracting DMEs above that in non-subcontracting ones. The compensation in meat, fish and grain mill and starch units raised the compensation in subcontracting units above that non-subcontracting units (Table 10.7).

In both NDMEs and DMEs, urban subcontracting units paid more than rural subcontracting units, but rural subcontracting units in meat, fruits and vegetables and grain mills and starch NDMEs and in dairy DMEs paid more than urban subcontracting units. Subcontracting units paid more, and work in urban DMEs was more profitable.

10.3.4 Factors Affecting Subcontracting in Unorganised Food Manufacturing

Finally, the factors that determine a unit's decision to subcontract from a parent firm (in 2015–16) were examined using a binary logit regression model. The role of certain key characteristics of production units indicating that they are progressive was examined in this section. The distribution of food manufacturing units in each of these parameters is discussed below.

Table 10.8 reveals that more than half of the non-subcontracting units and 33% of the subcontracting units were located outside the household premises. In subcontracting units, a larger proportion of rural units were located outside the household premises whereas in case of non-subcontracting units, it was mostly urban units.

Table 10.7 Emoluments per person engaged of subcontracting vs non-subcontracting units (2015–16) (Rs. thousand/person)

NIC 3-digit categories	Subcontracting total	Non–subcontracting total	Subcontracting units			
			NDME		DME	
			Rural	Urban	Rural	Urban
Meat	36.08	35.63	37.60	27.09	NA	NA
Fish	55.11	24.48	12.38	NA	52.59	57.99
Fruits and vegetables	31.90	39.39	56.03	11.86	26.55	71.16
Oils and fats	30.73	37.09	26.18	26.29	NA	74.34
Dairy	29.01	34.56	16.40	33.74	30.69	14.33
Grain mill and starch	31.13	27.22	19.97	15.18	35.79	67.74
Other foods	36.67	37.43	19.41	32.81	36.29	47.59
Animal feed	16.12	42.02	16.12	NA	NA	NA
Beverages	27.93	36.68	24.02	35.32	NA	26.69
Food manufacturing	36.50	34.93	27.94	29.95	37.24	50.55

Note: Figures presented are in real prices with 2011–12 as base year
Source: GoI- NSSO, 73rd round (2015–16)

Also located outside the household premises were a larger proportion of NDMEs and DMEs, and a lower proportion of OAMEs, among subcontracting and non-subcontracting units. All the subcontracting units in oils and fats and animal feed were located outside household premises.

Only 28.0% of non-subcontracting units but 41.0% of subcontracting units were registered under an actor authority. A higher percentage of rural subcontracting units were registered than urban subcontracting units. But in case of non-subcontracting units, more urban units were registered compared to the rural ones. Registration was very high among subcontracting units in meat (94.0%), oils and fats (78.0%) and beverages (68.0%).

Only 11.0% of subcontracting units, but 31.0% of non-subcontracting units exhibited an expanding status. Among both subcontracting and non-subcontracting units, a more of urban units expanded over the previous three years compared to rural units (Table 10.9). Out of all the subcontracting units, 100 % of animal feed and 60.0% of oils and fats units exhibited expanding status. A larger percentage of DMEs and NDMEs compared to OAMEs expanded over the previous three years.

Units that maintained accounts were in all probability more organised and had owners with better managerial skills. Among subcontracting and non-subcontracting units, a relatively low percentage of units has maintained accounts (5 and 6%, respectively), but in both cases a higher share of urban units, DMEs and NDMEs than rural units and OAMEs did the same (Table 10.7). A large proportion of beverage and oils and fats subcontracting units maintained accounts.

Table 10.8 Descriptive statistics of key factors affecting decision to subcontract

Percentage of units		Subcontracting units				Non-subcontracting units			
		OAME	NDME	DME	Total	OAME	NDME	DME	Total
Located outside household premises	Total	23.0	79.0	87.0	33.0	43.0	76.0	85.0	51.0
	Rural	29.0	79.0	71.0	36.0	39.0	73.0	92.0	45.0
	Urban	11.0	81.0	100.0	26.0	54.0	79.0	77.0	62.0
	Top 3 segments	Oils and fats, animal feed (both 100%) and beverages (68%)				Meat (81%), other foods and animal feed (both 68%)			
Registered under any act/authority	Total	36.0	61.0	78.0	41.0	22.0	55.0	53.0	28.0
	Rural	50.0	64.0	72.0	52.0	16.0	41.0	27.0	19.0
	Urban	10.0	55.0	84.0	21.0	37.0	66.0	82.0	47.0
	Top 3 segments	Meat (94%), oils and fats (78%) and beverages (68%)				Meat, oils and fats (both 42%) and fruits and vegetables (31%)			
With an expanding status over the last three years	Total	6.0	28.0	38.0	11.0	28.0	42.0	53.0	31.0
	Rural	7.0	15.0	61.0	9.0	29.0	41.0	57.0	31.0
	Urban	6.0	47.0	20.0	13.0	26.0	42.0	48.0	32.0
	Top 3 segments	Animal feed (100%), oils and fats (60%) and fruits and vegetables (44%)				Fruits and vegetables (40%), fish (36%), other foods and meat (both 34%)			
Maintaining accounts	Total	1.0	11.0	55.0	5.0	4.0	13.0	30.0	6.0
	Rural	1.0	9.0	49.0	3.0	3.0	10.0	15.0	5.0
	Urban	2.0	16.0	60.0	7.0	5.0	15.0	46.0	10.0
	Top 3 segments	Beverages (50%), oils and fats (40%) and dairy				Oils and fats (14%), fish (13%) and animal feed (11%)			

Source: GoI-NSSO, 73rd round (2015–16)

Table 10.9 Factors determining subcontracting in unorganised food manufacturing units (2015–16) (odds ratio)

Dependent variable	Subcontracting (yes = 1)	All	OAME	NDME	DME
Enterprise type	Ref. cat (DME)				
	OAME	0.71***	–	–	–
	NDME	0.71***	–	–	–
Sector	Ref. cat (urban)				
	Rural	0.55***	0.53***	0.44***	0.75***
Premises	Ref. cat (outside household)				
	Within household	0.28***	0.20***	0.95**	1.18***
Accounts maintained	Ref. cat (no)				
	Yes	1.01^{NS}	1.95***	1.03^{NS}	0.60^{NS}
Registration	Ref. cat (no)				
	Yes	0.23***	0.17***	0.59***	0.47***
Status	Ref. cat (not expanding)				
	Expanding	3.56***	4.89***	1.71***	1.76***
LnGVA (annual) per worker		1.59***	1.62***	1.37***	0.78***
Food categories	Ref. cat (beverages)				
	Meat	0.02***	0.01***	0.29***	–
	Fish	0.00***	0.00***	0.92^{NS}	0.01***
	Fruits and vegetables	0.01***	0.00***	0.81*	0.06**
	Oils and fats	0.20***	–	0.55***	1.28^{NS}
	Dairy	0.07***	0.04***	0.45***	0.09***
	Grain mills and starch	0.19***	0.10***	0.95^{NS}	0.15***
	Other foods	0.02***	0.01***	0.36***	0.11***
	Animal feed	0.24***	–	0.85^{NS}	–
Constant		24.30***	51.67***	2.66***	59.44***
Number of observations		16,135	8,632	6,230	1,273

Note: *, **, *** indicate significance of odds ratio values at 10, 5 and 1 per cent levels respectively; NS indicates non-significance

Source: Author's calculations from GoI-NSSO, 73rd round (2015–16)

The results for the binary logit regression are presented in Table 10.9. The first model "All" examines the role of enterprise type, sector, premises, maintenance of accounts, registration, status and value added per worker in the decision to subcontract in the unorganised food manufacturing sector overall.

Results of the first model revealed that units in urban areas, of DME type, located outside the household premises, and those that were expanding over the past three years were more likely to be in a subcontracting relationship with parent units than units in rural areas, of OAME type, located within the household premises that had not expanded in the past three years. Units registered under an Act or Authority were less likely to be subcontracting than those that were not. A unit's decision to subcontract was not significantly influenced by whether they maintained accounts. Lastly, labour productivity (GVA per worker) had a positive and significant influence on the decision to engage in subcontracting.

The disaggregated analysis pertaining to three types of enterprise (with the same dependent variables as "All") shows that urban units were more likely to forge linkages than rural units. Although OAMEs and NDMEs units located outside the household premises were more likely to be subcontracting, DMEs located inside the household premises were 1.18 times as likely to be subcontracting as DMEs located outside the household premises. An OAME that maintained accounts was 1.95 times as likely to be subcontracting as one that did not, but this variable is not significant in the case of NDMEs or DMEs. The odds ratio was higher for an OAME that had expanded in the past three years (4.89) than NDMEs (1.71) or DMEs (1.76); the association was positive for all enterprise types. The association of GVA per worker with subcontracting was positive and significant for OAMEs and NDMEs but negative for DMEs.

10.4 Conclusions

From 2005–06 to 2015–16, subcontracting grew in India's unorganised food manufacturing sector, especially in rural areas. During the same period, the assistance provided by parent units to subcontracting units in the form of equipment and raw material also increased. In both rural and urban areas, OAMEs made up the largest share of units. Assistance from parent units is especially useful for small and rural based units as they are otherwise not very likely to be able to afford the same. Based on the latest available data (2015–16) most of the subcontracting units were clustered around other foods and meat. However, the largest units were found in animal feed category which accounted for a negligible share of the total number of units.

Based on the technical coefficients of units, labour efficiency index (LEI) for both subcontracting and non-subcontracting units was constructed. The LEI values were very high for urban non-subcontracting units but negative for all enterprise types in rural areas. In subcontracting units, by sector and enterprise type all the values were close to 0, indicating that they performed optimally given their technical coefficients.

Compensation to workers in subcontracting units was higher than that of non-subcontracting units. Annual emoluments per worker were much higher in urban units compared to rural ones. Analysis of data by enterprise type revealed that DMEs paid their workers (Rs. 44,300 per annum) much more than NDMEs (Rs. 28,900 per annum). At the NIC 3-digit level, workers would benefit from working in urban DMEs in all segments with the exception of dairy units where rural DMEs compensated their workers much more than urban ones.

Finally, a look at the factors that determine a unit's decision to subcontract revealed that urban DMEs units were more likely than OAMEs, NDMEs especially rural units to be in a subcontracting relationship. OAMEs and NDMEs located outside the household premises were highly likely to be subcontracting. If a unit had been expanding, it had a positive and significant association with subcontracting. Also, OAMEs that maintained accounts were more likely to be in a subcontracting relationship than those that did not, but the association was not significant. Labour productivity had a positive and significant association with subcontracting for OAMEs and NDMEs, but the relationship was negative for DMEs.

Thus, positive and close to zero LEI values of subcontracting units in all sectors and enterprise types imply that units have been operating at an optimal level. Emoluments per worker for subcontracting units were higher than that of non-subcontracting units. Therefore, subcontracting in India's unorganised food manufacturing sector is not exploitative, as has been argued in the literature; in fact, improved productivity and growth have been seen in those units.

References

Ahmed, Y. (1981). Growth of partial factor productivity and economic efficiency in manufacturing sector of developing economy—A statistical analysis. *Margin, 13*(4), 53–63.

Basole, A., Basu, D., Bhattacharya, R. (2014). *Determinants and impact of subcontracting: Evidence from India's informal manufacturing sector* (Working Paper 2014-04, Economics Department Working Paper Series, 169) (pp. 1–40). https://www.umass.edu/economics/publications/2014-04.pdf.

GoI-NSSO. (1999–2000). *Informal non-agricultural enterprises survey, July 1999–June 2000, NSS 55th round*. Ministry of Statistics and Programme Implementation. Microdata Archive—DataCatalog. https://microdata.gov.in/nada43/index.php/catalog/92.

GoI-NSSO. (2005–06). *Unorganised manufacturing enterprises survey, July 2005–June 2006, NSS 62nd round*. Ministry of Statistics and Programme Implementation. Microdata Archive—DataCatalog. https://microdata.gov.in/nada43/index.php/catalog/112.

GoI-NSSO. (2015–16). *Unincorporated non-agricultural enterprises (excluding construction)—July 2015–June 2016, 73rd round*. Ministry of Statistics and Programme Implementation. Microdata Archive—DataCatalog. http://microdata.gov.in/nada43/index.php/catalog/139.

GoI-NSSO. (2017). *Key indicators of unincorporated non-agricultural enterprises (excluding construction) in India*. New Delhi: Ministry of Statistics and Programme Implementation, Government of India. https://www.mospi.gov.in/sites/default/files/publication_reports/NSS_KI_73_2.34.pdf.

Kimura, F. (2002). Subcontracting and the performance of small and medium firms in Japan. *Small Business Economics, 18*, 163–175. https://doi.org/10.1023/A:1015187507379.

Marjit, S. (2003). Economic reform and informal wage: A general equilibrium analysis. *Journal of Development Economics, 72,* 371–378. https://doi.org/10.1016/S0304-3878(03)00082-8.

Mehrotra, S., & Biggeri, M. (2007). *Child labour and subcontracted homebased manufacturing in low and middle-income Asia.* https://www.ucw-project.org/attachment/home_based_manufacturing.PDF.

Moser, C. O. N. (1978). Informal sector or petty commodity production: Dualism or dependence in urban development? *World Development, 6*(9/10), 1041–1064. https://doi.org/10.1016/0305-750X(78)90062-1.

NCEUS. (2007). *Report on conditions of work and promotion of livelihoods in the unorganised sector.* New Delhi: National Commission for Enterprises in the Unorganised Sector. https://dcmsme.gov.in/Condition_of_workers_sep_2007.pdf.

Portes, A., & Walton, J. (1981). *Labor, class, and the international system.* New York: Academic Press. https://doi.org/10.1016/C2013-0-11322-0.

Ranis, G., & Stewart, F. (1999). V–goods and the role of the urban informal sector in development. *Economic Development and Cultural Change, 47*(2), 259–288. https://doi.org/10.1086/452401.

Sahu, P. P. (2010). Subcontracting in India's unorganised manufacturing sector: A mode of adoption or exploitation? *Journal of South Asian Development, 5*(1), 53–83. https://doi.org/10.1177/097317411000500103.

Sen, K., & Rajesh Raj, S. N. (2016). *Out of the shadows?: The informal sector in post-reform India.* New Delhi: Oxford University Press.

Thomas, J. J. (2014). The demographic challenge and employment growth in India. *Economic and Political Weekly, 49*(6), 15–17.https://www.jstor.org/stable/24479252.

Tokman, V. E. (1978). An exploration into the nature of informal-formal sector relationships. *World Development, 6*(9/10), 1065–1075. https://doi.org/10.1016/0305-750X(78)90063-3.

Chapter 11
Investment Pattern and Sources of Finance in Micro, Small and Medium Agro-Processing Enterprises in India

Santosh Kumar

11.1 Introduction

Largely falling under the unorganised (informal) segment of manufacturing, agricultural processing enterprises (APEs) in India are traditionally small units run by family workers. The dominance of APEs in total enterprises and share in employment is sizeable. Approximately 99.89% of APEs are micro-size, 0.10% are small-size and 0.01% are medium-size,[1] according to the fourth all-India census of Micro, Small and Medium Enterprises (MSMEs 2006–07).

Micro-enterprises are generally the least productive household enterprises and employing less-skilled workers (Mazumdar and Sarkar 2008; Breman 2010). Concerted efforts have been made to make these enterprises productive by expanding their size and training for the family workers. The expansion of micro APEs has been attempted through an increase in investment, particularly in plant and machinery, by giving loans at lower rates of interest. The modernisation of small enterprises is effective in generating employment, rooting out poverty and facilitating higher productivity (Raj and Sen 2015), but their transition is largely hindered by inadequate finances.

Micro-enterprises depend largely on their own resources and, in some cases, on borrowings from non-institutional sources for finance. The census reported that 1.26% of all MSMEs faced a shortage of working capital. These MSMEs are informal, and their lack of access to institutional credit is a key constraint to the growth (Winker 1999; Beck et al. 2005; Beck 2007; Kuntchev et al. 2012). Registered, perennial and

---

[1] The Micro, Small and Medium Enterprises Development Act, 2006 categorises enterprises by the original value of investment in plant and machinery; it is up to INR 25 lakh for a micro-enterprise; between INR 25 lakh and INR 5 crore for a small enterprise; and between INR 5 crore and INR 10 crore for a medium-sized enterprise.

S. Kumar (✉)
Centre for the Study of Regional Development, Jawaharlal Nehru University, New Delhi, India
e-mail: santoshkdav@gmail.com

© The Author(s), under exclusive license to Springer Nature Singapore Pte Ltd. 2021
S. Bathla and E. Kannan (eds.), *Agro and Food Processing Industry in India*, India Studies in Business and Economics, https://doi.org/10.1007/978-981-15-9468-7_11

227

urban units are less likely to face the financial constraints than unregistered, seasonal, casual and rural enterprises.

Among the APEs, the dominant ones are engaged in grain mill products, starches and starch products; prepared animal feeds; spinning and weaving and finishing of textiles; other textiles and wearing apparel (except fur apparel). The average size of output is relatively large in the units engaged in the production, processing and preservation of meat, fish, fruits and vegetables, oils and fats; beverages; spinning, weaving and finishing of textiles; knitted and crocheted fabric articles; dressing and dyeing of fur and fur articles; and tanning and dressing of leather, luggage handbags, saddlery and harness. The census acknowledged that the number of APEs in various categories declined over time despite the significant potential of increase in the number of units, workers and output.

This chapter delineates the investment pattern in MSM APEs based on the original value of investment in plant and machinery and analyses their sources of finance. It empirically examines the determinants of investment in these enterprises based on the two-stage least squares (2SLS) model. A logistic regression model is also run to investigate the economic, social and locational factors that influence their access to institutional credit. The study utilises data from the all-India census of small-scale industries (SSI) and MSMEs pertaining to the years 1972, 1987–1988, 2001–2002 and 2006–2007. The investment pattern and sources of finance in APEs are analysed at the National Industrial Classification (NIC) 2004 three-digit level for the MSME categories.

Section 11.2 reviews the relevant literature to appraise the status of investment and financial constraints faced by MSM APEs. Section 11.3 explains the selection of variables and econometric approaches used to analyse the investment pattern and institutional credit. Section 11.4 examines the trends in investment in MSM APEs and their determinants; it focuses on the role of institutional credit. Section 11.5 examines the characteristics of loans taken by these enterprises and empirically analyses their access to institutional credit. Section 11.6 concludes and discusses policy implications.

11.2   Literature on Investment and Institutional Credit in MSM APEs

The literature on the investment patterns in MSM APEs and their sources of finance is scanty. The MSM APEs are informal, less developed and spread heterogeneously across the country. Outdated technology and financial constraints have adversely affected their growth. Despite these constraints, their number has grown, and they generate massive employment and contribute to the national income, but productivity in micro-units continues to be low, and a decline in the rate of employment and output growth has led to their closure in many states.

Agro-based industries use traditional labour-intensive techniques, and their modernisation requires capital-intensive methods (Srivastava 1989). Other constraints to development are high marketing costs, large expenditure on market development, high rates of interest on working capital from commercial banks and a high tax on processed products. The Small Industrial Development Bank of India (SIDBI) instituted credit schemes for SSIs, but probably, a lack of awareness led institutional credit to decline (Pillai 1993).

The smallest size group in the unorganised sector (own account enterprises (OAE)) is disadvantageously positioned in terms of backward linkages, raw material concentration index and market size (Sarkar 1995). The advantage for the OAE was diminishing due to dispersed raw material availability. The fixed assets of OAEs declined significantly with a sizeable increase in their direct and indirect linkages, raw material concentration index and market size. Sarkar suggested that the government should promote specialisation of agricultural production required by the APEs and expand market size.

In the 1980s, the investment in fixed assets per worker increased by 66% and in net value-added per fixed assets in SSIs by 38%, but insufficient institutional credit constrained their development (Abid Hussain Committee 1998) because the government authorities' instructions and guidelines often failed to reach the operational level and might not be compliant. The Abid Hussain Committee recommended that the government establish formal financial networks to ensure that SSIs receive adequate and timely credit at a low rate of interest.

Bhide (2000) opined that the absence of trust and understanding between bank officials and SSIs was the primary reason for poor access to institutional credit and suggested a collaborative relationship, in line with banks adopted in Germany, where bank representatives are appointed to the boards of borrowing companies to monitor operations. During a recession, a bank may consider reducing the interest rate, rescheduling a loan or making an additional loan. The number of SSIs increased rapidly between 1992 and 2003, but the share of bank credit to SSIs declined, partly because the incidence of non-performing assets was high (Rao et al. 2006). Other reasons for the decline may have been changing and complex monetary regulations, sectoral specific credit limits and the changing definitions of "unit".

Unorganised non-farm enterprises receive only 5–6% of the total institutional credit, though they contribute 30% of the gross domestic product (GDP) (GoI-NCEUS 2007). The enterprises with up to INR 500,000 investment dominant micro-enterprises, however the credit taken by this segment of the enterprises, accounted 2.3–3.6% of total credit. The National Commission on Enterprises in the Unorganised Sector (NCEUS), therefore, considered a supply-side intervention and recommended reserving 12% of the adjusted net bank credit for micro-enterprises and other needy enterprises, of which 5% of credit must be reserved for those where the investment was up to INR 500,000, an additional 3% for those where investment was between INR 500,000 and INR 2.5 million and remaining 4% for the remaining enterprises.

To provide banks adequate safety nets, the Commission recommended, for loans up to INR 500,000, raising the guarantee cover from 80 to 90% under a credit guarantee scheme and reducing the guarantee fee to 1% from 1.5% of the loan amount.

The Commission suggested, in the case of default, paying 80% (the current figure was 75%) of the default sum to banks on their first reporting of defaults. It recommended the adoption of a liberal approach and a simple system to analyse borrower risk. It suggested formulating policy for training personnel and posting them in rural and semi-urban branches and granting them special incentives with appropriate rules and regulations. To augment bank loans to enterprises, it recommended that at least, two representatives from this sector should be included in the board of directors of each public sector bank. The membership could be rotated every two years.

The government accepted many of the Commission's recommendations, but the growth and development of unorganised enterprises were tardy. Labour productivity, capital intensity and total factor productivity (TFP) slowed down between 1994–1995 and 2004–2005 (Kathuria et al. 2010). Micro-enterprises were concentrated in states where the agricultural sector dominates, and their productivity and capital intensity were low (Bathla 2014).

Investment in micro-enterprises is influenced by unit-specific factors (profit, sales and credit) and external factors (geographical location, public infrastructure and policies) that need to be considered in policymaking. Based on the firm-level panel data from a nationally representative survey on informal manufacturing sector in 364 districts from 1995 to 2010, Raj and Sen (2015) find financial constraints may lead to a 2% likelihood of the firm being traditional and less productive. Raj and Sen recommend that bank branches be established in rural and remote areas and enterprises be promoted by encouraging institutional loan through corpus funds and easier procedures. Only 5.18% of MSMEs had borrowed from institutional sources and 2.05% from non-institutional sources; the rest self-financed their investments (Dahale et al. 2015). Advertising regularly in newspapers and on television could enhance the awareness of credit sources, and financial institutions should reduce documentation and ease procedures (Singh and Wasdani 2016).

The analysis of MSMEs in the literature is comprehensive, but there is little focus on APEs, especially at the disaggregate enterprise-level in rural and urban areas. The literature indicates that micro- and small-scale APEs dominate in India's MSME and SSI sectors. These enterprises generate employment and contribute significantly to the GDP, but technological upgradation and development are constrained by their small size, unskilled labour, informality, rural location, credit constraints and dependence on non-institutional sources of credit. The rate of investment is declining more in smaller units, and the probability is higher that they will be less productive and discontinue operations.

This chapter adds to the literature by investigating the magnitude of investment made by the MSM APEs, their operational characteristics, location and sources of finance during the period from 1972–1973 to 2006–2007 to identify the changes. Another reason for choosing APEs is their strong backward linkages with agriculture for providing labour and raw material.

11.3   Selection of Variables and Empirical Approaches

The data have been compiled from published reports from three sources: the all-India census of SSIs for 1972–1973 and 1987–1988; the unit-level data of the third all-India census of SSIs (2001–2002); and the fourth all-India census of MSMEs (2006–2007).

The survey data for 1972–1973 and 1987–1988 provide information for registered SSI units only, and these are not comparable with that for 2001–2002 and 2006–2007, because the two latter censuses generated information for both registered and unregistered SSIs and included MSMEs. But all four depict the broad trends of MSMEs, which is currently missing in the literature. The analysis is carried out at NIC three-digit level, but the data are not concorded for the survey years, because there are differences in the coverage of units.

We use the compound annual growth rate (CAGR) to compute the rate of growth in key performance indicators in MSM APEs. We estimate important ratios such as investment per unit, investment per output and investment per labour (capital intensity). As regards the sources of finance, we group enterprises into institutional sources and non-institutional sources.[2] In analysing the determinants of investment in MSM APEs, the dependent variable taken is the log of the original value of investment in plant and machinery per unit at 2011–2012 prices.[3]

The independent variables considered are enterprise-specific characteristics: log of institutional loan per unit, log of profit per unit, log of expenditure on electricity and raw material per unit, registration status, location, managed by men or women APEs, account exists, ancillary unit, size of APEs and life span. These variables are converted into constant prices (2011–2012) using the GDP deflator. One independent variable, institutional loan, is found to be endogenous and correlated with the error term, which generated biased estimates on using the ordinary least squares (OLS) method. Therefore, we use an instrumental variable (IV) technique, based on the two-stage least squares (2SLS) method, to examine the significance of various factors in influencing investment in APEs. This method provides consistent estimates when controlled experiments are not possible. Then we use a logistic regression model to identify the determinants of APEs' access to institutional credit. The coefficients are estimated to predict a logit transformation of the likelihoods of the presence of a phenomenon based on another phenomenon:

$$\text{Logit}(p) = b_o + b_1 X_1 + b_2 X_2 + b_3 X_3 + \ldots + \mu_o$$

---

[2]Institutional sources comprise central, state and local governmental bodies; commercial banks; co-operative banks and societies; micro-finance institutions; and other institutional agencies. Non-institutional sources comprise moneylenders, business partners, contractors, relatives and friends.

[3]The original value of investment in plant and machinery is considered to be a better measure of investment because data are available for different points of time, because it does not provide information on the cumulative depreciation of capital (Ray 2002; Kumar 2006; Kathuria et al. 2010).

where

X_1 loan taken from institutional (1) or non-institutional sources (0).
v   registered enterprises (1) and not registered enterprises (0).
X_3 rural located (0) and urban located enterprises (1).
b_o constant and μ_o = standard error term and p is the probability.

Its logit transformation as the odds ratio,

$$\text{Oddsratio} = (\frac{p}{1-p}) = \frac{\text{probabilityofpresenceofthephenomena}}{\text{probabilityofabsenceofthephenomena}}$$

$$P = \frac{1}{1 + e^{-\text{logit}(p)}}$$

The interpretation is that the odds for a positive outcome in cases that enterprises have first phenomena are b_1 times higher than in cases of another phenomenon. For a better understanding of the effects of independent variables on the dependent variable, *marginal effects (dy/dx)* (first derivative) are computed for a change in the dummy variable from 0 to 1, assuming non-linearity of the model. The discrete change for a change of sigma in X_k equals,

$$\frac{\Delta \text{Pr}(y = 1|x)}{x_k} = \text{Pr}(y = 1|x, x_k + \delta) - \text{Pr}(y = 1|x, x_k)$$

The interpretation is that for a change in variable x_k from x_k to $x_k + \delta$, the predicted probability of an event changes by $\frac{\Delta \text{Pr}(y=1|x)}{x_k}$, holding all other variables constant.

11.4   Investment Pattern and Its Determinants in APEs

11.4.1   Investment Pattern in SSI APEs (1972–1973 and 1987–1988)

The number of SSI APEs, total workers and fixed investment per worker have increased; however, fixed investment per unit has declined in 1987–1988 over 1972–1973. Table 11.1 presents the total number of registered SSI APEs at the two-digit NIC level in 1972–1973 and 1987–1988 and their annual compound growth rate. It presents the total number of workers in these units and the investment per unit and investment per worker.

The number of APEs grew from 26,252 in 1972–1973 (about 19% of all SSIs) to 194,545 in 1987–1988 (about 33% of all SSIs); the percentage share in all SSIs grew about 13.3% per annum in 1972–1973 and 1987–1988. In 1972–1973, the number of wood units was high at 12,188, followed by readymade garments (6,718 units) and

Table 11.1 Investment patterns in SSI APEs at two-digit NIC level during 1972–1973 to 1987–1988

Enterprises Group	No. of APEs			Workers (Number in lakh)			Fixed Investment per Unit (INR in lakh)			Fixed Investment per Worker (INR in lakh)		
	1972–73	1987–88	CAGR (%)	1972–73	1987–88	CAGR (%)	1972–73	1987–88	CAGR (%)	1972–73	1987–88	CAGR (%)
Food Products	6,577	96,123	18.2	1.31	4.82	8.5	10.73	6.83	−2.8	0.54	1.36	5.9
Beverages, tobacco and tobacco products	769	3,669	10.3	0.05	0.73	18.9	6.87	9.54	2.1	1.15	0.48	−5.3
Hosiery and readymade garments	6,718	39,778	11.8	0.75	1.98	6.2	6.64	4.3	−2.7	0.59	0.86	2.4
Wood Products	12,188	54,975	9.9	0.95	2.30	5.7	4.29	3.87	−0.6	0.55	0.93	3.3
All APEs	26,252	194,545	13.3	3.06	9.83	7.6	6.58	5.53	−1.1	0.56	1.09	4.3
Share of APEs in SSI (%)	18.81	33.41	3.7	18.51	26.82	2.3	0.76[a]	1.60[a]	4.75	0.06[a]	0.25[a]	9.01

Note [a]Relative share (APEs/SSI). Source: Published Reports on First and Second All-India Census of SSIs

food (6,577 units). However, in 1987–1988, the number of food units was highest at 96,123, followed by wood (54,975 units) and readymade garments (39,778 units).

Food product enterprises are increased by 18.3% per annum, which was more than the overall increase in SSI APEs in terms of units in 1972–1973 and 1987–1988. This was followed by high annual growth in hosiery and readymade garments (11.8%), beverages, tobacco and tobacco products (10.3%) and wood products (9.9%). The total number of APEs and their workforce in total SSI was close to 30% in 1987–1988.

The expansion in SSI APEs provided employment opportunities: the total number of workers increased from 306,000 in 1972–1973 (19% of all SSI workers) to 983,000 in 1987–1988 (27% of all SSI workers), an annual increase of 7.6% per annum. During 1987–1988, the number of workers was highest at 482,000 in food products, followed by wood (229,000), hosiery, readymade garments (198,000) and beverages, tobacco and tobacco products (73,000). Between 1972–1973 and 1987–1988, the number of total workers increased by 18.9% per annum in beverages, tobacco and tobacco products, 8.5% per annum in food, 6.2% per annum in hosiery and readymade garments and by 5.7% per annum in wood.

Investment in fixed assets per unit declined from INR 658,000 in 1972–1973 to INR 553,000 in 1987–1988, a decline of 1.1% per annum. Fixed investment per unit in foods fell from INR 1073,000 in 1972–1973 to INR 683,000 in 1987–1988. In beverages, tobacco and tobacco products, investment rose from INR 687,000 in 1972–1973 to INR 954,000 in 1987–1988. In hosiery and readymade garments, investment fell from INR 664,000 in 1972–1973 to INR 429,000 in 1987–1988 and in wood from INR 430,000 in 1972–1973 to INR 387,000 in 1987–1988.

Fixed investment per unit was low in all enterprises, except in beverages, tobacco and tobacco products, where it increased by 2.1% per annum between 1972–1973 and 1987–1988. Fixed investment was low mainly in food (−2.8%), followed by hosiery and readymade garments (−2.7%) and wood (−0.7%). Accordingly, a decrease in fixed investment per unit may be due to higher increase in number of SSI APEs.

The investment in fixed assets per worker in SSI APEs increased 4.22% per annum—from INR 56,000 in 1972–1973 to INR 109,000 in 1987–1988. It was high at INR 115,000 in beverages, tobacco and tobacco products, followed by hosiery and readymade garments (INR 59,000), wood (INR 55,000) and food products units (INR 54,000) in 1972–1973. However, it was the highest in food (INR 136,000), followed by wood (INR 93,000), hosiery and readymade garments (INR 86,000) and beverages, tobacco and tobacco products (INR 48,000) in 1987–1988.

Fixed investment per worker improved in all groups of SSI APEs (except beverages, tobacco and tobacco products, where it declined by 5.4% per annum). The improvement was highest at 5.98% per annum in food, followed by wood (3.29%) and hosiery and readymade garments (2.39%).

The number of SSI APEs grew between 1972–1973 and 1987–1988, as did investment in fixed assets per worker. Food enterprises accounted for the highest growth rate in the number of units and in investment in fixed assets per worker. However, per unit investment in fixed assets declined in all groups of SSI APEs except in beverages, tobacco and tobacco products. And, the decrease was highest in food, hosiery and readymade garments and wood products, possibly because the number of micro APEs grew more than the number of large APEs.

11.4.2 Investment Patterns in MSM APEs During 2001–2002 and 2006–2007

The number of units, workers and investment pattern (original value of plant and machinery) in MSM APEs is extracted for 2001–2002 and 2006–2007. The growth in investment in plant and machinery per unit and worker is required for the development of MSM APEs. The number of MSM APEs, total workers, investment per unit and investment per worker has increased during 2001–2002 and 2006–2007. The growth per annum in investment per unit is less than the growth per annum in investment per worker. The growth per annum in number of MSM APEs is more than the growth per annum in total workers. Table 11.2 provides the estimates, and the annual rate of growth, at the NIC three-digit level between 2001–2002 and 2006–2007.

The number of APEs grew from 2.276 million in 2001–2002 (21.6% of all MSMEs) to 7.106 million in 2006–2007 (27.2% of all MSMEs), at about 21% per annum. Dressing and dyeing of fur and fur articles units declined at 30% per annum, and wood, cork, straw and plating materials units declined at 2% per annum. Other enterprises grew during the period, though with sizeable variations; the growth was higher in wearing apparel (except fur), dairy and sawmilling and planning of wood. Other enterprise types grew at a lower rate.

The number of workers in APEs grew from 6.413 million in 2001–2002 (25.72% of all MSME workers) to 17.669 million in 2006–2007 (29.71% of all MSME workers), at about 18.4% per annum. In dressing and dyeing of fur and fur articles units, the growth was—26% per annum; in wood, cork, straw and plaiting materials, the growth was—2.8% per annum. Growth was higher in spinning, weaving and finishing of textiles, wearing apparel and dairy (except in fur apparel and in sawmilling and planning of wood) than in MSM APEs overall.

The average per annum investment increased at 3.77%, mainly because investment increased in tobacco (38%), dressing, dyeing of fur and fur articles (26%) and spinning, weaving and finishing of textiles (23%). The growth rate was high in tanning and dressing of leather, luggage handbags, saddlery and harness (8.4%), beverages (14%), other textiles (10%), wood, cork, straw and plaiting materials (10%), other food (16%), production, processing and preservation of meat, fish, fruit vegetables, oils and fats (8.34%). The decline was visible in sawmilling and planning of wood (−5%), wearing apparel except fur apparel (−17%) and knitted and crocheted fabric articles (−3%), i.e. particularly in traditional and labour-intensive MSM APEs.

The investment in plant and machinery per worker (capital intensity) in APEs is increased by 6% per annum between 2001–2002 and 2006–2007. The highest per annum growth was recorded in tobacco (26%), followed by dressing and dyeing of fur and fur articles (20%), spinning, weaving and finishing of textiles (17%), other

Table 11.2 Industry-wise investment patterns in MSM APEs at three-digit NIC level during 2001–2002 and 2006–2007 (2011–2012 prices)

NIC 2004	Description	MSM APEs (units in lakh)			Workers (No. in lakh)			Investment per unit (INR in lakh)			Investment per worker (INR in lakh)		
		2001–2002	2006–2007	CAGR (%)	2001–2002	2006–2007	CAGR (%)	2001–2002	2006–2007	CAGR (%)	2001–2002	2006–2007	CAGR (%)
151	Production, processing, preservation of meat, fruit vegetables, oils and fats	0.96	1.21	3.90	3.57	4.05	2.14	2.12	3.42	8.34	0.57	1.02	10.21
152	Manufacture of dairy product	0.34	1.15	22.48	0.94	3.68	25.59	1.43	1.54	1.22	0.52	0.48	−1.29
153	Manufacture of grain mill products, starches and starch products, prepared animal feeds	7.61	18.54	16.00	15.86	37.44	15.40	1.00	1.22	3.38	0.48	0.61	3.92
154	Manufacture of other food products	1.96	3.25	8.77	7.56	14.95	12.04	1.03	2.51	15.99	0.27	0.54	12.60
155	Manufacture of beverages	0.27	0.27	0.20	0.83	1.05	3.96	2.76	5.91	13.52	0.90	1.54	9.41

(continued)

Table 11.2 (continued)

NIC 2004	Description	MSM APEs (units in lakh)		CAGR (%)	Workers (No. in lakh)		CAGR (%)	Investment per unit (INR in lakh)		CAGR (%)	Investment per worker (INR in lakh)		CAGR (%)
		2001–2002	2006–2007		2001–2002	2006–2007		2001–2002	2006–2007		2001–2002	2006–2007	
160	Manufacture of tobacco products	1.56	1.63	0.76	3.71	6.71	10.37	0.08	0.53	38.29	0.03	0.13	26.25
171	Spinning, weaving and finishing of textiles	1.24	3.22	17.29	4.81	16.89	23.29	1.79	6.26	23.16	0.46	1.19	17.17
172	Manufacture of other textiles	1.84	4.60	16.55	6.22	16.51	17.66	0.68	1.19	9.88	0.20	0.33	8.84
173	Manufacture of knitted and crocheted fabrics articles	0.21	0.25	2.91	1.43	1.53	1.16	4.64	3.87	−2.96	0.69	0.64	−1.28

(continued)

Table 11.2 (continued)

NIC 2004	Description	MSM APEs (units in lakh)		CAGR (%)	Workers (No. in lakh)		CAGR (%)	Investment per unit (INR in lakh)		CAGR (%)	Investment per worker (INR in lakh)		CAGR (%)
		2001–2002	2006–2007		2001–2002	2006–2007		2001–2002	2006–2007		2001–2002	2006–2007	
181	Manufacture of wearing apparel, except fur apparel	1.26	29.28	69.01	5.40	55.49	47.45	1.32	0.44	−16.83	0.31	0.23	−4.66
182	Dressing and dyeing of fur; manufacture of articles of fur	0.07	0.01	−30.04	0.26	0.04	−26.03	1.42	5.75	26.29	0.37	1.07	19.45
191	Tanning and dressing of leather, manufacture of luggage handbags, saddlery and harness	0.22	0.36	8.61	0.89	1.28	6.32	2.02	3.27	8.39	0.49	0.91	10.73

(continued)

Table 11.2 (continued)

NIC 2004	Description	MSM APEs (units in lakh)		CAGR (%)	Workers (No. in lakh)		CAGR (%)	Investment per unit (INR in lakh)		CAGR (%)	Investment per worker (INR in lakh)		CAGR (%)
		2001–2002	2006–2007		2001–2002	2006–2007		2001–2002	2006–2007		2001–2002	2006–2007	
192	Manufacture of footwear	0.94	1.13	3.20	2.26	2.99	4.77	0.63	1.30	12.86	0.26	0.49	11.17
201	Saw milling and planning of wood	0.38	2.59	37.92	1.34	6.44	29.85	1.74	1.28	−4.93	0.49	0.52	0.98
202	Manufacture of products of wood, cork, straw and plaiting materials	3.92	3.58	−1.53	9.05	7.63	−2.80	0.35	0.61	9.88	0.15	0.29	11.31
All APEs		22.76	71.06	20.90	64.13	176.69	18.40	0.98	1.22	3.77	0.35	0.49	5.95
Share APEs in MSMEs (%)		21.63	27.23	3.91	25.72	29.71	2.44	20.6[a]	206.6[a]	47	17.3[a]	189.3[a]	49

Note [a]Relative share (APEs/MSME). Source: All-India Census of SSIs/MSMEs of 2001–2002 and 2006–2007

food (13%), wood, cork, straw and plaiting materials (11% per annum), footwear (11%), luggage handbags, saddlery and harness (11%), meat, fish, fruits, vegetables, oils and fats (10%), beverages (9%), other textiles (9%) and others (less than the growth in total MSM APEs). Investment per worker declined by 4.7% in wearing apparel (except fur apparel), by 1.29% in dairy and by 1.28% in knitted and crocheted fabrics articles. The investment per worker is much higher in MSM APEs than in MSMEs overall.

Micro APEs made up 21.5% of all MSMEs in 2001–2002; in 2006–2007, that proportion grew to 27.1%. The proportion of small APEs grew from 0.10% in 2001–2002 to 0.11% in 2006–2007, and the proportion of medium APEs grew from 0.002% in 2001–2002 to 0.006% in 2006–2007 (Table 11.3). A few APEs are small- or medium-sized. Between 2001–2002 and 2006–2007, the annual growth rate in the number of units was 21% (micro MSM APEs), 18% (small MSM APEs) and 48% (medium MSM APEs); the annual growth rate in the number of workers was 18% (micro MSM APEs), 23% (small MSM APEs) and 56% (medium MSM APEs).

Annual investment in plant and machinery per unit grew at 4.39% in small APEs, 1.34% in micro APEs and 1.41% in medium APEs. Despite this, the average investment per unit in micro APEs was INR 65,000 in 2006–2007, much less than in small APEs (INR 9.038 million) and medium APEs (INR 86.8 million). In 2006–2007, investment per worker was only INR 28,000 in micro APEs, INR 232,000 in small APEs and INR 470,000 in medium APEs. The investment per worker increased in micro APEs (at 4% per annum) and in small APEs (at 0.09% per annum), but in medium APEs, it declined at 4% per annum.

This growth may be due to a higher increase in investment than in the number of workers, and a higher increase in the number of workers than in investment may be one of the important reasons of the decline in investment per worker in medium APEs. The number of micro-units increased phenomenally, due mainly to definitional changes and to an increase in demand for agro-processed products, due in turn to changes in consumption patterns in favour of processed products, government development initiatives and stagnant agricultural growth. The growth in investment per worker implies a shortage of investment in micro-units, which may be why capacity was under-utilised.

11.4.3   Determinants of Investment in MSM APEs

A firm's investment behaviour is explained by the flexible accelerator theory (Chenery 1952; Koyck 1954): capital is adjusted to its desired level by a certain proportion of the difference between the actual and the desired capital during each period, i.e. $I_t = K_t - K_{t-1} = (1-a)(K_t^* - K_{t-1})$, where $0 < a < 1$, and the actual capital stock is represented by a weighted average of the past desired capital stocks, i.e. $K_t = [1-a] \sum_{r=0} a^r K_{t-r}^* - \delta K_{t-1}$, in this model.

Chenery and Koyck proposed that the level of capital stock is proportionate to the expected output, and it is predicted based on the past output. The desired capital is

Table 11.3 Size-wise units, investment patterns in MSM APEs during 2001–2002 and 2006–2007 (2011–2012 prices)

Size of units	MSM APEs (units in lakh)		CAGR (%)	Workers (No. in lakh)		CAGR (%)	Investment per unit (INR in lakh)		CAGR (%)	Investment per worker (INR in lakh)		CAGR (%)
	2001–2002	2006–2007		2001–2002	2006–2007		2001–2002	2006–2007		2001–2002	2006–2007	
Micro	22.65 (21.5)	70.75 (27.1)	20.90	60.68 (24.3)	162.18 (27.3)	17.81	0.60	0.65	1.34	0.22	0.28	4.00
Small	0.11 (0.10)	0.29 (0.11)	18.23	3.24 (1.3)	11.40 (1.9)	23.31	69.86	90.38	4.39	2.31	2.32	0.09
Medium	0.00 (0.002)	0.02 (0.006)	48.27	0.21 (0.09)	3.11 (0.52)	56.40	798.38	868.18	1.41	5.95	4.70	-3.87
APEs	22.76 (21.6)	71.06 (27.2)	20.90	64.13 (25.7)	176.69 (29.7)	18.40	0.98	1.22	3.77	0.35	0.49	5.95

Note Parentheses represent shares in total MSMEs (%)
Source Ibid

the proportion of the profit (Tinbergen 1938) since it may be a profit expectations measurement (Grunfeld 1960), and the investment rate may be constrained by the supply of funds (Meyer and Kuh 1957; Anderson 1964; Meyer and Glauber 1964).

We use this theoretical framework and unit-level data to analyse the investment pattern in APEs for 2006–2007. Consistent time series data are not available. Therefore, we cannot estimate the profit earned by units and its adjustment partial or full over the time. To understand investment behaviour, we have taken enterprise-specific and peripheral factors and presented the summary statistics of variables in Table 11.4.

In all, 146,918 APEs were surveyed in 2006–2007; 85.78% were micro-enterprises, 12.55% were small enterprises, and 0.68% were medium-sized enterprises. The mean investment in plant and machinery was INR 375,000 in micro APEs, INR 9.26 million in small APEs and INR 91.2 million in medium APEs.

Per unit institutional loan was INR 1.1 million (micro APEs), INR 1.14 million (small APEs) and INR 75.7 million (medium APEs). The mean value of non-institutional loans was INR 81,000 (micro APEs), INR 844,000 (small APEs) and INR 5.3 million (medium APEs). It reveals that per unit non-institutional loans are much less than the institutional loans per unit.

The proportion of non-institutional loan in total loans is higher for micro APEs than for small or medium APEs. The mean value of profit was INR 1.739 million (micro APEs), INR 16.7 million (small APEs) and INR 121 million (medium APEs). The mean value of expenditure by micro APEs is INR 500,000 (electricity) and INR 8.8 million (raw material). The mean expenditure by small APEs was INR 4.4 million (electricity) and INR 81.7 million (raw material). The mean value of expenditure by medium APEs is INR 25.2 million (electricity) and INR 326 million (raw material).

In all, 56% of micro APEs were located in rural areas, 1.9% registered with any authority, 4% were ancillary, 90% were managed by men, and 46% had a bank account. In contrast, 43% of small APEs and 37% of medium APEs were located in rural areas; around 100% were registered; 9% were ancillary; 96% of small APEs and 98% of medium APEs were managed by men; and 93% of small APEs and 97% of medium APEs had a bank account.

The life of a micro APE may span more than 30 years, but these are outnumbered by micro APEs that fold in under 10 years (by 45%), in 11–20 years (by 35%) and in 21–30 years (by 13%). Small APEs older than 30 years are outnumbered by small APEs with a life span of up to 10 years (40%), 11–20 years (35% and 21–30 years (12%). Medium APEs older than 30 years are outnumbered by medium-sized APEs with a life span of up to 10 years (29%), 11–20 years (40%) and 21–30 years (15%).

The study examines the significant determinants of investment in plant and machinery for MSM APEs based on the 2006–2007 all-India census of MSMEs. The variables—value of investment, institutional loan, profit, expenditure on electricity and raw materials—are taken in log form at 2011–2012 constant prices. Dummies are taken for four categories of APEs based on life span, types of enterprise (micro, small and medium) and states (20 major states) in the empirical model.

Table 11.5 shows the results of 2SLS (first and second stages). The first column represents the coefficients of the first stage of the 2SLS models, and the third column represents the coefficients of the second stage. We treat institutional credit

Table 11.4 Summary statistics of MSM APEs based on all-India census of MSMEs, 2006–2007

Variables	Micro APEs			Small APEs			Medium APEs		
	Obs	Mean	Std. dev	Obs	Mean	Std. dev	Obs	Mean	Std. dev
Investment (INR lakh)	127,489	3.75	5	18,433	92.60	88	996	912	341
Institutional loan (INR lakh)	"	11.11	252	"	114	738	"	757	2,990
Non-institutional loan (INR lakh)	"	0.81	41	"	8.44	124	"	53	439
Profit (INR lakh)	"	17.39	541	"	167	1,170	"	1,210	4,430
Expenditure on electricity (INR lakh)	"	4.60	528	"	43.89	811	"	252	2,100
Expenditure on raw materials (INR lakh)	"	87.96	1900	"	817	4,840	"	3,260	8,550
Location (rural = 1 and urban = 0)	"	0.56	0.50	"	0.43	0.50	"	0.37	0.48
Registration (yes = 1 and not = 0)	"	0.019	0.14	"	1.00	0.04	"	1.00	0.03
Ancillary (yes = 1 and not = 0)	"	0.04	0.20	"	0.09	0.28	"	0.09	0.28
Manage by men (yes = 1 and not = 0)	"	0.90	0.30	"	0.96	0.19	"	0.98	0.14
Account exists (yes = 1 and not = 0)	"	0.46	0.50	"	0.93	0.25	"	0.97	0.16
Life span (above 30 years = base)									
Up to 10 years	"	0.45	0.50	"	0.40	0.49	"	0.29	0.45
11–20 years	"	0.35	0.48	"	0.35	0.48	"	0.40	0.49
21–30 years	"	0.13	0.34	"	0.12	0.32	"	0.15	0.36

Source All-India census of MSME, 2006–2007

Table 11.5 Determinants of investment in plant and machinery in MSM APEs: results based on 2 SLS, 2006–2007

Sr. No.	Dependent variable (log investment per enterprise)	2SLS			
		First stage		Second stage	
	Independent variables	Coefficient	Standard error	Coefficient	Standard error
1	Log institutional loan per unit			0.049^b	0.012
2	Log profit per unit (proxy of future expectations)	0.110^b	0.008	0.172^b	0.003
3	Log electricity value per unit (proxy of availability of energy)	0.046^b	0.004	0.111^b	0.001
4	Log value of raw materials per unit (proxy of backward linkages)	0.019^b	0.003	0.017^b	0.001
5	Location (rural = 1 and urban = 0)	0.267^b	0.029	−0.017	0.009
6	Ancillary	−0.044	0.062	0.048^b	0.017
7	Manage by men	0.127^b	0.047	0.214^b	0.013
8	Account exists	0.637^b	0.033	0.599^b	0.012
9	Life span (above 30 years = base)				
I	Up to 10 years	0.889^b	0.055	0.362^b	0.018
II	11–20 years	0.104^a	0.055	0.192^b	0.015
III	21–30 years	−0.069	0.061	−0.013	0.017
10	Instrumental variable: enterprise types (micro-units = base)				
I	Small enterprises	0.811^b	0.046	2.418^b	0.016
II	Medium enterprises	-0.413^b	0.166	4.257^b	0.047
11	Instrumental variable: registration	2.453^b	0.106	–	–
	Constant	5.263^b	0.157	7.693^b	0.095
	Observations	146,918		146,918	
	State dummies	Yes		Yes	
	R-square			0.588	

Note [b] and [a] signify the significant level of 1 and 10%

(an endogenous variable), size of APEs and their registration status as instrumental variables because they predict the ability of an enterprise to avail of institutional credit.

The second stage results show that the value of the coefficient of institutional loans is 0.049: an inclusive network of formal sources of finance that delivers low-interest loans in time significantly and positively impacts investment in plant and machinery in MSM APEs. The value of the coefficient for profit is estimated at 0.17: investment depends significantly on profit expectation (Tinbergen 1938), and it increases by 17% with an increase in profit.

Better infrastructure, i.e. energy, has a significant influence on investment. The adequate availability of electricity and raw material is likely to reduce cost and yield more profits. Moreover, the investment decreases by 1.70% in MSM APEs with change in location of the units from urban to rural areas. Investment in ancillary, men-managed APEs that have a bank account is greater than in non-ancillary, women-managed APEs that do not have a bank account. Compared to MSM APEs with 30 years above life span, the MSM APEs with up to 10 years life span and 11–20 years life spans have experienced 0.362 and 0.192 significant more impacts on investment, respectively. It implies that newly established enterprises tend to reap benefits by investing more in plant and machinery.

The model also includes types of APEs—micro, small and medium enterprises dummies. The estimates reveal that the investment in small and medium APEs is significantly more by 2.42 and 4.26 compared to micro APEs, respectively. It implies that investment per unit in micro APEs is lower than in small and medium APEs. It may be generalised that investment in plant and machinery is higher in APEs that obtain loans from institutional sources and earn high profit, have access to electricity and raw materials in time, have a bank account, are located in urban areas, are ancillary, are managed by men, are newly established and are large in size. Low-interest institutional credit could contribute to investment in APEs and, therefore, to their growth. It could be achieved by setting up a network of institutional sources of finance and raising awareness among processors in rural and urban areas. The subsequent section examines the determinants of MSM APEs' access to institutional credit.

11.5   Access of MSM APEs to Institutional Loans

Measures have been taken to promote financial inclusion, and the formal financial sector has expanded, but access to formal loans is not source-neutral; the informal sector cannot access credit and, hence, cannot grow. Only 7% of APEs had taken a loan in 2001–2002 and that percentage fell to 3% in 2006–2007; 57% of them borrowed money from formal sources of finance in 2001–2002 and 83% in 2006–2007, and the remaining 43% (in 2001–2002) and 17% (in 2006–2007) borrowed from informal sources. Almost 97% of APEs were excluded from the financial market; many may not have met the requirements (Table 11.6). Usually, small enterprises do not meet bank requirements and are excluded from the formal financial system; it may imply that access to formal loans is positively correlated with the size of APEs.

Table 11.6 Distribution MSM APEs as per loan access and their sources in 2001–2002 and 2006–2007

Source of loan	MSM APEs (lakh)		MSM APEs (in %)	
	2001–02	2006–07	2001–02	2006–07
Units taken loan	3	2	7	3
Units not taken loan	41	71	93	97
All APEs	44	'73	100	100
Units taken institutional loan	1.75	2.00	57	83
Units taken non-institutions loan	1.35	0.42	43	17
All APEs	3.10	2.42	100	100

Source All-India census of SSI/MSME, 2001–2002 and 2006–2007

Table 11.7 reveals that during 2001–2002, rural micro APEs that borrowed accounted for 54% of all APEs that borrowed from formal financial sources; the remaining 46% borrowed loan from informal financial sources. The share of rural micro APEs that borrowed from formal financial sources increased to 79% in 2006–2007. In 2001–2002, 70% of small APEs in rural areas borrowed from formal sources; the corresponding figure in 2006–2007 is 91%. Among medium APEs, the share of APEs that have borrowed from formal financial sources is 67% in 2001–2002 and 89% in 2006–2007.

Among urban micro APEs, 59% of the APEs have taken loans from formal financial sources in 2001–2002, and this share became 84% in 2006–2007. Among urban small APEs, 67% of the APEs have borrowed from formal financial sources in 2001–2002, and the share became 95% in 2006–2007. Among urban medium APEs, 68% of the APEs have borrowed from formal financial sources in 2001–2002, and it became 94% in 2006–2007.

As the size of an APE increases, its access to formal sources of finance increases and its access to informal sources decreases. Despite several measures to promote formal financial inclusion, access to formal loan is not size-neutral. A sizeable share of APEs still remains outside the ambit of the formal credit market; micro-units in rural areas are the most vulnerable.

According to the NSS 73rd round, most of the micro APEs borrowed loan from non-institutional sources—moneylenders, friends and relatives. The highest share, 29% of all micro APEs, borrowed from friends and relatives, followed by the share of micro APEs that borrowed from moneylenders and commercial banks. Small unincorporated APEs borrowed mainly from commercial banks and microfinance institutions, and medium unincorporated APEs mainly from commercial banks, business partners and suppliers and contractors. Other sources—central- and state-level term lending institutions, central, state and local government bodies, business partners and other agencies—played a minimal role in credit lending. Micro APEs are still more likely to depend upon non-institutional sources of finance for financial assistance.

Table 11.7 Size-wise distribution of MSM APEs with respect to sources of loan in 2001–2002 and 2006–2007 (in %)

Sources of loan	Rural						Urban					
	Micro		Small		Medium		Micro		Small		Medium	
	2001–2002	2006–2007	2001–2002	2006–2007	2001–2002	2006–2007	2001–2002	2006–2007	2001–2002	2006–2007	2001–2002	2006–2007
Institutional	54	79	70	91	67	89	59	84	67	95	68	94
Non-institutional	46	21	30	9	33	11	41	16	33	5	32	6
Total	100	100	100	100	100	100	100	100	100	100	100	100

Source Ibid

What determines MSM APEs' access to institutional loans? Bhavani and Bhanu-murthy (2014) mentioned that the proportion of owned assets, enterprise and owner-ship type, maintenance of account books and registration with the government agen-cies are the important determinants of financial access of small enterprises. We use a logit regression model using unit-level data from the all-India census of MSMEs (2006–2007). The dependent variable is categorical (Table 11.8). It contains enter-prises that have taken an institutional loan and not taken an institutional loan. The independent variables are enterprise-specific. The results portray that APEs that have higher output are more likely to obtain an institutional loans compared to enterprises that took a non-institutional loans or did not.

Keeping other variables unchanged, MSM APEs directly engaged in export activ-ities compared to non-exporting MSM APEs are more likely to avail of an insti-tutional loan. Enterprises engaged in indirect or both direct and indirect export activities compared to non-exporting units, small and medium units compared to micro-units, having quality certificate compared to not having quality certificate and a bank account compared to not having a bank account are significantly less likely to obtain an institutional loan. Importantly, MSM APEs located in rural areas compared to locate in urban areas, registered with any authority compared to unreg-istered, ancillary compared to non-ancillary, perennial and seasonal compared to casual and smaller life span (a proxy for experience) compared to large life span are more likely to obtain a loan from formal sources of finance than from informal sources of finance.

The estimated marginal effects, based on results from the logistic regression, show the effects of a discrete change in the base level on access to loan from institutional sources by MSM APEs. Units of the MSM APEs' accessed loan from institutional sources have significantly increased by 1.6% with continually increase in output. The units of MSM APEs borrowed from formal financial sources have significantly increased by 1.97%, 15.67%, 1.59%, 4.70%, 5.00% and 4.65% for units in rural areas, registered units, ancillary units, perennial units, seasonal units and units with 10 years life span with the change in the base characteristics, respectively. However, units of MSM APEs borrowed from formal financial sources have significantly decreased by 5.29%, 7.55%, 1.44%, 10.03%, 4.30%, 0.21% and 1.15% for units indirectly engaged export activities, units both directly and indirectly engaged in export activities, small units, medium units, units having quality certificate, units managed by men and units having account with change in the base characteristics, respectively.

11.6   Conclusion

This chapter investigated the pattern of investment in MSM APEs in India and their sources of finance. The analysis is carried out at NIC three-digit level as per type of enterprise in rural and urban areas. The data are taken from the published reports of the census for registered SSI 1972–1973 and 1987–1988 and from unit-level

Table 11.8 Determinants of MSM APEs' access to institutional loans: logit regression estimates

S. No.	Results of logit regression			Marginal effects	
	Dependent variable: units of the APEs which obtained institutional loan	Coefficient	Standard error	dy/dx	Standard error
1.	Continuous increase in gross output	0.1310^b	0.0206	0.166^b	0.0026
2.	Enterprises involved in export activity				
	(Non-exporting units: base)				
I	Direct export	0.0445	0.0057	0.0057	0.0055
II	Indirect export	0.0664	-0.0529^b	-0.0529^b	0.0104
III	Both direct and indirect export	0.0657	-0.0755^b	-0.0755^b	0.011
3.	Types of the enterprises (micro-units: base)				
I	Small units	0.0225	-0.0144^b	-0.0144^b	0.003
II	Medium units	0.0713	$-0.1,003^b$	$-0.1,003^b$	0.0128
4.	Location (rural = 1 and urban = 0)	0.1555^b	0.0161	0.0197^b	
5.	Registration status (registered = 1 and unregistered = 0)	1.2378^b	0.0461	0.1567^b	
6.	Ancillary units (yes = 1 and not = 2)	0.1256^b	0.0346	0.0159^b	
7.	Quality certificate (yes = 1 and not = 0)	-0.3398^b	0.0258	-0.0430^b	
8.	Operational status (casual = base)				
I	Perennial units	0.138	0.0470^a	0.0470^a	0.0213
II	Seasonal units	0.1414	0.0500^a	0.0500^a	0.0216
9.	Managed by (men = 1 and women = 0)	-0.0167	0.0275	-0.0021	
10.	Account exists (yes =1 and not = 0)	-0.0910^b	0.0172	-0.0115^b	
11.	Life span (above 30 years: base)				
I	Up to 10 years	0.0282	0.0465^b	0.0465^b	0.0038
II	11–20 years	0.0277	0.0059	0.0059	0.0039
III	21–30 years	0.0311	0.0037	0.0037	0.0044
12.	State dummies	Yes	–	Yes	–

(continued)

Table 11.8 (continued)

S. No.	Results of logit regression				Marginal effects	
	Dependent variable: units of the APEs which obtained institutional loan		Coefficient	Standard error	dy/dx	Standard error
	Constant		0.0276	0.151		
	Log likelihood = −60898.33	Observation	146,918		*Note*: dy/dx for factor levels is the discrete change from the base level	
		LR Chi-square (36)	5,962.45			
		Prob. > Chi-square	0.0000			
		Pseudo *R*-square	0.0467			

Note [b] and [a] show the statistical significance at 1 and 5% level

data from the census of registered and unregistered SSIs (2001–2002) and MSMEs (2006–2007).

The data collected during the first two survey years are not comparable with the recent two survey years, but broad trends are identified: the total number of registered SSI APEs increased from 26,252 in 1972–1973 to 195,000 in 1987–1988, and the workforce grew from 306,000 to 983,000. The subsequent surveys showed that the number of MSM APEs increased from 2.276 million in 2001–2002 to 7.106 million in 2006–2007 and the workforce from 6.413 million to 17.669 million. The investment per enterprise declined by about 1% per annum between 1972–1973 and 1987–1988 and increased by 3.77% per annum between 2001–2002 and 2006–2007.

Real investment per enterprise in registered APEs decreased from INR 658,000 in 1972–1973 to INR 553,000 in 1987–1988. In the subsequent census surveys (for registered and unregistered units), real investment per enterprise increased from INR 98,000 in 2001–2002 to INR 122,000 in 2006–2007 at 2011–2012 prices. The growth rate was much higher in dressing and dyeing of fur and articles of fur, tanning and dressing of leather, luggage handbags, saddlery and harness, beverages, spinning, weaving and finishing of textiles, tobacco, other food, meat, fish, fruits, vegetables, oils and fats and footwear units, but lower in other groups. The rate of growth is not found to be size-neutral. It was higher in micro APEs than in small and medium APEs, which could be due to alterations in the definition of micro, small and medium enterprises over the survey period.

The 2SLS analysis shows that the key determinants of investment into MSM APEs in 2006–2007 were institutional loans, profit earned, availability of raw material and energy. The easy and timely availability of raw material indicates that enterprises have strong backward linkages with agriculture and allied activities and they contribute to poverty reduction. Investments were made more in larger size MSM APEs. Investment significantly decreases with an increase in life span (a proxy of experience) of the units, inferring that compared to older units, newly established units make more investment and, hence, profit. Ancillary units that are managed by men and that have accounts are favourably positioned for attracting investments. The perception of the low investment in APEs may be due to poor access to institutional loans.

The results show that a sizeable proportion of APEs is outside the ambit of formal financial institutions. Usually, unregistered rural micro-enterprises are excluded from the formal financial system because they do not require loans. These micro-enterprises should be encouraged to access institutional loans. The logistic regression shows APEs' access to credit depends on growth in output, location of enterprise, registration status, ancillary, operating nature and size of enterprise. Setting up a well-organised network of institutional sources of finance is imperative, as is generating awareness among APEs and building trust between borrowers and sources of finance. Building infrastructure and markets and facilitating access to raw materials would help APEs increase output and, hence, profit, and it may improve access to institutional loans and accelerate investment.

Acknowledgements This study is a part of my doctoral research at the Centre for the Study of Regional Development, JNU, New Delhi.

References

Anderson, W. H. L. (1964). *Corporate finance and fixed investment: An econometric study* (Vol. 1). Division of Research, Graduate School of Business Administration, Harvard University.

Bathla, S. (2014). Agro-industry: The food processing sector. World Bank report: *India—Accelerating agricultural productivity growth* (Chap. 13).

Bhavani, T. A., & Bhanumurthy, N. R. (2014). Financial access-measurement and determinants: A case study of unorganised manufacturing enterprises in India. *Indian Economic Review,* 85–108.

Beck, T. (2007, April). Financing constraints of SMEs in developing countries: Evidence, determinants and solutions. In *KDI 36th Anniversary International Conference* (pp. 26–27).

Beck, T., Demirgüç-Kunt, A. S. L. I., & Maksimovic, V. (2005). Financial and legal constraints to growth: Does firm size matter? *The Journal of Finance, 60*(1), 137–177.

Bhide, S. (2000). Development of small scale industry. *Economic and Political Weekly, 35*(50), 4389–4390.

Breman, J. (2010). India's social question in a state of denial. *Economic and Political Weekly,* 42–46.

Chenery, H. B. (1952). Overcapacity and the acceleration principle. *Econometrica: Journal of the Econometric Society,* 1–28.

Dahale, S., et al. (2015). Critical analysis of role played financial institutions in development of Indian MSME's. *International Journal of Research and Scientific Innovation, 2*(3), 58–64.

Debroy, B., & Bhandari, L. (Eds.). (2005). *Small-scale industry in India: Large scale exit problems.* Academic Foundation.

Grunfeld, Y. (1960). *The determinants of corporate investment.* University of Chicago Press.

Kathuria, V., Raj, R., & Sen, K. (2010). Organised versus unorganised manufacturing performance in the post-reform period. *Economic and Political Weekly,* 55–64.

Koyck, L. M. (1954). *Distributed lags and investment analysis* (Vol. 4). North-Holland Publishing Company.

Kumar, N. (2006). *Emerging multinationals: Trends, patterns and determinants of outward investment by Indian enterprises* (No. 22108). East Asian Bureau of Economic Research.

Kuntchev, V., Ramalho, R., Rodríguez-Meza, J., & Yang, J. S. (2012). *What have we learned from the enterprise surveys regarding access to finance by SMEs.* Enterprise Analysis Unit of the Finance and Private Sector Development, The World Bank Group.

Mazumdar, D., & Sarkar, S. (2008). *Globalization, labor markets and inequality in India* (Vol. 79). IDRC.

Meyer, J. R., & Glauber, R. R. (1964). *Investment decisions, economic forecasting, and public policy* (No. 332.6/M61i).

Meyer, J. R., & Kuh, E. (1957). *The investment decision: An empirical study* (Vol. 102). Cambridge, MA: Harvard University Press.

Pillai, K. R. (1993). Finance for small industry. *Economic and Political Weekly, 28*(44), 374.

Raj, R. S. N., & Sen, K. (2015). Finance constraints and firm transition in the informal sector: Evidence from Indian manufacturing. *Oxford Development Studies, 43*(1), 123–143.

Raju, U. B. (1998). Future of small enterprises and small enterprises in future the Indian scenario. *Scientific Papers of the University of Pardubice. Series D, Faculty of Economics and Administration, 3.*

Rao, K. S. R., Das, A., & Singh, A. K. (2006). Commercial banks lending to small scale industry. *Economic and Political Weekly, 41*(11), 1025–1033.

Reddy, D. N. (2013). Formal credit and rural occupational diversification: Recent experience in India. *Journal of Land and Rural Studies, 1*(1), 1–24.

Sarkar, S. (1995). Size structure of agro-industry: A linkage analysis. Indian *Journal of Agricultural Economics, 50*(4), 634–648.

Sengupta, A. K. (2007). *National Commission for enterprises in the unorganized sector.* Report submitted to the Govt of India.

Singh, C., & Wasdani. (2016). *Finance for micro, small and medium-sized enterprises in India: Sources and challenge* (Working Paper) (p. 581). Japan: Asian Development Bank Institute.

Srivastava, U. K. (1989). Agro-processing industries: Potential, constrains, and task ahead. *Indian Journal of Agricultural Economics, 44*(3), 242–256.

Tinbergen, J. (1938). Statistical evidence on the acceleration principle. *Economica, 5*(18), 164–176.

Winker, P. (1999). Causes and effects of financing constraints at the firm level. *Small Business Economics, 12*(2), 169–181.

Part III
External Trade, Competitiveness and Determinants

Chapter 12
India's Trade in Agro-Processed Products: Revealed Comparative Advantage and Its Determinants

Ankur Jain and Elumalai Kannan

12.1 Introduction

Despite a structural change in the Indian economy in favour of the services sector, agriculture continues to provide employment to the vast majority of the rural population. Agriculture accounts for about 16% of GDP and 49% of the employment (GoI 2018). The composition of agricultural output changed from predominantly food grains to commercial crops, including fruits and vegetables, and then to livestock products. This is in line with the shift in policy focus, from sector-specific programmes to commodity-specific programmes, which aim to enhance output and then shift towards external trade orientation through increased integration with global markets. The latter was to be achieved through generating an adequate export surplus.

From being a ship-to-mouth food economy in the 1950s, India jumped to self-sufficiency in most food items by the 1980s. The green revolution was successful in irrigated areas, with the use of chemical fertilisers, seeds, extension and assured procurement at remunerative prices. Food grain production increased from about 50 million tonnes in 1950–51 to 275.7 million tonnes in 2016–17. Export controls, quantitative restrictions and export duties, used as instruments to restrict trade, were done away with during the 1990s. Economic reforms introduced in 1991, and the signing of World Trade Organization (WTO) agreements in 1995, led to the liberalisation of external trade. Since 2000, agricultural trade has been considered a tool for improving farm income and farmers' welfare.

A. Jain · E. Kannan (✉)
Centre for the Study of Regional Development, Jawaharlal Nehru University, New Delhi, India
e-mail: elumalaik@mail.jnu.ac.in

A. Jain
e-mail: ankurjain869@gmail.com

© The Author(s), under exclusive license to Springer Nature Singapore Pte Ltd. 2021
S. Bathla and E. Kannan (eds.), *Agro and Food Processing Industry in India*, India Studies in Business and Economics, https://doi.org/10.1007/978-981-15-9468-7_12

Agriculture was opened to international markets, and India's share in global exports of agriculture products rose from a mere 1% in the early 2000s to 2.2% in 2016. Globally, India is currently ranked ninth among the agricultural exporters. The USA is the largest export market for Indian agricultural products. The new agriculture export policy, instituted in December 2018, recommended that the export basket be diversified and high-value products boosted in global markets. The policy allows for the export of organic and processed products without any restriction. Trade agreements facilitated access to markets in Canada, China and South East Asian countries and helped enhance agricultural exports by 12–15% in recent years. Overall, agricultural exports increased from USD 6.1 billion in 2001 to USD 36.5 billion in 2018.

Boosting the export of processed agricultural products tends to increase employment, value addition and income. India's geographical location offers the unique advantage of connectivity to agriculturally less-surplus countries (such as in the Middle East and Japan, Singapore, Thailand, Malaysia and Korea), and there is a huge potential for increasing the export of processed food products to these countries.

However, there is little empirical evidence on whether India has the comparative advantage to export agricultural products, particularly processed products, to the world market. This chapter analyses the trends and patterns of India's agricultural trade, and the level of comparative advantage of the export of agricultural products, by using a revealed comparative advantage (RCA) index. The chapter analyses the determinants of changes in the RCA in the export of agricultural products.

12.2   Brief Review of Literature

Comparative advantage is the outcome of the interaction between factor endowment, technology, a country-specific characteristic, and factor intensity, an industry- or product-specific characteristic (Hirsch 1974). There are many measures of trade competitiveness or comparative advantage.

Vollrath (1991) theoretically analyses the various measures, identifies 10 alternative indexes and establishes the evolutionary linkages between them. Using Kunimoto (1977) integrative framework, Vollrath finds the most satisfying measures: the enlarged relative export share measure and three measures of RCA—relative trade advantage (RTA), relative export advantage (REA) and revealed competitiveness (RC).

Using longitudinal data from 1961 to 2011 and normalised RCA, Sarker and Ratnasena (2014) measured the international competitiveness of the wheat, beef and pork sectors in Canada. Canada enjoyed international competitiveness in wheat but not in pork, and competitiveness in beef improved rapidly since 1992. The exchange rate was the important driver of competitiveness, and decoupled farm policy did not have a significant impact.

Using the United Nations (UN) Comtrade database at the Harmonised System (Harmonized System) four-digit level for the 2004–2011 period, Oduro and Offei

(2014) investigated Ghana's RCA in the export of agro-processed products. The study used four indices: Balassa's RCA, RTA, logarithm of REA and RC. Ghana had an RCA in only 9 of 69 agro-processed product groups.

Mutambatsere (2007) evaluated the production and trade trends for maize and maize products in the South Africa Development Community (SADC) region for the 1996–2004 period. The region lacks a net comparative advantage in maize and maize flour production on a global scale, and competitiveness is restricted to a few countries that can produce and export significant quantities of maize.

Many studies have examined the trade competitiveness of India's agricultural products. Ansari and Khan (2015) analyse the direction, composition and potential of agriculture trade using Balassa's RCA to measure the export potential of various agricultural commodities. India has a comparative advantage in meat and edible meat offal, frozen fish, rice, wheat, oilseed, coffee and tea.

Ashish and Kannan (2015) analysed the RCA for the 2003–13 period in 116 agro-processed products, grouped into animal products, vegetable products and processed food products. The four variants of the RCA index were used to identify the products having comparative advantage to export. Statistical tests were conducted to examine the stability of these indices. India has the comparative advantage to export in 7 of 32 agro-processed animal products, 12 of 40 processed vegetable products and 7 of 44 processed food products.

Kannan (2010) used Balassa's RCA index and its alternative, the revealed symmetric comparative advantage (RSCA) index, to analyse India's trading pattern in the textile and clothing industry for the 1990–2007 period. India's export share in the world market did not improve much after the term of the Multi Fibre Agreement on Textile and Clothing (1974–1994); the values of RCA and RSCA declined for several clothing items, indicating a decrease in the efficiency of India's exports.

Studies have examined the interaction between factor endowments and factor intensity (Sachdev 1993). The RCA index of India's agricultural products was above unity till 1985. The share of agricultural exports in India's total exports declined from 40% in the mid-1960s to 17% in the early 1990s. The share of India's agricultural exports in world agricultural exports declined from 1.5% in 1960s to 0.8% by the end of the 1980s.

12.3 Data and Methodology

This chapter uses trade data compiled from the UN Comtrade database at the HS 4-digit level of classification for the 1998–2018 period. For the purpose of analysis, we group the 224 agricultural commodities by product type into.

1. Animal products (including fish) (66 products),
2. Cereals, oilseeds and vegetable oils (52 products),

3. Horticultural products (42 products),
4. Processed agricultural products (56 products) and
5. Agricultural raw materials (8 products).

Comparative advantage can be "revealed through examination of the real-world country/commodity trade patterns because actual exchange reflects relative costs as well as differences in non-price factors" (Balassa 1965). Balassa developed the RCA index, which can be written as

$$\text{RCA}_{ij} = \left(X_{ij}/X_j \right)/ \left(X_{iw}/X_w \right)$$

where, X_{ij} is value of export of product j of country i, X_i is value of total exports of country i, X_{jw} value of world exports of product j and X_w is value of world exports. If the value of RCA_{ij} is greater (less) than unity, then it means that country i has comparative advantage (disadvantage) in the export of the product j.

Balassa's RCA index is asymmetric; its value lies between zero and infinity. This index only conveys whether or not a country has a comparative advantage in a commodity or sector. Its magnitude has neither an ordinal property nor a cardinal property, and it can generate misleading results for countries with small market shares. Despite its shortcomings, this index is used widely to analyse changes in the trading pattern (Panchmukhi 1973; Yeats 1985; Amity 1999; Proudman and Redding 2000; Ferto and Hubbard 2003; Kannan 2010; Ashish and Kannan 2015).

The Balassa index is skewedly distributed towards the right, and its use in econometric analysis provides biased results. To overcome this problem, we modify it into the RSCA index, $(\text{RCA}_{ij} - 1)/(\text{RCA}_{ij} + 1)$. The RSCA values range from -1 to 1. It avoids the problem of zero values (Dalum et al. 1998), but the ordinary least square (OLS) method provides biased estimates. We estimate a panel tobit regression model to analyse the determinants of comparative advantage. The tobit random effects model can be specified as

$$Y_{it} = X_{it}\beta + v_i + u_{it}$$

where, Y_{it} is RSCA of commodity i measured at time t, X_{it} is vector of explanatory variables, v_i are random effects that are independently and identically distributed (i.i.d), u_{it} is error term with standard normal distribution independent of v_i.

12.4 Empirical Findings and Results

12.4.1 Composition of Agricultural Exports by Commodity Groups

Table 12.1 shows the composition of India's agricultural exports and the changes in its pattern across the various sub-groups. The value of total agricultural exports increased from USD 6.76 billion (triennium ending (TE) 1998) to USD 36.50 billion (TE 2018), but it varied by sub-category.

Exports increased for animal products, cereals, oilseeds and vegetable oils and agricultural raw materials, but decreased in the case of horticultural products and processed agricultural products. The share of animal products (including fish) rose from 21% in 1998 to 29.3% in 2018. In 2018, the exports of cereals, oilseeds and vegetable oils constituted the highest share of India's agricultural exports (31.7%), followed by animal products (29.3%), processed agricultural products (17.3%) and horticultural products (16.6%). It is worrisome to observe a decline in the share of processed agricultural products and a rise in share of agricultural raw materials.

Table 12.2 shows the export composition of animal products. In TE 2018, the highest share in exports was of milk and cream not concentrated (39.5%, down from 54.8% in 1998), meat of swine fresh or chilled (34%, up from 8.9% in 1998) and milk and cream concentrated (6.8%). This variation in the share of animal products may have been due to changes in the dietary pattern and the increasing preference for meat products in global markets.

Table 12.3 shows the export composition of the top 10 horticultural products from 1998 to 2018. In TE 2018, the highest share in exports was of tomatoes, fresh or chilled (14.5%); leguminous vegetables shelled or unshelled, fresh or chilled (13.8%); and fruits and nuts (12.1%). The export composition varied over time. The share of exports declined for tomatoes fresh or chilled; fruits and nuts; and cabbages and cauliflowers. But exports increased for leguminous vegetables shelled or unshelled, lettuce, ginger, saffron, turmeric, mate, vanilla, bananas and vegetables.

Table 12.1 Composition of India's agricultural products (%)

Items	1998	2001	2004	2007	2010	2015	2018
Animal products (including fish)	21.0	27.1	23.8	20.6	17.9	25.5	29.3
Horticultural products	25.5	28.8	21.9	20.7	18.6	13.8	16.6
Cereals, oilseeds and vegetable oils	29.4	26.7	33.9	28.1	28.5	36.6	31.7
Processed agricultural products	20.6	17.0	19.2	22.9	25.4	16.4	17.3
Agricultural raw materials	3.5	0.4	1.2	7.7	9.5	7.7	5.2
All	100.0	100.0	100.0	100.0	100.0	100.0	100.0
Total exports (million USD)	6,760	6,089	7,604	12,990	20,001	41,238	36,540

Source UN Comtrade

Table 12.2 Export composition of top 10 animal products (%)

Product code	Product description	1998	2001	2004	2007	2010	2015	2018
0201	Milk and cream, not concentrated	54.8	53.4	49.8	34.7	24.5	31.7	39.5
0202	Meat of swine, fresh, chilled or frozen	8.9	10.7	16.9	24.9	34.9	41.6	34.0
0203	Milk and cream, concentrated or containing added sugar	7.3	6.7	7.4	8.4	7.3	5.4	6.8
0204	Fish, dried, salted or in brine	14.3	14.1	9.9	10.1	10.2	6.4	6.5
0205	Crustaceans, whether in shell or not live, fresh, chilled, frozen, dried, salted or in brine; crustaceans, in shell, cooked by steaming or boiling in water, chilled or not, frozen, dried, salted or in brine	1.1	1.0	0.9	1.4	2.3	1.4	2.0
0206	Meat and edible offal, of the poultry	0.0	0.0	0.0	0.1	0.2	1.2	1.6
0207	Meat of horses, asses, mules	1.3	0.9	0.9	0.7	2.9	1.2	1.2
0208	Human hair, unworked, whether or not washed or scoured	0.1	0.1	0.7	0.6	1.1	0.9	0.9
0210	Birds' eggs, in shell, fresh, preserved or cooked	0.1	0.3	0.3	0.6	1.2	0.4	0.9
0301	Molluscs, whether in shell or not, live, fresh, chilled, frozen, dried, salted in brine; aquatic invertebrates	0.3	0.4	0.5	0.4	0.4	0.3	0.7

Source UN comtrade

Table 12.4 shows the export composition of the top 10 cereals, oilseeds and vegetable oils from 1998 to 2018. The major export items are rice (56.9%), vegetable saps and extracts (7.7%) and other fixed vegetable fats and oils (7.2%). There was an increase in the share of exports of rice, essential oils, groundnuts not roasted, maize and soya bean and a decrease in the share of vegetables saps and extracts, other oilseeds and plants and parts of plants. Rice accounted for over 50% of the share of total export of cereals, oilseeds and vegetable oil products.

The export composition of the top 10 processed agricultural products is given in Table 12.5. The top three products were cane or beet sugar (17.7%), oilcake and

Table 12.3 Export composition of top 10 horticulture products (%)

Product code	Horticultural products	1998	2001	2004	2007	2010	2015	2018
0702	Tomatoes, fresh or chilled	21.8	27.8	25.4	21.1	16.5	16.4	14.5
0708	Leguminous vegetables, shelled or unshelled, fresh or chilled	10.1	8.3	6.2	8.9	9.9	12.6	13.8
0812	Fruit and nuts, provisionally preserved	25.0	22.6	20.4	15.3	16.2	12.6	12.1
0704	Cabbages, cauliflowers, kohlrabi	19.4	11.8	9.1	10.5	9.2	9.7	9.4
0705	Lettuce (Lactuca sativa) and chicory	1.8	1.8	1.9	2.8	4.7	6.2	7.5
0910	Ginger, saffron, turmeric (curcuma)	3.4	3.3	7.2	8.1	11.6	8.1	7.0
0903	Mate	3.6	4.1	4.4	4.0	5.7	6.0	6.7
0905	Vanilla	0.8	0.7	1.2	1.9	2.7	3.7	4.9
0803	Bananas, including plantains, fresh	3.6	5.5	5.1	7.3	3.3	4.5	3.9
0710	Vegetables (uncooked or cooked by steam)	1.0	1.0	3.7	5.4	5.9	3.5	3.1

Source UN comtrade

Table 12.4 Export composition of top 10 cereals, oilseeds and vegetable oils products (%)

Product code	Product description	1998	2001	2004	2007	2010	2015	2018
1003	Rice	55.2	40.3	42.3	49.7	44.1	49.6	56.9
1004	Vegetable saps and extracts; pectic	8.4	10.7	6.2	8.9	7.8	13.5	7.7
1005	Other fixed vegetable fats and oils	7.4	11.6	5.3	7.0	8.9	4.9	7.2
1006	Essentials oils (terpeneless or not)	2.7	3.4	3.3	5.7	5.8	4.2	6.5
1007	Groundnuts, not roasted or otherwise	4.6	4.3	3.3	4.7	5.2	4.0	5.3
1008	Other oil seeds and oleaginous fruits	4.6	7.8	5.7	6.7	7.5	4.6	4.3
1101	Plants and parts of plants	3.3	3.9	2.6	2.5	2.2	1.5	2.5
1102	Maize (corn)	0.2	0.4	3.1	4.5	11.6	5.1	1.6
1103	Soya beans, whether or not broken	0.1	0.4	0.8	0.0	0.2	0.8	1.1
1104	Seeds, fruit and spores, of a kind	0.7	1.0	0.6	0.7	0.6	0.4	0.8

Source UN comtrade

Table 12.5 Export composition of top 10 processed agricultural products (%)

Product Code	Product Description	1998	2001	2004	2007	2010	2015	2018
1602	Cane or beet sugar and chemically preserved	7.4	12.6	16.6	18.3	15.4	16.1	17.7
1603	Oilcake and other solid residues,	45.9	38.9	34.8	33.9	34.9	22.1	10.7
1604	Unmanufactured tobacco; tobacco ref	13.7	14.4	11.8	9.4	13.0	10.7	9.9
1605	Crustaceans, molluscs and other aquatic	0.2	0.4	3.7	4.8	3.4	1.8	6.3
1701	Extracts, essences and concentrates	7.3	8.7	5.7	4.6	3.7	4.9	5.8
1702	Bread, pastry, cakes, biscuits and	0.5	0.7	2.1	2.6	2.6	4.5	5.4
1703	Oilcake and other solid residues,	7.4	1.5	3.8	5.2	6.0	7.3	4.2
1704	Preparations of a kind used in animal feeding	1.0	1.3	0.5	0.7	0.7	2.6	4.1
1801	Other manufactured tobacco and manufactured	1.1	1.7	1.8	1.9	1.8	2.2	4.1
1802	Food preparations not elsewhere specified or included	1.3	2.8	2.7	1.5	1.5	2.8	4.0

Source UN comtrade

other solid residues (10.7%) and unmanufactured tobacco; together, these accounted for over 33% of the total exports of processed products. The export composition varied considerably. There was an increase in the share of exports of cane or beet sugar, crustaceans, molluscs and other aquatic products, bread, pastry, cakes, biscuits, preparations of kind used in animal feeding, other manufactured tobacco and food preparations not elsewhere specified or included. There was a decrease in the share of exports of oilcakes and other solid residues, unmanufactured tobacco, extracts, essences and concentrates.

Table 12.6 shows the export composition of agricultural raw materials from 1998 to 2018. The export share is highest for agricultural raw materials, cotton not carded or combed (92.4%) and cotton waste including yarn waste (5.5%). The recent increase in the export of raw cotton, particularly to China, is a cause of concern for domestic cotton-based industries because a fall in supply can lead to price increases and capacity under-utilisation.

Table 12.6 Export composition of agricultural raw materials (%)

Product code	Product description	1998	2001	2004	2007	2010	2015	2018
5201	Cotton, not carded or combed	90.6	39.8	79.2	98.2	97.9	96.9	92.4
5202	Cotton waste (including yarn waste	8.9	17.8	3.1	1.2	1.7	2.4	5.5
5203	Cotton, carded or combed	0.3	39.7	16.2	0.5	0.1	0.0	0.1
5301	Flax, raw or processed but not spun	0.0	0.5	0.2	0.0	0.1	0.0	0.1
5302	True hemp (Cannabis sativa L.), raw	0.1	0.7	0.1	0.0	0.0	0.0	0.0

Source UN comtrade

12.4.2   Trends in RCA to Export

The status of RCA to export of agricultural products is shown in Table 12.7. India has an RCA in 34% of 224 products; 26% of animal products; 55% of horticultural products; 40% of cereals, oilseeds and vegetable oils; 23% of processed agricultural products; and 38% of agricultural raw materials.

The demand for India's buffalo meat in international markets has sparked a sudden increase in meat exports. The major export markets for buffalo meat and other animal products are Vietnam, Malaysia, Egypt, Arab Republic, Iraq and Saudi Arabia. Table 12.8 shows the RCA in case of animal products; 17 of 66 products (26%) have RCA. The RCA is highest in products such as human hair, unworked whether or not washed or scoured, waste of human hair (501); silk waste, including cocoons (5003); and crustaceans whether in shell or not (306). The RCA of most animal products declined gradually between 1998 and 2018.

Table 12.7 Status of RCA: 2016–2018

Items	Products (number)	Products with CA (number)	Products with CA (%)
Animal products	66	17	26
Horticultural products	42	23	55
Cereals, oilseeds and vegetable oils	52	21	40
Processed agricultural products	56	13	23
Agricultural raw materials	8	3	38
Total	224	77	34

Source UN comtrade

Table 12.8 RCA in Export of Animal Products

Product code	Product description	1998	2001	2004	2007	2010	2015	2018
0501	Human hair, unworked, whether or not washed or scoured	44.4	3.4	6.7	17.4	16.5	36.2	29.1
5003	Silk waste (including cocoons unsuitable)	20.6	17.1	5.2	6.4	6.2	12.0	16.6
0306	Crustaceans, whether in shell or not	15.1	11.4	9.0	6.4	4.2	8.1	9.7
0202	Meat of bovine animals, frozen	3.7	4.7	5.7	6.9	6.9	11.1	9.3
5103	Waste of wool or of fine or coarse	0.5	0.5	0.7	0.4	0.8	5.0	6.6
0307	Molluscs, whether in shell or not,	4.5	4.1	3.3	3.5	2.6	2.8	4.1
0506	Bones and horn-cores, unworked, defatted	18.9	21.3	21.0	16.6	9.0	4.8	2.9
0409	Natural honey	0.4	0.7	1.9	2.1	2.1	2.4	2.4
0408	Birds' eggs, not in shell, and egg	4.8	4.3	6.7	5.6	3.0	2.9	2.0
0303	Fish, frozen, excluding fish fillet	4.9	4.4	2.5	2.1	1.7	1.9	1.9
0507	Ivory, tortoise-shell, whalebone and whalebone hair	5.0	6.6	5.0	4.4	5.3	1.9	1.8
0510	Ambergris, castoreum, civet	2.4	2.2	5.4	2.0	0.6	1.6	1.8
3503	Gelatin and Gelatin derivatives	0.6	1.7	2.6	4.1	3.5	2.0	1.4
0508	Coral and similar materials, unworked	0.4	0.7	0.9	1.2	1.1	1.0	1.1
0206	Edible offal of bovine animals, swine	0.0	0.0	0.1	0.1	0.1	1.0	1.1
0204	Meat of sheep or goats, fresh, chilled	1.2	1.0	0.6	0.5	1.5	1.1	1.0
3501	Casein, caseinates and other casein	1.0	2.5	2.0	3.2	2.5	1.9	1.0

Source Computed based on UN comtrade

Of the 42 horticultural products, 23 (55%) have RCA. The RCA is highest for seeds of anise, badian, fennel, coriander (909), followed by mate (903) and coconuts, Brazil nuts and cashew nuts (803). The RCA fell for most horticultural products between 1998 and 2018, but it increased for products such as lettuce (*Lactuva sativa*) and chicory (705), grapes fresh or dried (806), carrot, turnip, salad, beetroot (706), vanilla (905), cloves (907), apricots, cherries, peaches (809), foliage branches and other parts (604) and cucumbers and gherkins (707) (Table 12.9).

In 2018–19, the major export destinations for cereals were Iran, Saudi Arabia, the United Arab Emirates (UAE), Nepal and Iraq (Table 12.10). The RCA was highest for products such as rice (1006), groundnuts not roasted or otherwise (1202) and other fixed vegetable fats and oils (1515). The RCA of most products declined gradually between 1998 and 2018—the RCA of rice fell from 34.8 to 17.8—but it increased for products such as copra (1203), essential oils (3301), flour, meal and powder of the dried (1106) and groundnut oil and its fractions (1508).

Of the 56 processed agricultural products, only 23% have the RCA to export (Table 12.11). The RCA is highest for oilcake and other solid residues (2305), vegetable fruit nuts and other (2001) and unmanufactured tobacco (2401). The RCA increased gradually for products such as jams, fruit jellies, marmalades (2007), other manufactured tobacco (2403), crustaceans, molluscs and other aquatic (1703) and other sugars (1702), but it fell for other products.

The trends of the RCA in export of agricultural raw materials are presented in Table 12.12. Only two of eight products—cotton waste (including yarn waste) and cotton not carded or combed—have an RCA, but its value varied significantly. The comparative advantage in the export of these products decreased till 2004 and then increased thereafter.

12.5 Determinants of Changes in RCA

This section analyses the determinants of comparative advantage in the export of agricultural commodities (Table 12.13). The likelihood ratio test shows that the panel tobit model is preferred to the pooled tobit model (chibar2(01) = 6,688.32 Prob > = chibar2 = 0.000). The GDP per capita captures the size of the domestic market, and its effect on comparative advantage is expected to be negative. This implies that larger the size of the domestic market for a product, lower its surplus available for export. The coefficient of GDP per capita is negative but not statistically significant. However, foreign direct investment (FDI) has a positive effect on RCA to export. This shows that FDI introduces new technology and promotes efficiency in production, which leads to improvement in competitiveness of agricultural commodities. As expected, the effect of exchange rate on RCA was positive, implying that a mild depreciation of currency enhances comparative advantage of India's exports in the international market.

12.6 Conclusions and Implications

The export composition of agricultural products changed between 1998 and 2018. The export share of non-traditional products—such as lettuce, grapes, cloves, jam

Table 12.9 RCA in Export of Horticultural Products

Product code	Product description	1998	2001	2004	2007	2010	2015	2018
0909	Seeds of anise, badian, fennel, coriander	33.1	22.7	10.7	19.6	25.5	22.2	12.3
0903	Mate	0.1	0.2	0.3	0.1	0.0	10.7	4.6
0801	Coconuts, Brazil nuts and cashew nut	70.1	53.9	33.5	23.3	13.7	6.6	3.8
0703	Onions, shallots, garlic, leeks	5.6	5.6	6.8	6.5	6.9	4.1	3.5
0908	Nutmeg, mace and cardamoms	11.0	9.3	8.4	6.4	5.6	5.3	2.8
0910	Ginger, saffron, turmeric (curcuma)	20.2	20.0	12.7	10.7	9.8	5.9	2.7
0904	Pepper of the genus Piper; dried	27.5	17.3	12.7	14.8	12.7	5.8	2.6
0902	Tea, whether or not flavoured	32.5	20.0	14.4	10.0	7.9	4.1	2.1
0705	Lettuce (*Lactuca sativa*) and chicory	0.0	0.0	0.0	0.0	0.0	2.0	1.8
0711	Vegetables provisionally preserved	7.9	7.9	6.9	9.1	7.2	2.8	1.7
0713	Dried leguminous vegetables, shelled	3.8	5.7	3.8	5.3	1.3	1.5	1.6
0806	Grapes, fresh or dried	0.8	0.6	0.7	1.0	1.0	1.6	1.5
0712	Dried vegetables, whole, cut, slice	2.1	3.1	2.0	2.8	1.5	1.8	1.4
0706	Carrots, turnips, salad beetroot	0.0	0.0	0.0	0.0	0.0	1.2	1.3
0905	Vanilla	0.1	0.4	1.3	3.2	4.7	1.6	1.3
0812	Fruit and nuts, provisionally preserved	34.0	45.3	24.1	3.5	2.3	0.5	1.3
0907	Cloves (whole fruit, cloves)	0.4	1.5	0.3	0.3	0.7	1.2	1.2
0809	Apricots, cherries, peaches	0.0	0.0	0.0	0.0	0.0	0.4	1.2
0604	Foliage, branches and other parts	0.5	1.1	2.7	2.9	1.9	1.2	1.2

(continued)

Table 12.9 (continued)

Product code	Product description	1998	2001	2004	2007	2010	2015	2018
0707	Cucumbers and gherkins, fresh or chilled	0.6	0.6	0.9	0.0	0.0	1.0	1.2
0804	Dates, figs, pineapples, avocados	2.5	1.7	3.0	3.7	3.3	1.4	1.1
0813	Fruit, dried	0.9	0.7	0.5	0.5	0.4	1.0	1.1
0901	Coffee, whether or not roasted or dried	5.2	3.4	2.5	1.9	1.2	1.1	1.1

Source Computed based on UN comtrade

and jellies—increased in recent years. These products appear to have huge export potential.

India has RCA in animal products such as human hair unworked whether or not washed or scoured, silk waste including cocoons and crustaceans whether in shell or not. In the case of horticultural products, the RCA was higher for seeds of anise, badian, fennel, coriander, followed by mate and coconuts, Brazil nuts and cashew nuts. Among cereals, oilseeds and vegetable oils, rice, groundnuts not roasted or otherwise and other fixed vegetable fats and oils have an RCA. In the case of processed agricultural products, RCA is found in oilcake and other solid residues; unmanufactured tobacco; vegetables and fruits; and nuts and other.

The major agricultural exports are in line with their RCA, though only 34% products have RCA. The FDI and the exchange rate are found to have a positive effect on RCA. These results imply that the government must focus more on products that have comparative advantage; the export of processed agricultural products can generate income, employment and value addition, and it should receive special attention. Commodity-specific export development programmes may help achieve these ends.

Table 12.10 Revealed Comparative advantage in Export of Cereals, Oilseeds, and Vegetable Oils

Product code	Product description	1998	2001	2004	2007	2010	2015	2018
1006	Rice	34.8	15.5	19.2	16.0	9.4	17.3	17.8
1202	Ground-nuts, not roasted or otherwise	15.1	12.6	11.5	15.5	14.8	15.1	13.6
1515	Other fixed vegetable fats and oils	16.8	21.1	11.1	11.2	12.5	11.3	11.5
1302	Vegetable saps and extracts; pectic	16.0	16.2	9.1	10.9	7.9	16.7	8.5
1207	Other oil seeds and oleaginous fruit	19.3	19.5	15.6	14.3	11.1	8.0	8.4
1203	Copra	6.0	0.3	0.3	1.5	10.5	7.7	8.1
3301	Essentials oils (terpeneless or not)	6.4	6.1	6.7	9.6	9.1	8.5	8.1
1301	Lac; natural gums, resins, gum-resin	41.7	38.7	29.8	12.7	6.9	10.2	7.8
1211	Plants and parts of plants	7.8	8.7	7.4	6.2	4.9	4.0	5.8
1404	Vegetable products not elsewhere specified	10.4	8.7	6.5	7.8	6.0	5.0	4.7
1106	Flour, meal and powder of the dried	2.9	3.2	2.6	3.3	3.5	4.2	3.3
1508	Ground-nut oil and its fractions	0.0	0.1	10.2	3.3	2.7	2.0	3.2
1008	Buckwheat, millet and canary seed	1.5	1.2	2.7	5.0	5.7	2.0	2.2
1208	Flours and meals of oil seeds	1.6	3.7	1.4	0.9	0.6	3.4	1.8
1103	Cereal groats, meal and pellets	1.0	0.5	2.2	0.5	0.5	1.2	1.4
1101	Wheat or meslin flour	2.6	1.6	4.0	0.5	0.2	1.5	1.1
1102	Cereal flours other than of wheat	0.7	0.4	1.2	1.8	1.7	0.8	1.1
1108	Starches; inulin	0.7	0.3	0.5	0.4	0.5	1.2	1.1
1516	Animal or vegetable fats and oils	1.7	1.9	1.5	0.8	0.7	1.0	1.0

Source Computed based on UN comtrade

Table 12.11 RCA in export of processed agricultural products

Product code	Product description	1998	2001	2004	2007	2010	2015	2018
2305	Oilcake and other solid residues	72.5	10.3	58.0	64.6	41.9	6.3	7.8
2001	Vegetables, fruit, nuts and others	4.5	5.6	4.7	6.6	6.0	4.9	4.5
2401	Unmanufactured tobacco; tobacco	5.2	3.9	3.6	3.5	4.6	3.5	3.3
1701	Cane or beet sugar and chemically preserved	2.1	2.0	3.1	3.0	3.0	2.5	2.5
2101	Extracts, essences and concentrates	6.8	6.3	3.9	3.1	2.4	2.3	2.5
2007	Jams, fruit jellies, marmalades	0.7	1.0	0.9	1.5	1.9	2.2	2.5
2306	Oilcake and other solid residues	10.1	2.1	4.5	7.6	6.1	4.1	2.4
2403	Other manufactured tobacco and manufactured	1.3	1.3	1.5	2.3	2.1	1.7	2.4
1703	Molasses resulting from the extract	8.9	5.4	1.8	5.1	4.2	1.9	2.0
1605	Crustaceans, molluscs and other aquatic	0.2	0.2	1.3	2.0	1.6	0.7	1.8
1903	Tapioca and substitutes therefor	2.8	1.2	1.8	3.0	2.5	1.4	1.5
2304	Oilcake and other solid residues	13.0	8.5	6.3	7.8	6.3	2.7	1.5
1702	Other sugars	0.6	0.4	0.6	0.5	0.6	0.9	1.0

Source Computed based on UN comtrade

Table 12.12 RCA in export of agricultural raw materials

Product code	Product description	1998	2001	2004	2007	2010	2015	2018
5202	Cotton waste (including yarn waste)	9.7	2.8	1.0	3.1	5.7	8.3	12.5
5201	Cotton, not carded or combed	5.5	0.3	1.0	10.2	12.6	12.6	7.9

Source Computed based on UN comtrade

Table 12.13 Determinants of changes in comparative advantage

Dependent variable: RSCA			
Variables	Variables	Z Value	Z Value
GDP per capita	−0.0057	−0.08	0.933
FDI	0.0253	2.34	0.020
Exchange rate	0.0732	1.63	0.101
Land productivity	−0.0778	−0.72	0.470
Constant	0.2530	0.23	0.818
Number of observations	4.704		
Log likelihood value	−1257.014		
Wald chi2(4)	15.32		
Prob > chi2	0.0041		

Source Authors' own estimates

References

Amity, M. (1999). Specialization patterns in Europe. *Weltwirtschaftliches Archiv, 135*, 573–593.

Ansari, S. A., & Khan, W. (2015). India's agricultural trade potential in post WTO period. *Agricultural Economics Research Review, 28*, 93–100.

Ashish, A., & Kannan, E. (2015). Analysis of India's revealed comparative advantage in agro-processed products. *Indian Journal of Economics and Business, 14*(1), 115–130.

Ballassa, B. (1965). Trade liberalization and revealed comparative advantage. *Manchester School of Economics and Social Studies, 33*, 99–123.

Benalywa, Z. A., Ismail, M. M., Shamsuddin, N. M., & Yusop, Z. (2019). Revealed comparative advantage and competitiveness of broiler meat products in Malaysia and selected exporting countries. *International Journal of Business and Society, 20*(1), 383–396.

Dalum, B., Laursen, K., & Villumsen, G. (1998). Structural change in OECD exports specialization patterns: De-specialization and stickiness. *International Review of Applied Economics, 12*, 447–467.

Ferto, I., & Hubbard, L. J. (2003). Revealed comparative advantage and competitiveness in Hungarian agri food sector. *World Economy, 26*(2), 247–259.

Government of India. (2018). *Agricultural statistics at a glance 2018*. New Delhi: Ministry of Agriculture and Farmers Welfare, Directorate of Economics and Statistics, Government of India.

Gupta, M., & Kumar, H. (2017). Revealed comparative advantage: An analysis of exports of Rwanda. *Journal of Economics and Finance, 8*(3), 69–76.

Hirsch, S. (1974). Capital or technology? Confronting the neo-factor proportions and the neo-technology accounts of international trade. *Weltwirtschaftliches Archiv, 110*, 535–563.

Kannan, E. (2010). Post quota regime and comparative advantage in export of India's textiles and clothing. *Journal of International Economics, 1*(2), 14–30.

Kunimoto, K. (1977). Typology of trade intensity indices. *Hitotsubashi Journal of Economics, 17*, 15–32.

Laursen, K. (1998). *Revealed comparative advantage and the alternatives as measures of international specialization* (DRUID Working Paper No 98-30). Danish Research Unit for Industrial Dynamics, Aalborg University.

Mutambatsere, E. (2007). Competitiveness and revealed comparative advantage in the SADC maize industry. In *AAAE Conference Proceedings* (pp. 57–62).

Oduro, A. D., & Offei, E. L. (2014). Investigating Ghana's revealed comparative advantage in agro-processed products. *Scientific Research Publication*, 384–390.

Panchamukhi, V. R. (1973). India's trade with the countries of the ECAFE region. *Economic and Political Weekly, 8*(2), 65–74.

Proudman, J., & Redding, S. (2000). Evolving patterns of international trade. *Review of International Economics, 8*(3), 373–396.

Sachdev, S. (1993). International competitiveness and agricultural export of India. *Indian Economic Review, 28*(2), 203–217.

Sarker, R., & Ratnasena, S. (2014). *Revealed comparative advantage and half a century competitiveness of Canadian agriculture: A case study of wheat, beef and pork sectors* (CATPRN Working Paper No. 2014-01). Canadian Agricultural Trade Policy and Competitiveness Research Network.

Vollrath, T. (1991). A theoretical evaluation of alternative trade intensity measures of revealed comparative advantage. *Review of World Economics, 127,* 265–280.

Yeats, A. J. (1985). On the appropriate interpretation of the revealed comparative advantage index: Implications of a methodology based on industry sector analysis. *Weltwirtchaftliches Archiv, 121*(1), 61–73.

Chapter 13
Trade Competitiveness of the Indian Dairy Industry: An Empirical Analysis

Yashobanta Parida, Avinash K. Ghule,
and Priyankkumar Tulsidas Dudhrejiya

13.1 Introduction

India is the largest milk producer in the world. Milk and other dairy products account for about 67% of the value of the livestock sector, and these products support the livelihoods of nearly 50% of India's rural households (GoI 2018). Milk production increased from merely 20 million tonnes (MT) in 1961 to 176 MT in 2017–2018, at a compound annual growth rate (CAGR) of 4%. In 2017–2018, India produced around 843 MT of milk, about 22% of the global production (FAO 2018). India's dairy sector is expected to reach INR 9.4 trillion (USD 146.2 billion) in 2020 (IBEF 2018).

Before 1999, India was a net importer of dairy products. The successful implementation of the Operation Flood programme increased the production of liquid milk, and the excess of production over consumption resulted in the production of value-added dairy products. India has been a net exporter of dairy products since 2000, and its share in world dairy exports increased marginally from 0.1% in 2001 to 0.2% in 2016.

India's share in world dairy imports also increased marginally from 0.018% in 2001 to 0.063% in 2016. The Middle East, South Asia, South East Asia and the USA are the major markets for India's dairy exports. India imports dairy products primarily from the European Union (EU), New Zealand, Australia, the United Arab Emirates (UAE) and the USA.

India is a cost-competitive milk producer (Ohlan 2012). The country is well endowed with the natural resources required for dairy production, and the industry

Y. Parida (✉) · A. K. Ghule
Verghese Kurien Centre of Excellence, Institute of Rural Management Anand, Anand, Gujarat, India
e-mail: yashobanta@irma.ac.in

P. T. Dudhrejiya
Ganpat University, Mehsana, Gujarat, India

© The Author(s), under exclusive license to Springer Nature Singapore Pte Ltd. 2021   273
S. Bathla and E. Kannan (eds.), *Agro and Food Processing Industry in India*, India Studies in Business and Economics, https://doi.org/10.1007/978-981-15-9468-7_13

can potentially increase the volume of its production and exports (World Bank 2011). India has the largest cattle population in the world, and it has a well-developed milk co-operative network. Milk production has increased, but dairy exports have been adversely affected by high input prices, poor milk quality, inadequate milk procurement and processing infrastructure and by trade restrictions, especially non-tariff barriers to trade (NTB).

This study examines the trade direction of Indian dairy products and their competitiveness. We propose and examine two hypotheses. Indian dairy products are competitive. The exchange rate and world GDP per capita enhance Indian dairy exports. The study uses dairy export data by-product for the period from 2001 to 2017 to estimate the nominal protection coefficient (NPC). It analyses the export and import performance of products and assesses the impact of currency exchange rates and world income on dairy export.

Section 13.2 briefly reviews the literature on the dairy sector's trade competitiveness. Section 13.3 analyses the major markets for Indian dairy products. The data sources, empirical methods and measures of competitiveness are discussed in Section 13.4. Section 13.5 describes the main findings and policy implications.

13.2   Review of Literature

The self-sufficiency ratio, defined as the ratio of global milk production to global milk consumption, is important in influencing the degree and direction of trade flows (FAO 2012; Shadbolt and Apparao 2016). Most trade theories focus on sources of comparative advantage while postulating that all nations can gain from trade by capitalising on their production-related strengths (Ortiz-Ospina 2018).

A few studies examined the Indian dairy industry's competitiveness. Ohlan (2014) studied the competitiveness of dairy exports and observed that the world market size, exchange rate and trade liberalisation are important determinants. Some NTBs play a significant role; for example, Indonesia imposed a blanket ban on the import of livestock products, including milk products, from India due to the foot-and-mouth disease. In June 2016, the Indonesian government introduced new regulations to allow the import of livestock or livestock products from certain zones of India free of foot-and-mouth disease (APEDA 2016).

Using the annual dairy trade data between 1975 and 2001, Rakotoarisoa and Gulati (2006) calculated the NPC to examine how world dairy policy affects the trade and competitiveness of the Indian dairy industry; whole milk powder, but not other dairy products, is competitive in world markets.

Jha (2004) examined the role of the tariff, milk price, milk production and employment opportunities and confirmed that the free import of milk had adversely affected employment opportunities in the dairy sector. Rajarajan et al. (2007) observed that India had been importing more dairy products from developed countries than developing countries; after the introduction of trade reforms, India gained competitive advantage in exporting skimmed milk powder, whole milk powder and ghee. Similarly, Kumar (2010) analysed the competitiveness of livestock products and determinants of livestock exports; trade liberalisation had enhanced the export performance of livestock products but not of milk or milk products.

13.3 Dairy Exports and Imports by Country

As per the FAO (2020), in 2016, Germany was the sixth-largest milk producer in the world, and it contributed 4% of global milk production. Its dairy exports fell from around 16% of world export in 2001 to 13% in 2016 (Table 13.1). New Zealand was the second-largest dairy exporter; it exported 12% of its dairy products, but it accounted for only 3% of milk production. Dairy exports from the Netherlands

Table 13.1 Dairy exports by major countries

Country	2001		2008		2016	
	Value (billion USD)	Share in world exports (%)	Value (billion USD)	Share in world exports (%)	Value (billion USD)	Share in world exports (%)
Germany	4.32	15.8	9.48	14.3	8.09	12.5
New Zealand	2.66	9.7	6.56	9.9	7.82	12.1
Netherlands	3.33	12.2	6.91	10.4	7.10	11.0
France	3.50	12.8	7.38	11.2	6.30	9.7
USA	0.60	2.2	2.98	4.5	3.33	5.1
Belgium	1.74	6.4	3.40	5.1	3.00	4.6
Italy	0.95	3.5	2.31	3.5	2.98	4.6
Denmark	1.29	4.7	2.56	3.9	2.28	3.5
Ireland	0.95	3.5	2.10	3.2	1.91	3.0
Belarus	0.15	0.5	1.09	1.6	1.82	2.8
UK	0.78	2.9	1.50	2.3	1.63	2.5
Australia	1.56	5.7	2.21	3.3	1.63	2.5
Poland	0.37	1.3	1.72	2.6	1.59	2.5
Austria	0.50	1.8	1.38	2.1	1.22	1.9
Saudi Arabia	0.13	0.5	0.66	1.0	1.16	1.8
India	0.04	0.1	0.27	0.4	0.13	0.2
Top 15	22.83	83.3	52.22	79.0	51.85	80.2
Rest of the world	4.56	16.7	13.92	21.0	12.80	19.8
Total	27.39	100	66.14	100	64.65	100

Source World integrated trade solutions (WITS)

accounted for around 11% of production, followed by France (10%) and the USA (3%). The Netherlands accounted for 1.8% of the production and the USA for 12%. The top five developed countries contributed over 50% of dairy exports worldwide and the top 15 countries 80%. India is a minor player; its export share increased marginally from 0.1% in 2001 to 0.2% in 2016, and its share of milk production increased from 14 to 22%.

Developed countries dominate the dairy export market, but dairy exports declined recently for Germany, the Netherlands, France, Belgium, Denmark, Ireland, the UK and Australia. Dairy exports increased for New Zealand, the USA, Poland, Belarus, Saudi Arabia, Italy and Austria (Table 13.1). Demand-related limitations from the Russian Federation had affected dairy exports from Belarus, but government efforts at identifying new export markets in Europe and beyond have stimulated output (FAO 2018).

From 2001 to 2016, Germany was the leading importer of dairy products; it accounted for 9% of the world's dairy imports in 2016 (Table 13.2). The other top importers were Italy (5.4%), China (5.25%), the Netherlands (5.21%), France (5.05%) and the UK (5%). The top 15 developed countries (except China) accounted for 61% of dairy imports worldwide. Dairy imports increased in China, the Russian Federation, Hong Kong, Saudi Arabia and the UAE, and the import share fell in the other countries in the top 15. China's demand for milk products, which has increased manifold in recent decades, attracts exporters in New Zealand, Europe, Australia and the USA (Gooch et al. 2017). India's share in world dairy imports rose from 0.018% in 2001 to 0.06% in 2016.

13.3.1 Trade Performance of the Indian Dairy Sector (1988–2017)

In the early 1980s, milk production was inadequate to meet the domestic consumption, and growing demand led India to depend heavily on subsidised dairy imports, especially from the EU, from the mid-1980s to 2000 (Joshi 2014). Imports continued till 1993–1994 when, just for once, exports surpassed imports. Between 1993–1994 and 1999–2000, imports and exports kept edging each other out, and since 2001, India has been a net exporter of dairy products (Goswami 2007).

India imports skimmed milk powder and other value-added milk products to meet domestic demand. After 2003, domestic milk production increased considerably and dairy exports picked up, but both exports and imports remained volatile. India's export share improved marginally from 0.013% in 1988 to 0.055% in 2017, but its import share fell from 0.393% to 0.009% (Table 13.3). Dairy exports overall fell between 2009–2010 and 2011–2012, evincing a negative trade balance in 2011.

In 2015, domestic food prices experienced high inflation, and the government restricted exports; exports and imports have been falling since then. The volatility in India's dairy exports could be attributed to fluctuating milk production and milk

Table 13.2 Dairy imports by major countries

Country	2001		2008		2016	
	Value (billion USD)	Share in world exports (%)	Value (billion USD)	Share in world exports (%)	Value (billion USD)	Share in world exports (%)
Germany	2.84	10.34	6.8	10.62	5.99	9.34
Italy	2.40	8.72	4.8	7.48	3.49	5.44
China	0.22	0.79	0.9	1.35	3.37	5.25
The Netherlands	1.65	5.98	3.2	4.99	3.35	5.21
France	1.84	6.71	3.3	5.20	3.24	5.05
UK	1.67	6.06	3.8	6.00	3.18	4.96
Belgium	1.86	6.77	3.4	5.37	3.13	4.89
USA	1.02	3.71	1.7	2.63	1.97	3.06
Russian Federation	0.39	1.42	1.5	2.33	1.91	2.97
Hong Kong	0.36	1.30	0.5	0.79	1.81	2.82
Saudi Arabia	0.54	1.96	1.6	2.56	1.78	2.78
Spain	1.03	3.74	2.6	4.11	1.62	2.53
Mexico	0.79	2.87	1.5	2.30	1.47	2.29
United Arab Emirates	0.27	0.99	0.8	1.28	1.30	2.02
Japan	0.74	2.69	1.3	2.10	1.20	1.88
India	0.00	0.018	0.0	0.024	0.04	0.063
Top 15	17.62	64.06	37.7	59.11	38.81	60.50
Rest of the world	9.88	35.94	26.1	40.89	25.34	39.50
Total	27.50	100	63.9	100	64.15	100

Source World integrated trade solutions (WITS)

quality, increasing domestic milk consumption and price instability in international markets.

13.3.2 International Markets

India's dairy exports increased from USD 97.03 million in 2006 to USD 209.87 million in 2017, and its export share to the top 15 countries increased from 63 to 91%. In 2017, India's largest markets were the Middle East (46%), South Asia (30%), South East Asia (11%) and the USA (5%) (Table 13.4). This high share could be due to lower transportation costs, similar tastes and cultural proximity. Between 2006 and

Table 13.3 Dairy trade performance (1988–2017)

Year	Export (value million USD) (value million USD)	Import (value million USD)	Export share (as % of total export)	Import share (as % of total import)
1988	1.8	76.1	0.013	0.393
1989	1.4	35.1	0.008	0.162
1990	1.3	2.1	0.007	0.009
1991	4.6	10.6	0.026	0.054
1992	3.2	18.7	0.016	0.077
1993	3.7	5.6	0.016	0.024
1994	12.2	9.8	0.047	0.034
1995	7.8	18.8	0.025	0.051
1996	3.4	1.5	0.010	0.004
1997	3.9	8.0	0.011	0.019
1998	4.1	10.1	0.012	0.024
1999	11.3	41.9	0.031	0.084
2000	15.6	14.1	0.037	0.027
2001	39.7	4.9	0.091	0.010
2002	24.9	13.1	0.050	0.023
2003	25.8	27.1	0.043	0.037
2004	50.5	13.1	0.067	0.013
2005	147.2	7.6	0.147	0.005
2006	109.2	21.7	0.090	0.012
2007	155.9	13.6	0.107	0.006
2008	270.0	15.2	0.148	0.005
2009	89.0	63.4	0.050	0.024
2010	115.3	183.8	0.052	0.053
2011	75.4	177.4	0.025	0.038
2012	157.3	101.2	0.054	0.021
2013	575.4	34.6	0.171	0.007
2014	311.6	47.1	0.098	0.010
2015	121.5	45.0	0.046	0.012
2016	130.5	40.4	0.050	0.011
2017	161.1	41.3	0.055	0.009

Source World integrated trade solutions (WITS)

Table 13.4 Dairy exports from India

Country	2006		2017	
	Value (million USD)	Export share (as % of total dairy export)	Value (million USD)	Export share (as % of total dairy export)
UAE	14.55	15.0	38.45	18.3
Egypt	12.43	12.8	26.85	12.8
Bhutan	0.33	0.3	19.7	9.4
Afghanistan	2.03	2.1	14.58	6.9
Nepal	4.94	5.1	12.5	6.0
Philippines	2.62	2.7	12.24	5.8
Singapore	2.34	2.4	10.43	5.0
Bangladesh	10.8	11.1	10.2	4.9
USA	2.26	2.3	9.78	4.7
Qatar	0.18	0.2	8.16	3.9
Oman	1.51	1.6	8.02	3.8
Saudi Arabia	2.61	2.7	5.62	2.7
Kuwait	0.87	0.9	5.58	2.7
Pakistan	3.58	3.7	5.32	2.5
Bahrain	0.48	0.5	4.6	2.2
Rest of the world	35.5	36.6	17.84	8.5
Total	97.03	100	209.87	100

Source Export import data *Bank Version 7.1*, Ministry of Commerce and Industry, Government of India

2017, exports to neighbouring countries such as Bangladesh and Pakistan declined, due possibly to geopolitical factors.

India's dairy imports increased from USD 23.5 million in 2006 to USD 43.8 million in 2017. In 2017, India imported 25.7% from France, followed by Denmark (7.8%), Italy (6.7%), Germany (6.5%) and New Zealand (4.8%) (Table 13.5). About 65% of India's dairy imports were from 12 developed countries—55% from the EU and the rest from New Zealand, Australia, the UAE and the USA.

Table 13.6 shows the product-wise (HS-4 digit) distribution of India's dairy exports in 2006–2017. India's export share of milk and cream, not concentrated products, increased from 2.4% in 2006 to 4% in 2017, at a CAGR of 14%. Its export share of butter and other fats and oils increased from 11 to 52% and of cheese and curd products from 2 to 17%.

The export share fell for milk and cream, concentrated (dairy products containing added sugar or other sweeteners), buttermilk, curdled milk and cream and whey and other natural milk constituents. The growth rate was negative for products other than whey and other natural milk constituents. These trends imply that there is great scope

Table 13.5 Dairy imports to India

Country	2006		2017	
	Value (million USD)	Import share (as % of total dairy import)	Value (million USD)	Import share (as % of total dairy import)
France	2.7	11.6	11.3	25.7
Denmark	1.9	8.0	3.4	7.8
Italy	0.5	2.0	2.9	6.7
Germany	0.3	1.3	2.9	6.5
New Zealand	12.5	53.0	2.1	4.8
UK	0.4	1.8	1.9	4.3
Netherland	0.8	3.5	1.7	3.9
Nepal	2.1	9.0	1.4	3.1
Australia	0.2	0.9	0.7	1.5
Switzerland	0.1	0.3	0.2	0.4
UAE	0.1	0.2	0.1	0.2
USA	0.7	2.8	0.0	0.1
Rest of the world	1.3	5.5	15.4	35.1
Total	23.5	100	43.8	100

Source Export import data bank version 7.1, Ministry of Commerce and Industry, Government of India

Table 13.6 Dairy exports by-product (%)

HS codes	Dairy products	2006	2010	2014	2017	CAGR (%) (2006–2017)
0401	Milk and cream, not concentrated	2.44	1.87	5.12	4.11	13.60
0402	Milk and cream, concentrated	78.81	43.83	59.84	25.24	– 1.07
0403	Buttermilk, curdled milk and cream	1.10	0.74	0.20	0.84	6.33
0404	Whey and other natural milk constituents	4.43	1.94	0.06	0.28	– 13.65
0405	Butter and other fats and oils	10.78	44.87	24.82	52.28	24.07
0406	Cheese and curd	2.44	6.74	9.97	17.25	28.02

Source Export import data bank version 7.1, Ministry of Commerce and Industry, Government of India

Table 13.7 Dairy imports by-product (%)

HS codes	Dairy products	2006	2010	2014	2017	CAGR (%) (2006–2017)
0401	Milk and cream, not concentrated	0.19	0.08	1.18	2.30	33.48
0402	Milk and cream, concentrated	7.71	52.40	14.99	10.02	10.88
0403	Buttermilk, curdled milk and cream	0.92	0.30	0.22	3.59	21.55
0404	Whey and other natural milk constituents	18.41	7.00	56.83	52.56	18.40
0405	Butter and other fats and oils	60.33	36.11	9.54	10.97	– 5.88
0406	Cheese and curd	12.45	4.11	17.24	20.56	13.12

Source Export import data bank version 7.1, Ministry of Commerce and Industry, Government of India

for enhancing the export of milk and cream, not concentrated, butter and other fats and oils and, cheese and curd.

Table 13.7 shows the distribution of dairy imports by-product and the growth rate of imports by-product, between 2006 and 2017. In 2017, India imported whey products (more than 50%); cheese and curd (21%); butter and other fats (11%); milk and cream; concentrated (10%); buttermilk, curdled milk and cream (4%); and milk and cream and not concentrated (2.3%). The import share of all products (except butter and other fats and oils) increased between 2006 and 2017.

Indian dairy products could not penetrate European or South American markets (Joshi 2014) because the product quality was inadequate, tariff rates high and input costs for producing milk in India were higher than in other countries such as Australia and New Zealand (International Farm Comparison Network, Dairy Report, 2018).

13.4   Competitiveness of India's Dairy Sector

We extracted the export and import data by country and product from the World Integrated Trade Solutions (WITS) and from the Export Import Data Bank, Ministry of Commerce and Industry, Government of India. We took the data on world per capita income and exchange rates from the World Development Indicators (WDI).

13.4.1   Nominal Protection Coefficient (NPC)

The competitiveness of a product or commodity can be measured in various ways, but the NPC is a popular measure (Gulati et al. 1990; Rakotoarisoa and Gulati 2006;

Ohlan and Vedpal 2006; Elumalai and Sharma 2008; Ohlan 2010). It is defined as

$$NPC_i = \frac{P_i^d}{P_i^w}$$

where NPC_i is the NPC of the ith commodity, P_i^d is the domestic price of ith commodity adjusted for transportation cost in domestic market, and P_i^w is the international reference price of the ith commodity adjusted for transportation cost in the world market.

The NPC is the ratio of the adjusted domestic price to the adjusted world reference price. The NPC explains a commodity's competitiveness in the world market. This study estimates the NPC under the exportable hypothesis, and it compares the unit prices of exportable goods in India with the world unit price of those goods without adjustment of the domestic transportation cost of these commodities (Rajarajan et al. 2007; Kumar 2010). Thus, the NPC formula is

$$NPC_i = \frac{\text{India}_i^X}{\text{World}_i^X}$$

where India_i^X is the export price of ith commodity in India, and World_i^X is the export price of the ith commodity in world.

$$\text{India}_i^X = \frac{\text{Export Value}_i}{\text{Export Quantity}_i}, \text{World}_i^X = \frac{\text{Export Value}_i}{\text{Export Quantity}_i}$$

If $NPC_i < 1$, the export price of ith commodity in India is less than the export price of ith commodity in the world, or a particular product is competitive in the world market; it is unprotected and obtainable in a free trade scenario.

If $NPC_i > 1$, the export price of ith commodity in India is greater than the export price of the commodity in the world; it is protected, and it is less competitive in the world market.

To assess the dairy industry's competitiveness between 2001 and 2017, we estimated the NPC under the exportable hypothesis of various dairy products (HS four digit). The NPC is 1.1–2.0, implying that Indian dairy products are not export-competitive (Table 13.8). The probable reasons are that rising input costs increase the price of raw milk (Hemme et al. 2015); milk processing and other transaction costs make Indian dairy products more expensive; export (including input) subsidies in other countries make Indian dairy products expensive in international markets (Knips 2005); and some NTBs, like quality issues and technical barriers, constrain exports (Ohlan 2014).

For milk and cream and not concentrated products (HS 0401), the NPC value was less than unity between 2005 and 2015 (except 2013). But the NPC value exceeded unity for most products (except 0401 and 0406) for most of the study period. India

Table 13.8 Trends in nominal protection coefficient (NPC)

Year	HS codes and corresponding dairy products category						All dairy products
	0401 Milk and cream, not concentrated	0402 Milk and cream, concentrated	0403 Buttermilk, curdled milk and cream	0404 Whey and other natural milk constituents	0405 Butter and other fats and oils	0406 Cheese and curd	
2001	3.118	0.809	1.407	2.479	1.357	0.926	1.248
2002	5.668	0.797	2.715	1.641	1.235	0.677	1.077
2003	1.999	0.910	1.800	1.703	1.132	0.448	1.170
2004	2.243	1.012	2.096	1.586	1.039	0.590	1.215
2005	0.874	0.865	1.520	1.838	0.859	0.564	1.077
2006	0.930	1.035	1.090	1.650	0.905	0.641	1.132
2007	0.778	1.144	2.072	1.739	0.964	0.735	1.302
2008	0.853	1.066	4.760	1.935	0.846	0.779	1.343
2009	0.974	1.065	1.054	1.221	1.163	0.628	1.223
2010	1.097	0.969	1.275	0.935	0.929	0.983	1.222
2011	0.743	0.853	1.702	2.026	0.953	0.701	1.153
2012	0.942	0.964	1.510	2.361	1.227	0.816	1.252
2013	1.457	1.023	4.351	1.590	1.066	1.621	1.802
2014	0.736	0.965	1.342	2.077	1.146	0.772	1.252
2015	1.304	1.127	1.020	2.756	1.546	0.970	1.711
2016	1.221	1.166	2.107	2.631	1.647	1.017	1.811
2017	1.447	1.281	1.850	2.805	1.149	1.075	2.048

Source Estimated based on world integrated trade solutions (WITS)

is competitive for exporting milk and cream, therefore, but dairy products are not competitive overall. For milk and cream and concentrated products (HS 0402), the NPC is less than unity during 2005–2009, 2011–2012 and 2014 and greater than unity for the rest of the years, or milk and cream concentrated products were competitive only for a few years.

The butter and other fats and oils product group (HS 0403) were somewhat competitive between 2005 and 2011 (except 2009); it was not competitive in the rest of the period. The NPC values of buttermilk, curdled milk and cream (HS 0403) and whey and other natural milk (HS 0404) products were above unity throughout the study period; this product group was uncompetitive. The export price of India's cheese and curd is lower than the world export price, and it gives India a comparative advantage.

13.4.2 Assessing the Impact of Exchange Rate and World Income on Dairy Exports (1988–2017)

We employed the autoregressive distributed lag (ARDL) model because it is a cointegration technique that estimates the long-run relation between export of dairy products, exchange rate and world income; the error correction term of the estimated ARDL model is negative and significant. The ARDL model is used if the variables are stationary at the level I(0) and stationary at first difference I(1). This model controls for endogeneity of the variables by choosing the optimal lag length of the variables. The estimated model is given as

$$lnexport_t = \alpha + \beta_1 lnwpc_t + \beta_2 ER_t + \beta_3 EUP_t + \beta_4 D2001 + \varepsilon_t \quad (13.1)$$

where $lnexport_t$ is the natural logarithm of India's dairy export to total export, ER_t is the exchange rate (rupee per US\$), EUP_t is the export unit price of India' dairy products over world export unit price of dairy products, and D2001 is the dummy variable for removal of trade restrictions relevant to the Indian dairy trade. We estimated the Eq. (13.1) using the ARDL model (Table 13.9).

The coefficient of world per capita income is positive and significant; an increase in world per capita income raises the demand for Indian dairy products. The coefficient of the exchange rate is positive and significant, which is a theoretically correct sign. The results confirm that demand for Indian dairy exports rises when prices fall, and we conclude that the exchange rate plays a significant role.

The coefficient of the 2001 dummy is positive and insignificant, implying that lifting trade restrictions against India raised its dairy exports to some extent only. The coefficient of unit export price to world unit export price of dairy is negative and significant, implying that Indian dairy exports fall when prices rise.

Table 13.9 Long-run coefficient of ARDL (1,2,1,3)

Variable	Coefficients	Std. Error
ln world per capita income	30.018***	7.265
Exchange rate (INR/US\$)	0.285***	0.080
Export unit price/World export price	−8.388***	2.163
Dummy 2001 (Relaxation of dairy trade restriction for India)	0.454	0.634
Error correction term	−0.8407***	0.2266

Note Dependent variable: ln (Dairy export/total export). In this regression, we include time and a constant term. F-statistic = 4.621 shows that there exists a long-term relationship between the variables. ***, ** and * denotes the 1%, 5% and 10% level of significance

13.5 Conclusion and Implications

India is a minor player in the international market for dairy products; its share of exports in terms of percentage of the total world dairy trade increased only marginally from 0.1% in 2001 to 0.2% in 2016. The import share, too, increased concomitantly, though slightly—from a paltry 0.018 to 0.063%. India became a net exporter of dairy products from 2000 onwards, but exports remained volatile and even dipped below imports in the year 2010–2011, probably due to fluctuations in milk production; its reliability as a supplier of milk products to the world is a cause for concern. South Asia, the Middle East and South East Asia are the major export markets for India's dairy products, and India imports largely from developed nations, Nepal being one exception.

We evaluated the trade performance of dairy products, India exports around 50% of butter and other fats and oils out of its total dairy exports, followed by milk and cream, concentrated (25%), cheese and curd (17%) and whey and other natural milk constituents (0.28%), which is lowest among the products. In 2017, India imported primarily whey and other natural milk, cheese and curd (21%), butter and other fats, and oils (11%) and milk and cream, not concentrated (2.3%).

Around 18% of India's dairy exports were sold to the UAE, and more than 25% of its dairy imports were purchased from France. India exported around 72% of butter and other fats and oils to the UAE and imported around 87% whey and other natural milk constituents from France. Much of its dairy-related international trade in some products occurs with the UAE (exports) and France (imports). The contours of the foreign market keep changing, and relying on a few countries for international trade invites certain risks. These risks may be minimised by closely monitoring global business conditions and focusing on the relevant countries.

We evaluated the dairy industry's competitiveness overall and by-product using the NPC for the period from 2001 to 2016. The NPC coefficient reveals that the Indian dairy industry is, generally speaking, not competitive enough in exporting dairy products. One reason is that India's export prices exceed world export prices. India is relatively competitive in cheese and curd exports; their prices are lower than the world export price.

The results based on the ARDL estimates show that world per capita income and the exchange rate are key determinants of increasing dairy exports, while also plays a significant role in enhancing dairy exports. The results also show that the higher unit price of dairy products adversely affects dairy exports, while diminishing tariff rate of dairy products can increase dairy exports to some extent.

To improve the export competitiveness of dairy products, the state and central governments should increase public investment to develop the primary processing infrastructure in the diary sector. They must devise dairy management policies to increase the milk yield and raise procurement and farmer income. It is critical to invest in technology and in research and development to improve traceability and the quality of milk and dairy products and to reduce the cost of production. The government must reduce the tariff rate on dairy products, negotiate the non-tariff and technical barriers and strengthen international cooperation and policy dialogues to restrict developed countries from levying export and input subsidies.

References

APEDA. (2016). https://apeda.gov.in/apedawebsite/SubHead_Products/Onions.htm. Accessed on July 14, 2020.

Elumalai, K., & Sharma, R. K. (2008). Trade protection of India's milk products: Structure and policy implications. *Indian Journal of Agricultural Economics, 63*(1), 67–83.

FAO. (2012). *FAO statistical yearbook 2012—World food and agriculture.* Available at: https://www.fao.org/docrep/015/i2490e/i2490e00.htm.

FAO. (2018). *Dairy market review.* Rome: Food and Agriculture Organization (FAO).

FAO. (2020). https://www.fao.org/faostat/en/#data/QP. Accessed on July 14, 2020.

Government of India (GoI). (2018). *Production enhancement through productivity gains* (Report of the Committee for Doubling Farmers' Income) (Vol. 8, p. 13).

Gooch, E., Hoskin, R., & Law, J. (2017). *China dairy supply and demand* (A report from the Economic Research Service, LDPM-282-01). USDA, Economic Research Service.

Goswami, B. (2007). Can Indian dairy cooperatives survive in the new economic order? In *WTO PUBLIC FORUM 2007 "How Can the WTO Help Harness Globalization"?*, October 4–5, 2007, Geneva (p. 4).

Gulati, A., Hanson, J., & Pursell, G. (1990). *Effective incentives in India's agriculture* (Policy Planning and Research Working Paper) (p. 332).

Hemme, T., Saha, A., & Tripathi, P. (2015). *Dairy farming in India: A global comparison.* IFCN Dairy Research Network, Germany; Food and Agribusiness Strategic Advisory and Research Group (FASAR), YES BANK.

IBEF. (2018). *Agriculture and allied industries report* (p. 26). India Brand Equity Foundation. Retrieved from https://www.ibef.org/download/Agriculture-and-Allied_Industries-Report-May-2018.pdf.

Jha, B. (2004). *India's dairy sector in the emerging trade order.* Institute of Economic Growth.

Joshi, R. M. (2014). India's dairy exports: Opportunities, challenges and strategies. Invited Article. National Seminar on "Indian Dairy Industry—Opportunities and Challenges". AAU Anand.

Knips, V. (2005). *Developing countries and the global dairy sector, part I—Global overview* (PPLPI Working Paper No. 30). FAO.

Kumar, A. (2010). Exports of livestock products from India: Performance, competitiveness and determinants. *Agricultural Economics Research Review, 23*(347–2016–17, 033), 57.

Ohlan, R. (2010). *WTO and Indian agriculture.* New Delhi: Global Research Publications.

Ohlan, R. (2012). Global competitiveness in dairy sector. *Agricultural Situation in India, 69*(5), 257–264.

Ohlan, R. (2014). Competitiveness and trade performance of India's dairy industry. *Asian Journal of Agriculture and Development, 11*(2), 18–37.

Ohlan, R., & Pal, V. (2006). India's comparative advantage in farm trade in the emerging trade order. *Foreign Trade Review, 41*(2), 35–61.

Ortiz-Ospina, E., Beltekian, D., & Roser, M. (2018). *Trade and globalization.* Our World in Data.

Rajarajan, T. R., Saravana Kumar, V., & Singh, R. V. (2007). Implications of trade liberalisation on indian dairy sector: An empirical analysis. *Indian Journal of Agricultural Economics, 62*(3), 426–439.

Rakotoarisoa, M., & Gulati, A. (2006). Competitiveness and trade potential of India's dairy industry. *Food Policy, 31*(3), 216–227.

Shadbolt, N. M., & Apparao, D. (2016). Factors influencing the dairy trade from New Zealand. *International Food and Agribusiness Management Review*. Special Issue–19 B (pp. 241–255).

World Bank. (2011). Demand-led transformation of the livestock sector in India: Achievements, challenges, and opportunities. In *Liberalization of wheat: Production, prices and trade*. Washington, D.C.: World Bank.

Chapter 14
Protection Structure and Comparative Advantage in Primary and Processed Agriculture Exports

Abhishek Jha and Seema Bathla

14.1 Introduction

India has substantially reduced tariffs and non-tariff barriers in agriculture, industry and services sectors—following rapid transformations in the world trade and the Structural Adjustment Program of the World Bank, and in consonance with the stipulations of the World Trade Organization (WTO).India has a comparative advantage in rice, fish, meat, sugar, oilseeds and spices, and it has become a net exporter of agriculture commodities, but it still ranks poorly among agriculture-exporting countries. This chapter investigates the composition of its exports and imports, to see whether India has moved away from exporting primary agricultural products to processed agricultural commodities, and to estimate the level of protection and comparative advantage each commodity has and their implications for farmers, industry and consumers.

The United Nations Conference on Trade and Development (UNCTAD) categorises the exports and imports of agricultural commodities into.

1. Category I. Live Animals and Animal Products, ITC HS[1]Chaps. 1–5;
2. Category II. Vegetable Products and Cereals, ITC HS Chaps. 6–14;
3. Category III. Animal or Vegetable Fats and Oils and their Cleavage Products; Prepared Edible Fats; Animal or Vegetable Waxes, ITC HS Chap. 15; and

---

[1]**ITC-HS** Codes, known as Indian Trade Clarification based on Harmonized System of Coding was adopted in India for import–export operations.

A. Jha (✉) · S. Bathla
Centre for the Study of Regional Development, Jawaharlal Nehru University, New Delhi, India
e-mail: Jhaeconrlae@gmail.com

S. Bathla
e-mail: seema.bathla@gmail.com

© The Author(s), under exclusive license to Springer Nature Singapore Pte Ltd. 2021
S. Bathla and E. Kannan (eds.), *Agro and Food Processing Industry in India*, India Studies in Business and Economics, https://doi.org/10.1007/978-981-15-9468-7_14

4. Category IV. Prepared Foodstuffs; Beverages, Spirits and Vinegar; Tobacco and Manufactured Tobacco Substitutes, ITC HS Chaps. 16–24.

The agri-commodities in Category I (HS Chaps. 1–5) and Category II (HS Chaps. 6–14) are termed primary as these require little processing; mainly, these require cleaning, sorting and freezing, and cereals need to be transformed into rice and flour. Processing these commodities requires basic technology and skills in the agriculture and industrial sectors, and reasonable logistics; traders or the industry procure produce from farmers or wholesalers and sell to exporters or other industries that, in turn, export the commodities. Products that are highly processed, using sophisticated technology and skills, are included in Categories III (HS Chap. 15) and IV (HS Chaps. 16–24). Barley, for example, is processed at multiple stages to make value-added products such as oats, wafers and beer. Such commodities are usually exported directly by the industry or through distributors and exporters.

We analyse the prospects of exports from agriculture and the steadily growing food industry to help in formulating policy decisions. Our hypothesis is that India's trade in highly processed agricultural items (Categories III and IV) has grown faster than in primary agricultural items (Category I and II), and that India's comparative advantage in processed agricultural items exceeds that in primary agricultural items.

Section 14.2 examines the composition of agriculture exports and imports under each category at the ITC HS four-digit level. Section 14.3 measures the degree of protection given to each commodity based on the nominal rate of protection (NRP),[2] and the consequent reduction in distortions, if any. Time period considered for our analysis will be from 2001 to 2017. Section 14.4 provides estimates on revealed comparative advantage that each commodity has and empirical results on the structural shift. Section 14.5 concludes and draws implications.

The analysis is based on data on exports and imports (2001–17) at a disaggregate ITC HS from the UN COMTRADE database. The annual rate of growth in exports and imports is estimated, and the results are presented for the triennium average (TE) because some commodities are price sensitive and tend to be highly volatile.

The domestic and international price series are generally unavailable for most processed commodities, and we use the unit value of their exports or imports to estimate the nominal protection coefficient (NPC).[3] We use the NPC as a proxy for free on board (FOB) and cost insurance and freight (CIF) price, as the estimated price does not consider the freight and insurance between foreign destinations, port handling costs, transportation costs or marketing margins. The unavailability of estimates on transportation cost, marketing margins etc. for a longer time period may be treated as the main limitation of the study. We calculate the NRP as NPC—1, which is estimated under both exportable and importable hypothesis. A lowering of

---

[2]The nominal rate of protection (NRP) on any good is the proportional difference between its domestic and international price arising from the trade policies in question. The major policies include import tariffs, export taxes, quantitative and other restrictions, licensing requirements, rules of origin, local purchase requirements, etc.

[3]The Nominal Protection Coefficient (NPC) is the simplest measure of trade protection. The NPC of a commodity is defined as the ratio of its domestic price to its international reference price.

the value of the NPC and, hence, a negative value of the NRP may indicate a reduction in restrictions and, hence, distortions. The NPC is also considered a price-based measure, and it is used to assess a commodity's comparative advantage in the international markets. If a commodity's NPC exceeds 1, or its domestic price exceeds the import reference price, that commodity is termed "import-competing" in that year. If the value of a commodity in a year is less than 1, or its domestic price is less than the export reference price, the commodity is termed "export-competing".

Greater openness in external trade is perceived to contribute to productivity growth in agriculture and industry. To gauge the openness of trade in primary and processed products, we delineate the changes in the applied duty rate in each product at the four-digit level and compare it with the WTO bound rate. We estimate the trade competitiveness of primary and processed products using the transformed revealed competitiveness (RC)[4] index, based on the original Balassa index, proposed by Vollrath (1991) and Dalum et al. (1998). To determine whether India's agricultural export basket underwent structural change between 2001 and 2017, we estimate a Galtonian regression, separately for primary and processed agri-products.

14.2 Trends in Primary and Processed Agriculture Exports and Imports

Agriculture exports from India began to accelerate mainly from 1995, following the signing of the Uruguay Round Agreement on Agriculture under the auspices of the WTO. External trade was facilitated by favourable changes in the export policy and reductions in quantitative restrictions and in tariff and non-tariff barriers. Primary agricultural commodities such as basmati rice, spices, groundnut seed, soyabean seed and meals were seen to have a comparative advantage, and these commodities continue to have a dominant share in total agriculture exports, though the commodity basket has undergone rapid changes.

From 2001 to 2017, India's share of primary agricultural exports (Categories I and II Chaps. 1–14) in total agricultural exports (Chaps. 1–24) was much higher than the analogous world's scenario. The share fell from 53.5% in 2001 to 48.5% in 2017; the corresponding figure for the world plummeted from 75% in 2001 to 64.5% in 2008 and, after fluctuating wildly, returned to 75% in 2017. Primary agricultural commodities dominated in both the Indian and world markets.

India's total agricultural exports increased in value terms, from USD 6.3 billion in 2001 to USD 35.7 billion in 2017, but seen in terms of share in world agricultural exports the increase—from 1.4% to only 2.3%—was unimpressive. There are large year-to-year variations in the share of agriculture exports in India's total exports; it was high at 14.4% in 2001 but hardly 2% in 2017. The value of all agricultural

---

[4]The RC index is a measure of how able a country is in the allocation of resources for exports adjusted for imports in comparison to the rest of the world. If a country's value of RC in a commodity is greater than zero or positive, it indicates to possess comparative advantage to export (Vollrath 1991).

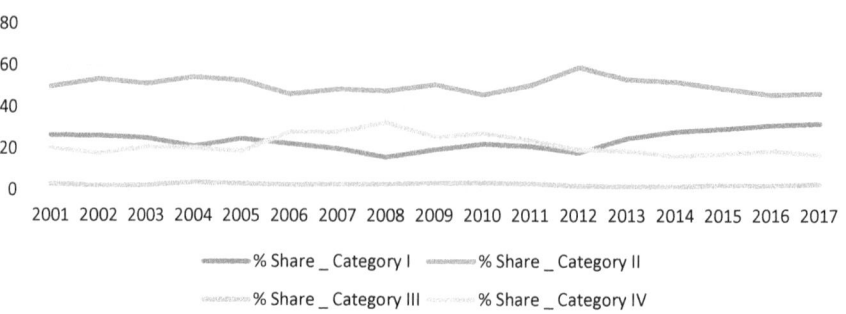

Fig. 14.1 % share of agricultural exports in total agricultural exports (by categories). *Source* Author's calculations based on data from COMTRADE

imports increased from USD 2.67 billion to USD 25.2 billion. The share of India's agricultural imports in world agricultural imports is minimal, at 1.6%, and its share in the country's total imports (agricultural + non-agricultural) has been consistently close to 5.5% from 2001 to 2017.

Within agriculture, a closer look at the share of exports by category between 2001 and 2017 reveals a maximum, almost 50% share of vegetable products in Category II; it fell slightly to 46.8% in 2017. The share of live animals, in Category I, in total exports increased from 26.5 to 32.4%. The share of these two categories grouped as, primary commodities, increased by four percentage points between 2001 and 2017. This indicates that almost 76% of exports are of products from the primary categories and the remaining (24%) is from the other two categories, highly processed products comprising edible oils, prepared food, spirits and tobacco (Fig. 14.1).

India's dependence on imports is greater on processed commodities in Categories III and IV; their share in total imports is high, though it fell from 62.73% in 2001 by about four percentage points to 58.92% in 2017. In 2017, the imports from Category III much exceeded those from Category IV. In fact, imports of animal and vegetable fats and oils (under category III), remained 47%, signalling their significant imports. The low share of imports of primary commodities indicates that India has a comparative advantage and that it depends on foreign markets mainly for value-added commodities; and its food industry is not equipped to produce highly processed products such as edible oils (Fig. 14.2).

14.2.1 Composition of Primary and Processed Agriculture Exports and Imports

The food industry fulfils its requirements mainly through domestic markets; it does not depend much on imports because of either cost or high tariffs. In 2011–12, imports comprised mainly raw and intermediate goods, such as cocoa, which are not produced domestically (Chap. 2 of this book). We analyse the composition of

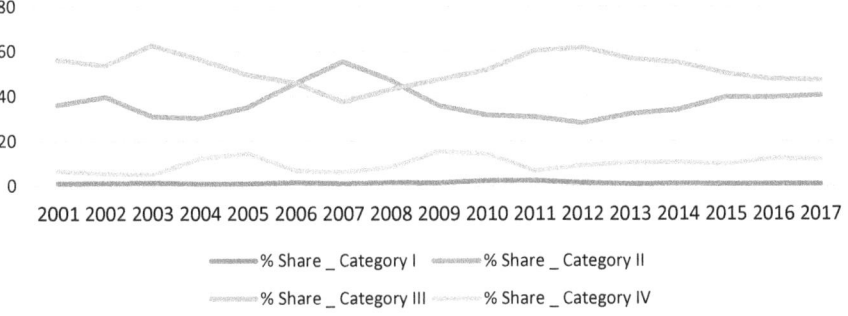

Fig. 14.2 % share of agricultural imports in total agricultural imports (by categories). *Source* Author's calculations based on data from COMTRADE

imports to determine whether industry prefers to import intermediate goods or final goods. We begin with the trends in major exports and imports under Categories I–IV; their share in total agricultural exports and imports; and the annual rate of growth from 2001 to 2017.

The value of major exports under Category I, Live Animals, etc. (Chaps. 1–6) increased significantly from USD 17.34 million in TE 2003 to USD 1021 million by TE 2017. The annual growth rate was high, ranging between 10 and 54%. The value of exports of raw products improved considerably since 2001. The highest increase in the share in total agriculture exports, at nearly 12%, was in edible offal of bovine animals and meat of bovine animals. In total agricultural exports, the share of meat of bovine animals increased from 3.87 to 11.92%; the share fell slightly for crustaceans from 14.3 to 11.8% and of frozen fish from 3.6 to 2%. The share of all products together in Category I rose from 25.97% in TE 2003 to 31.34% in TE 2017, at the compound annual growth rate (CAGR) of 15–16%.

The value of products in Category II much exceeded that in Category I; it grew from USD 3493 million in TE 2003 to USD 15,447 million in TE 2017—an increase of almost five times and a growth rate 13.38% per annum. The export value rose for rice, groundnut, grapes and dates, figs, pineapples, avocados, guavas, mangoes and tea. The maximum share in total agriculture exports in TE 2017 was that of rice (19.2%), coconut (2.8%), vegetable saps and extracts (2.7%), pepper (2.7%) and tea (2.2%). Over the years, there was a decrease in the share of tea; coffee; oleaginous fruits; dried leguminous vegetables; brazil nuts, cashew nuts and coconuts; and other oilseeds.

The value of the exports of processed agricultural products under Category III grew at 13.5% per annum—it rose from USD 174 million in 2001 to USD 1014 million in 2017—but it was still much less than that of Category I or Category II. The exported value increased the most, are for boiled, oxidised, dehydrated animal oil and fats and oils and their fractions of fish or marine, which surged between 10 and 30% per annum. The share of Category III exports in total agricultural exports has remained the same, around 3%, over the years.

Category IV comprises highly processed products—prepared foodstuffs; beverages, spirits and vinegar; and unprocessed tobacco and manufactured tobacco substitutes. Their export value grew from USD 1320.50 million in TE 2003 to USD 7635 million USD in TE 2013, but then fell to USD 5918 million in TE 2017. The rate of growth, estimated at nearly 13% per annum, is about the same as in the other two product categories. The export value of products under Category IV is much higher than that under Category III. An increase in demand is visible for cane/beet sugar; crustaceans and molluscs; food preparations; and unmanufactured tobacco. The value increased significantly for food preparations such as breads, pastries, cakes and biscuits. The products in Category IV, as in Category III, have a lower share in total agricultural exports. The share of the products in Category IV is 18.2%; cane/beet sugar, at 3.7%, has the highest share. The shares of cane and unmanufactured tobacco raw exports as a percentage of agricultural exports decreased over time. Oilcake and other solid residues experienced a major setback in their share in total agricultural exports.

We estimated the value of major imports under each category, their annual growth rate and their share in total agricultural imports from TE 2001 to TE 2017. The value of imports under Category I increased from USD 41.2 million in TE 2003 to USD 185 million in TE 2017. A major increase is seen in animal products, from USD 4.34 million to USD 22.95 million. Other imports viz. whey, fish fillets and crustaceans too grew at over 12% per annum. Imports of primary commodities grew at 13% per annum, but their share in total agricultural imports was less than 0.10%. The value of primary imports in Category II is much higher than that of Category I. Imports in Category II grew at 15% per annum, and their value jumped from USD 1145 million to USD 9045 million. The highest share among primary importable in total agriculture imports is of dried leguminous vegetables (16.9%), coconuts (5.9%) and other nuts (4.44%). The share in total agriculture imports is less than 1% for most of the other products, such as apples and other fruits, oilseeds, coffee and lac.

India imports many primary products, and their share in total imports has not changed, but the share of wheat imports in total imports fell from 9.48% in 2001 to 1.22% in 2013 and rose to 2.56% in 2017. Clearly, India imports wheat only in situations of need. Milk and cream imports fell from USD 5.79 million to USD 3.22 million. The value of imports in Category III is the highest among the four categories considered; it increased from USD 1882 million to USD 10,949 million. Palm oil and edible oils, mainly soya bean oil and sunflower oil, had the major share. The share of soya bean in total agricultural imports increased from 1.73% in 2001 to 6.59% in 2017, but the share of soya bean oil fell from 16.1% in TE 2001 to 12.4% in TE 2017 and that of palm oil from 36.4% in TE 2001 to 26.8% during TE 2017. Most of the importable items in Categories I, II and III are for direct consumption, and these grew at more than 14% per annum.

The value of imports of processed products in Category IV increased from USD 184 million to USD 2562 million, but it is much less than the value of products under Category II or III. The value of imports of processed products increased steadily, as did their share in total agricultural imports; and the growth rate of products was much higher, above 20% per annum, than of primary commodities (Categories I and

II). The increase in the value of cane/beet sugar imports was the largest, from USD 6.67 million in 2001 to USD 825.76 million in 2017, at 40.78% per annum. The share of cane/beet sugar imports in total agriculture imports increased from 0.20% in 2001 to 3.63% in 2017.

The share in total agricultural imports increased mainly for the products such as preparations used in animal feeding; undenatured ethyl alcohol of an alcoholic strength spirits; water; chocolate and other food preparations; cocoa beans, butter, etc.; and other sugars. The share in agricultural imports is less than 1% for most of these said products, but their value increased beyond 100% between 2001 and 2017. The manufacturing sector uses cocoa and food preparations as intermediate products in making final consumables. Overall, the industry uses the importable items under Category IV for raw or intermediate consumption.

14.3 Measuring Protection in Primary and Processed Agricultural Commodities

Agricultural trade is a sensitive issue in most developing countries, including India, because commodity prices in world markets are highly volatile, and their impact on food security and on poor farmers is a serious concern, as are quality issues and standards and the possibilities of an import surge. Therefore, countries restrict exports and imports by imposing high tariff and non-tariff barriers, though the Uruguay Round Agreement on Agriculture mandates member countries to convert non-tariff barriers to tariff equivalents. India's market is better integrated with the world market than earlier, but how much have liberal trade policies—reduced tariff and non-tariff barriers—raised the growth rate of exports and imports? We measure the magnitude of protection provided to major exportable and importable commodities and compares it with their respective applied tariffs. The protection is measured based on the NRP separately under the exportable and importable hypotheses. The major limitation is that domestic and world prices are not available for several agricultural commodities at the disaggregate commodity level. Therefore, we estimate the unit value of the selected commodities in each category.

The NPC indicates the incentive or disincentive that the growers or industry have in a free trade regime. The estimated NRP indicates the percentage tariff imposed on a product as it enters a country. When the NPC for a commodity exceeds 1, the support price exceeds the border price, and producers receive higher price; it reflects producer subsidies (protection), since the producer earns more than the market would pay. Consumers would have to pay a higher price; hence, they are not protected. If the NPC of a commodity is less than 1, or its domestic price (support price) is less than the border price, the protection accorded is termed negative, implying that farmers get a lower price. The consequent negative NRP suggests a tax or restriction on trade. If the value of NPC is 1, the protection is considered neutral. The NPC is a crude, price-based measure of a commodity's competitiveness or comparative advantage.

If a commodity's NPC is less than 1, it is considered competitive in the international market, and it carries positive incentives for exports.

Table 14.1 shows the NPC and NRP of products in Categories I–IV under the exportable hypothesis from 2001 to 2017. The NPC of the major tradable items in Category I at four-digit level is less than 1 (0.81); the NRP is negative (0.19), implying that primary agricultural products are highly unprotected and hardly favour farmers and that the trade policy is biased towards consumers, as Saini and Gulati (2017) point out in analysing selected agricultural commodities. The average NPC of the primary products in Category II is 1.36; the NRP (0.36) is positive, which indicates that some protection is provided to the edible offal of bovine animals, milk, cream and butter, dried leguminous vegetables, bananas, peel of citrus fruit or melons, rye, oats, wheat or meslin flour, fodder roots and lac.

Highly processed and value-added products in Categories III and IV receive more protection. The NPC is more than 1 for most items—except malt, prepared foods, breads and pastries—though it fell during the study period. The magnitude of protection for all commodities together in Category III increased from 1.76 in 2001 to 3.37 in 2017; the NRP rose from 0.76 to 2.37. The average NPC of highly processed commodities in Category IV shot up from 0.97 to 1.80, with a change from a negative NRP at 0.03 in 2001 to a positive one at 0.80 in 2017. The average NPC of products in Category IV is less than that in Category III.

Our analysis of the protection structure for primary agricultural commodities indicates that India's agriculture trade policy is biased against farmers, as the free market prices of most primary commodities are much higher than their respective domestic prices (Fig. 14.3).The food processing industry appears to be highly protected, in contrast, as the domestic prices of manufactured agricultural products are higher than their respective free market prices. Such distortions in processed items may indicate that the consumers are at a loss as they have to pay a higher price on account of protection. Farmers would not benefit if primary agricultural commodities were less protected or processed agricultural commodities were more protected, as their produce fetches prices much less than the free market prices.

The estimated NPC and NRP are slightly different under the importable hypothesis. The NPC of primary commodities fell from 4.67 to 1.82 over the study period, but it still exceeds 1. The NRP was positive, 3.67 in 2001 and 0.82 in 2017, and it implies that agriculture was highly protected by tariff and non-tariff barriers. In contrast, the NPC for Category II products was much lower, at 1.52 in 2017; the NRP (0.52), though, indicates protection. For selected primary commodities, the value of NPC is less than 1, which shows the potential for accelerating trade. The NPC is more than 1 for other raw commodities, vegetables, uncooked or cooked by steaming or boiling in water, frozen flour, meal and powder of peas, beans, lentils and other dried leguminous vegetables. High tariffs are levied on the imports of meat and meat products to restrict imports into India.

The protection accorded to edible oils in Category III fell considerably; the NPC is close to 1, and the NRP is 0.07, indicating neutral protection (Fig. 14.4 and Table 14.2). The protection structure is in favour of industry and against consumers, however; the average NPC of products in Category IV is greater than 1. The only

Table 14.1 Nominal rate of protection in major agriculture commodities under exportable hypothesis in India (FOB prices)

HS CODE	Product label	NPC 2001	NPC 2017	NRP 2001	NRP 2017
	Category I	*0.85*	*0.81*	*0.15*	*0.19*
201	Meat of bovine animals, fresh or chilled	0.333	0.734	0.667	0.266
202	Meat of bovine animals, frozen	0.536	0.74	0.464	0.26
203	Meat of swine, fresh, chilled or frozen	0.474	0.952	0.526	0.048
204	Meat of sheep or goats, fresh, chilled or frozen	0.712	1.022	0.288	0.022
206	Edible offal of bovine animals, swine, sheep, goats, horses, asses, mules or hinnies, fresh, …	1.228	1.206	0.228	0.206
302	Fish, fresh or chilled (excluding fish fillets and other fish meat of heading 0304)	1.792	0.401	0.792	0.599
304	Fish fillets and other fish meat, whether or not minced, fresh, chilled or frozen	0.5	0.794	0.5	0.206
305	Fish, fit for human consumption, dried, salted or in brine; smoked fish, fit for human consumption	0.293	–	0.707	–
306	Crustaceans, whether in shell or not, live, fresh, chilled, frozen, dried, salted or in brine	0.858	0.701	0.142	0.299
401	Milk and cream, not concentrated nor containing added sugar or other sweetening matter	3.044	1.762	2.044	0.762
405	Butter, incl. dehydrated butter and ghee, and other fats and oils derived from milk; dairy	1.475	1.198	0.475	0.198
406	Cheese and curd	0.906	0.806	0.094	0.104
409	Natural honey	0.851	1.223	0.149	0.223
410	Turtles eggs, birds' nests and other edible products of animal origin, n.e.s	0.077	0.272	0.923	0.728
	Category II	*1.45*	*1.36*	*0.45*	*0.36*
701	Potatoes, fresh or chilled	0.564	0.545	0.436	0.455
702	Tomatoes, fresh or chilled	0.285	0.38	0.715	0.62
703	Onions, shallots, garlic, leeks and other alliaceous vegetables, fresh or chilled	0.531	0.43	0.469	0.57

(continued)

Table 14.1 (continued)

HS CODE	Product label	NPC 2001	NPC 2017	NRP 2001	NRP 2017
704	Cabbages, cauliflowers, kohlrabi, kale and similar edible brassicas, fresh or chilled	1.666	0.513	0.666	0.487
705	Lettuce "Lactuca sativa" and chicory "Cichorium spp.", fresh or chilled	0.592	0.329	0.408	0.671
706	Carrots, turnips, salad beetroot, salsify, celeriac, radishes and similar edible roots, fresh or chilled	0.831	1.068	0.169	0.068
707	Cucumbers and gherkins, fresh or chilled	0.482	0.932	0.518	0.068
708	Leguminous vegetables, shelled or unshelled, fresh or chilled	0.808	1.288	0.192	0.288
711	Vegetables provisionally preserved, e.g. by sulphur dioxide gas, in brine, in sulphur water...	0.68	0.782	0.32	0.218
712	Dried vegetables, whole, cut, sliced, broken or in powder, but not further prepared	0.841	0.315	0.159	0.685
713	Dried leguminous vegetables, shelled, whether or not skinned or split	3.398	2.379	2.398	1.379
802	Other nuts, fresh or dried, whether or not shelled or peeled (excluding coconuts, Brazil nuts	1.276	0.65	0.276	0.35
803	Bananas, incl. plantains, fresh or dried	1.462	1.102	0.462	0.102
804	Dates, figs, pineapples, avocados, guavas, mangoes and mangosteens, fresh or dried	0.647	0.811	0.353	0.189
806	Grapes, fresh or dried	0.934	0.821	0.066	0.179
808	Apples, pears and quinces, fresh	0.667	0.598	0.333	0.402
809	Apricots, cherries, peaches incl. nectarines, plums and sloes, fresh	0.631	0.849	0.369	0.151
814	Peel of citrus fruit or melons, incl. watermelons, fresh, frozen, dried or provisionally preserved	2.647	1.037	1.647	0.037
901	Coffee, whether or not roasted or decaffeinated; coffee husks and skins; coffee substitutes	0.764	0.908	0.236	0.092

(continued)

Table 14.1 (continued)

HS CODE	Product label	NPC 2001	NPC 2017	NRP 2001	NRP 2017
902	Tea, whether or not flavoured	1.049	0.61	0.049	0.39
905	Vanilla	0.08	1.351	0.92	0.351
907	Cloves, whole fruit, cloves and stems	0.563	1.107	0.437	0.107
910	Ginger, saffron, turmeric "curcuma", thyme, bay leaves, curry and other spices (excluding pepper…	0.69	1.128	0.31	0.128
1001	Wheat and meslin	0.573	1.354	0.427	0.354
1002	Rye	3.192	4.297	2.192	3.297
1004	Oats	4.365	1.475	3.365	0.475
1006	Rice	1.164	0.783	0.164	0.217
1101	Wheat or meslin flour	0.559	1.616	0.441	0.616
1102	Cereal flours (excluding wheat or meslin)	1.161	1.292	0.161	0.292
1105	Flour, meal, powder, flakes, granules and pellets of potatoes	0.641	0.616	0.359	0.384
1201	Soya beans, whether or not broken	0.654	1.481	0.346	0.481
1206	Sunflower seeds, whether or not broken	2.345	0.924	1.345	0.076
1211	Plants and parts of plants, incl. seeds and fruits, of a kind used primarily in perfumery	0.782	0.736	0.218	0.264
1213	Cereal straw and husks, unprepared, whether or not chopped, ground, pressed or in the form	1.642	1.58	0.642	0.58
1214	Swedes, mangolds, fodder roots, hay, alfalfa, clover, sainfoin, forage kale, lupines, vetches	18.772	7.429	17.772	6.429
1301	Lac; natural gums, resins, gum–resins, balsams and other natural oleoresins	2.928	2.163	1.928	1.163
	Category III	*1.76*	*3.37*	*0.76*	*2.37*
1505	Wool grease and fatty substances derived therefrom, incl. lanolin	0.952	0.757	0.048	0.243
1506	Other animal fats and oils and their fractions, whether or not refined, but not chemically	3.635	8.466	2.635	7.466

(continued)

Table 14.1 (continued)

HS CODE	Product label	NPC 2001	NPC 2017	NRP 2001	NRP 2017
1507	Soyabean oil and its fractions, whether or not refined (excluding chemically modified)	0.988	1.668	0.012	0.668
1508	Groundnut oil and its fractions, whether or not refined, but not chemically modified	2.125	0.962	1.125	0.038
1509	Olive oil and its fractions obtained from the fruit of the olive tree solely by mechanical	1.647	1.009	0.647	0.009
1510	Other oils and their fractions, obtained solely from olives, whether or not refined	0.913	0.659	0.087	0.341
1511	Palm oil and its fractions, whether or not refined (excluding chemically modified)	3.105	2.285	2.105	1.285
1514	Rape, colza or mustard oil and fractions thereof, whether or not refined, but not chemically	1.613	2.333	0.613	1.333
1516	Animal or vegetable fats and oils and their fractions, partly or wholly hydrogenated, inter–esterified	1.188	1.238	0.188	0.238
1517	Margarine, other edible mixtures or preparations of animal or vegetable fats or oils and edible	1.982	1.372	0.982	0.372
1518	Animal or vegetable fats and oils and their fractions, boiled, oxidised, dehydrated, sulphurised	2.436	2.724	1.436	1.724
1520	Glycerol, crude; glycerol waters and glycerol lyes	1.726	10.397	0.726	9.397
	Category IV	*0.97*	*1.80*	*0.03*	*0.80*
1601	Sausages and similar products, of meat, offal or blood; food preparations based on these products	1.009	1.481	0.009	0.481
1602	Prepared or preserved meat, offal or blood	0.623	1.619	0.377	0.619
1704	Sugar confectionery not containing cocoa, incl. white chocolate	0.9	0.465	0.1	0.535
1803	Cocoa paste, whether or not defatted	4.511	2.3	3.511	1.3

(continued)

Table 14.1   (continued)

HS CODE	Product label	NPC 2001	NPC 2017	NRP 2001	NRP 2017
1804	Cocoa butter, fat and oil	2.075	0.865	1.075	0.135
1805	Cocoa powder, not containing added sugar or other sweetening matter	2.458	1.183	1.458	0.183
1806	Chocolate and other food preparations containing cocoa	0.904	1.338	0.096	0.338
1901	Malt extract; food preparations of flour, groats, meal, starch or malt extract	0.91	0.948	0.09	0.052
1902	Pasta, whether or not cooked or stuffed with meat or other substances or otherwise prepared	2.283	0.97	1.283	0.03
1903	Tapioca and substitutes therefor prepared from starch, in the form of flakes, grains, pearls	1.068	0.86	0.068	0.14
1904	Prepared foods obtained by the swelling or roasting of cereals or cereal products, e.g. corn	0.502	0.647	0.498	0.353
1905	Bread, pastry, cakes, biscuits and other bakers wares, whether or not containing cocoa	0.543	0.518	0.457	0.482
2002	Tomatoes, prepared or preserved otherwise than by vinegar or acetic acid	0.983	0.923	0.017	0.077
2003	Mushrooms and truffles, prepared or preserved otherwise than by vinegar or acetic acid	0.904	16.101	0.096	15.101
2004	Vegetables prepared or preserved otherwise than by vinegar or acetic acid, frozen	2.178	1.738	1.178	0.738
2006	Vegetables, fruit, nuts, fruit–peel and other edible parts of plants, preserved by sugar	0.57	0.452	0.43	0.548
2007	Jams, fruit jellies, marmalades, fruit or nut purée	0.765	0.565	0.235	0.435
2103	Sauce and preparations	0.865	1.347	0.135	0.347
2105	Ice cream and other edible ice, whether or not containing cocoa	1.89	0.966	0.89	0.034
2106	Food preparations, n.e.s	0.646	0.45	0.354	0.55
2304	Oilcake	1.036	1.186	0.036	0.186
2401	Unmanufactured tobacco; tobacco refuse	0.656	0.689	0.344	0.311

(continued)

Table 14.1 (continued)

HS CODE	Product label	NPC 2001	NPC 2017	NRP 2001	NRP 2017
	Average of All Commodities	**1.25**	**1.58**	**0.25**	**0.58**

Source Based on data from COMTRADE

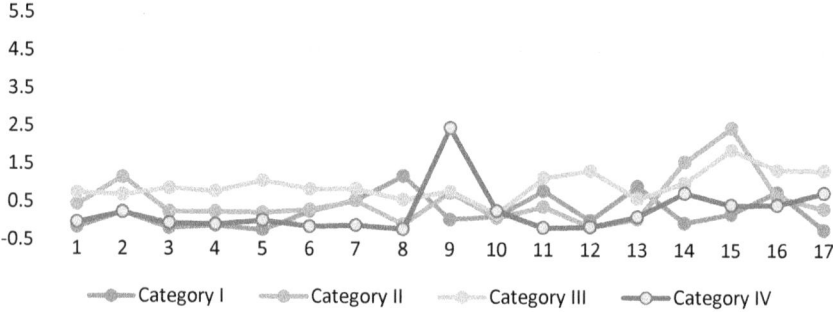

Fig. 14.3 Nominal Rate of Protection (NRP) under Exportable Hypothesis: 2001 to 2017. *Source* Author's calculations based on data from COMTRADE

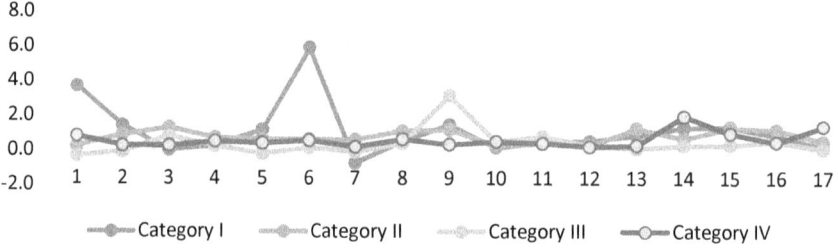

Fig. 14.4 Nominal Rate of Protection (NRP) under Importable Hypothesis: 2001 to 2017. *Source* Author's calculations based on data from COMTRADE

exceptions are in the case of sugar, cocoa powder, extracts and food preparations; the food industry uses these as intermediate goods and, hence, the tariffs on these goods are lower.

We now compare the applied most favoured nation (MFN) rates and bound rates for important importable commodities to the magnitude of protection accorded to agriculture. As shown in Table 14.3, the applied MFN rate has been reduced from 41 to 35.3% for all agricultural commodities. The applied tariff rate has been reduced slightly for meat, fish, crustaceans and natural honey (Category I), except in the case of honey, but the tariff on each product is much below the bound rate. The tariff rates did not change between 2001 and 2017 for Category II (cereals, oilseeds, vegetables, plants and figs). The bound rate for each category is 100, or above; if imports surge, India has considerable scope for raising the tariff. India has a comparative advantage in rice, tea and coffee, and a steady export market, and so the tariffs are high. Tariffs

Table 14.2 Nominal rate of protection in major agriculture commodities under importable hypothesis (CIF Prices)

HS CODE	Products	NCP 2001	NCP 2017	NRP 2001	NRP 2017
	Category I	*4.67*	*1.82*	*3.67*	*0.82*
202	Meat of bovine animals, frozen	3.914	1.802	2.914	0.802
203	Meat of swine, fresh, chilled or frozen	2.308	1.837	1.308	0.837
204	Meat of sheep or goats, fresh, chilled or frozen	3.969	1.704	2.969	0.704
304	Fish fillets and other fish meat, whether or not minced, fresh, chilled or frozen	1.225	0.295	0.225	−0.705
405	Butter, incl. dehydrated butter and ghee	0.551	0.667	−0.449	−0.333
406	Cheese and curd	1.422	1.244	0.422	0.244
409	Natural honey	0.947	2.075	−0.053	1.075
	Category II	*1.23*	*1.52*	*0.23*	*0.52*
701	Potatoes, fresh or chilled	0.289	0.96	−0.711	−0.04
702	Tomatoes, fresh or chilled	3.412	1.646	2.412	0.646
703	Onions, shallots, garlic, leeks and other alliaceous vegetables	1.247	0.468	0.247	−0.532
704	Cabbages, cauliflowers, kohlrabi, kale and similar edible brassicas, fresh or chilled	0.153	0.104	−0.847	−0.896
708	Leguminous vegetables, shelled or unshelled, fresh or chilled	0.237	1.588	−0.763	0.588
709	Other vegetables, fresh or chilled (excluding potatoes, tomatoes, alliaceous vegetables)	1.735	1.449	0.735	0.449
710	Vegetables, uncooked or cooked by steaming or boiling in water, frozen	11.355	0.793	10.355	−0.207
713	Dried leguminous vegetables, shelled, whether or not skinned or split	0.849	0.825	−0.151	−0.175
801	Coconuts, Brazil nuts and cashew nuts, fresh or dried, whether or not shelled or peeled	0.397	0.866	−0.603	−0.134
802	Other nuts, fresh or dried, whether or not shelled or peeled (excluding coconuts, Brazil nuts)	0.838	0.867	−0.162	−0.133
804	Dates, figs, pineapples, avocados, guavas, mangoes and mangosteens, fresh or dried	0.257	0.555	−0.743	−0.445

(continued)

Table 14.2 (continued)

HS CODE	Products	NCP 2001	NCP 2017	NRP 2001	NRP 2017
806	Grapes, fresh or dried	0.962	1.901	−0.038	0.901
807	Melons, incl. watermelons, and papaws (papayas), fresh	0.447	1.489	−0.553	0.489
808	Apples, pears and quinces, fresh	1.118	1.04	0.118	0.04
809	Apricots, cherries, peaches incl. nectarines, plums and sloes, fresh	0.899	1.111	−0.101	0.111
901	Coffee, whether or not roasted or decaffeinated; coffee husks	0.834	0.48	−0.166	−0.52
902	Tea, whether or not flavoured	0.569	0.694	−0.431	−0.306
903	Mate	1.413	3.514	0.413	2.514
904	Pepper of the genus Piper; dried or crushed or ground fruits of the genus Capsicum	0.974	1.212	−0.026	0.212
907	Cloves, whole fruit, cloves and stems	1.291	1.049	0.291	0.049
910	Ginger, saffron, turmeric "curcuma", thyme, bay leaves, curry and other spices	0.234	1.455	−0.766	0.455
1004	Oats	0.93	1.158	−0.07	0.158
1006	Rice	0.863	1.55	−0.137	0.55
1101	Wheat or meslin flour	0.688	1.376	−0.312	0.376
1105	Flour, meal, powder, flakes, granules and pellets of potatoes	1.281	0.936	0.281	−0.064
1106	Flour, meal and powder of peas, beans, lentils and other dried leguminous vegetables	2.455	3.025	1.455	2.025
1109	Wheat gluten, whether or not dried	1.025	0.988	0.025	−0.012
1201	Soya beans, whether or not broken	1.656	1.562	0.656	0.562
1202	Groundnuts, whether or not shelled or broken (excluding roasted or otherwise cooked)	1.531	0.878	0.531	−0.122
1203	Copra	0.778	1.46	−0.222	0.46
1204	Linseed, whether or not broken	1.103	1.278	0.103	0.278
1213	Cereal straw and husks, unprepared, whether or not chopped, ground, pressed or in the form	0.376	1.175	−0.624	0.175
	Category III	*0.66*	*1.07*	*−0.34*	*0.07*

(continued)

Table 14.2 (continued)

HS CODE	Products	NCP 2001	NCP 2017	NRP 2001	NRP 2017
1505	Wool grease and fatty substances derived therefrom, incl. lanolin	0.689	1.171	−0.311	0.171
1510	Other oils and their fractions, obtained solely from olives, whether or not refined	1.818	1.031	0.818	0.031
1515	Fixed vegetable fats and oils, incl. jojoba oil, and their fractions	0.646	0.66	−0.354	−0.34
1520	Glycerol, crude; glycerol waters and glycerol lyes	0.632	1.022	−0.368	0.022
	Category IV	*1.79*	*2.37*	*0.79*	*1.37*
1601	Sausages and similar products, of meat, offal or blood; food preparations based on these products	1.017	1.168	0.017	0.168
1602	Prepared or preserved meat, offal or blood (excluding sausages and similar products)	0.496	1.454	−0.504	0.454
1603	Extracts and juices of meat, fish or crustaceans, molluscs and other aquatic invertebrates	0.822	20.818	−0.178	19.818
1604	Prepared or preserved fish; caviar and caviar substitutes prepared from fish eggs	2.906	1.428	1.906	0.428
1605	Crustaceans, molluscs and other aquatic invertebrates, prepared or preserved (excluding smoked)	0.461	0.639	−0.539	−0.361
1704	Sugar confectionery not containing cocoa, incl. white chocolate	0.69	0.532	−0.31	−0.468
1801	Cocoa beans, whole or broken, raw or roasted	1.017	0.936	0.017	−0.064
1802	Cocoa shells, husks, skins and other cocoa waste	2.32	1.05	1.32	0.05
1803	Cocoa paste, whether or not defatted	1.347	1.087	0.347	0.087
1804	Cocoa butter, fat and oil	0.964	1.019	−0.036	0.019
1805	Cocoa powder, not containing added sugar or other sweetening matter	0.883	0.856	−0.117	−0.144
1806	Chocolate and other food preparations containing cocoa	0.865	1.098	−0.135	0.098

(continued)

Table 14.2 (continued)

HS CODE	Products	NCP 2001	NCP 2017	NRP 2001	NRP 2017
1904	Prepared foods obtained by the swelling or roasting of cereals or cereal products, e.g. corn	0.194	0.975	−0.806	−0.025
1905	Bread, pastry, cakes, biscuits and other bakers wares	0.614	0.787	−0.386	−0.213
2001	Vegetables, fruit, nuts and other edible parts of plants, prepared or preserved by vinegar	0.527	1.062	−0.473	0.062
2002	Tomatoes, prepared or preserved otherwise than by vinegar or acetic acid	1.094	0.913	0.094	−0.087
2003	Mushrooms and truffles, prepared or preserved otherwise than by vinegar or acetic acid	6.424	3.853	5.424	2.853
2004	Vegetables prepared or preserved otherwise than by vinegar or acetic acid	1.733	4.574	0.733	3.574
2005	Other vegetables prepared or preserved otherwise than by vinegar or acetic acid, not frozen	1.754	0.828	0.754	−0.172
2006	Vegetables, fruit, nuts, fruit − peel and other edible parts of plants, preserved by sugar	2.084	1.168	1.084	0.168
2007	Jams, fruit jellies, marmalades, fruit or nut purée and fruit or nut pastes	1.247	1.282	0.247	0.282
2106	Food preparations, n.e.s	1.941	1.644	0.941	0.644
2305	Oilcake and other solid residues, whether or not ground or in the form of pellets, resulting	0.788	1.136	−0.212	0.136
2309	Preparations of a kind used in animal feeding	3.039	1.919	2.039	0.919
2401	Unmanufactured tobacco; tobacco refuse	1.254	0.991	0.254	−0.009
2403	Manufactured tobacco and manufactured tobacco substitutes and "homogenised" or "reconstituted"	1.731	1.288	0.731	0.288
	Average All Commodities	**3.86**	**1.62**	**2.86**	**0.62**

Source Based on data from COMTRADE

Table 14.3 Import tariff (applied and bound rates) in major agriculture commodities

HS	Product	Applied MFN Rate (%)					Bound Rate (%)	
		TE 2003	TE 2009	TE 2012	TE 2017		TE 2003	TE 2017
Category I								
0202	Meat of bovine animals, frozen	32.5	30	29.8	30		150	100
0204	Meat of sheep or goats, fresh, chilled or frozen	32.5	30	29.8	30		150	100
0206	Edible offal of bovine animals,	32.5	30	29.8	30		100	100
0302	Fish, fresh or chilled	33.5	29.81	28.9	30		NA	150
0303	Frozen Fish	33.5	29.81	28.9	30		NA	150
0304	Fish fillets and other fish meat,	33.5	29.81	28.9	30		NA	150
0305	Fish, fit for human consumption, dried, salted	33.5	29.81	28.9	30		NA	150
0306	Crustaceans	35	29.81	28.9	30		NA	150
0307	Molluscs	35	29.81	28.9	30		NA	150
0409	Natural honey	30	60	60	60		100	100
Category II								
1006	Rice	77.5	71.7	60	77.5		100	100
0801	Coconuts, Brazil nuts and cashew nuts,	44.2	38.3	47.1	45.7		150	100
1302	Vegetable saps and extracts	30	26.3	26.3	26.3		100	100
0904	Pepper, dried or crushed	70	70	70	68.9		150	150

(continued)

Table 14.3 (continued)

		Applied MFN Rate (%)			Bound Rate (%)	
0902	Tea	100	100	100	150	150
1202	Groundnuts,	30	30	30	100	100
0901	Coffee, whether or not	100	100	100	150	150
1207	Other oil seeds and oleaginous fruits	35	38	29	100	100
0703	Fresh/Chilled Onions, shallots, garlic,	35	49.2	43.3	100	100
0910	Ginger, saffron, turmeric	30	30	30	150	150
0909	Seeds of anis, badian, fennel, coriander, cumin	30	30	30	150	150
1211	Plants and parts used primarily in perfumery	31	18.8	18.8	100	100
0806	Grapes, fresh or dried	72.5	65	65	100	100
0713	Dried leguminous vegetables, shelled,	32.2	11.1	32	100	100
0804	Dates, figs, pineapples, avocados, guavas, mangoes and mangosteens, fresh or dried	30	30	30	100	100
Category III						
1515	Fixed vegetable fats and oils, incl. jojoba oil, and their fractions	100	32.4	4.3 / 73.7	300	300

(continued)

Table 14.3 (continued)

		Applied MFN Rate (%)			Bound Rate (%)	
1516	Animal or vegetable fats and oils	30	36.9	36.9	38.8	300	300
1513	Coconut "copra", palm kernel or babassu oil and fractions	100	3.8	3.8	73.4	300	300
1518	Boiled, oxidised, dehydrated animal oil	30	27.5	20.4	23.6	300	300
1504	Fats and oils and their fractions of fish or marine	30	30	30	30	300	300
Category IV						
1605	Crustaceans, molluscs and other aquatic invertebrates, prepared or preserved (excluding smoked)	30.5	37	37	37	150	100
1701	Cane or beet sugar and chemically pure sucrose, in solid form	100	100	60	60	150	100
1905	Bread, pastry, cakes, biscuits and other bakers wares, whether or not containing cocoa	35	30	30	30	150	150
2101	Extracts, essences and concentrates, of coffee, tea	30	30	30	30	150	150
2106	Food preparations, n.e.s	95	42	90	90	150	150

(continued)

Table 14.3 (continued)

		Applied MFN Rate (%)			Bound Rate (%)	
2304	Oilcake and other solid residues, whether or not ground or in the form of pellets	30	15	15	100	100
2306	Oilcake and other solid residues	30	15	13.6	100	100
2309	Preparations of a kind used in animal feeding	30	25	25	150	150
2401	Unmanufactured tobacco; tobacco refuse	30	30	30	100	100
2403	Manufactured tobacco and manufactured tobacco substitutes	30	30	30	150	150

Source WITS, UNCTAD

have been reduced to 50% for plants and parts used in perfumery, fresh and dried grapes and dried leguminous vegetables. The applied tariff rates for vegetable oils (Category III) has been cut from 100 to 73%, and for animal oils from 100 to 38%, though the bound rate is 300% for both. Tariffs have not been changed for most commodities in Category IV, but for oilcake and solid residues, it has been reduced from 30 to 15%.

Therefore, India's tariff structure in primary and processed agricultural commodities is well within the limits prescribed by the WTO. The applied tariff rates for several commodities have been static since 2001. The tariffs are higher for primary commodities (cereals, pepper, fruits-vegetables, coffee, honey and tea) than for processed commodities (Categories III and IV), perhaps on grounds of food security, price volatility and farmers' interest. Imports of primary commodities are more protected than processed items (palm oil and edible oils, Category III). The tariffs for tobacco, extracts, essences and concentrates, coffee, tea and seeds remain the same and very much below the WTO bound rates.

Notwithstanding a lower protectionist regime for several agricultural commodities, India has placed quantitative restrictions on the import of sensitive commodities on grounds of food security and health. Exports face non-tariff barriers such as sanitary and phytosanitary measures, technical barriers to trade, price control measures, quality control, contingencies and measures (Mehta 2005; Goyal et al. 2017). Non-tariff barriers are on the rise, and often held to hinder integration with economies such as the Association of South East Asian Nations (ASEAN); but these are little understood, and we need to understand the existing non-tariff barriers urgently and make these transparent, especially because of the several tariff and non-tariff barriers to agriculture exports from India (Chaudhari et al. 2012). Food quality and safety and health-related issues are examples of non-tariff barriers that have surfaced in key markets such as the United States (US), the European Union (EU) and ASEAN.

14.4 Comparative Advantage in Primary and Processed Commodities and Structural Shift

We estimate the competitiveness of primary and processed agriculture exports adjusted for imports. Going by Balassa (1965, 1977), the RCA index is estimated as.

$$\text{RCA}_{Ai} = (X_{Ai} / \Sigma_{j \in P} X_{Aj}) / (X_{Wi} / \Sigma_{j \in P} X_{Wj})$$

where

P is the set of all products (with $i \in P$),
X_{Ai} is the country A's exports of product i,
X_{Wi} is the worlds' exports of product i,

$\Sigma_{j \in P} X_{Aj}$ is the country A's total exports (of all products j in P), and.
$\Sigma_{j \in P} X_{Wj}$ is the world's total exports (of all products j in P).

When a country has a revealed comparative advantage for a given product (RCA > 1), it is inferred to be a competitive exporter of that product relative to a country producing and exporting that good at or below the world average. A country with a revealed comparative advantage in product i is considered to have an export strength in that product. The higher the value of a country's RCA for product i, the higher its export strength in product i.

The index suffers from a few limitations: its distribution is unstable over time; its ordinal ranking property is feeble; and it can capture exports only (Yeasts 1996; Hinloopen and Van Marrewijk 2001). The value of the index varies from 0 to ∞, and that makes it hard to compare the RCA of an exportable that has a value of more than 1.

The RCA considers the intrinsic advantage of an export commodity, and it is consistent with the changes in an economy's relative factor endowments and productivity. These are its main advantages. But it cannot distinguish between improvements in factor endowments and the pursuit of appropriate trade policies by a country (Batra and Khan 2005). And it suffers from the asymmetry problem: a "pure" RCA is not comparable on both sides of unity, as the index ranges from 0 to 1, if a country is not specialised in a given commodity; if a country is specialised, the index ranges from 1 to ∞. Several variants of the Balassa index have evolved to address these limitations; two indexes merit attention (Vollrath 1991; Dalum et al. 1998).

Vollrath proposed three alternative measures:

1. Relative trade advantage (RTA), the difference between revealed export advantage (RXA) and revealed import advantage (RMA), and written as $RTA_{Ai} = RXA_{Ai} - RMA_{Ai}$, where $RXA = (X_{Ai}/\Sigma_{j \in P} X_{Aj})/(X_{Wi}/\Sigma_{j \in P} X_{Wj})$, RMA (for imports) $= (M_{Ai}/\Sigma_{j \in P} M_{Aj})/(M_{Wi}/\Sigma_{j \in P} M_{Wj})$ and X and M denote exports and imports;
2. The logarithmic transformation of RCA $= \ln (RXA_{Ai})$; and
3. Revealed competitiveness (RC), the difference between the logarithm of the relative export advantage and the logarithm of the relative import advantage: RC $= \ln (RXA_{Ai}) - \ln (RMA_{Ai})$. A positive value of each index indicates a revealed comparative advantage whereas a negative value indicates a revealed comparative disadvantage.

Dalum et al. (1998) proposed a symmetrical RCA (SRCA), an approximation of the log transformation of the Balassa index, ranging from−1 to + 1 with 0 as a neutral point. It is expressed as: $SI_{ij} = \frac{BI_{ij}-1}{BI_{ij}+1}$ where BI_{ij} is the Balassa index of country i and commodity j. Country i will have a comparative advantage for product j if the value of SRCA is greater than zero and disadvantage if it is less than zero. The distribution of the Dalum index fulfils the normality assumption more often than the Balassa index, making it propitious to use for econometric analysis (Laursen 1998).

Figure 14.5 and Table 14.4 depict the estimated average revealed competitiveness (RC) index during triennium ending (TE) for selected categories. It considers imports

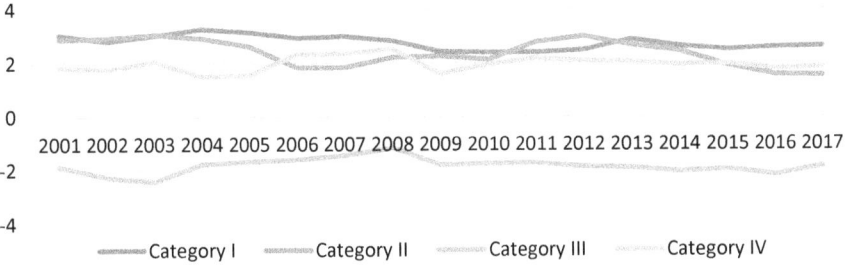

Fig.14.5 Revealed Competitiveness (RC) in Primary and Processed Agriculture Commodities: 2001 to 2017. *Source* Author's calculations based on data from COMTRADE

also from 2001 to 2017, as imports are adjusted to have net exports, explained in pointer number 3 above. As per the competitiveness indices calculated, the results indicate that competitiveness is much higher for primary commodities in Categories I and II. The value of index was almost 3 during 2001; it fell in the period from 2008 to 2011 and picked up thereafter. The competitiveness of the products in Categories II and IV declined 2013 onwards, though the index is positive and more than 1 throughout. The processed products in Category III, mainly edible oils, show a disadvantage as the value of the index remained negative.

Within each category, the revealed comparative index shows mixed results. India has a comparative advantage in the meat of bovine animals, crustaceans, molluscs and tea (Category I) and in onions and other vegetables, pepper, rice, groundnuts and oilseeds (Category II). Only a few primary products have a positive, but low RC, but many products have a negative RC, indicating a lack of competitiveness in the world markets, although the price-based measure, NPC, is less than 1 (or domestic prices are less than world prices). The RC is negative also for most highly processed foods and beverages in Category III. The only exceptions in Categories III and IV, or the products that are competitive, are fixed vegetable fats and oils, cane/beet sugar, extracts, essences and concentrates of coffee, tea, oilcakes and solid residues and unmanufactured and manufactured tobacco.

We turn to examine the structural shift of trade specialisation between India and the world for primary and processed agriculture exports. The Galtonian regression (Hart and Praise 1956) is used. It is expressed as.

$\text{RCA}_{ij}^{t2} = \alpha_i + \beta_i \text{RCA}_{ij}^{t1} + \varepsilon_{ij}$, where t_1 is the average exports in the initial period (TE 2003) and t_2 is the average exports in the later period (TE 2017); RCA_{ij} is the Dalum index,[5] called symmetric revealed comparative advantage index, α_i and β_i are the standard regression coefficients, and ε is the error term.

The null hypothesis is H_0: $\beta i = 0$, and the alternate hypothesis is H_A: $\beta i \neq 0$). Galtonian regression permits us to relate two cross-sections at two distinct points

---

[5]The use of the Balassa index in regression is problematic because its distribution is non-symmetrical. It violates the assumption of the normal distribution of error terms, which makes the t-statistics invalid. In contrast, the Dalum index has a symmetric nature, as its value equals $\frac{BI_{ij}-1}{BI_{ij}+1}$.

Table 14.4 India's Revealed Competitiveness (RC) in Agriculture Commodities

HS Codes		TE 2003	TE 2007	TE 2010	TE 2013	TE 2017
Category I						
0202	Meat of bovine animals, frozen	0.77	0.82	0.84	1.05	1.07
0204	Meat of sheep or goats, fresh, chilled or frozen	−0.21	−0.33	0.16	0.05	0.02
0206	Edible offal of bovine animals,	−1.37	−1.36	−1.03	0.01	0.07
0302	Fish, fresh or chilled	−1.00	−1.09	−1.49	−0.89	−0.61
0303	Frozen Fish	0.52	0.22	0.20	0.24	0.32
0304	Fish fillets and other fish meat,	−0.56	−0.65	−0.48	−0.42	−0.31
0305	Fish, fit for human consumption, dried, salted	−0.41	−0.52	−0.63	−0.44	−0.40
0306	Crustaceans	0.86	0.75	0.59	0.83	0.89
0307	Molluscs	0.50	0.50	0.41	0.46	0.55
0409	Natural honey	−0.52	0.18	−0.03	0.32	0.34
	Overall Category I	2.96	3.02	2.55	2.57	2.54
Category II						
0703	Onions, shallots, garlic, leeks and other alliaceous vegetables, fresh or chilled	0.43	0.78	0.86	0.61	0.77
0713	Dried leguminous vegetables, shelled, whether or not skinned or split	−58.52	−31.71	−44.05	−34.71	−31.59
0801	Coconuts, Brazil nuts and cashew nuts, fresh or dried, whether or not shelled or peeled	−33.99	−31.55	−16.68	−14.19	−10.92
0804	Dates, figs, pineapples, avocados, guavas, mangoes and mangosteens, fresh or dried	−0.38	0.00	−0.01	−0.15	−0.18
0806	Grapes, fresh or dried	−0.32	−0.24	−0.09	−0.09	−0.02
0901	Coffee	−9.53	−50.12	−56.95	−60.58	−29.52
0902	Tea	0.96	0.87	0.81	0.78	0.81
0904	Pepper of the genus Piper; dried or crushed or ground	−25.14	−32.40	−29.91	−24.40	−22.12

(continued)

Table 14.4 (continued)

HS Codes		TE 2003	TE 2007	TE 2010	TE 2013	TE 2017
0909	Seeds of anis, badian, fennel, coriander, cumin or caraway; juniper berries	−2.43	−2.91	−1.66	0.01	−1.61
0910	Ginger, saffron, turmeric "curcuma", thyme, bay leaves	−0.95	−3.24	−1.91	−1.30	−1.50
1006	Rice	1.23	1.19	1.09	1.05	1.03
1202	Groundnuts, whether or not shelled or broken (excluding roasted or otherwise cooked)	0.98	1.15	1.18	1.30	1.36
1207	Other oil seeds and oleaginous fruits, whether or not broken (excluding edible nuts, olives,...	0.50	0.10	−0.30	0.25	0.46
1211	Plants and parts of plants used primarily in perfumery	−4.19	−5.42	−2.66	−4.21	−4.03
1302	Vegetable saps and extracts; pectic substances, pectinates and pectates; agar − agar and other	−3.14	−1.15	−1.36	−0.67	−0.52
	Overall category II	2.96	2.10	2.19	2.80	1.64
Category III						
1504	Fats and oils and their fractions of fish or marine mammals, whether or not refined	−3.63	−2.58	−2.25	−1.10	−1.08
1513	Coconut "copra", palm kernel or babassu oil and fractions thereof, whether or not refined	−2.12	−2.36	−2.01	−1.81	−1.52
1515	Fixed vegetable fats and oils, incl. jojoba oil, and their fractions, whether or not refined	0.85	0.90	0.96	1.01	1.12
1516	Animal or vegetable fats and oils and their fractions, partly or wholly hydrogenated	−2.80	−4.19	−1.78	−0.21	−0.14

(continued)

Table 14.4 (continued)

HS Codes		TE 2003	TE 2007	TE 2010	TE 2013	TE 2017
1518	Animal or vegetable fats and oils and their fractions, boiled, oxidised, dehydrated	−1.96	0.26	0.24	−0.56	−1.08
	Overall category III	−2.18	−1.58	−1.58	−1.86	−2.02
Category IV						
1605	Crustaceans, molluscs and other aquatic invertebrates, prepared or preserved (excluding smoked)	−0.16	0.31	0.24	−0.16	−0.11
1701	Cane or beet sugar and chemically pure sucrose, in solid form	0.46	−1.84	−1.61	−2.20	−1.29
1905	Bread, pastry, cakes, biscuits and other bakers wares, whether or not containing cocoa	−0.80	−0.49	−0.46	−0.43	−0.40
2101	Extracts, essences and concentrates, of coffee, tea	0.67	0.52	0.41	0.35	0.39
2106	Food preparations, n.e.s	−1.09	−1.09	−1.18	−1.49	−1.02
2304	Oilcake and other solid residues, whether or not ground or in the form of pellets	0.61	0.82	0.87	0.70	0.71
2306	Oilcake and other solid residues	−14.00	−16.81	−14.52	−16.55	−14.04
2309	Preparations of a kind used in animal feeding	−9.75	−8.66	−7.93	−9.59	−9.38
2401	Unmanufactured tobacco; tobacco refuse	0.49	0.50	0.61	0.54	0.58
2403	Manufactured tobacco and manufactured tobacco substitutes	0.16	0.28	0.39	0.27	0.26
	Overall category IV	1.88	2.08	2.02	2.08	1.84

Source Based on data from COMTRADE

Table 14.5 Structural transformation in agriculture exports based on Galtonian regression: 2001 and 2017

Category I	Coefficient	Standard error	t-statistic
RCA (Dalum Index) 2001 (β_i)	0.43	0.187	2.31
Constant (α)	0.98	0.813	1.21
R-square	0.11	F-statistic	5.33
Category II	Coefficient	Standard error	t-statistic
RCA (Dalum Index) 2001 (β_i)	0.97	0.009	101.3
Constant (α)	0.08	0.05	1.61
R −square	0.99	F-statistic	10,379
Category III	Coefficient	Standard error	t-statistic
RCA (Dalum Index) 2001 (β_i)	0.89	0.011	79.2
Constant (α)	0.03	0.03	0.91
R-square	0.98	F-statistic	6375
Category IV	Coefficient	Standard error	t-statistic
RCA (Dalum Index) 2001 (β_i)	1.05	0.02	37.01
Constant (α)	−0.013	0.03	−0.37
R − square	0.96	F − statistic	1369

of time and articulate the transformation in the configuration of trade specialisation in a country that has transpired between the periods of interest. It is also helpful to examine the patterns of technological specialisation (Cantwell 1989) and to analyse the convergence of productivity (Hart 1995).

14.4.1   Interpretation

1. If the value of $\beta_i = 1$, the degree of the country's specialisation did not change between the two time periods.
2. If value of $\beta_i > 1$, the country's existing specialisation increased in those commodity groups that have a comparative advantage and weakened in those that do not have a comparative advantage.
3. If the value of β_i lies between 0 and 1 ($0 < \beta_i < 1$) and if the product categories with initially high values of RCA experience a decline between the selected time periods while those with initially low scores experience growth, then a β score in this range indicates that the specialisation pattern has not changed.
4. If value of $\beta_i < 0$, there has been a sharp reversal in the comparative advantage.

Table 14.5 presents the empirical results for each category of agriculture exports. The value of β_i is 0.43 for primary products in Category I and 0.97 for primary products in Category II. Both the values are statistically significant, and they lie between 0 and 1, indicating that the specialisation of Indian exports was phlegmatic over the years and commodities that initially possessed a strong RCA value declined in competitiveness. The value of products in Category III were static, and it changed slightly for commodities Category IV—their β value was 1.05. It implies that a structural transformation may have begun in processed commodities such as prepared foodstuffs, spirits, beverages and tobacco.

14.5 Conclusions and Implications

India's market is better integrated with the world markets now, and the exports and imports of agriculture and processed agricultural commodities have increased significantly. This chapter analysed the trends in imports and exports from 2001 to 2017 at the four-digit level by categorising products as primary (less processed) or secondary (processed). We used the nominal rate of protection (NRP), and the changes in the applied tariff rates vis-à-vis the respective bound rates, to examine the extent of protection accorded to primary and processed products, and we evaluated their revealed competitiveness (RC) using the transformed RCA approach.

In each of the categories considered, the composition of agricultural exports and imports had changed substantially, but the aggregate-level share of exports and imports in total agricultural exports and imports had not changed much. The share of primary exports in total agricultural exports increased, due primarily to the export of meat and basmati rice, but the share of value added (processed) exports (Categories III and IV) had remained static. Not much change was seen in the case of imports except in the case of processed palm oil and edible oils.

India is a net exporter of agricultural products in the world markets, and its potential for accelerating primary exports is vast. There is a bias against farmers and towards consumers in the exports of primary commodities, as the domestic prices of most commodities is far less than their free market prices. Under the exportable scenario, primary commodities receive little protection. Low prices are deliberately maintained in domestic markets to favour consumers and at the expense of producers, or farmers. The only exceptions are sugar and wheat; their NPC is slightly above 1.

An increase in trade in some commodities that have an NPC of more than 1 is explained by several factors: geographical location, smaller distance between a port and the border of another country, low transport and handling cost, export subsidies given by the government and the devaluation of the Indian rupee versus the US dollar (Shweta and Gulati 2017). When growers' prices in domestic markets are lower than the free market price, such low prices may act as a disincentive to growers. But the imports of primary commodities such as cereals are protected by high tariff and non-tariff barriers. India has long been pursuing a policy of self-sufficiency in food, and it imports only in cases of shortage and emergency. A policy of neither encouraging primary exports nor allowing their imports is of a piece with the broader trade policy.

India must accelerate agricultural exports and encourage industry to add value. Value-added or highly processed products enjoy greater protection than primary commodities, implying that industry is favoured at the expense of consumers, who have to pay more for such products than the free market allows. The government should follow a liberal trade policy and lower protection to let imports reduce such distortions. The industry should be provided with better technology and skills and encouraged to compete with imported processed food items. Ironically, India's policy of providing little support to primary agriculture commodities does not allow farmers (producers) to gain from higher prices in the world market and, concomitantly, the high protection accorded to processed agri-commodities and, hence, industry negates the gains to consumers from lower prices in a free trade regime. This is done mainly to encourage industry, as it is a provider of wage goods and an important source of employment.

The processed food industry is increasingly becoming competitive, but its competitiveness is less than that of primary commodities. The value of the RC of processed foods is positive at 1.6, but it is much less than the value of the RC of primary commodities, estimated at 2.6. There was a change in the export and import baskets over the period. The imports constituted mainly palm oil, selected edible oils and intermediate products such as cocoa and cocoa powder used in the industry for making consumables. Few of India's processed (industrial) products (Categories III and IV) are competitive. Competitiveness is higher in primary commodities (Categories I and II) and in some products in Category III, mainly intermediate products used in industry. The Galtonian regression validates that little structural transformation took place in the primary and processed agricultural products, and India's agricultural exports were static between 2001 and 2017. It is imperative that the food industry becomes price-competitive by making the requisite investments in technology and skills and in creating agricultural value chains.

References

Balassa, B. (1965). Trade liberalization and "revealed" comparative advantage. *Manchester School of Economic and Social Studies, 33,* 99–123.

Balassa, B. (1977). Revealed comparative advantage revisited: An analysis of relative exports shares of the industrial countries, 1953–1971. *Manchester School of Economic and Social Studies, 45,* 327–344.

Balassa, B., & Noland, M. (1989). Revealed comparative advantage in Japan and the United States. *Journal of International Economic Integration, 4*(2), 8–22.

Batra, A., & Khan, Z. (2005). *Revealed comparative advantage: An analysis for India and China* (Working Paper No.168) (pp. 1–53). New Delhi: Indian Council for Research on International Economic Relation (ICRIER).

Cantwell. (1989). *Technological innovation and multinational corporations.* Oxford: Basil Blackwell; reprinted, 1990, xvi + 239 pp.

Chaudhari, M. B., Giedraitis, V., & Kapse, P. (2012). Barriers to export from India to the European Union. *Ekonomika, 91*(2), 38–48.

Dalum, B., Laursen, K., & Villumsen, G. (1998). Structural change in OECD exports specialization patterns: De-specialization and stickiness. *International Review of Applied Economics, 12,* 447–467.

Goyal, T. M., Mukherjee, A., & Kapoor, A. (2017, September). *India's exports of food products: Food safety related issues and way forward* (ICRIER, Working Paper No. 345).

Hart, P. E., & Praise, S. J. (1956). The analysis of business concentration: A statistical approach. *Journal of the Royal Statistical Society Series A, 119,* 150–191.

Hart, O. (1995). *Firms, contracts, and financial structure.* Oxford and New York: Oxford University Press, Clarendon Press.

Hinloopen, J., & Van Marrewijk, C. (2001). On the empirical distribution of the balassa index. *Weltwirtschaftliches Archiv, 137,* 1–35.

Laursen, K. (1998). *Revealed comparative advantage and the alternatives as measures of international specialisation* (DRUID Working Papers 98–30). DRUID, Copenhagen Business School, Department of Industrial Economics and Strategy/Aalborg University, Department of Business Studies.

Mehta, R. (2005, June). *Non-tariff barriers affecting India's exports* (RIS Discussion Paper No. 97). Research and Information System for Non-Aligned and other Developing Countries.

Saini, S., & Gulati, A. (2017). *Price distortions in Indian agriculture.* Indian Council for Research on International Economic Relations (ICRIER) and World Bank. http://icrier.org/publications/reports/.

Vollrath, T. L. (1991). A theoretical evaluation of alternative trade intensity measures of revealed comparative advantage. *Weltwirtschaftliches Archive, 127,* 265–279; *Review World Economic, 127,* 265–280

Yeats, A. (1996). *Does Mercosur's trade performance justify concerns about the effects of regional trade arrangements? Yes!* (mimeo) World Bank. https://doi.org/10.1080/00472330480000241. (PDF) Competitiveness in Agricultural Trade under India ASEAN Trade Agreement. Available from: https://www.researchgate.net/publication/317822729_Competitiveness_in_Agricultural_Trade_under_India_ASEAN_Trade_Agreement. Accessed January 14, 2020.

Chapter 15
Protection Structure and Total Factor Productivity Growth in India's Organised Food Industry

Seema Bathla

15.1 Introduction

An evaluation of the level of protection accorded to primary agricultural products (Categories I and II) and processed agricultural products (Categories III and IV)—based on the data at four-digit level of the harmonised system (HS)—finds that the average applied tariff rate fell from 41% in 2001 to 35.3% in 2017, though with large variations (Chap. 14 of this book). The value of the nominal rate of protection (NRP), another measure of protection, fell significantly, but it is more than 1 for many products. Under the importable hypothesis, the fall in the value of the NRP was higher for products in Category I (live animals, etc.) and Category III (edible oils, etc.) than for products in Category II (cereals, etc.) and Category IV (food preparations, wine, spirits, etc.). Under the exportable hypothesis, in contrast, the fall in the value of the NRP was higher for commodities in Categories I and II. In other words, India provides more protection to value-added agricultural products than to primary (less processed) products. This chapter explores whether such protectionism impacts growth in the total factor productivity (TFP) and the technical efficiency (TE) of the organised foods and beverages industry.

TFP measures an increase in the total output not accounted for by an increase in the total inputs. TFP also indicates the efficiency in the use of inputs in the production process. The processed food industry's total factor productivity growth (TFPG) has been improving since the 1980s, though the returns to scale have been constant and for some years decreasing. From the 1980s to the early 2000s, its TFPG was attributable largely to differences in TE, which in turn was influenced positively by infrastructure and negatively by the share of agriculture income in total income (Mitra 1999; Mitra et al. 2002; Hashim et al. 2009). Between 1980 and 2008, the all-India TFPG was positive, though interstate differences were large (Bathla 2014). Within

S. Bathla (✉)
Centre for the Study of Regional Development, Jawaharlal Nehru University, New Delhi, India
e-mail: seema.bathla@gmail.com

© The Author(s), under exclusive license to Springer Nature Singapore Pte Ltd. 2021   321
S. Bathla and E. Kannan (eds.), *Agro and Food Processing Industry in India*, India Studies in Business and Economics, https://doi.org/10.1007/978-981-15-9468-7_15

the organised processed foods sector, productivity differed by state, due to differences in technology, infrastructure development and the regulatory and institutional environment. Bathla (2014) finds, contrary to Mitra et al. (2002), that agricultural linkages significantly impacted TFPG, which implies that the relative size of an agricultural economy helped improve productivity, especially in the laggard states. Productivity is determined also by investor-friendliness and urbanisation, as access to markets and consumer demand are important. The TFPG is also influenced positively and significantly by workers' education (skill development) but negatively and insignificantly by economic reforms (Bathla 2018).

The role of trade liberalisation in improving the TFPG of the agricultural and processed foods industry has not been established yet; the debate over the issue is wide and varied. Productivity does not necessarily grow in an economy that is open to external trade (Tybout and Westbrook 1995). The protection structure, competitiveness and domestic policy vary by each subsector in India's manufacturing sector and influence their exports and imports and, hence, their growth rate of productivity and employment (Rodriguez and Rodrik 1999; Goldar 2002; Goldar and Veeramani 2005). A disaggregated industry-level analysis in Nouroj (2001) finds that India's high tariff structure makes its industrial exports less attractive. The manufacturing sector is more protected in India than in other countries, but the protection does not significantly affect productivity or efficiency, especially in the food industry. During the study period 1970 to 1988, productivity growth was influenced less by external trade than by domestic demand—captured by capacity utilisation, or the deviation of the output from the trend. The commodities were classified as industry-based, trade-based or input-based. The analysis was based on the nominal rate of protection (NRP) and the effective rate of protection (ERP) for these commodity groups. The analysis shows that the weighted average ERP fell from 118% in 1987–88, the pre-reform period, to 41% in 1997–98, the post-reform period. The nominal rate of tariff (weighted) fell in agriculture from 45.7% to 11.2% and in the food industry from 97.4% to 29.9%; the quantitative restrictions were reduced but remained high.

India is globally competitive in dairy products, but in high protection levels, a measure of trade openness, in the 1990s and 2000s, adversely affected the industry's employment and TE; dismantling the protection structure would raise exports and improve performance in the dairy industry (Kannan and Birthal 2010) and also in primary and processed agriculture products (Saini and Gulati 2017). The net protection coefficient (NPC) was estimated for 15 agricultural commodities from 2004–05 to 2013–14; on average, their domestic prices were below export parity prices 72% of the time, above import parity prices 11% of the time and between export parity prices and import parity prices 17% of the time. The domestic prices of value-added industrial products such as sugar and skimmed milk powder were above the import parity prices in most years, which indicates a lack of comparative advantage.

India's policy complex has a pro-consumer, anti-farmer bias. Policy-makers protect industry and do not let consumers benefit from lower free market prices, and for many years they used restrictive export policies to keep the domestic prices of primary products artificially low. The economic reforms in India reduced the protection of agricultural and processed food products.

This chapter examines whether the reduced protection influenced the TFPG and employment in the organised foods and beverage industry. We test two hypotheses. First, alterations in the protection structure have positively influenced the TFPG, TE and employment in the processed food industry in India. Secondly, high value-added agricultural commodities have a higher comparative advantage than primary agricultural commodities, and this competitiveness has positively influenced the industry's TFPG.

We use the estimates on protection—NRP and tariffs—for agricultural commodities calculated by Jha and Bathla (Chap. 14, this book). To estimate the TFP, the nonparametric Malmquist index using the data envelopment analysis program (DEAP) is used. The productivity change is decomposed into its meaningful components—technical change (TC), technical efficiency change (TEC) and scale efficiency—to calculate their relative contribution to changes in the TFP.

We estimate the correlation coefficient to analyse the impact of the NRP and tariffs on the TFPG and employment in the organised food industry. The analysis is carried out from 1980–81 to 2014–15 for all states together and also separately for 17 major Indian states. We hold that the reforms took place in phases during this period and that we can assign a decade to a phase; for example, we study the 1980–89 decade to gauge the performance in the pre-reform period; the 1990–99 decade to study the first phase of the post-reform period and the 2000–09 period to study the second phase of the post-reform period. We study the 2010–15 period separately.

Section 15.2 explains the data sources and methodological approach followed to estimate the TFP and TEC. Sections 15.3 and 15.4 present the results and discussion, and an analysis of the effect of the NRP (protection structure) accorded to primary and processed agriculture commodities on TFPG from 2001 to 2015. Section 15.5 concludes and draws implications.

15.2 Estimating Total Factor Productivity (TFP): Data Sources and Methodology

TFP is computed as the ratio of an index of aggregate output to an index of aggregate inputs. The TFP is deemed to be the broadest measure of productivity and efficiency in the use of resources. It aims at decomposing the changes in production due to changes in quantity of inputs used and in residual factors such as change in technology, capacity utilisation, quality of factors of production and learning by doing. We use the Malmquist productivity index through the data envelopment analysis (DEA) to measure the TFPG (Annex A). Under this approach, TFP is defined as the ratio of two output distance functions, i.e. it measures the change in TFP between two data points by calculating the ratio of the distances of each data point relative to a common technology.

The DEA decomposes TFP growth into TC (progress or regress; innovation/frontier shift effect), TEC (catching-up effect) and scale efficiency change between time periods. The DEA also enables us to identify the sources of growth and use that information to suggest policy measures that will improve productivity growth. The TEC can be decomposed further into pure technical efficiency change (under variable returns to scale (VRS)) and scale efficiency change. Technological change comprises advancements in knowledge relating to the art of production, which may take the form of new goods, processes or new modes of organisation. These abilities give the DEA an advantage over other methods.

The TEC indicates the efficiency at which factors of production are used to generate output, or the capacity utilisation. The TC is conceptualised in terms of shifts in the production function (Solow 1957), and the TEC measures the distance between the actual output and the frontier or maximum attainable output level (Bettesse 1990). The index is obtained under the VRS assumption in an output-oriented model (increase in output with given inputs). The TEC is a key component of the TFP, and it indicates the extent of inefficiency in inputs use. A case of overcapacity, overcapitalisation and/or underutilisation can help in drawing implications for institutional and other reforms.

The TFP estimations are based on the Malmquist index, which explains the change in the gross value of output (GVA) at the given level of two inputs, labour (persons engaged) and capital stock estimated at 2004–05 prices. An output-oriented model (increased output at given inputs) under the VRS assumption is specified in the DEAP software. The state-level data for 17 major states from 1980–81 to 2014–15 is taken from National Accounts Statistics (NAS), Ministry of Statistics and Programme Implementation (MOS&PI), Government of India (GoI). It provides Annual Survey of Industries (ASI) database at two-digit level for the food–beverage industry. The variables are converted into real price (2004–05) using the gross domestic product (GDP) and gross fixed capital formation (GFCF) deflators sourced from the National Accounts Statistics, MOS&PI, GoI. Annex B furnishes details on the construction of each variable and its source.

15.3   Results and Discussion

In most states, the food industry is operated at IRS in the 1980s and 1990s, when private investment was initiated. The industry slowed down in several states in the 1990s and improved in the 2000s except in Himachal Pradesh, Jammu and Kashmir and West Bengal. A move towards IRS, or an increase in production, in most states except West Bengal is apparent between 2010 and 2014 (Table 15.1).

Table 15.2 provides decadal averages of TEC, TC and TFP scores in food and beverage industry from 1980–81 to 2014–15. For all the selected states together, the TFP index was 1.05 during the 1980s, increasing a little to 1.14 during the 1990s and falling slightly in later periods. The TFP score was more than 1, implying that productivity improved due to TEC and TC. All three indexes show considerable variations since 1981; their score increased significantly in the 1990s, fell up to the mid-2000s and then jumped sharply, because TEC increased in industry in Gujarat

Table 15.1 Returns to scale in organised food–beverage industry: 1980–81 to 2014–15

State	1980–89	1990–99	2000–09	2010–14
Andhra Pradesh	IRS	IRS	IRS	IRS
Assam	IRS	DRS	IRS	IRS
Bihar	IRS	DRS	IRS	IRS
Gujarat	IRS	IRS	IRS	IRS
Haryana	IRS	DRS	IRS	IRS
Himachal Pradesh	IRS	DRS	CRS	IRS
Jammu and Kashmir	IRS	DRS	CRS	IRS
Karnataka	IRS	DRS	IRS	IRS
Kerala	IRS	DRS	IRS	IRS
Madhya Pradesh	DRS	DRS	IRS	IRS
Maharashtra	IRS	CRS	IRS	IRS
Odisha	IRS	IRS	IRS	IRS
Punjab	IRS	IRS	IRS	IRS
Rajasthan	IRS	IRS	IRS	IRS
Tamil Nadu	CRS	IRS	IRS	IRS
Uttar Pradesh	CRS	IRS	IRS	IRS
West Bengal	IRS	IRS	IRS	CRS

Note CRS: Constant return to scale; IRS: Increasing returns to scale; DRS: Decreasing return to scale

and Haryana. It is evident from the pattern in Fig. 15.1 that the rate of change in TFP is attributable to both TEC and TC.

Table 15.2 and Fig. 15.2 show the state-level TFP index for three decades—the 1980s, 1990s and 2000s—and the five-year average from 2010 to 2014. The TFP was greater than 1 during the 1980s, 1990s and 2000s in some states, and it was less than 1 in Andhra Pradesh, Assam, Bihar, Gujarat, Haryana and Himachal Pradesh in the 1990s and 2000s. The TFP remained low in these states and in Rajasthan, Tamil Nadu, Uttar Pradesh and West Bengal in the 2000s, but it rose in most of these states between 2010 and 2014. Growth picked up in the food industry during the 1990s. The average decadal TFP tended to be higher and more than 1 in Kerala, Punjab, Madhya Pradesh, Rajasthan, Tamil Nadu, Uttar Pradesh and West Bengal in the first phase of the reform period. The TFP was higher in Jammu and Kashmir, Karnataka, Kerala, Odisha, Rajasthan, Punjab, Madhya Pradesh and Odisha in the 2000s, and it increased later in almost every state.

Table 15.2, Figs. 15.3 and 15.4 reveal the results of the average TEC and TC (progress). Both TEC and TC brought in changes in TFP, though its magnitude varied by state; during the 2000s, the TC for all states together on average, at 1.05, was slightly higher than the TEC. Both the TEC and TC varied in magnitude by state during the selected periods. The TEC, an indicator of better capacity utilisation, shows that efficiency was low during the 1980s; it improved to 1.02 during the 1990s

Table 15.2 State-level estimates on TEC, TC and TFP change in organised food–beverage industry

	TEC				TC				TFP			
	1981–89	1990–99	2000–09	2010–14	1981–89	1990–99	2000–09	2010–14	1981–89	1990–99	2000–09	2010–14
Andhra Pradesh	0.986	1.047	1.000	0.995	1.026	0.900	0.922	0.997	1.011	0.942	0.922	0.991
Assam	1.015	0.982	1.018	1.043	1.043	0.883	0.938	1.000	1.060	0.867	0.955	1.042
Bihar	0.991	1.009	1.008	1.009	1.054	0.905	0.928	1.036	1.045	0.914	0.936	1.046
Gujarat	1.043	1.000	1.027	0.968	1.050	0.916	0.944	0.985	1.095	0.916	0.968	0.952
Haryana	1.060	1.008	0.997	0.964	1.065	0.917	0.971	0.986	1.129	0.925	0.968	0.951
Himachal Pradesh	1.015	0.997	1.019	0.945	1.066	0.956	0.947	0.992	1.082	0.954	0.964	0.937
Jammu and Kashmir	1.038	0.888	1.119	0.953	1.069	0.973	0.927	0.993	1.110	0.864	1.038	0.946
Karnataka	1.018	0.926	1.079	0.977	1.077	0.979	0.960	0.995	1.097	0.907	1.036	0.971
Kerala	1.030	0.920	1.088	0.991	1.086	0.970	0.990	0.994	1.119	0.893	1.076	0.984
Madhya Pradesh	0.999	0.973	1.017	1.022	1.096	0.936	0.986	1.002	1.095	0.911	1.003	1.024
Maharashtra	1.009	0.990	1.010	0.982	1.106	1.036	0.989	1.005	1.116	1.026	0.999	0.987
Odisha	0.979	0.996	1.020	1.013	1.097	1.008	0.985	1.013	1.074	1.004	1.004	1.027
Punjab	0.861	1.139	1.034	0.974	1.097	1.031	0.982	1.019	0.944	1.174	1.016	0.992
Rajasthan	0.955	1.034	1.003	1.020	1.065	1.094	0.970	1.022	1.017	1.130	0.973	1.043
Tamil Nadu	0.931	1.043	0.983	1.069	1.070	1.081	0.970	1.030	0.996	1.128	0.954	1.101
Uttar Pradesh	0.759	1.244	1.010	1.064	1.063	1.076	0.961	1.037	0.807	1.338	0.970	1.103
West Bengal	1.037	0.996	1.003	0.977	1.084	1.100	0.969	1.035	1.123	1.095	0.971	1.011
17 States	0.953	1.022	1.022	0.975	1.099	1.111	0.980	1.048	1.047	1.135	1.001	1.021

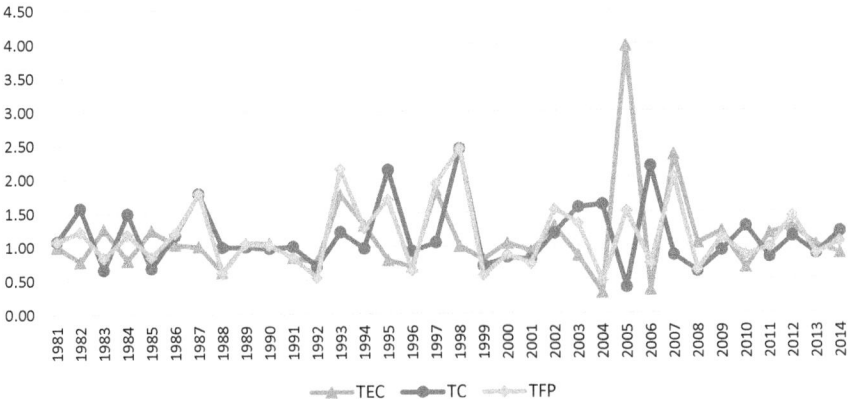

Fig. 15.1 TFP, TEC and TC in organised food–beverage industry: 1980–81 to 2014–15

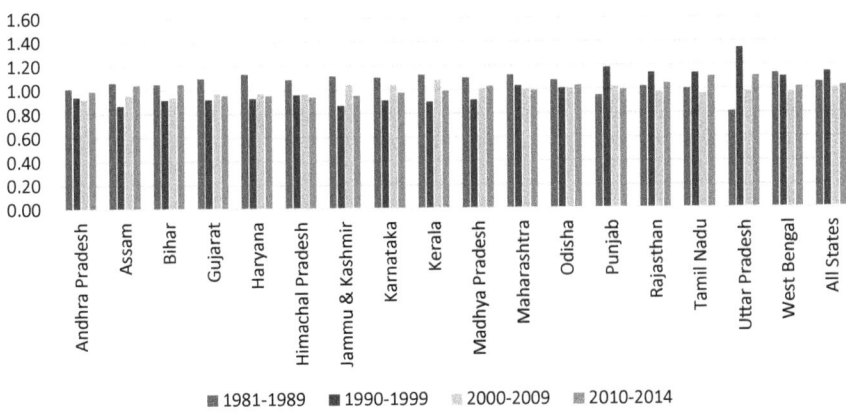

Fig. 15.2 TFP change in food–beverage industry: decadal averages

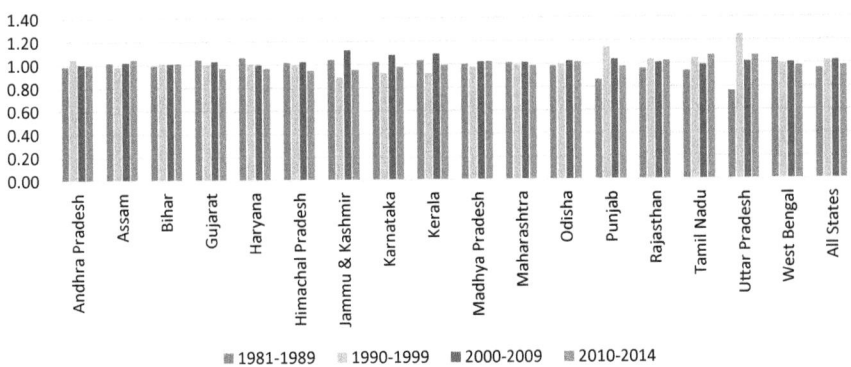

Fig. 15.3 Technical efficiency change in food–beverage industry: decadal averages

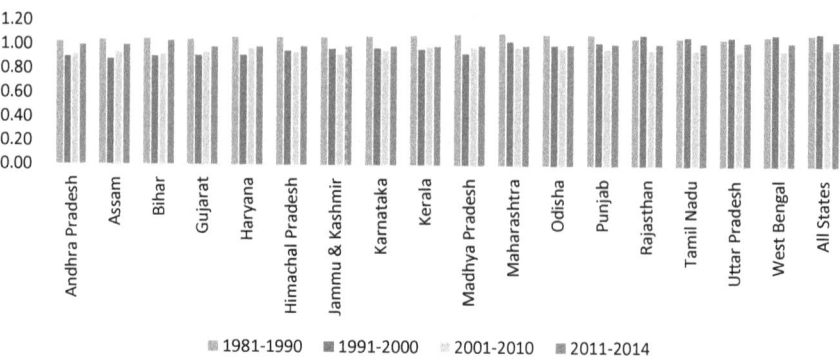

Fig. 15.4 Technical change in food–beverage industry: decadal averages

except in Assam, Jammu and Kashmir, Karnataka, Kerala and Madhya Pradesh; and it improved in almost every state during the 2000s. At the aggregate level, the TEC remained at 1.02 during the 2000s, and it fell to 0.97 in the 2000–14 period. The frontrunners in TEC in recent years were Assam, Gujarat, Madhya Pradesh, Odisha, Rajasthan, Tamil Nadu and Uttar Pradesh. The TC is marginally lower than the TEC in most states; in the 2010–14 period, however, the TC score (1.05) was slightly above the TEC (0.978).

A bifurcation of the TEC into pure TE and scale efficiency change in processed food provides interesting insights into the relative position of states. Table 15.3 presents the decade-wise average estimated scores on pure TEC (VRS) and scale efficiency in the organised food industry. The average TEC for all 17 states in the 1980s was 0.95; it increased to 1.03 during the 1990s and 2000s and then fell to 0.98. The average scale efficiency has remained around 0.99 over the period, though it has varied by state. The industry is at the high end of the efficiency scale in several states, including Haryana, Himachal Pradesh, Jammu and Kashmir, Karnataka, Maharashtra and Odisha, Punjab, Rajasthan, Tamil Nadu, Uttar Pradesh and West Bengal, implying that there is potential for easier gains. The TEC of the processed foods sector has been increasing, overall, and its scale efficiency has been improving, except in a few states—both TEC and scale efficiency decreased in Gujarat and Punjab between 2010 and 2014. Improving the pure TE can substantially increase the low TE in the food industry.

Finally, we look at the annual growth rate of three performance indicators (Table 15.4). For all states together, the average TFPG from 1981–82 to 1989–90 was—1.18%, explained primarily by the low TEC. In the subsequent decade, the TFP turned out to be positive and high at 3.26%, due to the 3.30% growth in TC and implying that new technology adopted by the industry helped during this period. The growth rate in the TEC was low and negative, because scale efficiency slowed down. From 2000 to 2009, the TFPG was positive, because the TEC grew at a high rate, implying that the proper use of technology and an efficient combination of inputs led to gains in efficiency.

Table 15.3 TEC into pure TEC and SE change in organised food–beverage industry

	TEC				Pure TEC				Scale efficiency			
	1981–89	1990–99	2000–09	2010–14	1981–89	1990–99	2000–09	2010–14	1981–89	1990–99	2000–09	2010–14
Andhra Pradesh	0.986	1.047	1.000	0.995	0.973	1.025	1.000	1.000	1.013	1.022	1.000	0.995
Assam	1.015	0.982	1.018	1.043	0.999	0.968	1.020	1.036	1.017	1.015	0.998	1.006
Bihar	0.991	1.009	1.008	1.009	0.981	1.017	0.993	1.003	1.010	0.993	1.015	1.007
Gujarat	1.043	1.000	1.027	0.968	1.058	0.987	1.027	0.983	0.986	1.013	1.000	0.985
Haryana	1.060	1.008	0.997	0.964	1.042	1.001	0.998	1.003	1.017	1.007	0.998	0.962
Himachal Pradesh	1.015	0.997	1.019	0.945	0.992	0.997	1.017	0.996	1.023	1.000	1.002	0.949
Jammu and Kashmir	1.038	0.888	1.119	0.953	1.000	0.888	1.126	1.000	1.038	1.000	0.994	0.953
Karnataka	1.018	0.926	1.079	0.977	1.002	0.932	1.080	1.000	1.016	0.993	0.999	0.977
Kerala	1.030	0.920	1.088	0.991	1.018	1.011	1.000	0.987	1.012	0.910	1.087	1.004
Madhya Pradesh	0.999	0.973	1.017	1.022	0.999	1.000	0.997	1.006	1.000	0.972	1.021	1.015
Maharashtra	1.009	0.990	1.010	0.982	1.006	1.000	1.000	0.983	1.004	0.991	1.009	0.999
Odisha	0.979	0.996	1.020	1.013	0.976	1.001	1.017	1.011	1.003	0.995	1.003	1.002
Punjab	0.861	1.139	1.034	0.974	0.850	1.139	1.033	0.977	1.013	0.999	1.001	0.996
Rajasthan	0.955	1.034	1.003	1.020	0.992	1.000	1.002	1.024	0.962	1.034	1.001	0.995
Tamil Nadu	0.931	1.043	0.983	1.069	0.963	1.012	0.985	1.076	0.966	1.031	0.998	0.994
Uttar Pradesh	0.759	1.244	1.010	1.064	1.010	0.958	1.008	1.067	0.751	1.298	1.001	0.997
West Bengal	1.037	0.996	1.003	0.977	1.034	1.000	1.000	0.980	1.003	0.996	1.003	0.996
17 States	0.953	1.022	1.022	0.975	0.958	1.031	1.008	0.982	0.995	0.990	1.014	0.993

Table 15.4 Annual rate of growth in TEC, TC and TFP in organised food–beverage industry (at 2004–05 prices)

	1981–89			1990–99			2000–09			2010–14		
	TEC	TC	TFP	TEC	TC	TFP	TEC	TC	TFP	TEC	TC	TFP
Andhra Pradesh	0.39	−1.10	−0.74	3.05	−0.84	2.19	4.15	−0.07	4.09	2.01	4.41	6.50
Assam	1.19	−0.95	0.22	0.91	−1.24	−0.33	0.39	0.06	0.43	2.72	−0.45	2.23
Bihar	2.39	−0.60	1.77	0.99	−0.21	0.78	1.27	−0.01	1.25	5.52	−4.15	1.16
Gujarat	−1.07	−0.01	−1.07	0.05	−0.03	0.04	3.71	0.48	4.21	5.17	0.77	5.99
Haryana	0.14	0.11	0.23	6.12	−0.13	6.00	4.06	1.68	5.80	8.99	0.40	9.41
Himachal Pradesh	1.96	0.39	2.36	3.72	0.71	4.44	3.80	0.94	4.78	4.33	0.72	5.06
Jammu and Kashmir	0.89	0.54	1.43	−2.47	2.36	−0.18	−3.98	1.73	−2.32	2.27	0.68	2.96
Karnataka	1.64	0.98	2.64	−0.83	1.68	0.84	0.12	0.20	0.32	4.03	0.84	4.89
Kerala	1.36	1.10	2.48	−0.93	0.71	−0.22	−0.93	−1.29	−2.22	5.98	1.05	7.08
Madhya Pradesh	5.14	2.04	7.27	1.75	1.45	3.22	1.61	−1.20	0.38	10.16	1.91	12.26
Maharashtra	5.10	2.10	7.31	3.91	2.47	6.48	3.97	−1.03	2.91	5.47	2.16	7.77
Odisha	2.78	1.71	4.53	1.25	3.24	4.54	1.22	−1.08	0.14	0.35	−0.24	0.11
Punjab	−7.37	1.64	−5.83	−7.04	4.22	−3.12	2.32	−1.20	1.09	2.22	0.03	2.26
Rajasthan	0.55	−0.83	−0.28	0.37	2.97	3.36	0.81	−1.66	−0.86	1.24	−1.53	−0.30
Tamil Nadu	−0.04	−0.24	−0.29	−0.11	2.95	2.84	0.56	−1.63	−1.07	−1.62	−0.96	−2.58
Uttar Pradesh	−14.18	−0.07	−14.24	−11.52	2.86	−8.99	−2.21	−1.92	−4.09	−4.21	−1.32	−5.44
West Bengal	−0.02	0.71	0.68	4.50	3.48	8.14	2.64	−2.00	0.59	10.02	−0.92	9.01
17 States	−1.19	0.02	−1.18	−0.04	3.30	3.26	3.06	−1.78	1.22	3.99	−0.83	3.12

The state-level analysis provides a mixed picture. The TFPG was high and positive in most states during the 1990s and the 2000s. The growth of the TEC is positive and high in all states except Tamil Nadu and Uttar Pradesh, but the growth rate of TC is negative in many states. The TFP fell in these states because capacity utilisation is low in the industry and resources and skills are inadequate. Overall, TFP and GVA growths have a positive correlation, which indicates that input use efficiency is growing. These findings are in line with that in Mitra et al. (2002): inefficiency adversely affected food industry growth in some states in the 1980s. The scenario changed from 2000: the TFPG exceeded 2%, primarily because the TEC improved, in all states except Bihar, Rajasthan, Odisha, Tamil Nadu and Uttar Pradesh.

Recently, the TFPG was higher in Andhra Pradesh (6.5%), Gujarat (5.99%), Haryana (9.41%), Kerala (7.08%), Madhya Pradesh (12.3%), Maharashtra (7.77%) and West Bengal (9.01%). This high rate may be explained by the higher rate of growth in agriculture, better technology, the growing demand for processed foods and favourable policy changes. The frontier effect (TC) and the catching-up effect, or the movement towards the best frontier (TEC), contributed to higher TFPG in the food industry in the 1980s and 1990s. During the 2000s, however, scale efficiency change and pure TEC drove the TFPG, and pure TE and scale efficiency deteriorated, though the deterioration was greater in the case of scale efficiency. These findings suggest that TEC contributed more to the TFPG in processed foods in the 2000s than in the 1990s or the 1980s.

The TFPG in several states in the 2000s is due more to changes in TE than to technological progress; the TEC grew at a much higher rate than the TC in most states, indicating efficient resource use. Pure TEC and scale efficiency are the main components of TEC, and the growth rate of pure TEC much exceeds that of scale efficiency; one may say that the production frontier has shifted, due perhaps to an increase in capital, as labour input has not increased much. There is considerable scope for improving productivity in the organised food industry in Odisha, Rajasthan, Tamil Nadu and Uttar Pradesh by increasing the TE, suggesting that resource use is inefficient.

In most states, the food and beverage industry is scale-inefficient. Innovations can help improve its TC, and the food industry can improve efficiency scores by taking measures to exploit their comparative advantage in offering lower transaction and transport costs (for raw material), better economies of scale and cheap labour. A favourable policy of appropriate incentives and enabling environment offers promise; Himachal Pradesh has a small share in the food industry in terms of factories, workers, investment and output but much higher efficiency and productivity. Himachal Pradesh and Uttarakhand offer fiscal measures to encourage private investment.

15.4   Impact of Protection on Total Factor Productivity Growth and Employment

The extant literature on India's food industry, though scant, attributes productivity growth to differences in the TE, taken to be positively influenced by net value-added, technology acquisition, infrastructure, urbanisation, investor-friendliness, skill development of workers and share of agriculture income in total income. Productivity growth is found to be negatively impacted by the protection level on agricultural products (trade openness), a finding negated in a few studies. We investigate the impact of trade openness—NRP and applied tariff rates on TFP and employment—in the organised foods and beverages industry from 2001–02 to 2014–15. The protection accorded to the primary and processed agricultural products is expected to have a negative impact on industry's TFP.

Table 15.5 provides the estimates of the correlation coefficients between TFP, employment (workers per factory), industry-specific variables (GVA per factory, labour productivity and capital intensity) and protection measures (average tariff rate and NRP) for each of the categories taken. As expected, the correlation coefficients between TFP and the protection level (tariffs and NRP) are negative and significant at 10 per cent level, implying that openness in agricultural trade has contributed to productivity growth in the processed food, but not significantly. The correlation between the level of protection and GVA per factory, though negative, is statistically insignificant, which may suggest that a reduction in protection to agricultural commodities would positively affect output. Across primary and processed products, Categories II, III and IV have a negative and insignificant relationship with TFP under the exportable hypothesis; under the importable hypothesis, only Categories III and IV products have a negative and insignificant relationship with TFP.

A higher TFP in foods and beverage industry may not be explained solely by a less protective regime; a greater role is played by domestic factors, such as improvements in infrastructure and investment climate, increasing demand for processed food and the easy availability of raw material from the agricultural sector. Lowering the protection of agricultural commodities has not adversely affected employment; in fact, the slow rate of growth in employment could have been due to increase in capital intensity, as the sign of coefficient is 0.69 and significant at 1% level. The size of industry (captured through GVA per factory) has a positive effect on employment.

15.5   Summing up and Implications

We use the Malmquist index to estimate the TFP for all the states together, and also separately for each state, under the assumption of IRS, and based on an output-oriented model. We decompose the TFP into TC and TEC, and bifurcate the TEC further into pure TEC and scale efficiency. Their relation with the NRP and tariffs is seen for each of the four categories of agricultural products.

Table 15.5 Correlation coefficient between TFP and protection indicators during 2001–02 to 2014–15

	TFP	Applied Tariff Rate	NRP-Exportable Hypothesis	Category I	Category II	Category III	Category IV	NRP-Importable Hypothesis	Category I	Category II	Category III	Category IV	GVA/Factory	Labour Productivity	Worker/Factory	Capital Intensity
TFP	1															
Applied Tariff Rate	-0.44***	1														
NRP-Exportable Hypothesis	-0.35	-0.03	1													
Category I	0.45***	-0.44***	-0.03	1												
Category II	-0.33	-0.01	0.91*	-0.13	1											
Category III	-0.27	-0.22	0.52**	-0.12	0.54**	1										
Category IV	-0.38	0.21	0.67*	-0.21	0.35	0.09	1									
NRP-Importable Hypothesis	-0.05	0.50**	0.18	-0.19	0.27	-0.09	0.08	1								
Category I	0.06	0.15	0.03	-0.14	0.10	-0.04	-0.02	0.78*	1							
Category II	0.36	-0.04	0.44***	0.34	0.35	0.16	0.31	-0.03	-0.13	1						
Category III	-0.10	0.19	0.39	0.02	0.06	-0.05	0.79*	-0.13	-0.09	0.36	1					
Category IV	-0.01	-0.19	0.46**	-0.25	0.48**	0.30	0.23	0.22	0.13	-0.10	-0.16	1				
GVA/Factory	0.08	-0.41	0.16	0.48**	-0.08	-0.20	0.36	-0.37	-0.27	0.12	0.38	-0.12	1			
Labour Productivity	0.04	-0.56**	0.26	0.57**	0.03	0.10	0.29	-0.46***	-0.28**	0.11	0.31	0.01	0.87*	1		
Worker/Factory	0.10	0.29	-0.19	-0.15	-0.23	-0.62*	0.15	0.17	0.02	0.03	0.14	-0.28	0.31	-0.20	1	
Capital Intensity	0.01	-0.49**	0.48**	0.30	0.41	0.42	0.21	-0.32	-0.22	0.17	0.12	0.43***	0.27	0.64*	-0.69*	1

The results show that the TFP index score improved between 1980–81 and 2014–15. During the pre-reform period (1981–82 to 1989–90), the national-level TFP grew at—1.18% on average, primarily because the TEC was low. In the subsequent decade, the TFP turned out to be positive and high, at 3.26%. This high growth is explained by the 3.30% growth in TC, implying that the new technology adopted by industry helped. The growth in the TEC was low and negative because the scale efficiency slowed down. The TFPG was positive from 2000 to 2009 because the TEC grew at a high rate, implying that the proper combination of inputs and use of technology led to gains in efficiency.

The state-level analysis shows that the growth in TEC is positive and high in all states, except in Tamil Nadu and Uttar Pradesh, but the growth rate was negative in most states. A decline in TFP may be attributed to low capacity utilisation in industry and inadequate resources and skills. Overall, a positive correlation is found between TFP and GVA growth, which indicates that input use efficiency is growing. These findings validate the literature that inefficiency adversely affected food industry growth in some states during the 1980s.

The scenario changed from 2000: the TEC improved and raised TFPG above 2 per cent except in Bihar, Rajasthan, Odisha, Tamil Nadu and Uttar Pradesh. In recent years, the TFPG was high in Andhra Pradesh (6.5%), Gujarat (5.99%), Haryana (9.41%), Kerala (7.08%), Madhya Pradesh (12.3%), Maharashtra (7.77%) and West Bengal (9.01%). It can be explained by a revival in the agricultural growth rate, better technology, growing demand for processed food and favourable policy changes.

The frontier effect (TC) and the catching-up effect, or the movement towards the best frontier (TEC), raised productivity growth in the 1980s and 1990s; in the subsequent decade, however, the contribution of TEC was more prominent; scale efficiency change and pure TEC drove the improvement. But, in the 2000s, scale efficiency change and pure TEC deteriorated in many states, and scale efficiency change deteriorated more than the pure TEC. These findings suggest that TEC drove TFPG in the processed foods industry more in the 2000s than in the 1990s or the 1980s.

Productivity growth decelerated in some states because capacity utilisation declined continually and agricultural growth was dismal, especially from 1995 to 2002 and then from 2012 to 2015. An uptick in productivity growth, especially in laggard states, could be attributed to the increase in the TE and scale efficiency, a favourable investment climate, availability of infrastructure and backward linkages with agriculture played a crucial role—as reported in the literature.

Trade liberalisation was not significant in accelerating processed food productivity, contrary to the expectation, and indicating that the dependence of food and beverages industry on external trade is low. The correlation coefficient between TFP and the level of protection accorded to primary and processed agricultural commodities, through NRP and their respective tariff rates, is negative, but statistically significant only at 10 per cent level. It means that trade in primary and processed agricultural commodities did contribute to productivity growth in food industry during the 2000s, but not in a significant way. Similarly, a negative correlation between the level of protection and GVA per factory may suggest that a reduction in the protection of agricultural commodities would positively affect output. Internal factors—such as improvements in infrastructure, investment climate, increase in demand and easy availability of raw materials from the agricultural sector—have a greater role to play. As regards employment, the lower rate of protection on primary and processed agricultural commodities has not adversely affected industrial employment. In fact, the slow rate of growth in employment is due to increase in capital intensity, which is verified through a highly significant value of correlation coefficient at 0.69. The size of industry (captured through GVA per factory) has a positive effect on employment.

The implications of the analysis are clear. The organised food and beverage industry has considerable scope for expanding and accelerating productivity growth. The agriculturally dominant states, where investment and productivity are picking up, can exploit their comparative advantage in offering lower transaction and transport costs, better economies of scale and cheap labour. These states can attract private investment by offering the appropriate incentives, improving the ease of doing business, developing infrastructure and enacting favourable policies. Private investment can improve the growth rate, and technological advancements can boost productivity and efficiency.

Despite a perpetual increase in exports and imports—owing to an array of reform measures—India's manufacturing sector is somewhat protected (Chap. 14, this book). This protective regime persists mainly due to industry's potential to pull surplus labour from agriculture and contribute to economic growth. India's agricultural products are increasingly competitive in the world markets, but this competitiveness is restricted largely to low-value primary products; the foods and beverages industry is not cost-competitive, and this lack of cost-competitiveness may deter exports. India protects many processed agricultural products and, therefore, industry, and prevents consumers to gain from lower prices in a free trade regime. A lower support to primary agriculture commodities prevents farmers (producers) from gaining from higher prices in the world market. Therefore, India must reduce the protection it accords to processed agricultural products.

If India's foods and beverages industry can improve technology and resource use efficiency and become price-competitive in the export market, it would compete with global players such as China, the European Union (EU), Canada, the USA and Australia. India would also have to overcome non-tariff measures (NTM) imposed by the importing countries. Key export markets—the USA, the EU and the Association of South East Asian Nations (ASEAN)impose NTMs on primary and processed agricultural exports, and the topmost are related to food quality and to health-related, sanitary and phytosanitary issues. India would require to undertake several domestic measures to improve the quality of its fresh and processed products and upgrade standards. The public sector, in tandem with support from the private sector, can be instrumental in delivering the skills and infrastructure required for implementing good agricultural practice standards germane with international requirements and with maintaining the safety and quality in the agricultural food chain.

The consciousness about food safety and health standards is growing worldwide but, while the incidence of NTMs has not been increasing, the existing restrictions are not transparent, and these are poorly understood (Cadot et al. 2016; Cadot and Ing 2015). Poor design harms many regulations and complicates the business and fails to protect the public. For instance, the rules for pharmaceutical imports, are complex in many countries, but the traffic in counterfeits is widespread, and it continues unabated. This is because, typically, NTMs span the competencies of several ministries, and they rarely have a mechanism to coordinate among themselves and make the trade-offs necessary. Also, many administrations are anti-business and enforce regulations in punitive ways.

India's agriculture export policy (GOI 2018) needs a mechanism to deal with NTMs and with sanitary and phytosanitary issues. Simultaneously, India must initiate a dialogue at the World Trade Organization (WTO) to standardise NTMs and ensure that, if there is a discrepancy or if importing countries set unreasonably high standards, exporters and export promotion agencies can raise the concerns at bilateral and multilateral forums. To establish this case, India needs scientific research and adequate data.

Annex A

DEA Approach to Estimate TFP

Productivity is defined as the ratio of output to input(s). Productivity can be measured by using the single (or partial) factor productivity (SFP) and multifactor or TFP. The SFP is defined as the ratio of output (or value-added) to the quantity of factor of production. Three broad measures are used as follows:

1. Labour productivity, or output per labour;
2. Capital productivity, or output per capital and
3. Capital intensity, or capital per labour.

These partial measures of productivity do not capture the overall changes in the productive capacity of a firm or industry, and these are affected by changes in the composition of inputs.

The TFP represents the overall productivity or efficiency in input use. That is its advantage over other measures. An increase in TFP is termed TC. Several methods are used to estimate the TC and often include economies of scale and TE gains.

In a two-factor production model, the rate of growth of output is determined by capital stock, labour input and a "residual", which is interpreted broadly as TC or technological progress in growth economics. The "residual" measures the rate of disembodied, autonomous, exogenous and neutral TC. The technical progress could also be embodied, induced, endogenous or non-neutral to factors of production. It could be labour-saving or capital-saving in nature (Goldar 1986; Balakrishnan and Pushpangadan 1994).

"Technological progress" and "TFP" are used interchangeably, but TFP captures only one aspect of technological progress—its effect on the overall efficiency of input use. TFP is considered to include both technological progress (regress) and change in

TE. Technological progress is taken to be the advancement in knowledge relating to the art of production, which may take the form of new goods, processes or new modes of organisation. TE is defined as the efficiency with which factors of production are combined to generate output. While technological progress is conceptualised in terms of shifts in the production function (Solow 1957), the latter measures the distance between the actual and the frontier or maximum attainable levels of output (Bettesse 1990).

To estimate TFP, the literature has identified various techniques (non-frontier and frontier), which are classified into nonparametric and parametric approaches. Non-frontier techniques include the growth accounting and econometric methods. The frontier approach includes the Malmquist index, stochastic and deterministic frontier function.

In the parametric method, an explicit functional form is specified, and the parameters are estimated econometrically, implying that the estimates are sensitive to the selection of a particular functional form and the problem of simultaneity bias may arise. The nonparametric method does not impose any functional form; therefore, no direct statistical test can be performed (Goldar 2004; Das and Ghosh 2006; Kathuria et al. 2013).

The frontier approach aims to find the best obtainable position given the inputs or prices (Mahadevan 2003). It enables the decomposition of TFP into technical progress and TEC. The non-frontier approach assumes TE on the part of firms.

There is no consensus in the literature on the best approach for computing TFP. Many studies use non-frontier approaches, especially the nonparametric techniques. A few recent studies use the frontier approach and the parametric technique (Balakrishna et al. 2000; Marjit and Kar 2009).

The main methods are the growth accounting approach, multilateral TFP index, DEA analysis, Translog/Tornqvist index and the Levinsohn–Petrin method.

We employ the DEA approach, a nonparametric method, under the frontier approach, because it helps to overcome the shortcomings of the growth accounting approach, and it identifies the components of productivity change by decomposing the TFP index (Charnes et al. 1978). The TFP change is estimated using the Malmquist productivity index. It is defined as the ratio of two output distance functions. In other words, it measures the TFP change between two data points by calculating the ratio of the distances of each data point relative to a common technology. The variables usually used are cost of capital, labour, raw material consumed, energy used and gross value of output. Malmquist TFP index and efficiency scores are obtained by using the DEAP software.

The distance function is useful to describe a multi-input, multi-output technology without specifying the behavioural objectives of the firm (Kannan 2011). We use the concept of the output distance function to define the Malmquist TFP index. The output distance function measures maximal proportional expansion of output vector given input vector. Following Färe et al. (1994), for each time period $t = 1, 2, \ldots T$, the production technology set S^t consists of all feasible input vector $x^t \in R_+^N$ and output vector $y^t \in R_+^M$ such that x can produce y. The technology set is represented as follows:

$$S^t = \left\{ (x^t, y^t) : x^t \text{canproduce } y^t \right\}$$

The following output distance function is defined at t.

$$D_0(x^t, y^t) = \min\left\{ \theta : (x^t, y^t/\theta)\varepsilon \ S^t \right\}$$

$D_0(x^t, y^t)$ represent the distance of a firm using x input vector to produce y output vector in period t relative to the reference technology in period t. The distance function $D_0(x^t, y^t)$ will take a value of less than or equal to one if (x^t, y^t) is an element of technology set S^t. Further, $D_0(x^t, y^t)$ will take a value of 1 if (x^t, y^t) is located on the boundary of the technology, and it will take a value greater than 1 if located outside the feasible technology set. The distance function is measured by using DEA, as in linear programming, by assuming constant returns to scale (Coelli 1996; Coelli and Rao 2003).

Following Färe et al. (1994), the Malmquist TFP index between period t and $t + 1$ can be represented as the geometric mean of output-oriented indexes: one using technology in period t as a reference technology and another using technology frontier in period $t + 1$ as the reference. The Malmquist TFP index is written as follows:

$$M_0\left(x^{t+1}, y^{t+1}, x^t, y^t\right) = \left[M_0^t\left(x^{t+1}, y^{t+1}, x^t, y^t\right) \times M_0^{t+1}\left(x^{t+1}, y^{t+1}, x^t, y^t\right) \right]$$

$$= \left[\frac{D_0^t\left(x^{t+1}, y^{t+1}\right)}{D_0^t(x^t, y^t)} \times \frac{D_0^{t+1}\left(x^{t+1}, y^{t+1}\right)}{D_0^{t+1}(x^t, y^t)} \right]$$

The Malmquist productivity index, defined in terms of distance functions above, evaluates whether the observed input/output combination has improved relative to reference technology in period t and relative to reference technology in period $t + 1$. The TFPG is positive if the value of productivity index (M_0) is greater than 1; negative if less than 1; and stagnant between periods t and $t + 1$ if 1. Following Färe et al. (1994), the Malmquist productivity index can be written as follows:

$$M_0\left(x^{t+1}, y^{t+1}, x^t, y^t\right) = \frac{D_0^{t+1}\left(x^{t+1}, y^{t+1}\right)}{D_0^t(x^t, y^t)}$$

$$\times \left[\left(\frac{D_0^t\left(x^{t+1}, y^{t+1}\right)}{D_0^{t+1}\left(x^{t+1}, y^{t+1}\right)} \right) \times \left(\frac{D_0^t\left(x^t, y^t\right)}{D_0^{t+1}(x^t, y^t)} \right) \right]^{1/2}$$

The component outside the square bracket is the ratio of TE in period t to TE in period $t + 1$. This efficiency change component indicates how far the observed production is getting closer or farther from the frontier. The expression inside the bracket indicates the shift in the technology frontier (TC) between the period t and t

+ *1*. It is measured as the geometric mean of shift in technology between two periods evaluated at input levels x^t and x^{t+1}. If the value of efficiency change component is greater than 1, the production unit is catching up to the frontier in period $t + 1$ as compared to the period t. The improvement in TC provides evidence of innovation between two periods, and the value of TC greater than 1 shows technical progress.

Annex B

Construction of Variables and Sources of Data

The organised manufacturing sector in India comprises factories registered under Sections 2m (i), 2 m(ii) and 85 of the Factories Act, 1948. Under Section 2m, "factory" means any premises including the precincts thereof:

2 m(i) wherein ten or more workers are working or were working on any day of preceding 12 months and in any part of which a manufacturing process is being carried on with the aid of power or is ordinarily so carried on;

2 m(ii) where in 20 or more workers are working or were working on any day of proceeding 12 months and in any part of which a manufacturing process is being carried on without the aid of power or is ordinarily so carried on and does not include a mine subject to the operations of the Indian Mines Act, 1923, or railways run school. Under Section 85 of the Factories Act, 1948, the state government is empowered to notify any factory not covered under the above two sections.

The study is based on ASI annual data on organised manufacturing and National Sample Survey (NSS) quinquennial data on unorganised manufacturing sectors. It is important to mention that till 1988–89 the classification of industries was based on the National Industrial Classification (NIC) 1970 and from 1989–90 onwards based on NIC-1987 and then replaced by NIC-1998.

The Economic and Political Weekly Research Foundation (EPWRF) database has prepared concordance between NIC-1998 and NIC-1987 from 1976–77 to 2003–04. During 2000, the industrial classification changed to NIC-2004 and from 2008–09 replaced by NIC-2008. Many new industries have emerged and reclassified even at two-digit level. For instance, for long, manufacture of tobacco was considered as part of the food and beverage (NIC codes 20 and 21), which was taken to be a separate industry under NIC 2004 (code 16). Further, as per NIC-2004, code 15 represents food and beverage together which under NIC-2008 is changed to code 10 for food and code 11 for beverage.

To make a comparable time series on food and beverage industry in each state, a concordance matrix between three-digit classes of NIC-1998, NIC-2004 and NIC-2008 is prepared. From 1976–77 to 1997–98, data is extracted at NIC three-digit level based on NIC-1998 and from 1998–99 to 2013–14 from the Ministry of Statistics and Programme Implementation, Central Statistical Office. The industries falling under NIC three-digit level codes—151, 152, 153, 154 and 155—are categorised under processing of food and beverage. The industrial code 151 refers to production, processing and preservation of meat, fish, fruit, vegetables, oils and fats; 152 is the manufacture of dairy products; 153 is the manufacture of grain mill products, starches and starch products and prepared animal feeds; 154 is the manufacture of bakery and other food products; and 155 is the manufacture of beverages, including liquor.

Industry-Specific Variables

The following variables at nominal prices are extracted from the ASI processed data base, taken from the EPWRF database and the CSO.

Labour

Data on labour is obtained by adding production workers and non-production workers. As per the definition provided by the ASI, production workers relate to all persons employed directly or through only agency whether for wages or not and engaged in any manufacturing process or in cleaning any part of the machinery or premises used for manufacturing process. Persons holding positions of supervisor or management or employed in the administrative office, storekeeping section and welfare section, engaged in the purchase of raw material, etc., are included in non-production workers. Total number of persons engaged is taken to represent labour.

Gross Fixed Capital Stock

Studies done on productivity show that the measurement of capital stock is afflicted by many conceptual problems, which explain the considerable differences in the estimation methodologies employed. The NAS makes benchmark estimates available, and, therefore, national-level estimates are easy to construct, but state-level estimation is hard and disaggregated industry-level estimation is harder still (for a full discussion see, among others, Roychaudhury (1977), Goldar (1986), Sarma and Rao (1990), Singh and Ajit (1995), Kumar (2001), and Sharma and Upadhyay (2008)).

The perpetual inventory method is most widely used in empirical research. For constructing a time series on gross fixed capital stock at constant prices, we require a series on gross investment, an asset price deflator, depreciation rate and a benchmark capital stock, and we adopt the following three-step procedure.

Step 1.

The most important prerequisite is the figure of capital stock in the benchmark (initial) year, i.e. K_0. To obtain K_0, it is assumed that the value of finished equipment of a balanced age composition would be exactly half the value of equipment when it was new. Hence, twice the book value of fixed assets in the benchmark year at 2004–05 prices is taken as a rough estimate of replacement value of fixed capital, i.e. $K_0 = 2 \times B_0$ (where B_0 is the book value of fixed capital net of the depreciation in the benchmark year).

Step 2.

After obtaining the estimate of K_0, gross real investment (I_t) is obtained by using the following relationship:

$$I_t = \frac{B_t - B_{t-1} + D_t}{P_t}$$

where $B_t =$ book value of fixed capital in the year t, $D_t =$ value of depreciation of fixed assets in year t, and $P_t =$ implicit deflator for GFCF for registered manufacturing given in the NAS.

Step 3.

Given the estimate of K_0, the following relationship has been used to construct a series of gross fixed capital stock at 2004–05 prices:

$$K_t = K_{t-1} + I_t + d K_{t-1}$$

where $K_t =$ gross fixed capital at 2004–05 prices in the year t, $I_t =$ gross real investment in the year t, and $d =$ annual rate of discarding capital. Following studies done on the subject, the annual rate of discarding of capital is taken to be equal to 5 per cent.

Measurement of Gross Value Added

The GVA is arrived at by deducting the cost of total input from the value of total output. The figures of "total output" comprise the total ex-factory value of products and by-products manufactured as well as other receipts from non-industrial services rendered to others, work done for others on material supplied by them, value of electricity produced and sold, sale value of goods sold in the same conditions purchased, addition in stock of semi-finished goods and value of own construction.

However, "total inputs" comprise the total value of fuels, materials consumed and expenditures such as cost of contract and commission work done by others on materials supplied by the factory, cost of materials consumed for repair and maintenance work done by others to the factory's fixed assets, inward freight and transport charges, rate and taxes (excluding income tax), postage, telephone and telex expenses, insurance charges, banking charges, cost of printing and stationery and purchase value of goods sold in the same condition as purchased. Rent and interest paid are not included.

The GVA in organised manufacturing total is deflated by the wholesale price index (WPI) of all commodities and food manufacturing by the WPI of food. A GVA measure based on a single deflation procedure may produce a bias in the estimates if material prices do not move parallel to output prices (Balakrishnan and Pushpangadan 1994; Kathuria et al. 2010), but this study uses the single deflation method because of the lack of state and industry-level deflators and other measurement problems in the use of the double deflation method.

Measurement of Gross Output

To obtain gross output, the figures of depreciation are added to net output. The ASI defines "depreciation" as the consumption of fixed capital due to wear and tear and obsolescence during the accounting year. It is taken as provided by the factory owner or is estimated on the basis of cost of installation and working life of fixed asset.

We use gross output figures instead of net output figures because depreciation charges in Indian industries are known to be highly arbitrary, as these are fixed by the income tax authorities and seldom represent true or actual capital consumption. However, the figures of net output consist of total value of all the products and by-products produced by the firm. This variable is deflated by the WPI.

Measurement of Wages (Emoluments)

The ASI provides data on emoluments paid to workers and includes all remuneration in monetary terms and also payable more or less regularly in each pay period to workers as compensation for work done during the accounting year. It includes direct wages and salary (i.e. basic wages/salaries and payment of overtime and dearness, compensatory, house rent and other allowances); bonus; paid holiday, etc.

The wages are expressed in terms of gross value, i.e. before deductions. Since we have taken the number of persons engaged, wage is represented by total emoluments and employer's provident fund contribution. The monetary figures of emoluments have been deflated at constant 2004–05 prices using the consumer price index (CPI) of industrial workers. We use the splicing method to make a common base for the index. Data on deflators and other variables is extracted from NAS, CSO, Report on Currency and Finance, RBI, Handbook of Statistics on Indian Economy, RBI. Each variable specified in the functional form above is extracted from the ASI data at two-digit level for the organised foods industry.

References

Balakrishnan, P., & Pushpangadan, K. (1994). Total factor productivity growth in manufacturing industry: A fresh look. *Economic & Political Weekly, 29*(31), 2028–2035.

Banga, R., & Bathla, S. (2012). Impact of trade on labour markets in the unorganised sector in India: An empirical approach. In K. Pushpangadan & V. N. Balsubramanyam (Eds.), *Impact of growth on development: India's record since liberalization*. New Delhi: Oxford University Press.

Banker, R. D., Charnes, A., & Cooper, W. W. (1984). Some models for estimating technical and scale inefficiencies in data envelopment analysis. *Management Science, 30*(9), 1078–1092.

Bathla, S. (2014). Agro-industry: The food processing sector. In *World Bank Study (2014), Republic of India: Accelerating agricultural productivity growth*. Washington D.C.: The World Bank

Bathla, S. (2018). Productivity in food processing industry under varying trade regimes: Analysis across the Indian States. In A. Mitra (Ed.), *Economic growth in India: Its various dimensions (Essays in honour of Prof. B.B. Bhattacharya)*. Hyderabad: Orient BlackSwan.

Battese, G. E., & Coelli, T. J. (1995). A model for technical inefficiency effects in a stochastic frontier production function for panel data. *Empirical Economics, 20,* 325–332.

Cadot, O., et al. (2016). *Non-tariff measures in ASEAN, economic research institute for ASEAN and East Asia and United Nations Conference, on Trade and Development* (pp. 26–36)

Cadot, O., & Ing, L. Y. (2015). *NTM harmonization in RCEP* (ERIA Discussion Paper No. 61). Jakarta: ERIA.

Charnes, A., Cooper, W. W., & Rhodes, E. (1978). Measuring the efficiency of decision making units. *European Journal of Operational Research, 2,* 429–444.

Coelli, T. J. (1996). *A guide to DEAP Version 2.1: A data envelopment analysis (Computer) Program* (CEPA Working Paper 96/08). University of New England, Armidale.

Coelli, T. J., & Prasada Rao, D. S. (2005). Total factor productivity growth in agriculture: A malmquist index analysis of 93 countries, 1980–2000. *Agricultural Economics, 32*(Supplement), 115–134.

Coelli, T. J., Prasada Rao, D. S., & Battese, G. E. (1998). *An introduction to efficiency and productivity analysis*. Boston: Kluwer Academic Publishers.

Coelli, T. J., Prasada Rao, D. S., O'Donnell, C. J., & Battese, G. E. (2005). *An introduction to productivity and efficiency analysis* (2nd ed.). USA: Springer.

Das, D. K., Wadhwa, D., & Kalita, G. (2009). *The employment potential of labor intensive industries in India's organized manufacturing* (Working Paper No. 236). Indian Council for Research on International Economic Relations (ICRIER).

Farrell, M. (1957). The measurement of productive efficiency. *Journal of the Royal Statistical Society, Series A, 120,* 253–281.

GoI-Central Statistical Organisation. (1980 to 2015). *Annual survey of industries (ASI)*. New Delhi: Government of India.

Goldar, B. (1986). *Productivity growth in Indian industry*. Delhi: Allied Publishers.

Goldar, B., & Kumari, A. (2003). Import liberalization and productivity growth in Indian manufacturing industries in the 1990s. *Developing Economies, 41*(4), 436–60.

Goldar, B. (2004). *Productivity trends in Indian manufacturing in the pre- and post-reform periods* (Working Paper No. 137). Indian Council for Research on International Economic Relations (ICRIER).

Goldar, B. (2017). Growth, productivity and job creation in Indian manufacturing. In U. Kapila (Ed.), *India's economy pre-liberalisation to GST: Essays in honour of Raj Kapila* (pp. 619–652). New Delhi: Academic Foundation.

Goldar, B., & Aggarwal, S. C. (2010). *Informalization of industrial labour in India: Are labour market rigidities and growing import competition to blame?* New Delhi: Institute for Economic Growth.

Government of India (GOI). (2018). Agriculture export policy, Department of Commerce, Ministry of Commerce and Industry, GOI, India.

Hashim, D. A., Kumar, A., & Virmani, A. (2009, October). *Impact of major liberalization on productivity: The J curve hypothesis* (Working Paper No 5/2009). Department of Economic Affairs, Ministry of Finance.

Kannan, E. (2011). *Total factor productivity growth and its determinants in Karnataka agriculture* (ISEC Working Paper 265). Bangalore: Institute for Social and Economic Change (ISEC).

Kannan, E., & Birthal, P. S. (2010). Effect of trade liberalization on the efficiency of Indian dairy industry. *Journal of International and Area Studies, 17*(1), 1–15.

Kathuria, V., Rajesh Raj S. N., & Sen, K. (2010, June 12). Organised versus unorganised manufacturing performance in the post-reform period. *Economic and Political Weekly, XLV*(24).

Mitra, A. (1999). Total factor productivity growth and technical efficiency in Indian industries. *Economic and Political Weekly, 34*(31), M98–M105.

Mitra, A., Varoudakis, A., & Veganzones, M. A. (2002). Productivity and technical efficiency in Indian States' manufacturing: the role of infrastructure. *Economic Development and Cultural Change, 50*(2), 395–426.

Nouroz, H. (2001). *Protection in Indian manufacturing: An empirical study.* Macmillan India Ltd.

Ray, S. C. (2004). *Data envelopment analysis: Theory and techniques for economics and operations research.* Cambridge, United Kingdom: Cambridge University Press.

Rodriguez, F., & Rodrik, D. (1999). *Trade policy and economic growth: A skeptic's guide to cross national evidence.* Mimeo.

Saini, S., & Gulati, A. (2017). *Price distortions in Indian agriculture.* International Bank for Reconstruction and Development and World Bank.

Seiford, L. M., & Thrall, R. M. (1990). Recent developments in DEA: The mathematical programming approach to frontier analysis. *Journal of Econometrics, 4*, 7–38.

Solow, R. M. (1956). A contribution to the theory of economic growth. *Quarterly Journal of Economics, LXX*(1), 65–94.

Solow, R. M. (1957). Technical change and the aggregate production function. *Review of Economics and Statistics, XXXIX*(1), 312–320.

Topalova, P. (2003). *Trade liberalization and firm productivity: The case of India.* Yale University. www.econ.yale.edu/seminars/NEUDC03/topalova1.pdf.

Tybout, J. R., & Westbrook, D. M. (1995). Trade liberalization and dimensions of efficiency change in Mexican manufacturing industries. *Journal of Development Economics, 39*, 53–78.

Chapter 16
Productivity, Competitiveness and Export Performance: A Plant-Level Analysis of India's Wearing Apparel Industry

Bishwanath Goldar and Yashobanta Parida

16.1 Introduction

To eliminate poverty in India in the foreseeable future, the Indian economy needs to grow at the rate of about 8% per year, or higher, for the next two decades; manufacturing-sector growth must accelerate markedly, too[1]; ample employment opportunities need to be created. For boosting growth in the manufacturing sector and ensuring concomitant large-scale job creation in it, the prime focus has to be on export-oriented labour-intensive manufacturing industries.[2]

---

[1] To eliminate poverty in India and turn it into an upper-middle-income country by 2035, Mohan (2019) emphasises the need for stepping up the growth rate of the Indian economy in the next two decades. According to him, to reverse the deceleration in the economy's growth rate since 2008–09 and raise the growth rate to 8–9% per annum, certain key macroeconomic tasks, such as sustained increase in savings and investment, need to be performed, and one crucial area of action is to accelerate growth in the manufacturing sector. The need for manufacturing-led growth in India in the coming years has been emphasised also by Ghose (2015, 2016) and Mitra (2015).

[2] To accelerate growth in the manufacturing sector in India, the greatest need in the next decade or two is to induce a major expansion in labour using export-oriented manufacturing, similar to what has been done by China and other East Asian countries over the past 30–40 years (Mohan 2019, p. 41).

B. Goldar (✉)
Institute of Economic Growth, Delhi, India
e-mail: goldarbng@rediffmail.com

Y. Parida
Verghese Kurien Centre of Excellence, Institute of Rural Management Anand, Anand, Gujarat, India
e-mail: yashobanta@irma.ac.in

This paper is concerned with one such industry, the wearing apparel industry, and its focus is on exports.[3] The core empirical analysis presented in the paper is confined to the organised or formal segment of this industry, and the analysis is based on the unit-level data of the *Annual Survey of Industries* (ASI), brought out by the Central Statistics Office (CSO), Ministry of Statistics and Programme Implementation, Government of India. Some analysis of the aggregate-level export performance of India in wearing apparel (which includes exports from both formal and informal sector plants) is also presented.

The wearing apparel industry in India is important to study because of the potential it has for the creation of jobs. Readymade garments as a product category is one of the important items of India's exports. The readymade garment industry has substantial potential for generating employment through increased exports.[4] The current global economic situation is marked by sluggish growth in world trade, and it severely constrains the possibility of adopting a predominantly export-led manufacturing-sector-growth strategy in India, as also in other emerging economies. Perhaps the situation is unlikely to change much in the near future. Arguably, thus, there is a case for a two-pronged strategy for manufacturing-sector growth in India based on both domestic markets for manufactured products and serving the international demand for such products. However, it is important to realise that to attain an annual growth

---

[3]In the context of the "Make in India" programme, Veeramani and Dhir (2017) observe that two groups of industries have the potential for export growth and employment generation. The first group is traditional unskilled-labour-intensive manufactured products, such as textiles, clothing, footwear and toys. The other group consists of products with an internationally fragmented manufacturing process where the production activity is controlled mainly by multinational enterprises and their global production networks. Evidently, Veeramani and Dhir (2017) recognise the importance of the wearing apparel industry as a potential thrust area for future economic development. It should be added here that the focus of the "Make in India" programme is on 25 sectors, and one of these 25 sectors is textiles and clothing.

[4]To substantiate this assertion, some statistics and estimates may be given. According to the estimates presented in a paper of the Export–Import Bank of India (2016), total employment (direct plus indirect) supported by exports of readymade garments and miscellaneous textile products was about 8.2 million in 2012–13. The corresponding figures on employment generation supported by exports were only 0.09 million for petroleum products, 0.31 million for drugs and medicines and 0.05 million for organic and inorganic chemicals; these are important items of exports from India. In 2012–13, the share of machinery in total exports was 5.2%, and the employment supported by machinery exports was 1.5 million; the share of transport equipment in total exports was 3.4%, and the employment supported by exports was 1.14 million. By contrast, the share of readymade garments and miscellaneous textile products in total exports was 3.94% in 2012–13 and employment supported by exports was much higher at 8.2 million. It should be mentioned here that the potential for employment generation is higher also in the exports of gems and jewellery. According to the aforementioned estimates of the Export–Import Bank of India, the share of gems and jewellery in total exports in 2012–13 was 10.22%, and the total employment supported by exports of gems and jewellery in that year was about 4.9 million. It needs to be pointed out, however, that compared to readymade garments, gems and jewellery exports have greater dependence on imports. Thus, the domestic value-added content in gems and jewellery exports is smaller than that in exports of readymade garments. According to the estimates of Goldar et al. (2017), in the case of readymade garments, the domestic value-added content in exports in 2007–08 was 84%, and in the case of gems and jewellery it was 63%.

rate of 10% or more in manufacturing, so that the overall growth rate of the economy could be raised to 8% or higher, India needs to exploit more fully than before the potential that exists in the export markets of labour-intensive manufactured products.[5]

The rest of the paper is organised as follows. The next section deals with the trends in India's exports of readymade garments/wearing apparel. This analysis is done at the aggregate level, covering the period 1987–88 to 2017–18 for some analyses, and a shorter period for others. Besides looking at the trends in India's readymade garment exports, a comparison of India's export performance is undertaken with China, Bangladesh and Vietnam, which are important exporters of readymade garments. An analysis of the export intensity of organised sector plants in the wearing apparel industry in India is presented in Section 16.3. This analysis is based on unit-level data of the ASI, and the period covered for the analysis is 2008–09 to 2014–15.[6] Section 16.4 presents an econometric analysis of determinants of export intensity of organised sector plants in wearing apparel industry. The analysis is based on a panel data set for period 2008–09 to 2012–13. A panel Tobit model is estimated, investigating some important determinants of the export intensity of plants—with a particular focus on the impact of productivity improvement on the export performance of wearing apparel plants. Also, the role of labour market regulations in influencing the export performance is considered in this section.[7]

The impact of changes in the real effective exchange rate (REER) on India's export performance in respect to wearing apparel products[8] is presented in Section 16.5.

---

[5] Veeramani and Dhir (2016) examine the export performance of India in unskilled-labour-intensive manufactured products (which include textiles and wearing apparel) in a comparative perspective using a gravity model, which is estimated on the basis of data for the year 2011. They compare India with China and several other developing countries in South Asia and South-East Asia. Based on the results of their analysis, they conclude that India has been an underperformer. They hold the opinion that flexible labour market regulations and improved infrastructure facilities will help in enhancing the growth of labour-intensive manufacturing in India.

[6] The ASI provides data on the share in products and by-products directly exported by plants, hereafter referred to as the export share in production or export intensity. Such data are available only from 2008–09 onwards. Hence, the analysis based on plant-level data presented in Sect. 16.3 and that presented subsequently in the paper are confined to the period from 2008–09 onwards.

[7] That labour market rigidities may be constraining the growth performance of labour-intensive export-oriented industries in India is recognised by Veeramani and Dhir (2016). How labour market conditions make a difference to the performance of organised sector plants in textiles and wearing apparel industry in India is studied by Ahluwalia et al. (2018). They employ a difference-in-difference estimation strategy. There used to be quota restrictions on the exports of apparel and textile products by developing countries to the developed world; these restrictions were abolished in 2005. Ahluwalia et al. (2018) consider the impact of the abolition and find that it led to significant gains in employment and wages in textile- and apparel-producing plants in the organised sector of the industry in Indian states that had more flexible labour market regulations as compared to the states with inflexible labour market regulations.

[8] On the question whether the exchange rate channel is effective in supporting exports, views differ. Doubts have been expressed on whether substantial gains in India's exports can accrue from exchange rate depreciation. Some studies find that a depreciation in the exchange rate does not positively affect India's manufactured exports (see, e.g., Bhanumurthy and Sharma 2013), but several empirical studies find that the exchange rate significantly impacted India's exports, depreciation having a favourable effect and appreciation having an unfavourable effect (see, e.g., Veeramani

An analysis is undertaken using time series data at the aggregate level. In one econometric exercise, India's exports of wearing apparel vis-à-vis the exports of China, Bangladesh and Vietnam are considered, and how the inter-temporal changes in the relative export performance are impacted by movements in the REER of India vis-à-vis those in the other three countries is investigated. In another econometric exercise, attention is confined to India's exports of readymade garments vis-à-vis the world exports of such products. An econometric model is estimated to assess the impact of domestic production and the REER on India's export performance (i.e. India's share in world exports) in readymade garments. For both sets of regressions, the autoregressive distributed lag (ARDL) model is applied. In the subsequent analysis, the impact of India's REER on export performance is examined using plant-level data. The period covered in this analysis is 2008–09 to 2014–15. The fixed effects model is used for the regression analysis. Unlike the analysis in the previous section, here the focus is on the impact of changes in the exchange rate and global demand. In addition, the impact of output growth on the export intensity of plants is examined.

The exchange rate and productivity are two important pillars of competitiveness of industries in international markets. These two aspects are taken into consideration in analysing the export performance of plants in the Indian wearing apparel industry in Sections 16.4 and 16.5, respectively. The final section presents the main findings of the study.

16.2 Analysis of Trends in Export Performance–Wearing Apparel

16.2.1 Trends in India's Exports of Readymade Garments

As mentioned above, readymade garment as a product group is one of the important items of India's exports. In 2017–18, it formed about 5.5% of India's total merchandise exports (Reserve Bank of India 2019). Other important items include engineering goods (25.9% share in total exports in 2017–18), gems and jewellery (13.7%), petroleum products (12.3%), drugs and pharmaceuticals (5.7%) and organic and inorganic chemicals (5.3%). The share of all textile products taken together (including yarn, carpets and made-up products) in India's total exports was about 11% in 2017–18, and out of this, the share of readymade garments was about 50%.

India's exports of readymade garments (in USD) grew at the trend rate of about 9.0% per annum during 1987–88 to 2004–05 (the time series is presented in Fig. 16.1 along with yearly growth rates). The year 2005 is a watershed because the Multi-Fibre Agreement (MFA) quota system was abolished (see, in this context, Ahluwalia et al. 2018). One might expect that the phasing-out of the MFA quota system would

---

2008; Cheung and Sengupta 2013; Kapur and Mohan 2014; Chinoy and Jain 2019). The need for a "realistic and competitive" exchange rate for India has been emphasised by Mohan (2019) as a requirement for attaining 8–9% annual growth rate in the Indian economy in the years ahead.

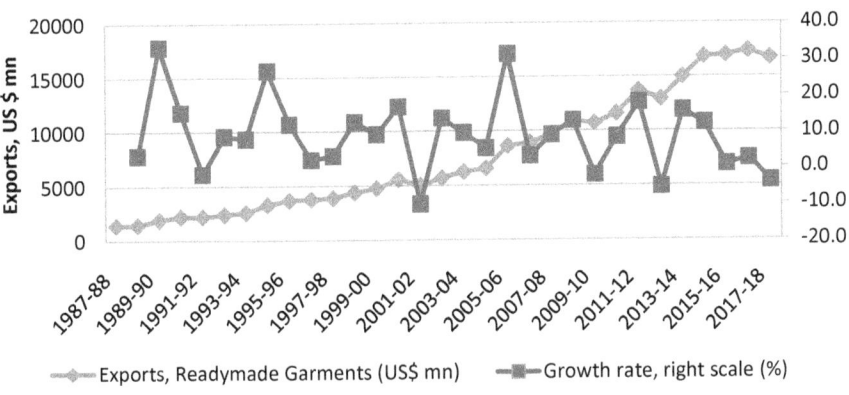

Fig. 16.1 India's exports of readymade garments. *Source* Prepared by authors based on Reserve Bank of India (2019)

have raised the growth rate of the production and exports of readymade garments in India. Indeed, India's exports of readymade garments did increase sharply, by about 31% in 2005–06 over the previous year, but exports of readymade garments in the post-2005 period did not grow faster than during the 1987–2004 period; rather, the growth was slower. The trend growth rate in India's exports of readymade garments (in USD) during 2004–05 to 2017–18 was about 7.0% per annum, lower by about two percentage points than the trend growth rate achieved during the 1987–2004 period. The share of readymade garments in India's total merchandise exports was about 12% in 1990–91, and about the same in 1994–95 (Fig. 16.2), but it fell between

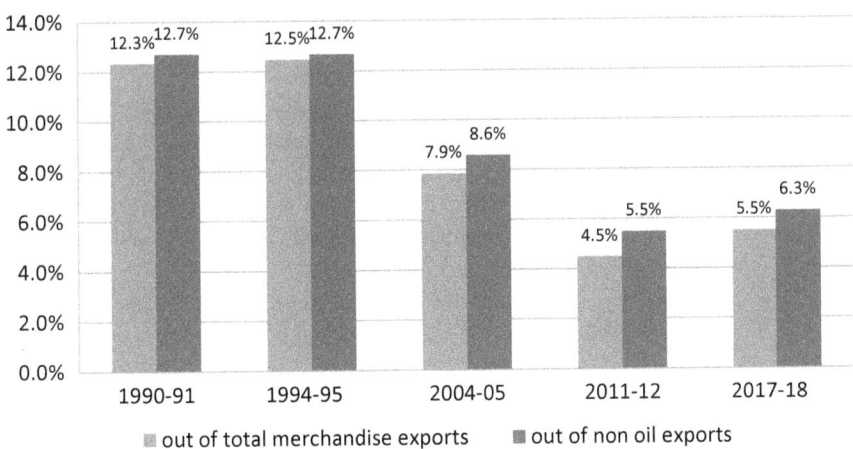

Fig. 16.2 Share of readymade garments in India's merchandise exports. *Source* Authors' computations based on Reserve Bank of India (2019)

1994–95 and 2004–05 and also between 2004–05 (about 8%) and 2011–12 (about 4.5%).

The exports of petroleum products from India increased markedly in the 2000s and later, and it would be appropriate to consider additionally the share of readymade garment exports out of non-oil exports. Even for this ratio, a clear downward trend is observed between 1994–95 and 2004–05 and also between 2004–05 and 2011–12. It is only after 2011–12 that there has been a reversal of the trend and some increase in the share of readymade garments in aggregate merchandise exports.

16.2.2 Comparative Analysis: India Compared with China, Bangladesh and Vietnam

India's share in the world exports of articles of apparel and clothing accessories was 2.3% in 1985; it rose to 3.5% in 2000 and fell to 3.2% in 2005 (Government of India 2019). The share increased again between 2005 and 2015—from 3.2 to 3.9%—and it remained at the same level in the next two years, 2016 and 2017. Although the compound annual growth rate (CAGR) of India's exports of apparel and clothing accessories was slower between 2005 and 2017 (about 6%) than that between 1990 and 2005 (about 10%), India could still raise its share in world exports because its growth rate was faster than the growth rate in world exports of articles of apparel and clothing accessories (about 4% per annum).

A comparative analysis is made between India's share in global exports of wearing apparel and that of China, Bangladesh and Vietnam, which are among the important exporters of wearing apparel from Asia. For making this comparison, we take the export data for wearing apparel (code 181 of the International Standard Industrial Classification of All Economic Activities (*ISIC*), *Revision 3*) from the World Integrated Trade Solution (WITS) database.

Figure 16.3 shows the share of the aforementioned four countries in world exports of wearing apparel. China's export share of wearing apparel is much higher than that of India, Bangladesh and Vietnam. China's share increased significantly in the period between 2001 and 2015; by comparison, the increases were much lower in the cases of India, Bangladesh and Vietnam. Comparing India with Bangladesh and Vietnam, it is found that during the 2000s and later, Vietnam's share in world exports of wearing apparel, as well as Bangladesh's share, increased faster than that of India. In the years 2014–2017, the export share of Vietnam exceeded that of India (Fig. 16.4).

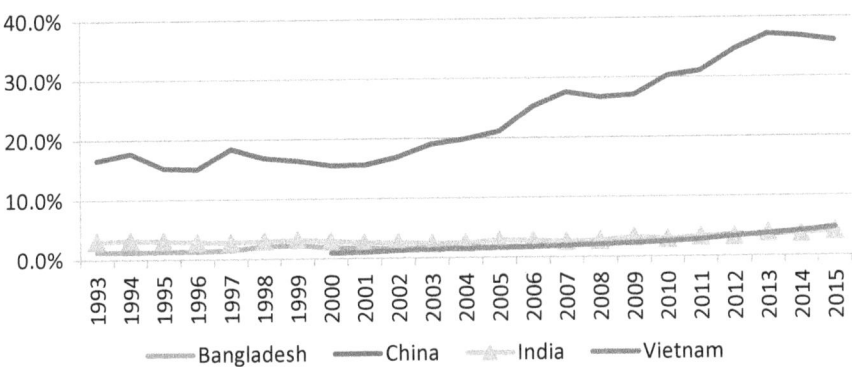

Fig. 16.3 Share in world exports of wearing apparel: Bangladesh, China, India and Vietnam. *Source*
Authors' own calculations based on data taken from the WITS database

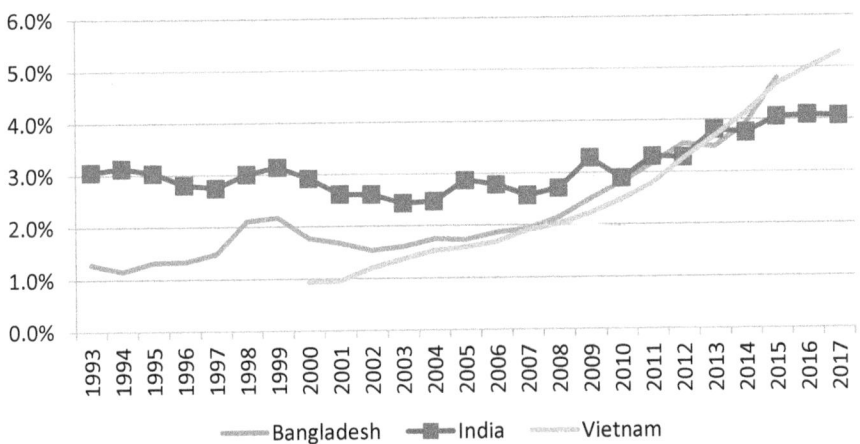

Fig. 16.4 Shares of Bangladesh, India and Vietnam in world exports of wearing apparel. *Source*
Authors' own calculations based on data taken from the WITS database

16.3 Export Intensity of Organised Sector Plants in the Wearing Apparel Industry

An examination of plant-level data on export intensity (share of products and by-
products directly exported by the plant, in terms of value) for the years 2008–09
to 2014–15 reveals concentration at two ends—zero export intensity and very high
export intensity (Table 16.1). It is interesting to observe that a little over 10% of the
factories in the wearing apparel industry are 100% export-oriented units, and about
one-fourth of the factories export in the range of 75–100%. The average export
intensity of plants in the wearing apparel industry ranges from 23 to 27%. There is
no clear upward or downward trend in average export intensity.

Table 16.1 Export intensity of organised sector plants belonging to wearing apparel industry (distribution by export intensity, %)

Export share in value of products and by-products (%)	2008–09	2009–10	2010–11	2011–12	2012–13	2013–14	2014–15
Nil	70	70	71	66	69	69	73
>0–75%	6	5	6	8	4	5	5
75–99%	11	11	10	12	16	15	11
100%	14	14	12	13	11	12	11
All	100	100	100	100	100	100	100
Average export intensity (%)	26.4	26.3	24.0	27.3	27.2	25.2	23.5

Source Authors' computations based on unit-level ASI data

16.4   Determinants of Export Intensity—Plant-Level Analysis

To investigate the important determinants of the export intensity of organised sector plants in the wearing apparel industry and, in particular, ascertain the impact of productivity, a multiple regression analysis is undertaken using plant-level panel data for the years 2008–09 to 2012–13.[9]

The explanatory variables considered for the analysis are the

1. extent of the use of imported materials input[10] (hereafter referred to as material import intensity);
2. extent of the use of purchased manufacturing services[11] (hereafter referred to as outsourced manufacturing services intensity);
3. size of the plant, measured by a dummy variable for small-size plants[12];
4. share of contract workers out of total workers employed (hereafter called contract worker intensity); and
5. location of the plant—one dummy variable representing whether the plant is located in an urban area rather than a rural area, and another dummy variable

---

[9]Estimates of the total factor productivity (TFP) of the plants have been made for the period from 1998–99 to 2012–13. Data on export intensity are available from 2008–09 onwards. Hence, the analysis is confined to the period from 2008–09 to 2012–13.

[10]The value of material input directly imported by the plants is divided by total materials used (indigenously procured and imported).

[11]The value of manufacturing services purchased is normalised by dividing it by the value of fixed capital.

[12]Considering the distribution of plant-year observations (for wearing apparel industry) in terms of the real value of fixed capital, the 25th percentile is considered, and plants with real fixed capital stock below the 25th percentile are treated as small plants. Accordingly, a dummy variable is formed and used.

representing whether it is located in a state marked by inflexible labour market regulations.[13]

In addition, a set of dummy variables for years have been included in the estimated model to allow for year-specific effects. Besides the five explanatory variables listed above, a key explanatory variable considered for the regression analysis is the level of total factor productivity (TFP) of the plants (taken in logarithms in the specified model). For estimating the TFP level of the plants in various years, the Levinsohn and Petrin (2003) method has been applied. For this purpose, a two-input Cobb–Douglas production function has been estimated from panel data. The ASI unit-level data for the years 1998–99 to 2012–13 have been used for estimating the production function and deriving the estimates of TFP. The plant-level data on real gross value-added (GVA)[14] have been taken as the measure of output; the number of persons employed as the measure of labour input; and the deflated fixed capital stock[15] as the measure of capital input. The deflated value of the energy used is taken as a proxy variable for capturing productivity shocks. Only those plants observed in the data set for at least three years during the period from 1998–99 to 2012–13 are considered in the estimation of the production function and, hence, in the estimation of TFP. The number of observations used for the estimation of production function and, hence, TFP is reduced further because all the observations in which the ratios of GVA to fixed capital and GVA to labour input are too high or too low (based on the 2nd and 98th percentile) have been removed.

The estimated regression equations are presented in Table 16.2. The share of exports in production (export intensity) is the dependent variable. Since the share is zero in a very high proportion of the observations (about 70%), and in about 10% of the observations export intensity is 100%, a Tobit model is appropriate to use. Because a panel data set is used for the regression analysis, the panel Tobit model has been applied, allowing for random effects.

The first two regressions (Table 16.2) differ in regard to the inclusion of the TFP variable. In the first regression, it is included. In the second regression, it is dropped to find out if the coefficients of other explanatory variables change much with the exclusion of the TFP variable. Since TFP estimation has been done only for a subset of observations as explained above, the total number of observations used for model estimation in regression 2 is much higher than that in regression 1. The third regression is similar to the first regression, except that the year dummies have

---

[13]The dummy variables for plants located in states with inflexible labour market regulations have been formed using the list of states with flexible, inflexible and neutral labour market regulations provided in and used by Ahluwalia et al. (2018).

[14]The gross value-added (GVA) has been deflated by the wholesale price index (WPI) for wearing apparel.

[15]A blanket deflation procedure has been used for deriving the estimates of fixed capital stock at constant prices rather than using the perpetual inventory method, which would have been more appropriate. The ASI-reported data on fixed capital stock (net fixed assets, closing figure for the year) for various plant-year observations have been deflated by the implicit deflator for gross fixed capital formation for manufacturing obtained from the *National Accounts Statistics*.

Table 16.2 Determinants of export intensity, organised sector plants in wearing apparel industry, panel Tobit model (random effects)

Explanatory variables	Regression 1	Regression 2	Regression 3
ln(TFP)	7.9 (1.99)**		8.0 (2.02)**
Small plant size (dummy)	−96.7 (−12.19)***	−71.6 (−10.14)***	−96.7 (−12.19)***
Located in urban area (dummy)	34.1 (4.05)***	29.7 (4.06)***	34.0 (4.04)***
Located in a state with inflexible labour market regulations (dummy)	−9.3 (−0.82)	−22.0 (−2.54)**	−9.2 (−0.81)
Manufacturing services purchased/capital stock	17.5 (9.05)***	14.2 (10.47)***	17.4 (9.01)***
Imported material input intensity	100.1 (4.10)***	125.3 (5.59)***	99.0 (4.05)***
Contract worker intensity	43.4 (4.87)***	47.8 (6.10)***	43.8 (4.90)***
Time trend			3.0 (1.75)*
Year dummies	Yes	Yes	No
Number of observations	5100	8368	5100
Log-likelihood	−9858.3	−15,236.3	−9863.5
Wald chi-square and P-value	277.0 (0.00)	268.2 (0.00)	269.6 (0.00)

Source Authors' computations based on unit-level ASI data

Note t-values in parentheses. *, ** and *** statistically significant at 10%, 5% and 1% level, respectively

Dependent variable: share of exports in value of products and by-products (%)

been dropped and instead a time trend variable has been included. The purpose is to find out if this makes a major difference to the results.

It is seen from the regression results (Table 16.2) that imported material input intensity and TFP have positive and statistically significant coefficients. In other words, these explanatory variables bear a positive relationship with the export intensity of plants in the wearing apparel industry. These results are in line with the findings of several earlier studies on Indian manufacturing. A positive effect of TFP on export intensity, for instance, has been found for Indian manufacturing in Goldar et al. (2018). A positive effect of imported material intensity on export intensity has been found for Indian manufacturing in Goldar (2013) and Goldar et al. (2018). The coefficient of the small plant size dummy variable is negative and statistically significant. This indicates that a plant of relatively small size in the wearing apparel industry has a disadvantage in exporting their products as compared to a large plant.

For the contract worker intensity variable and the outsourced manufacturing services variable, a significant positive relationship with export intensity is found. These results are along the expected lines. The interpretation of these empirical findings is that, other things remaining the same, a plant that makes more extensive use of subcontracting of manufacturing activity, or makes relatively greater use of contract labour within the plant (or both), enjoys relatively higher competitiveness in selling its products in international markets.

As regards the impact of labour market regulations, the results are not strong. When the TFP variable is included in the model, the dummy for labour market inflexibility has a negative coefficient but not statistically significant. When the TFP variable is dropped from the equation, the coefficients of other explanatory variables do not change much except in the case of the labour market rigidity dummy variable whose coefficient goes up in (absolute) numerical value and turns negative and statistically significant. This finding is indicative of a negative effect of labour market rigidity on export performance of organised sector plants of wearing apparel industry.

16.5 Impact of REER on India's Export Performance in Wearing Apparel

16.5.1 Analysis Based on Time Series Data on Aggregate Level of Wearing Apparel Exports

To examine the impact of the REER on the exports of wearing apparel from India, the ARDL model has been applied to estimate the following equation:

$$\ln(\text{rel\_export}_t) = \alpha + \beta_1 \ln(\text{rel\_REER}_t) + \beta_2 T + \varepsilon_t \qquad (16.1)$$

where $\ln(\text{rel\_export}_t)$ is the natural logarithm of India's exports of wearing apparel[16] to that of a competitor (China, Bangladesh and Vietnam are alternatively considered), rel_REER$_t$ is the ratio of India's REER[17] to that of her competitor (China, Bangladesh and Vietnam are alternatively considered) and T denotes the time trend. The long-run coefficients in the ARDL estimates are shown in Table 16.3.

In Models 2 and 3, the coefficient of ln(REER) is negative, and it is statistically significant in the case of Model 2, which compares India with China. Based on these results, it may be inferred that a depreciation of India's REER leads to an increase in export of wearing apparel from India. In Model 1 (which compares India with Bangladesh), by contrast, the coefficient ln(REER) is positive, which is not an expected result. There are perhaps some factors other than those considered in the model which had a major impact on growth in wearing apparel exports from Bangladesh. These factors have probably impacted the ratio of India's export of

---

[16]Data on exports (in US$) have been taken from the WITS database (https://wits.worldbank.org/about_wits.html).

[17]Data on the REER (base 2007 = 100) have been taken from a data set on REER published by Bruegel (https://bruegel.org/publications/datasets/real-effective-exchange-rates-for-178-countries-a-new-database/). For details, see Darvas (2012a, b).

Table 16.3 Long-run coefficients of ARDL model

Variables	Model 1 ARDL (1, 2): dependent variable ln(exports of wearing apparel in India/Bangladesh)	Model 2 ARDL (3, 3): dependent variable ln(exports of wearing apparel in India/China)	Model 3 ARDL (2, 0): dependent variable ln(exports of wearing apparel in India/Vietnam)
ln(REER)@	0.5839 (0.4694)	−2.8451*** (0.3648)	−0.2656 (0.3249)
Time trend	−0.0498*** (0.0085)	−0.0244*** (0.0025)	−0.0685*** (0.0049)
Constant	0.9959*** (0.1794)	−1.9816*** (0.0655)	0.8683*** (0.0572)
Number of observations included	21	22	16
Time period	1993–2015	1993–2017	2000–2017
F	4.4694*	18.6558***	9.7733**
ECM	−0.6601*** (0.1240)	−1.2666*** (0.2872)	−1.1211*** (0.2905)

Source Authors' own calculations

Note Standard errors in parentheses; ***, ** and * denote, respectively, the 1%, 5% and 10% level of significance

In all models, optimal lag selection is based on AIC.

@ In model 1, the REER is the ratio of REER of India over REER of Bangladesh

In model 2, the REER is the ratio of REER of India over REER of China

In model 3, REER is the ratio of REER of India over REER of Vietnam

wearing apparel to that of Bangladesh, resulting in an incorrectly signed coefficient of the relative REER. The coefficient of the time trend is negative and significant in all models, which implies that some factors have caused India's export of wearing apparel to grow slower than that of China, Bangladesh and Vietnam leading to a decline in the relative exports over the years. The F-statistics is statistically significant in all the three models, and this fact confirms the long-run relation between the relative REER and the relative exports of wearing apparel—exports from India divided by that from the other three countries considered.

To pursue further the analysis of impact of exchange rate on India's exports of readymade garments, the export determination model has been specified as follows:

$$EXP_I = f(EXP_W, REER_I, REER_C, Q_I, T) \tag{16.2a}$$

India's exports of readymade garments (EXP_I) are taken as a function of the world exports of readymade garments (EXP_W), capturing the effect of growth in income in importing countries, REER of India ($REER_I$) and that of its important competitors ($REER_C$), domestic production of readymade garments in India (Q_I) capturing the supply-side effect, and a time variable (T) representing other factors that have changed with time. For the purpose of estimation, Eq. (16.2a) is transformed and the following equation estimated:

Table 16.4 Long-run coefficients of ARDL estimate

Variables	ARDL (1, 2, 1): dependent variable ln(export of wearing apparel, India/World)
ln(R_REER)	−0.974** (0.370)
ln(domestic production)	0.293 (0.179)
Time trend	0.005 (0.016)
Constant	−14.91*** (2.38)
ECM (−1)	−0.635 (0.150)***
Number of observations	22
Time period	1993–94 to 2016–17
F-statistic	7.25
W-statistic	21.78

Source Authors' own calculations
Note Standard errors in parentheses; *** and ** denote, respectively, 1% and 5% level of statistical significance. Optimal lag selection is based on AIC
R_REER is the ratio of India's REER to the average REER of her important competitors from Asia

$$\ln\left(\left[\frac{EXP_I}{EXP_W}\right]_t\right) = \alpha + \beta_1 \ln(R\_REER_t) +_2 \ln(Q_t) + \beta_3 T + \varepsilon_t \qquad (16.2b)$$

In this equation, $[EXP_I/EXP_W]_t$ denotes the ratio of India's exports of readymade garments to the world exports of wearing apparel in year t,[18] R_REER_t denotes the ratio of India's REER to the average REER of its important competitors from Asia in year t,[19] and Q_t denotes the value of output of India's wearing apparel industry at constant prices in year t.[20] The equation contains a trend term denoted by T. Equation (16.2b) has been estimated by using the time series data from 1993–94 to 2016–17. The ARDL model has been applied. From the estimates of long-run coefficients (Table 16.4), it may be seen that the relative REER variable has a negative and statistically significant coefficient. This indicates that India's REER (relative to competitors) has a negative effect on exports—an appreciation in the exchange rate

---

[18]Data on India's exports of readymade garments have been taken from the *Handbook of Statistics on Indian Economy*, Reserve Bank of India, and data on world exports on wearing apparel have been taken from the WITS database. It should be pointed out that while data on India's exports are presented for the financial year (April–March) the data on world exports are presented for the calendar year.

[19]The REER index with base 2007 (= 100)—the previously mentioned data set on REER published by Bruegel—is used. India's REER has been divided by a weighted average of the REER indices for Bangladesh, Cambodia, China, Hong Kong, Indonesia, Malaysia, Pakistan, Sri Lanka, Thailand and Vietnam to get a measure of R_REER. The weights are the exports of clothing from these countries during 2012 to 2017.

[20]The series on value of output of wearing apparel industry (Code 18 of NIC 1998/2004) has been taken from the database prepared by the Economic and Political Weekly Research Foundation (EPWRF) using ASI data. It should be noted that production data relate only to the organised segment of the industry whereas data on exports cover both the organised and unorganised segments.

tends to lower the exports of wearing apparel. A positive long-run coefficient is found for the domestic production variable. The t-value is 1.64, and if the one-sided test is applied, which seems logical and justified, the coefficient is found to be statistically significant at the 10% level. It may be inferred, therefore, that an improvement in the growth rate of the domestic production of the wearing apparel industry will increase the growth in the exports of the industry's products.

The error correction term is negative and statistically significant. Since the coefficient is -0.635, it follows that about 64% adjustment takes place in the first year. The long-term equilibrium is reached shortly. The F-statistic and W-statistic are higher than the estimated bounds, which shows the existence of co-integration, and it be may be inferred accordingly that there exists a long-run relation among the variables.

16.5.2 Analysis Based on Plant-Level Data on Export Intensity

The analysis of the impact of REER on export performance based on plant-level data uses the following model:

$$(XI_{it}) = \alpha + \beta_1(REER_{t-1}) + \beta_2(REER\_vol)_{t-1} +_3 \ln(Q_{it}) + \beta_4 \ln(WX_t) + \varepsilon_{it}$$
$$(16.3)$$

In this equation, XI_{it} is the export intensity (export share in production, in %) of plant i in year t, and ΔXI_{it} is the change in export intensity in plant i between years $t - 1$ and t. $\Delta \ln(Q_{it})$ is the growth rate in real value of output in plant i in year t over the previous year. $\Delta \ln(WX_t)$ is the growth rate in world exports of wearing apparel in year t over the previous year. $\Delta(REER_{t-1})$ is the change in REER between years $t - 2$ and $t - 1$. $REER\_vol_{t-1}$ denoted volatility in REER in the year $t - 1$. Note that while the change in plant-level export intensity and growth in world exports are considered for the current year (over the previous year), the change in REER and the extent of volatility in REER are taken with one-year lag.

The model in Eq. (16.3) above is similar to the model used by Cheung and Sengupta (2013). They use firm-level panel data for the non-financial sector firms in India from the Prowess database of the Centre for Monitoring Indian Economy (CMIE); data for the period from 2000 to 2010 are taken. They confine their analysis to exporting firms. In the model estimated by them, they take the change in export intensity as the dependent variable and the change in the REER as one of the explanatory variables. Other explanatory variables considered are the exchange rate volatility and the change in the level of foreign income, which is computed as the trade-share-weighted average income of India's top five trading partners. They also consider some firm characteristics as explanatory variables. In the model adopted for this analysis, the basic structure is similar to that in Cheung and Sengupta (2013), but the change in the REER and the extent of volatility in the REER have been included in this model with one-year lag.

Equation (16.3) is estimated using the fixed effects model. Data on export intensity have been obtained from ASI unit-level data. Data for the years 2008–09 to 2014–15 have been used. The change in the REER for each year is computed by using the 36-currency index of the REER (base 2004–05 = 100) prepared by the Reserve Bank of India using trade weights (Reserve Bank of India 2019). The REER series is for financial years, and hence it is more appropriate to use with the export intensity data reported in ASI.

For getting a measure of volatility in REER, the monthly series on the trade-weighted REER of the Reserve Bank of India (RBI) has been used. Following Cheung and Sengupta (2013), the volatility in REER is measured by the standard deviation of monthly REER indices in a (financial) year. Data on the value of output at plant-level have been taken from ASI unit-level data. These have been deflated appropriately. Data on world exports of wearing apparel (which are in calendar year) have been taken from the WITS database.

The regression results are reported in Table 16.5. The results clearly indicate a positive effect of global demand on exports of wearing apparel from Indian organised sector plants. The coefficient of the world export variable is found to be positive and statistically significant. The results also show a positive effect of output growth in

Table 16.5 Explaining change in plant-level export intensity, organised sector plants in wearing apparel industry, fixed effects model

Explanatory variables	Regression 1	Regression 2	Regression 3	Regression 1a
Change in REER ($t - 1$)	−0.442 (−2.20)**	−0.491 (−2.46)**	0.481 (−2.51)**	−0.594 (−2.15)**
Volatility in REER ($t - 1$)	−0.374 (−0.45)	−0.268 (−0.33)		−0.591 (−0.51)
Growth rate in world exports of wearing apparel	49.6 (4.07)***	47.3 (3.16)***	52.8 (3.90)***	67.6 (3.23)***
Growth in real value of output in the plant	4.50 (4.07)***		4.48 (4.06)***	7.42 (4.28)***
Number of observations	6525	6678	6525	4350
R-squared	0.01	0.002	0.01	0.017
F-statistic and P-value	7.84 (0.000)	4.5 (0.004)	10.4 (0.000)	8.29 (0.000)

Source Authors' computations

Note t-values in parentheses. Robust standard errors, corrected for plant-level clustering. Regression-1a excludes plants for which reported export intensity is zero for all observations during 2008–09 to 2014–15. ** and *** statistically significant at 5% and 1% level, respectively

Dependent variable: change in the share of exports in value of products and by-products (in percentage points)

the plants on their export intensity. In this case, again, the coefficient is positive and statistically significant.

The coefficient of change in the REER is negative and statistically significant. This is in agreement with the findings of Cheung and Sengupta (2013). Also, this is broadly consistent with the findings from the analysis presented in the previous section. The coefficient of the variable representing the extent of volatility in REER is negative, as would be expected, but it is not found to be statistically significant. In the estimates made by Cheung and Sengupta (2013) using data on non-financial sector firms in India, the coefficient of volatility was found to be negative and statistically significant. However, when they made separate estimates for exports of goods and exports of services, the coefficient of volatility in the case of exports of goods was found to be negative and statistically insignificant. Thus, the empirical results obtained in this study in respect to the variable representing the volatility of the REER are similar to that in Cheung and Sengupta (2013).

16.6 Conclusions

To boost the growth rate of the manufacturing sector in India in the years ahead and, thereby, step up the growth rate of the Indian economy, a major focus has to be on the labour-intensive export-oriented industries. One such industry, the wearing apparel industry, was taken up for study in this paper. Wearing apparel is an important item of India's exports, and it has good employment-generation potential. The focus of the analysis was on export performance and what factors impacted export performance. Most of the analysis presented in the paper was based on the plant-level data of the ASI. The analysis was, thus, confined to the organised or formal segment of India's wearing apparel industry. In addition, some analyses based on aggregate-level series data on wearing apparel exports were undertaken.

The study finds that the export intensity of plants in the organised sector of India's wearing apparel industry is positively impacted by plant size, use of imported materials, purchase of manufacturing services from other plants (outsourcing) and the use of a relatively higher proportion of contract workers. Total factor productivity (TFP) has a significant positive effect on the export intensity of wearing apparel plants. Wearing apparel plants located in urban areas have an advantage in selling their products in international markets. There is some indication that labour market rigidities tend to lower the export intensity of wearing apparel plants in India.

The empirical evidence indicates that faster growth in the global exports of wearing apparel, reflecting faster growth in global demand, has a positive effect on the export performance of India's wearing apparel industry. Also, the analysis at both industry and plant level shows that growth in the domestic industry positively affects export performance. It may thus be inferred that the policies which promote the growth of the wearing apparel industry—and this is, perhaps, true also for other domestic labour-intensive export-oriented industries—say, through infrastructure development, will automatically boost the industry's exports growth.

Another important finding that emerges from the analysis is that an appreciation in the exchange rate has a negative effect on the exports of wearing apparel from India and, conversely, a depreciation in the exchange rate has a positive effect. This finding has important implications for exchange rate policy. Some scholars and researchers emphasise the need for a "realistic and competitive" exchange rate for India to enhance its competitiveness in global markets, as it will augment growth in the manufacturing sector. The evidence presented in this chapter supports that view. Several studies have looked into the impact of the exchange rate on India's exports at the aggregate level (e.g. Veeramani 2008), and the micro-evidence on this issue in the Indian context is virtually non-existent. To the knowledge of the present authors, Cheung and Sengupta (2013) is perhaps the only study available where the impact of exchange rate on exports has been analysed using micro-level data. Their analysis was at the firm-level; the present study has taken a step further and explored the issue at the factory level. There is need for more such micro-level research into India's labour-intensive export-oriented industries.

References

Ahluwalia, R., Hasan, R., Kapoor, M., & Panagariya, A. (2018). *The impact of labor regulations on jobs and wages in India: Evidence from a natural experiment* (Working Paper No. 2018-02). Deepak and Neera Raj Center on Indian Economic Policies, School of International and Public Affairs, Columbia University.

Bhanumurthy, N. R., & Sharma, C. (2013). *Does weak rupee matter for India's manufacturing exports?* (Working Paper No. 2013-115). New Delhi: National Institute of Public Finance and Policy.

Cheung, Y.-W., & Sengupta, R. (2013). Impact of exchange rate movements on exports: An analysis of Indian non-financial sector firms. *Journal of International Money and Finance, 39,* 231–245.

Chinoy, S. Z., & Jain, T. (2019). What drives India's exports and what explains the recent slowdown? New evidence and policy implications. In S. Shah, B. Bosworth, & K. Muralidharan (Eds.), *India policy forum 2018* (Vol. 15). National Council of Applied Economic Research. New Delhi: Sage.

Darvas, Z. (2012a). *Real effective exchange rates for 178 countries: A new database* (Working Paper 2012/06). Bruegel.

Darvas, Z. (2012b). *Compositional effects on productivity, labour cost and export adjustment* (Policy Contribution 2012/11). Bruegel.

Export-Import Bank of India. (2016). *Inter-linkages between exports and employment in India* (Occasional Paper No. 179). Export-Import Bank of India.

Ghose, A. K. (2015). *India needs rapid manufacturing-led growth* (Working Paper No. WP 01/2015). New Delhi: Institute for Human Development.

Ghose, A. K. (2016). *India employment report 2016: Challenges and the imperative of manufacturing-led growth.* New Delhi: Institute for Human Development, Oxford University Press.

Goldar, B. (2013). Determinants of import intensity of India's manufactured exports under the new policy regime. *Indian Economic Review, 48*(1), 221–237.

Goldar, B., Das, D. K., Sengupta, S., & Das, P. C. (2017). *Domestic value addition and foreign content: An analysis of India's exports from 1995 to 2011* (Working Paper No. 332). New Delhi: Indian Council for Research on International Economic Relations.

Goldar, B., Banga, R., & Banga, K. (2018). India's linkages into global value chains: The role of imported services. In S. Shah, B. Bosworth, & K. Muralidharan (Eds.), *India policy forum 2017–18* (Vol. 14). National Council of Applied Economic Research. New Delhi: Sage.

Government of India. (2019). *Economic survey 2018–19*. Ministry of Finance, Government of India.

Kapur, M., & Mohan, R. (2014). *India's recent macroeconomic performance: An assessment and way forward* (IMF Working Paper No. WP/14/68). Washington, DC: International Monetary Fund.

Levinsohn, J., & Petrin, A. (2003). Estimating production functions using inputs to control for unobservables. *The Review of Economic Studies, 70*(2), 317–341.

Mitra, A. (2015). Manufacturing-led growth, competition and challenges. *Yojana, 59,* 13–16.

Mohan, R. (2019). *Moving India to a new growth trajectory: Need for a comprehensive big push* (Brookings India Research Paper No. 072019).

Reserve Bank of India. (2019). *Handbook of statistics on the Indian economy, 2018–19*. Reserve Bank of India.

Veeramani, C. (2008). Impact of exchange rate appreciation on India's exports. *Economic and Political Weekly, 43*(22), 10–14.

Veeramani, C., & Dhir, G. (2016). India's exports of unskilled labour intensive products: A comparative analysis. In C. Veeramani & R. Nagaraj (Eds.), *International trade and industrial development in India: Emerging trends, patterns and issues*. Hyderabad: Orient Blackswan.

Veeramani, C., & Dhir, G. (2017). Make what in India? In S. Mahendra Dev (Ed.), *India development report 2017*. New Delhi: Oxford University Press.

Chapter 17
Import Content, Value-Added and Employment Generation: An Input–Output-Based Analysis of India's Exports

Devender Pratap and Shibananda Nayak

17.1 Introduction

Since 1991, India's economic integration with the global economy has significantly increased its dependence on the rest of the world, and this increasing dependence could well be viewed in terms of the rising share of international trade of goods and services in its gross domestic product (GDP).

India's merchandise trade increased from USD 95.1 billion in 2000–01 to USD 795.3 billion in 2011–12, and then to USD 844.1 billion in 2018–19. India's share in world merchandise exports increased from 0.8% in 2003 to 1.7% in 2017, and the share of merchandise imports increased from 0.9 to 2.5% during the same period (WTO 2019). Merchandise trade increased from 20.3% of GDP in 2000–01 to 31.0% in 2018–19, and merchandise exports rose from 9.5% of GDP to 12.1%.

The global fragmentation of production has raised the trade in intermediate goods in the manufacturing sector, which necessitates an evaluation of the extent of import intensity—the degree of value addition of an imported item that is subsequently exported—and domestic value addition in the output and exports of specific countries, and of global participation in joint production sharing. In the context of developing countries, it is imperative to assess the extent of domestic value addition in exports, and in turn, the extent of employment generated by domestic manufacturing activity.

This chapter is an abridged and revised version of the report '*Estimating Import Intensity, Domestic Value-Addition and Employment*' submitted to the Centre for WTO Studies, Indian Institute of Foreign Trade, New Delhi. The authors express their gratitude to Professor Abhijit Das, Centre for WTO Studies, New Delhi for his critical comments.

D. Pratap (✉)
National Council of Applied Economic Research, New Delhi, India
e-mail: dpratap@ncaer.org

S. Nayak
MSME, Government of India, Vikas Sadan, Cuttack, India
e-mail: Shibananda.nayak@gmail.com

© The Author(s), under exclusive license to Springer Nature Singapore Pte Ltd. 2021
S. Bathla and E. Kannan (eds.), *Agro and Food Processing Industry in India*, India Studies in Business and Economics, https://doi.org/10.1007/978-981-15-9468-7_17

The literature shows that trade reforms have a positive relationship with industrial growth (Neogi and Ghosh 1998). The import inflows used as intermediate goods in the production process or as final consumption goods significantly affect productive capacity. A large part of imports used as intermediate inputs for industrial output bears a critical link to the economy. In India, non-oil imports—particularly in the form of capital goods, raw materials and intermediate goods—could certainly be viewed as complementary to industrial production.

Sathe (1997) assesses, in a different context, whether a rise in the imported raw material leads to an equivalent rise in exports and argues that imports are required mainly for domestic consumption and production; only a small fraction of imports that enter production is intended for export. If the import intensity of exports is very high, the balance-of-trade problem will continue to afflict the economy—even if exports grow at a phenomenally high rate. However, such relationships are country-specific and require probing.

The Indian economy is increasingly becoming dependent on exports and imports. Is its increasing import dependence critical for India's exports? How much of its imports translates into exports? One approach to gauge the effect of imports could be evaluating the import intensity of exports. Gems and jewellery constitute an example of export products that have high import intensity.

A brief review of studies conducted on the import intensity of India's exports reveals the importance of imports as intermediate inputs to the producing sector. The firm-level analysis of the top 100 importing companies shows that they accounted for about 50% of the manufacturing exports in the late 1990s, which increased to 80% in 2008. The import intensity of these firms, defined as share imports in sales, almost doubled between 1999 and 2008 (RBI 2010). The import intensity rose in many sectors in the late 1970s and mid-1980s (Pitre 1981; Bhattacharyya 1989; Siddharthan 1989; Mani 1991; Singh 1994). The Export Import Bank of India (1991) showed that the index of import intensity of exports by the manufacturing sector increased from 21.2% in 1980–81 to 41.7% in 1988–89; it declined marginally to 38% in 1989–90 and continued declining till the early 1990s (10.10–11.45%). The import intensity of exports improved after the mid-1990s (Sathe 1997; Burange 2001).

Sarma (1990) estimated the relationship between export performance and imported raw material requirement in an input-output (I-O) framework and found a high value of rank correlation coefficient at 0.94 in 1983–87. The import intensity of exports increased at different times (Bhat et al. 2007; Bhat and Paul 2009; Sengupta and Das 2011), due to an increase in non-traditional exports (Sathe 1995). Imports have a unidirectional impact on industrial output (RBI 2010) and positively affect industrial output and manufacturing output. These studies point to the relevance of export-linked import liberalisation in India.

The total direct and indirect import requirements are known as the 'import content of exports' (ICE) or 'embodied imports' (OECD 2012; Loschky and Ritter 2006). The literature shows that the import intensity of India's exports rose at the aggregate level, but there is no disaggregated analysis of the import intensity of exports or ICE. India's exports, which increasingly embody imported intermediate inputs, tend to boost domestic output and contribute value-added (income) and employment at the aggregate and disaggregate levels.

This chapter aims to fill this gap based on an I-O analysis. Methodologically, in a slight departure from the existing literature, this chapter examines the direct and indirect contributions of imports per unit of final demand in general and exports in particular. The changes in the import intensity of exports evaluated at both domestically supplied inputs and those of sourced by imports are assessed with the help of I-O based analysis in the Indian context. The multiplier index is computed with the help of the Leontief inverse matrix, which enumerates the total direct and indirect requirement in the economy, and is based on domestic intermediate flows only.

17.2 Database and Methodology

This chapter uses I-O transaction tables published by the Central Statistical Office (CSO), Government of India (GoI), for the years 1998–99, 2003–04, 2006–07 and 2007–08. Other data required are employment or workforce numbers that use the unit-level data given in the National Sample Survey (NSS) employment and unemployment surveys for three different rounds—55th (1999–2000), 61st (2004–05) and 66th rounds (2009–10).

The employment estimates are extracted at five-digit level and then re-estimated at three points of time, each corresponding to the years of estimation of the I-O tables. The employment numbers are mapped with the I-O table with a well-defined mapping scheme. The 55th round of NSS uses the National Industrial Classification (NIC)-1998; the other two rounds are based on the NIC 2004. The mapping scheme between these two classifications is prepared.

In the case of employment, labour input or number of jobs generated criteria are used. The concept is based on adding multiple workers into the NSS definition of usual status workers (usual principal status (UPS) and usual subsidiary status (USS)). The methodology for estimating the workforce during the 55th and 61st rounds is explained in Kolli et al. (2008). We use the labour input (numbers) from NSS 55th round for extrapolating the employment numbers for 1998–99; for extrapolating the employment numbers for 2003–04, we use the labour input (numbers) from NSS 61st round.

The employment figures extracted at the five-digit level are calibrated to match the economy-wide published numbers. Mapped with the 115 or 130 sectors of the I-O table, these numbers provide us the direct employment headcount per unit of gross value of output (in hundred thousand rupees (INR)). The estimates are based on the NSS employment status (UPS + USS) data, along with the multiple workers, which become number of jobs. There is a considerable time lag for which I-O data are available in the public domain; the reporting lag in the case of the present I-O table (2007–08) is five years.

The structure of Input–output (IO) models consisting of n sector economy is explained here. The material balance of the economy in terms of intermediate and final uses could be explained as follows.

$$X_i = \sum_j X_{ij} + F_i i, \quad j = 1, 2, 3, \dots n$$

where,

X_i is the total output of ith sector

X_{ij} is the output of ith sector consumed in jth sector

F_i is the total final demand for ith sector consisting of Private consumption, Government consumption, gross fixed capital formation, change in stocks, and net exports (exports less imports).

Where $\sum_j X$ and F_i are total intermediate and final demand of the total output of sector i, respectively. In other words, output of ith sector is equal to the total output consumed by other sectors including the sector itself and different components of final demand. This could further be explained in terms of coefficients which are as follows.

$$X_{ij} = a_{ij} X_j$$

where, a_{ij} is the output of sector i used as input by sector j for producing one unit of output. The a_{ij} are also called as structural or technical coefficients which explain sectoral interdependence in the economy. The above balance equation could be explained as follows.

$$X_i = a_{ij} * X_j + F_i$$

The equation could further be explained in matrix form.

$$(I - A)X = F$$

where A is coefficient matrix of input coefficients a_{ij}; I is the identity matrix where diagonal elements are equal to unity and off diagonal elements are equal to zero. X and F are vectors of total output and final demand. The input coefficients matrix (a_{ij}) gives the direct input requirement of the ith sector for producing one unit of output of jth sector. Hence, with the help of IO model, we can estimate the direct and indirect requirements of producing an additional unit of a sector. The equation could further be manipulated as follows.

$$X = (I - A)^{-1} F$$

$$X = R * F$$

where $R = [r_{ij}]$ is called Leontief inverse or multiplier. Each coefficient of r_{ij} shows direct and indirect amount of ith input required one unit of final demand in sector j.

In the present paper, the concept of total linkages is further analysed by distinguishing the intermediate inputs X_{ij} into domestically supplied and imported intermediates in the I-O framework.

$$X_i = \sum_j (X_d + X_m)_{ij} = F_i i = i, j = 1, 2, 3, \ldots n$$

$$A_d = X_{d_{ij}}/X_j$$

$$A_m = X_{m_{ij}}/X_j$$

where,

X_{ij} is the output of ith sector consumed in jth sector

$X_{d_{ij}}$ is the domestically supplied ith input used in one unit production of jth sector

$X_{m_{ij}}$ is the imported ith input used in one unit production of jth sector

A_d is the technical coefficient matrix for domestically supplied inputs

A_m is the technical coefficient matrix for imported inputs

Distinguishing the intermediate inputs X_{ij} into domestically supplied or sourced from imports would help identifying direct and indirect multipliers accruing due to domestic supply or from import demand. This has further been used in computing ICE and other related concepts in the present paper.

17.2.1 Import Content of Exports (ICE)

Assuming that all the goods produced by an industry are homogenous, we can calculate the total imports embodied directly and indirectly within exports as follows.

$$\text{ICE} = \left[M * (I - A_d)^{-1} * X \right]/E$$

M is a $i * n$ matrix Mj (the ratio of imports to output in industry, j)

$(I - A_d)^{-1}$ is the Leontief inverse matrix $(n * n)$

X is a $x * 1$ vector of exports

E is $\sum_i^n X_i$, gross value of exports.

17.2.2 Contribution of Domestic Value-Added in Exports (DVA-Exports)

Similarly, we can estimate the total indirect and direct contribution of exports to value-added by replacing the import vector M above with an equivalent vector that shows the ratio of value-added to output (V).

$$\text{DVA} - \text{Exports} = \left[V * (I - A_d)^{-1} * X\right]/E$$

where V is a $1 * n$ vector with components Vj (the ratio of value-added to output in industry j) and other notations are the same as in the import content formula.

17.2.3 Employment Multiplier of Exports (EMP-Exports)

We calculate the direct and indirect contribution of exports in generating employment:

$$\text{EMP} - \text{Exports} = \left[L * (I - A_d)^{-1} * X\right]/E$$

where L is ratio of labour input to gross value of output in each sector and other notations are the same as in the import content formula.

The methodological superiority of this kind of analysis is manifold. The multiplier or total (direct and indirect) linkage analysis, which is based on both backward and forward linkages, and how much of those are attributed to domestic production, are the most essential uses. These further depend on the specific objectives of the research. The I-O analysis enables an understanding of the import intensity of domestic production.

This chapter analyses the ICE for a specific component of final use, i.e. exports. The direct requirement for imports into intermediate outputs is multiplied with a direct and indirect requirement matrix, which is a Leontief inverse matrix computed for domestic coefficients. The employment and value-added contribution of exports are computed; the analysis computes the import dependency of India's economy and estimates the contribution of exports to value-added and employment.

The intermediate and final use flows are not distinguished into domestic and imported inputs. That is a major computational difficulty in I-O analysis. In the standard United Nations (UN) convention, country I-O tables are presented in the form of supply and use tables, where the imports column appears in the outer orbit of final use. The I-O table (2006–07) for India is presented in this format (Kolli and Sharma 2011). That could, in a way, help us benchmark the table to the National Accounts Statistics (NAS).

The two core I-O matrices—available in the form of absorption and make matrices—could be used for constructing a symmetric table on uniform basis (commodity × commodity basis). We arrive at the import flow matrix—also available at commodity × commodity basis—by apportioning the total import column pro rata, and we exclude 'exports' and 'change in stock' from the final use.

We distinguish between intermediate and final use flows by domestic and imported content at the sectoral level and balance the I-O table. Then, we estimate the import intensity of exports, or ICE—i.e. direct and indirect imports embodied in the domestic production per unit of final demand.

17.3 Empirical Results

17.3.1 Import Content of Exports (ICE)

Table 17.1 presents the ICE for the aggregate economy. It improved from 13.1% in 1998–99 to 13.6 in 2003–04 to 20% in 2006–07 and to 21.5% in 2007–08. That points to the rising import dependence of the services and manufacturing sectors. In the case of the manufacturing sector, the ICE fell from 15.2% in 1998–99 to 13.6% in 2003–04 and jumped to 26.3% in 2006–07 and to 29.2% in 2007–08. In the services sector, the ICE fell from 9.2% in 1998–99 to 6.8% in 2003–04 before rising to 8.7% in 2006–07 and to 13.3% in 2007–08 (Fig. 17.1).

We analyse the ICE by sector and find that it grew over time. In 2006–07, the ICE was high in the major manufacturing sectors—ships and boats, aircrafts and spacecraft, petroleum products, fertilisers, electrical wires and cables, non-ferrous basic metals, gems and jewellery, organic heavy chemicals, synthetic fibres and resin, miscellaneous metal products, iron and steel foundries, other non-electrical machinery, electrical industrial machinery and tractor and agricultural implements. The ICE for these sectors exceeded 30% in 2007–08.

The import content for coal tar products nearly doubled from 15.4% in 1998–99 to 33.7% in 2007–08. In the case of fertilisers, the ICE almost doubled between 1998–99 and 2007–08. Its value-added rose from 26.4% in 2003–04 to 31.1% in 2006–07. The ICE of the batteries sector rose from 26–27% in 1998–99 and 2003–04 to 32.8% in 2006–07 to 35% in 2007–08. The import content for petroleum products grew—from 40.5% in 1998–99, to 52.0% in 2003–04, to 55.6% in 2006–07 and to 65.8% in 2007–08.

The import content for ships and boats increased nearly five times from 16.8% in 1998–99 to 82% in 2007–08; the ICE value was 42.9% in 2003–04 and 42.9% in 2006–07. The import content for gems and jewellery increased by 8.7 percentage

Table 17.1 Import content of exports and value-added contribution due to exports in major manufacturing sectors of India

Year	1998–99			2003–04			2006–07			2007–08		
Commodity	ICE	Exports	TVA	ICE	Exports	TVA	ICE	Exports	TVA	IC	Exports	TVA
Petroleum products	40.54	3.57	2.12	52.04	115.66	55.46	55.56	236.02	105.50	65.83	698.58	238.71
Coal tar products	15.36	0.01	0.01	30.48	1.96	1.36	35.37	4.39	2.83	33.66	3.29	2.18
Inorganic heavy chemicals	18.82	25.05	20.34	20.80	14.83	11.74	25.68	27.99	20.59	34.45	32.63	21.39
Organic heavy chemicals	19.64	43.50	34.95	19.50	93.35	75.15	24.45	195.25	146.16	36.24	234.20	149.33
Fertilisers	25.52	0.37	0.28	26.36	0.35	0.26	31.14	0.45	0.31	50.30	1.22	0.61
Synthetic fibres, resin	19.01	3.78	3.06	21.62	35.15	27.55	27.25	75.86	54.84	33.17	62.09	41.50
Iron and steel foundries	13.78	6.64	5.72	23.66	16.17	12.34	27.86	12.40	8.90	31.28	106.29	73.04
Non-ferrous basic metals	23.63	7.71	5.89	25.97	36.08	26.71	29.12	118.14	83.06	37.95	159.74	99.12
Miscellaneous metal products	16.95	21.02	17.46	21.48	34.47	27.07	25.63	52.84	39.07	31.56	55.57	38.03
Tractors and agri. implements	14.41	0.59	0.50	19.04	3.86	3.13	24.04	12.50	9.37	30.20	13.14	9.17
Industrial machinery (F&T)	20.56	4.37	3.47	19.94	10.96	8.78	24.58	19.03	14.23	33.75	18.95	12.56
Other non-electrical machinery	16.94	20.96	17.41	19.24	81.84	66.09	24.14	132.46	99.56	31.71	166.94	114.01
Electrical industrial Machinery	20.69	8.00	6.34	20.74	12.06	9.56	26.66	55.51	40.18	31.53	62.26	42.63
Electrical wires and cables	30.25	2.20	1.54	30.53	3.00	2.09	36.27	13.40	8.46	38.82	14.58	8.92
Batteries	25.75	1.49	1.11	26.73	2.04	1.49	32.84	5.44	3.61	34.74	2.75	1.79
Communication equipment	18.11	27.04	22.14	22.12	26.75	20.83	27.59	189.25	134.51	35.03	39.72	25.80
Other electrical machinery	20.85	4.76	3.77	22.26	20.47	15.91	27.67	84.42	60.37	32.60	59.81	40.31

(continued)

Table 17.1 (continued)

Commodity	1998–99			2003–04			2006–07			2007–08		
Year	ICE	Exports	TVA	ICE	Exports	TVA	ICE	Exports	TVA	IC	Exports	TVA
Electronic equipment (incl. TV)	23.65	2.31	1.76	23.32	19.27	14.78	28.78	37.36	26.02	35.56	17.10	11.02
Ships and boats	16.75	2.59	2.16	42.91	5.59	3.19	45.04	47.80	25.75	82.00	77.91	14.02
Gems and jewellery				34.39	337.92	221.70	43.10	1504.94	841.68	36.61	186.22	118.04
Aircraft and spacecraft				13.82	3.44	2.96	16.23	2.24	1.87	78.29	27.00	5.86
Manufacturing	15.05	1322.34	1123.39	17.63	2481.64	2044.09	26.25	5733.05	4228.05	29.22	4922.18	3483.83
Services	9.24	681.53	618.54	6.76	1439.04	1341.70	8.65	3121.91	2851.99	13.27	4659.03	4040.73
Total economy	13.07	2003.87	1741.93	13.64	3920.69	3385.80	20.04	8854.97	7080.04	21.47	9581.22	7524.56

Source Authors' computations based on input-output (IO) transaction tables

Note ICE is import content of Exports, %; TVA is total direct and indirect value-added contribution due to exports, and exports are in Rs billion. The sectors having ICE exceeding 30% in 2007–08 are ultimately analysed here

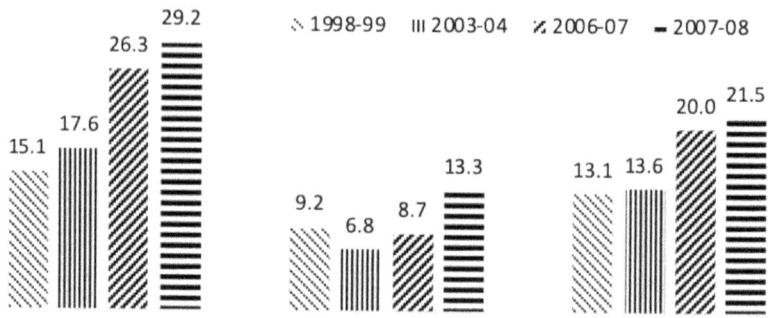

Fig. 17.1 Import content of exports in India (%). *Source* Authors' estimates

points, from 34.4% in 2003–04 to 43.1% in 2006–07, but fell subsequently to 36.6% in 2007–08. The ICE of the electrical wires and cables sector was 38.3% in 2007–08; its import content improved from a little over 30% at the two earlier points of time to 36.3% in 2006–07.

The import content rose over these four years in other sectors: inorganic heavy chemicals (34.5%), synthetic fibres and resin (33.2%), iron and steel foundries (31.3%), non-ferrous basic metals (38%), miscellaneous metal products (31.2%), electrical industrial machinery (31.5%), other electrical machinery (32.6%) and electronic equipment including television sets (35.6). Their ICE exceeded 30% in 2007–08.

The ICE exceeded 30% in the four years; the percentage shares of exports in total manufacturing exports were 14.1%, 35.3%, 49.3% and 41.5%, respectively in four points of time. In 1998–99, the ICE exceeded 25% in sectors like petroleum products, fertilisers, electrical wires and cables, batteries and miscellaneous manufacturing; the share of exports in total exports was 14.26%.

In 2007–08, the ICE exceeded 30% in certain new sectors like coal tar products, non-ferrous basic metals, ships and boats and gems and jewellery. Petroleum products and electrical wires and cables exceeded 30% ICE in 1998–99. The share of exports of these goods with import content exceeding 30% rose significantly in 2007–08.

The import content increased in sectors like silk textiles, art silk, synthetic fibre textiles, plastic products, pesticides, drugs and medicines, soaps, cosmetics and glycerine, other non-metallic mineral products, iron and steel casting and forging, hand tolls, hardware, industrial machinery (other), machine tools, electrical appliances, motor vehicles, medical and precision and optical instruments; in 2007–08, the import content was 25–30%.

The import content increased in manufacturing sectors like printing and publishing, rubber products, paints, varnishes and lacquers, other chemicals, cement, iron, steel and ferrous alloys, rail equipment, motor cycles and scooters, bicycles, cycle rickshaws, other transport equipment and service sectors like land transport, water transport, business services and other services; over these four years, the import content was 20–25%.

In 2007–08, the import content was 15–20% in sectors like carpet weaving, ready-made garments, miscellaneous textile products, paper, paper products and newsprint, structural clay products and service sectors like construction, electricity and air transport.

Between 1998–99 and 2007–08, the import content declined in sectors like tobacco products, structural clay products, watches and clocks and miscellaneous manufacturing sectors, and in services like education and services and medical and health. The value of exports by these specific sectors is low or zero, and that may have been the reason for the decline.

17.3.2 Total Direct and Indirect Value-Added (TVA) Contribution Due to Exports

India depends on imported raw materials for around 50% of its commodity basket of total exports—the rest is produced domestically—but the contribution of exports to total value addition, direct and indirect, has been declining over the years (Fig. 17.2). We compute the total valued-added (TVA) by exports (using the methodology in Sect. 17.2) for the economy. The TVA declined—from 86.9% in 1998–99 to 86.4% in 2003–04 to 80% in 2006–07 to 78.5% in 2007–08. But the decline in the TVA was greater in the manufacturing sector—from 84.9% in 1998–99 to 70.8% in 2007–08. The TVA due to exports by the services sector varied. The domestic value addition in exports was more than 98% in 1998–99 for sectors like rubber, other livestock products and gobar gas, forestry and logging and copper ore; but their TVA declined in the other three years.

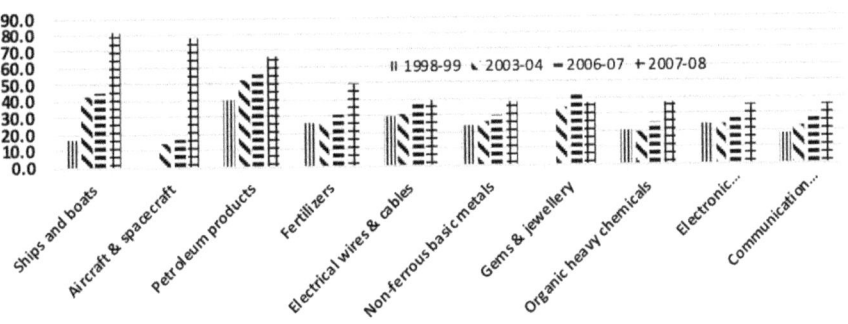

Fig. 17.2 Import contents of broad manufacturing sectors (%).
Source Authors' estimates as given in Table 17.1. The ICE estimates for gems and jewellery and aircraft and spacecraft are available for 1998–99

17.3.3 Employment Generation Due to Exports

The total direct and indirect employment generated by exports is another important indicator. The indicator is based on sector-wise direct employment per unit of gross value of output (GVO); it is the sector-wise labour input number per unit of GVO or output (in hundred thousand rupees). It should not be interpreted as man-days or man-hours per unit of output. If the direct employment coefficient per unit of output is 0.05, it could be interpreted as 0.05 jobs per hundred thousand rupees of output.

The employment content can be interpreted as the number of jobs created additionally per unit of direct employment in a sector. Such a concept is useful where we use the employment multiplier to appraise a project in well-known impact assessment studies. The total direct and indirect employment contribution could be differentiated from the indices explained earlier. We restrict our analysis to the sectors where the ICE exceeds 30%, and that is why important sectors like food products do not feature here.

In 2007–08, the import content of the gems and jewellery sector was 36.6%; it generated 740,000 jobs (direct and indirect), fewer than in 2003–04 or 2006–07. The import content of the organic heavy chemicals sector was 36.2%; it generated 700,000 jobs (direct and indirect) (Table 17.2), continuing its rising trend over the four years 1998–99, 2003–04, 2006–07 and 2007–08.

The import content of the other non-electrical machinery sector was 31.71% in 2007–08; the number of jobs generated, 350,000, fell from the 430,000 in 2003–04 and 420,000 in 2006–07. The import content of the non-ferrous basic metals sector was nearly 38% in 2007–08; it generated 340,000 jobs. The import content of the iron and steel foundries sector was 31.3% in 2007–08; it generated 280,000 jobs. The import content of the petroleum products was high, as were its contribution to exports and value-added; it generated 250,000 jobs in 2007–08, more than the 100,000 jobs in 2003–04 and the 150,000 in 2006–07.

The import content was 32–33% in sectors such as miscellaneous products, synthetic fibre resin, and electrical industrial machinery; these generated around 150,000 jobs. The import intensity of the ships and boats sector was 82% in 2007–08; it generated 700,000 jobs. The import intensity of the spacecraft and aircraft sector was 78.3% in 2007–08; it generated 1.1 million jobs.

The import content of the fertiliser sector was 50.3% in 2007–08, up from 25.5% in 1998–99, 26.4% in 2003–04 and 31.1% in 2006–07, but its contribution to total employment was not significant. The import content was high in sectors such as tractors and agricultural implements, electrical wires and cables, coal tar products and batteries, but employment generation was low. It would have been instructional to gauge total employment contribution in terms of broader groups—raw material and intermediates; capital goods; and consumer durables and non-durables.

The import content of the petroleum products sector was high, as were its exports and contribution to value-added; it generated nearly 250,000 jobs in 2007–08, up from 100,000 in 2003–04 and 150,000 in 2006–07.

Table 17.2 Employment generated in major manufacturing sectors of India

Commodity	1998–99			2003–04			2006–07			2007–08		
	Exports (Rs billion)	EC	Emp. generated (million)	Exports (Rs billion)	EC	Emp. generated (million)	Exports (Rs billion)	EC	Emp. generated (million)	Exports (Rs billion)	EC	Emp. generated (million)
Petroleum products	3.57	0.29	0.01	115.66	0.09	0.11	236.02	0.06	0.14	698.58	0.04	0.25
Coal tar products	0.01	1.20	0.00	1.96	0.39	0.01	4.39	0.27	0.01	3.29	0.13	0.00
Inorganic heavy chemicals	25.05	0.55	0.14	14.83	0.51	0.08	27.99	0.35	0.10	32.63	0.3	0.10
Organic heavy chemicals	43.5	0.65	0.28	93.35	0.55	0.51	195.25	0.37	0.72	234.2	0.3	0.70
Fertilisers	0.37	0.44	0.00	0.35	0.36	0.00	0.45	0.24	0.00	1.22	0.22	0.00
Synthetic fibres, resin	3.78	0.89	0.03	35.15	0.42	0.15	75.86	0.28	0.21	62.09	0.24	0.15
Iron and steel foundries	6.64	0.85	0.06	16.17	0.57	0.09	12.4	0.35	0.04	106.29	0.26	0.28
Non-ferrous basic metals	7.71	0.89	0.07	36.08	0.43	0.15	118.14	0.27	0.32	159.74	0.22	0.34
Miscellaneous metal products	21.02	0.79	0.17	34.47	0.58	0.20	52.84	0.36	0.19	55.57	0.28	0.15
Tractors and agri. implements	0.59	2.12	0.01	3.86	0.7	0.03	12.5	0.43	0.05	13.14	0.27	0.04
Industrial machinery (F&T)	4.37	1.28	0.06	10.96	0.5	0.06	19.03	0.32	0.06	18.95	0.22	0.04
Other non-electrical machinery	20.96	0.83	0.17	81.84	0.5	0.41	132.46	0.32	0.42	166.94	0.21	0.35

(continued)

Table 17.2 (continued)

Commodity	1998–99			2003–04			2006–07			2007–08		
	Exports (Rs billion)	EC	Emp. generated (million)	Exports (Rs billion)	EC	Emp. generated (million)	Exports (Rs billion)	EC	Emp. generated (million)	Exports (Rs billion)	EC	Emp. generated (million)
Electrical industrial machinery	8.0	0.82	0.07	12.06	0.47	0.06	55.51	0.3	0.17	62.26	0.24	0.15
Electrical wires and cables	2.2	0.65	0.01	3.00	0.39	0.01	13.4	0.26	0.03	14.58	0.24	0.03
Batteries	1.49	0.70	0.01	2.04	0.65	0.01	5.44	0.38	0.02	2.75	0.37	0.01
Communication equipment	27.04	0.75	0.20	26.75	0.47	0.13	189.25	0.31	0.58	39.72	0.21	0.08
Other electrical machinery	4.76	1.47	0.07	20.47	0.48	0.10	84.42	0.31	0.26	59.81	0.24	0.15
Electronic equipments(incl.TV)	2.31	1.6	0.04	19.27	0.81	0.16	37.36	0.46	0.17	17.1	0.45	0.08
Ships and boats	2.59	0.78	0.02	5.59	0.57	0.03	47.8	0.38	0.18	77.91	0.09	0.07
Gems and jewellery			0.00	337.92	0.82	2.76	1504.94	0.47	7.06	186.22	0.4	0.74
Aircraft and spacecraft			0.00	3.44	1.81	0.06	2.24	1.21	0.03	27	0.42	0.11
Manufacturing	1322.34		28.63	2481.64		43.02	5733.05		56.94	4922.18		40.24
Services	681.53		6.94	1439.04		12.98	3121.91		21.96	4659.03		23.42
Total economy	2003.87		35.57	3920.69		55.99	8854.97		78.91	9581.22		63.66

Source Our computation based on IO tables for relevant years. EC reflects direct employment content, i.e. total labour inputs per unit Rs Lakh gross value of output

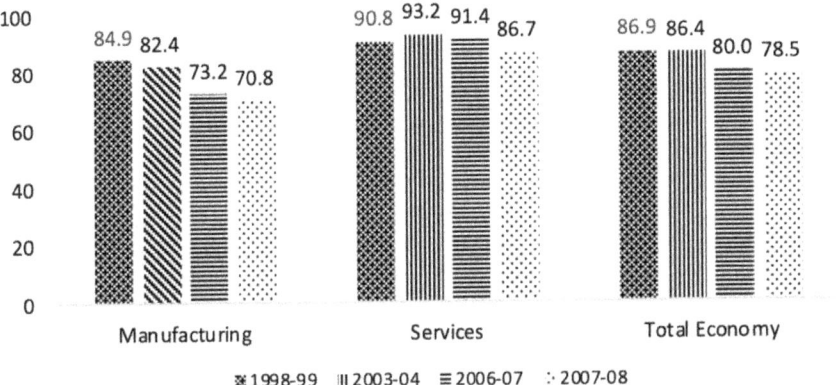

Fig. 17.3 Total direct and indirect value-added due to exports in India (%). *Source* Authors' estimation

17.3.4 Import Content of Exports (ICE) and Employment Generated Due to Exports

Exports increased over the years, as did the ICE—from 13.1% in 1998–99 to 21.5% in 2007–08 (Fig. 17.3). The import content of the manufacturing sector almost doubled—from 15.1% in 1998–99 to 29.2% in 2007–08. The import content of the service sector increased from 9.2% in 1998–99 to 13.3% in 2007–08. The increasing import content of the Indian economy led the contribution of exports to total value addition, direct and indirect, to decline.

Employment generation increased from 1998–99 to 2006–07 and dipped in 2007–08; exports created 63.66 million total direct and indirect jobs. The economy generated 35.55 million jobs in 1998–99; this number improved to 55.99 million jobs in 2003–04 and to 78.91 million in 2006–07.

The employment generated by manufacturing exports grew from 28.56 million jobs in 1998–99 to 56.94 million in 2006–07 and fell to 40.24 jobs in 2007–08. But the employment generated by the services sector has increased—from 6.99 million in 1998–99 to 23.42 million jobs in 2007–08. Total exports increased for the economy as a whole, and gross manufacturing sector exports increased from 1998–99 to 2006–07 and fell in 2007–08.

17.4 Conclusion and Policy Remarks

The total (direct and indirect) import intensity of exports of the Indian economy rose in 1989–90, 2003–04, 2006–07 and 2007–08. The rise in the import intensity of domestic production is unavoidable. The results obtained at the aggregate level validate the literature.

The results at the sectoral level are in sharp contrast to the earlier findings, however, and one must be careful in interpreting the results. The import content is computed for all sectors given in the I-O table but, while explaining the results, we consider the sectors exceeding 30% of import content in 2007–08: ships and boats, aircrafts and spacecraft, petroleum products, fertilisers, electrical wires and cables, non-ferrous basic metals, gems and jewellery, organic heavy chemicals and synthetic fibres and resin.

There was a decline in the contribution of exports to the TVA of the manufacturing sector and the economy overall, but the contribution of the services sector was mixed. The import content of two sectors—gems and jewellery, and organic heavy chemicals—was a little over 36%. The gems and jewellery sector contributed 740,000 jobs (direct and indirect), and the organic heavy chemicals contributed 700,000 jobs (direct and indirect). Total employment in the gems and jewellery sector turned lower in 2003–04, but turned significantly higher in 2006–07 and 2007–08.

The contribution to total employment of the other sectors that had an import content above 30% varied in 2007–08. Other sectors—non-electrical machinery, non-ferrous basic metals and iron and steel foundries—generated 280,000–350,000 jobs. The petroleum products sector generated 250,000 jobs. Other sectors—miscellaneous products, synthetic fibre resin and electrical industrial machinery—added 150,000–160,000 jobs. The import intensity of the ships and boats sector is 82%; it generated 69,000 jobs in 2007–08. The import intensity of the spacecraft and aircraft sector is 78.3%; it generated 110,000 jobs. The import content of the fertiliser sector was 50.3% in 2007–08; it could not generate employment. Other sectors that did not generate much employment are tractors and agricultural implements, electrical wires and cables, coal tar products and batteries.

Further investigation is needed into the employment generated by broader groups—raw material and intermediate goods; capital goods; consumer durables and non-durables. Our findings confirm that the rising import content of exports should not be a problem as long as exports rise at a sufficiently high pace (Sathe 1997). A sector's contribution to employment, direct and indirect, could be another important yardstick in this regard.

References

Bhat, T. P., & Paul, M. (2009). Measurement of import intensity of exports in India. *The Journal of Income and Wealth, 31*(1).

Bhat, T. P., Guha, A., Paul, M., & Sahu, P. P. (2007). *Estimates of import intensity of India's manufacturing exports: Recent trends and dimensions* (ISID Working Paper 2007/08). https://isidev.nic.in/pdf/WP0708.PDF.

Bhattacharyya, M. (1989). Import-intensity of exports: A case study of Indian economy. *Indian Economic Journal, 36*(3), 94.

Burange, L. G. (2001). Import-intensity in the registered manufacturing sector of India. *The Indian Economic Journal, 49*(2), 42–52.

EXIM Bank of India. (1991, December). *How import intensive are Indian exports* (Occasional Paper, No 16).

Government of India. *Export import data bank*. New Delhi: Department of Commerce.

Government of India. (1998–99, 2003–04, 2006–07 and 2007–08). *Input-output transaction table*. New Delhi: Central Statistical Organisation.

Indian Institute of Foreign Trade. (1990). *Impact of import liberalisation on exports*.

Kolli, R., & Sharma, A. C. (2011). Supply and use tables for Indian economy, 2006–07. *The Journal of Income and Wealth, 33*(1), 66–78.

Kolli, R., Sharma, S., & Sinharay, A. (2008). Estimates of workforce from NSS-61 round, 2004–05. *The Journal of Income and Wealth, 30*(1), 34–67.

Loschky, A., & Ritter, L. (2006). Import content of exports. In *OECD, Statistics Directorate. Paper for 7th OECD International Trade Statistics Expert Meeting (ITS) and OECD-Eurostat Meeting of Experts in Trade-In-Services (TIS)*, Paris.

Mani, S. (1991, July). Export liberalisation and import dependence. *Economic and Political Weekly*, pp. 1693–1696.

Neogi, C., & Ghosh, B. (1998, February 28). Impact of liberalization on performance of Indian industries: A firm level study. *Economic and Political Weekly*.

OCED. (2012). *Trade in value added: Concepts, methodologies and challenges* (Joint OECD-WTO Note).

Pitre, V. (1981). A study of trends in India's imports, 1960–61 to 1974–75. *Economic and Political Weekly*, Vol. 16, No. 19, p. 851.

Pitre, V. (1992, May). Import intensity in the Indian economy. *RBI Studies*.

RBI. (2010). *The report on currency and finance 2002–03* (p. 260). https://rbidocs.rbi.org.in/rdocs/Publications/PDFs/51010.pdf.

Sarma, A. (1990, September). Import intensities of Indian industries in the context of new economic policy: An analysis in input-output framework. *Man and Development*.

Sathe, D. (1995). Impact of diversification of composition of exports: An analysis of the linkages of Indian exports. *Indian Economic Journal, 42*(3), 114.

Sathe, D. (1997). Import intensity of India's exports—Some fresh evidence. *Economic and Political Weekly*, Vol. 32, No. 8, p. M-31.

Siddharthan, N. S. (1989). Impact of import liberalisation on export intensities—A study of the Indian private corporate sector. *Indian Economic Journal, 37*(2), 103–111.

Singh, D. (1994). Impact of import liberalization on exports. *Reserve Bank of India Occasional Papers*, Vol. 15, No. 1.

WTO. (2019). *International trade statistics*. Geneva. https://www.wto.org/english/res_e/statis_e/its2012_e/its2012_e.pdf.